CURTIS MAYFIELD

People Never Give Up

Printed in the United Kingdom by MPG Books Ltd, Bodmin

Published by Sanctuary Publishing Limited, Sanctuary House, 45–53 Sinclair Road, London W14 0NS, United Kingdom

www.sanctuarypublishing.com

Cover photographs: front cover by Dana Lixenberg, courtesy of Warner Bros Records; rear cover courtesy of *Black Music* magazine

ISBN: 1-86074-457-5

CURTIS MAYFIELD

People Never Give Up

Peter Burns

Sanctuary

About The Author

Peter Burns was born in Lambeth towards the end of World War II. He grew up and was educated in southeast London. Whilst pursuing a career in Graphic Design, Peter was amongst the earliest writers published in *Blues & Soul* magazine. From the early '70s, he began to make freelance contributions to many other music weeklies, fanzines and magazines. At 30 he returned to full-time education at the University of Kent, where he obtained a BA (Hons) and a teaching degree whilst moonlighting as a mobile DJ in the evenings and at weekends. For almost 20 years he lectured in Graphic Design at Ealing, Barnet and Croydon Colleges until the mid-'90s, when he quit education to set up his own graphic-design studio and the Echo Archive.

Contents

Acknowledgements

When you spend almost a decade writing a book, inevitably you talk to a great many people about your project. My closest friends and family have been very patient and supportive, my sincere thanks goes to them. Candy, my wife has been like a rock throughout the whole process. Many thanks to Norman Jopling and Terry Chappell for long-term advice and encouragement. Trevor Churchill for all his constant help, encouragement and informed opinion. Bob Fisher for his thoughtful contributions and soulful support. To Faith Aarons, Russell Jones, Russell and Pauline Gardner for help with American coverage, tapes and US press clippings, my sister Janet Rapp also helped here. Nick Marcus for archival info from the BBC. The folks at Ace/Kent for their involvement and help: Ady Croasdell, Roger Armstrong, Tony Rounce, Bob Dunham, Chris Poppin, Neil Scaplehorn and Carol Fawcett. Kev Featherstone for many rare items and music, Rob Hughes for discographical and practical help and Steve Bryant for music and info. The *Blues & Soul* connection, Bob Killbourn and John Abbey. The Sanctuary/Castle connection, Roger Semon, Sam Szczepanski and John Reed. Also honourable mentions go to John & Christina Hazell, Jeulie Palliser, Mike Hart, Roger St Pierre, Joe Boake, Rick Davie, Mick Anderson, Chris Phylactou, Cliff Clifford and Roy Simonds. Special thanks to Iain MacGregor for believing in my book, Anna Osbourne and Claire Musters for their editorial skills, and the team at Sanctuary – Jess, Michelle, Laura and Alan. My sincere apologies to anyone that I may have left out in the rush to publication.

PHOTOGRAPHS

Thank you to the following people for their particular help in supplying photos (many of which have not been used here but reside in the Echo Archive). From Curtom Neil Bogart and Clarice Pollock sent me many between 1969–'80. Thanks to Bob Killbourn at *Blues & Soul*, Bob Fisher at Acrobat, Noreen Woods at Atlantic, Rick Davie and Seamus McGarvey.

INTERVIEWS

Curtis Mayfield, Churchill Hotel, London 7/71
Curtis Mayfield, Astoria, London, 2/72
Curtis Mayfield, Camden, London, 6/88
Curtis Mayfield, Telephone, Atlanta, 10/96
Jerry Butler, Fountain Productions, Chicago, 10/72
Calvin Carter, Fountain Productions, Chicago, 10/72
Billy Butler, Fountain Productions, Chicago, 10/72
Larry Wade, Fountain Productions, Chicago, 10/72
Terry Callier, Fountain Productions, Chicago, 10/72
Terry Callier, Jazz Café, Camden, LOndon, 11/2000
Ollan Christopher Telephone and Internet 10/99
Sam Gooden, Fred Cash, Leroy Hutson, Speakeasy, London, 7/72
Impressions, Royal Garden Hotel, London, 2/01
Melvin Jones, Telephone London, correspondence 8/98
Neil Bogart, Interview, London, 10/69
Neil Bogart, Interview, New York, 9/72
Neil Bogart, Telephone and correspondence 6/70
Carl Davis, Telephone, Chicago, 10/72
Sam Gooden, Telephone and Internet '01-03
Donny Hathaway, Telephone, Chicago, 9/72
Ron Ainsfield, Curtom, Chicago, 10/72
Clarice Pollock, Curtom, Chicago, 10/72
Clarice Pollock, correspondence '72–'80
Marv Heiman, Curtom, Chicago, 10/72
Richard Tufo, Curtom, Chicago, 10/72

1 Initial Impressions

'I read a sign somewhere that said
"Everyone walkin' can always stumble over truth"
But never you mind –
'Cause we always get right back up and leave it there.'
— *'Something To Believe In', Curtis Mayfield, 1980*

In the past 40 years, Curtis Mayfield's music and poetry have grown into an impressive and truly individual body of work. His songs of love, peace and understanding have entertained and enlightened millions of us during this period. Curtis has written some of the most remarkable sociologically aware and poetically lyrical love songs ever published. Since 1957 Mayfield has been prolific as a songsmith. Hundreds of his songs have been recorded by artists from all over the world and, as a singer and musician, his message has reached, influenced and inspired millions. His poetry, personal conviction and powers of communication have artistically put him in the illustrious company of other great transatlantic troubadours like Lennon, Dylan, Ray Charles, Johnny Cash and Dion.

By the time Curtis set up his own label, Curtom, in '68 he'd already had more success than most people achieve in a lifetime. He had made significant contributions to the careers of Jerry Butler, Gene Chandler, Major Lance and a host of other Chicagoan recording artists. His music had already influenced the work of Bob Marley, Marvin Gaye, Jimi Hendrix and was yet to touch Prince and countless others. He had also steered his own group the Impressions through a ten-year period that had spawned a cluster of R&B and pop single hits.

During a ten-year association, the Impressions also enjoyed a dozen hit albums, as well as their 30 singles with ABC Records. In 1970 Curtis launched his own solo career with classic albums like *Curtis* and *Roots* that became big hits all over the world and this personal success introduced him to Hollywood and the movie soundtrack, the first of which gave him his biggest career album, *Superfly*. These are just some of the highlights from the Curtis Mayfield story and to fill in the gaps you need to go back 60 years...

Curtis Mayfield was born in Chicago on 3 June 1942 and grew up in the city of music, which helped to shape him and his music. To many of us, Chicago – like New York, LA or Hollywood – appears to be a tangled kaleidoscope filled with the images of romance, violence and corruption, which have been profiled by the movies and TV in recent decades. However, in the '30s, if you were a black share-cropper working for slave wages in the south, Chicago was a vision of the promised land. As the city evolved into an industrial magnet, it drew millions of black Americans with the lure of freedom, the opportunity of jobs and a better life and created the greatest migration in American history.

In the south, generations of blacks had suffered from the iniquities of slavery and, since its abolition, continued appalling treatment and prejudice. Field workers were locked out of the towns and cities. In the north they were locked into neighbourhoods and boroughs that were later rebuilt as the instant ghettos called the 'projects'. Chicago was to become the largest railway centre in the world, and was also celebrated by many as the heartland of urban blues and gospel music and some say the birthplace of soul music.

This was a city that had already established its ethnic separation as routine because racial integration had always been unacceptable in the past. As such, the black community soon secured its own businesses, churches and entertainment. Many blues artists like Memphis Slim, Big Bill Broonzy and Muddy Waters were drawn to the city and some settled. Chicago blues began to be recorded, according to Mike Rowe in *Chicago Blues* (Eddison Press Ltd, 1973), with Tampa Red's 'How Long, How Long Blues' (Vocalion in 1928) and 'It's Tight Like That'. The record companies that catered for the 'Race' market began to record artists like Big Bill Broonzy and Bumble Bee Slim in the north. Their music later became known as urban blues and it was this form that became popular with record buyers in the late 1930s. Sonny Boy Williamson began to record in Chicago in 1937. He and other singers like Homesick James, Lonnie Johnson and JB Lenoir played long hours for a few dollars at the southside clubs like The Three Deuces, The Boulevard Lounge, The Square Deal and The Circle Inn. The southside of Chicago soon became honeycombed with blues clubs, which regularly featured the established artists of the time as well as the newer talents attracted by the magnet that was to become the legendary 'home of the blues'.

Leonard and Phil Chez, two Polish immigrants who owned and ran the Macomba Lounge situated on the southside, found themselves increasingly anxious to record the acts that played at the club, who were often unskilled factory workers by day and blues artists by night. When the Blues Brothers set up their first label Aristocrat in 1947, their original intention was to record jump jazz music but this quickly gave way to the blues. Muddy Waters, who had first moved to Chicago in 1943, signed to Aristocrat five years later with 'Sunnyland' Slim. There were many fine blues labels in the city but Len and Phil created the most internationally famous of them all with the Chess label in 1950. There were great early releases from Gene Ammons and Jimmy Rogers but it was Muddy Waters who gave them their earliest hit with 'Louisiana Blues' that went to #10 on the R&B charts in January '51. Chess went on to unparalleled success in their field over the next 30 years as they extended their catalogue to encompass R&B, rock 'n' roll and soul music through the addition of sister labels Checker and Cadet. In 1959 the company was sold to GRT Tape Company but four years later Chess set up WVON (Voice Of The Negro), a 24-hour black-run radio station, the first in Chicago. WVON ran a black community and civil rights programme and sold products, via advertising, to black Chicago. Of course, the music that DJs like Don Cornelius and Herb Kent played carried the soul message.

By the mid 1940s and early 1950s all the strands of black music were reaching a wide and varied audience via record, radio and live performances in small clubs and at theatres like the Regal and the Savoy. Through these media, gospel music reached a wider audience and created even more followers. Gospel had existed on the North American continent as long as the Christian church and, as a consequence of segregated worship, the black communities, in both the northern and southern states, grew up using their churches as meeting houses. For most of them, the church became the centre of community life. In the southern states where the greatest concentration of slave labour had been employed, they could not travel around easily, so every church and prayer house formed its own choir. Through worship they began to articulate their struggle and from that time the black gospel tradition began to evolve.

Containment laws still prevented southern blacks from migration, but in other parts of the country 'Gospel Travelers' began to spread their message nationwide, performing at festivals, fairs and meeting halls. Two of the most famous and influential of these groups were The Soul Stirrers and The Pilgrim Travelers, both founded in Houston, Texas in the early 1930s, and from their ranks later evolved two of Chicago's most celebrated sons, Sam Cooke and Lou Rawls.

Sam Cooke's crossover to popular music, as well as his identification and establishment of the genre of soul music, caused great controversy in gospel circles and this attitude rapidly spread to the music business in general. Sam quit The Stirrers and got a rough ride for a while (especially from his gospel fans, who regarded his move as scandalous and viewed his early rewritings of traditional gospel tunes as sacrilegious) but his public eventually forgave him and he continued to pioneer gospel/soul into the mainstream of popular music. His 35 R&B chart singles all crossed over to pop during the 1950s and early '60s right up until his murder at a Los Angeles motel in December 1964. Many soul music fans believe that Sam 'Mr Soul' Cooke was the architect of the genre and that the birthplace of soul music was the city of Chicago in the late '50s. It was in this environment, with its plethora of musical influences, that young Curtis Mayfield first started to make music.

Curtis cited his own early influences as those of his maternal grandmother Annabell Mayfield who was a preacher with her own Traveling Soul Spiritualists' Church, and his mother who sang and played the piano. The church was housed in a converted storefront in the city where Annabell administered to her small congregation. She also practiced as a 'healer' from her small apartment. Quite often, other family members would have to sit patiently for long periods in the kitchen waiting for her to finish with her clients. The Mayfields may have been poor but what they did have was a strong family support system, which extended through their church to the local community. Though poor, they were rich in genuine concern and affection for each other. Although the children did not believe everything that they learned from this environment, Curtis stated that he developed a respect for the attendant grown ups in his childhood, as they all shared the struggle that bound their community together. These community values persisted into the '70s until the combination of hard drugs and street gang culture destabilized them for all future generations.

It was the poetry of Paul Lawrence Dunbar that inspired Curtis' mother Marion and she would often recite at home and in church. She also encouraged Curtis to sing at an early age and taught him songs at the piano. Marion's earliest recollection of Curtis singing publicly was aged three when he gave a spirited rendition of 'Pistol Packin' Mama', which he must have heard on the radio (it had first been a big hit by Al Dexter on OKeh in late '43 and went on to be an even bigger national hit for Bing Crosby). She has described Curtis as an introverted but inquisitive child, who worked most things out for himself.

Fortunately for the Mayfields, Marion had the personal discipline and inner strength that it took to bring up her five children on her own in the Cabrini Green area of Chicago. Times were tough and the family lived in near poverty much of the time but their struggle for survival made them a strong family unit. Mayfield said that his mother had a fair and reasonable approach to discipline and always talked any problems through with the children, which helped to create a close harmony and understanding. Curtis was the eldest and so often watched over his two sisters and two brothers, especially Kirby, who was retarded and depended on him more than the others. Kirby died, aged 18, of an enlarged heart.

It was as part of his natural development that Curtis, aged seven, joined the Northern Jubilee Singers, a gospel quintet who sang at his grandmother's church, during the early '50s. (Jubilee was a secularized form of church music, which was deemed to be acceptable entertainment in clubs and concert halls). It was here that he met and became friends with Jerry Butler who along with two of Mayfield's cousins, Charles and Tommy Hawkins, and bassman Eddie Patterson aka 'Paddyfoot' completed the group's line-up at that time. They would hang out at the Mayfield household and it was in these conducive surroundings that Curtis and Jerry grew up as brothers instinctively working together through their musical apprenticeship, soaking up the very roots of gospel as it began its evolutionary transformation into soul.

After the war, Chicago saw another peak in the numbers of its southern immigrants. By the 1940s and 1950s, the city had developed a long and deep black musical tradition that ranged from jazz and ragtime, to the blues and R&B. This was also the music that provided Curtis and Jerry with a rich diet of mainstream influences via records and the radio. It was common practice for the various churches in Chicago to visit each other at their places of worship. So the Northern Jubilee Singers were exposed to the music of many fine choirs and other quartets/quintets from all over the city, which provided the young group with a rich vein of influences and experiences with which to develop their own unique vocal identity.

While still in his early teens, Curtis started to teach himself the guitar on an instrument that had been discarded by an uncle and left at his grandmother's house. He unconventionally tuned it himself from the black notes on the piano in his home and he began to write some of his earliest songs. Because of this unique tuning (which unknown to him at the time was in the key of F$\sharp$), Mayfield began to play and write in a style that set him apart from the others. He and Jerry formed the Modern Jubiliares, a gospel quartet who didn't really last long due to differences of opinion within the line-up. Butler left to join The Quails and Curtis put together his own new vocal group. The Alphatones were a quintet consisting of Curtis, Earl Boyce, James Waine and two other boys named 'Finease' and 'Dallas' Dixon. They practised their vocal routines at West Side Grammar and at the Mayfield home with Jerry occasionally sitting in. Although they had all been singing for most of their lives, they were still relatively young and totally inexperienced in the ways of the music business.

Butler, who was four years older than Curtis, parted company with The Quails, and went on to meet and team up with three singers who had just arrived in Chicago from Chattanooga, Tennessee, where they had been part of a group known as The Roosters. Jerry persuaded a somewhat reluctant Curtis to leave his own group and play guitar for this more experienced outfit. Curtis, who was barely 15, had never been an 'A' student – there had been frequent moves before the family settled in Cabrini Green and his school studies had always taken second place to his music. He convinced his mother that he saw his future in music and that he should take this opportunity. Curtis quit his classes at West Side Grammar and became the youngest Rooster in the group.

After a period of intense rehearsal, the new Roosters positively bristled with latent talent. Sam Gooden talked in a recent interview (London, February 2001) about the early days and how the Impressions were formed. Back in Chattanooga, the original Roosters were comprised of two brothers (Richard and Arthur Brooks) a brother and sister (Emanuel and Catherine Thomas who was resident 'chick' lead from time to time) and two close friends from childhood (Fred Cash and Sam) who sang lead vocals. In answer to the question as to why they didn't cut any records, Sam admitted, 'We just weren't very good. There were four or five better outfits in Chattanooga at that time. I really wanted to play professional baseball and I managed to get a trial with the Chicago Cubs, so Richard and Arthur came along for the ride. While I was trying out at the club, they met up with Jerry and by the time I got back they had decided to team up.' It was Jerry's town, so he became the natural leader. The only spot left vacant was bassman, so Sam took it and has remained there ever since. It was then that Jerry suggested Curtis and his guitar should complete their line-up.

Eddie Thomas, then working as a salesman, was looking for a way to break into the entertainment business when he met the Roosters at a talent show and was inspired by what he witnessed. He was convinced that this group had something special and began working part-time as their manager. His first challenge was to come up with a new and more memorable name. They were all beginning to tire of the crows and barnyard sounds that they had been getting from the young audiences at their initial gigs. It became obvious to them that people in the city of Chicago were unlikely to wake up to the rural sound of The Roosters – what they needed now was urban sophistication and a name that reflected these values. One thing that they all agreed upon was that above all they wanted to impress with their performances and so their new name – the Impressions – was born.

2 The Vee-Jay Years

Thomas began promoting the Impressions in the Chicago area, hustling for gigs and record deals. This meant that Eddie spent much of his time in and around 'Record Row', which had grown to become the centre of the Chicago record industry. Record Row was situated on South Michigan Avenue and ran for a 'golden' mile between 12th and 24th streets. Here is where many of the greatest independent labels set up home, including Decca, Capitol, Mercury, Chess, Chance, Onederful, Vee-Jay and King and almost 20 record distributors were also gathered there, including United, the only all-black distribution company in the business. However, Thomas could not find any takers for the Impressions at this time.

The first label to show any interest was Bandera Records, a small independent run by Bernie Harville and his mother, who apparently liked what they heard and signed the group but did not release any records immediately. So Thomas kept on trying to interest the larger, more established record labels in town.

Events took a positive turn for the Impressions in June '58 when fate played its part in persuading Calvin Carter, A&R Director and Principal Producer for Vee-Jay Records, to listen to their demo tape. Thomas in his role as manager had arranged for the quintet to audition for the legendary Chess Records but he had only been able to fix them an appointment on a Saturday morning. There was much excitement and anticipation when they dispersed after rehearsal that Friday night. When the Impressions arrived carrying their instruments and amplifiers they found to their surprise that the front door to Chess Records was firmly locked and they couldn't raise anyone from within. Bassman Sam Gooden recalled, 'There was a doorman sittin' at the desk and we could see him but he just ignored us.' Overnight, unexpectedly, there had been a late spring snowstorm, which had piled up several feet deep in some places. This wasn't about to deter the Impressions from what might be their lucky break but most people in Chicago were unwilling to leave the house.

As fate would have it Vee-Jay was situated directly opposite across the street and Carter (who was working despite the weather) ushered them in and took them upstairs to the studio where Ewart Abner Jr (General Manager) was also present. Initially Calvin was unmoved by what he heard on their demo tape. 'Pretty Betty (Baby)', 'My Baby Loves Me' and the other four songs had been recorded in Mayfield's kitchen and, as Curtis said later, 'They sounded like it.' Once he heard the final track on their tape, 'Your Precious Love', which they had recently added, he really became interested and got the Impressions to perform this song again, after which he was convinced that with a few improvements he had a potential hit on his hands. He signed the Impressions to the VJ subsidiary Falcon, (soon to change its name to Abner, to avoid confusion with an earlier Falcon logo). He negotiated rights with Vi Muszynski, Bandera's label boss who still had some plans for them herself and struck a deal with her to record the group at VJ.

Carter felt this deal was hot and wanted a record right away. Jerry recalled in '72, 'We recorded "For Your Precious Love" on the Wednesday and it was in the shops the following Monday.' In the next two weeks the record sold 150,000 copies and rapidly became the runaway summer R&B hit of '58. Listening to it now, this may be a little hard to believe because, brilliant as the piece is, it does not seem to possess any of the characteristics of a hit record. It begins with the slow, measured backbeat of a funeral lament accentuated by the plodding bass line. Butler's suffering baritone juxtaposes perfectly with the sweet and sour backing vocals of the other four and delivers this plea with devastating sincerity. The two wailing high tenors of Curtis and Arthur reinforce the eerie atmosphere that Carter's superbly controlled production had created. The song was arranged by Riley Hampton (one of the finest musical arrangers in Chicago) and this further enhances the ballad's powerful atmosphere. Everybody got it just right. It's a masterpiece and it strikes a chord deep within anyone who listens to it, which probably, as much as anything, accounted for its huge success. Mayfield's understated guitar works beautifully supporting this resigned but eternally hopeful prayer. It's all here – despair, loneliness, sincerity and persistence. All these elements, and much more, make this record a milestone in the evolution of soul music. Steady sales pushed it to #11 on Billboard's Hot 100/pop (#3 R&B) by 16 July '58. Today, all the original pressings of 'For Your Precious Love' fetch big money on the collectors' market but the first few copies that Carter pressed up on Vee-Jay to garner local music biz opinion are said to be worth £6000 each.

The success of their first hit was confined to America and the record meant little to the rest of the world at the time of its issue. Jerry was featured as lead singer but without consultation with the band – Carter decided to press the record with credits going to 'Jerry Butler and the Impressions'. Curtis later said, 'It somewhat created hard feelings among the fellas, that we were all striving equally and trying to make it.'

It caused a ripple of tension within the group but, before things came to a head, they were out on the road touring America playing all the famous venues that up until then they had only dreamed about. Despite the ongoing differences between the members of the group and their lack of professional performance time, when the Impressions played the Apollo in June '58 it created a massive audience response. They broke the box-office attendance records and it has been estimated that there were 5000 fans on the street outside the theatre who came each night to see them perform. The story goes that it was DJ Doug 'Jocko' Henderson who booked them into the Apollo after he'd caught their act at the Uptown Philadelphia. Curtis, who celebrated his 16th birthday during their weeks residence, said that it was while he was jamming with the musicians at the Apollo between shows that he first became aware of the F♯ tuning on his guitar and the slight problems it caused the band (when they had no knowledge of this).

'For Your Precious Love' was a very special record and, hard as they tried, the Impressions could not duplicate its success over the following 18 months. 'The Gift Of Love' written by Butler, Richard Brooks and Mayfield as the sequel was not used immediately and instead Carter cut

'Come Back My Love', written by Roy Hamilton (and Clyde Otis). Roy had scored regularly on the American charts with a string of hits since the mid '50s and Carter presumably considered Hamilton's songs a better commercial bet (he later recorded several of their compositions with Butler solo). The record was good but despite everyone's efforts it only managed to reach #29 R&B and created no discernible pop interest. On reflection, perhaps they should have followed up with 'The Gift Of Love'. It did, in fact, become their third Abner single, but, by then, the momentum was lost and the single didn't register on either chart. Within seven months and with a lot of encouragement from Carter, Jerry had left the Impressions for a solo career.

While it was clear that Carter always had his own agenda for Butler, this left the Impressions in a bit of a hole. Richard Brooks must have assumed that he would be the natural successor to Butler as lead singer. After all it was his song, written with Arthur and Jerry, that had established the Impressions in the first place. With peacemaker Butler gone, there was an uneasy tension between Richard and the 'kid' who was now the only native Chicagoan left in the line-up.

Curtis had written and recorded more Impressions records as lead voice than any of the others, except Butler, and Brooks' influence began to wane as Mayfield's began to rise. Curtis, now just 16, occupied the Impressions' vacant lead spot while ex-Rooster Fred Cash was summoned from Chattanooga to fill out the quintet. Mayfield attempted to 'lighten up' the Impressions' material and they cut 'Senorita I Love You'/'That You Love Me' for use as their fourth single. 'Senorita' is in a similar vein to 'At The County Fair' on which Curtis sang lead while Jerry was still present and which was used as a B-side to 'Gift'. These songs showed more doo wop influences than gospel, but the single could not pick up sales again and the group struggled to find a comfortable identity as VJ began to lose interest. However, Vi Muszynski at Bandera could still see a future for the group and took the Impressions to Hall Recording Studios to cut a speculative session. Muszynski, who produced, hired Riley Hampton to supply the arrangements and continuity. Despite their best efforts 'Listen' – written by Jerry Butler and sung by Sam Gooden (whose vocal range was most similar to Jerry's) – and flipside 'Shorty's Got To

Go', hastily cobbled together by Curtis from an old song he had learned from his mother, could only create local interest.

The local interest in 'Listen' was enough to prompt Carter to offer the Impressions what turned out to be their final Abner session. The ensuing single 'A New Love', was a forerunner to Mayfield's much-recorded 'Little Young Lover' and a clear indication of how the Impressions would later evolve. But it could only continue the downturn in record sales and in 1960, when VJ absorbed Abner Records, they did not re-sign the luckless quintet. It could not have helped matters that Curtis had recently had a run in with Carter and Abner over the publishing royalties to his songs. Despite local high regard for their talent, Thomas could not immediately secure a recording contract for the Impressions and they all had to take non-music jobs whilst he scouted around for new opportunities. Mayfield had married his first wife Helen and the other Impressions had also taken on commitments that meant that they could no longer hang on and wait for things to improve, so the group went into temporary suspension.

Carter admired Mayfield's ability to play guitar and write songs but was not a big fan of his vocal style that at the time he thought was weak and unmemorable. Jerry did not agree and, while he was on tour in New York, he called Curtis to come down and replace Phil Upchurch, who played guitar in Butler's road band but had a hot single of his own (the superb 'You Can't Sit Down') and naturally wanted leave to chase the hit. Jerry sent Curtis a plane ticket and bought him an amp and they joined forces once more to tour America over the next year promoting Butler's solo career. Curtis was still only 18 in 1960. The tour with Jerry gave him much needed experience and practice, and he quickly became a better guitarist and a stronger and more confident singer. He met and worked with many stars, his heroes. Everybody he admired was out there on the road touring and, as a result of colour prejudice, they often had to room in close quarters because they couldn't stay in hotels or eat at restaurants. This all brought the performers closer together.

As well as just playing the guitar, Curtis wrote (and co-wrote) many songs during this period. He always had a treasure chest of song ideas to which he constantly added, changed and rewrote. When inspired, he used to put down verses and ideas on tape and go back to finish them at a later date. Between 1960 and '64, Jerry Butler recorded 14 songs that were written with or by Mayfield and four of them hit the Top 40. Their first big hit 'He Will Break Your Heart' (co-written with Carter) took Butler to #1 on the R&B charts and gave him his first solo Hot 100 hit when it went to #7 pop in October 1960. This song became a classic inspiring many later versions by artists such as Ben E King, Freddie Scott, Dawn and many others. Butler's next hit 'Find Another Girl' reached #27 pop in April '61, 'I'm A Telling You' made #25 later that year and 'Need To Belong' became a Top 30 record in December '63. On the back of this kind of songwriting success, Curtis would gradually expand his freelance production activities, but his first hits came with Jerry Butler. In an interview in '72, Butler said, 'Curtis and I always inspired each other writing and singing. Sometimes we'd fight about this or that, but when it came together it was beautiful.'

While Jerry and Curtis enjoyed huge chart success with a sell-out tour of America, the other four Impressions languished in near obscurity. At the tail end of 1960 Curtis Mayfield and Eddie Thomas took, for then, an unprecedented step and formed Curtom, their own music publishing company. (Sam Cooke had become a partner with JW Alexander in his already established Kags Music the previous year). For black artists at this time, this kind of move was unheard of. It had long been the practice of the more unscrupulous label owners and managers to coerce artists to share their songwriting credits or sell them. The argument that they used was that there was no money in publishing and that the singers would make much more cash from their tours and public performances. The reverse was true. Mayfield had already encountered these kind of tactics and regarded it as theft. He was determined to protect his songs so he formed his own company to ensure his and their future. They reformed the Impressions and, in early '61, signed to a long-term contract with a major, ABC Paramount Records in New York.

3 Gypsy Woman, ABC And OKeh

During the year that Curtis Mayfield toured with Jerry Butler, he put together enough money to cut a speculative recording session with the Impressions in New York in July '61, which yielded the classic 'Gypsy Woman'. ABC Paramount's MD, Larry Newton signed them to a five-year contract and they released the single in the winter months of '61 – it rapidly became the Impressions' first international hit. Within a month of release, it climbed to #20 on Billboard's Hot 100 (pop) and scored #2 on the R&B singles chart. The song, allegedly first written by Curtis aged 14 (but only recently completed), was one of Mayfield's finest fantasy vignettes, in the tradition of 'At The County Fair' and 'Minstrel & Queen'.

Mal Williams, Maxine Brown's manager/husband, co produced all the Impressions' New York sessions with Curtis, through his and Maxine's Mal-Max Productions. Curtis had met Maxine while on tour with Jerry and had given her a song ('I Don't Need You No More') for her first session with ABC. Roy Glover, the arranger on the Impressions' New York sessions, added cleverly to the musical atmosphere created on 'Gypsy Woman' as guitar and castanets counterpointed Mayfield's lament for a gypsy dancer.

The song's huge success shot the Impressions into a hectic schedule of live appearances at such famed venues as the Apollo (New York), the Regal (Chicago), the Uptown (Philadelphia), the Howard (Washington) and the Royal (Baltimore). Dick Clark featured them twice on his nationally televised *American Bandstand* on ABC-TV and they made countless other appearances on television and radio. This song was destined to become a standard with other notable versions by Bobby

Womack, Brian Hyland and Lou Johnson, amongst many others. It was also a big hit on the London club scene and was iconized by the highly fashionable Mods of the time.

The Impressions went on to record another 11 songs in New York (cutting nine in a two-day period on 21 and 22 March '62). However, these records did not have a commercial impact anywhere except for 'I'm The One Who Loves You'. This was the only one released in Britain and it found the groove again with the dancers and signalled clearly what was to come. The other songs produced, including 'Can't You See', 'Minstrel & Queen' and 'Little Young Lover' were all of an earlier Mayfield style, which failed to excite the public.

During this period, Richard Brooks, who had previously been quite an influential writer and group member since their first hit, seemed largely overshadowed by Curtis and only turned in one song 'I Need Your Love', a rewrite of 'Give Me Your Love', which had been cut on VJ with Jerry singing lead in 1958 but had been rejected for release as an A-side. Brooks, it seems, got stuck behind this song as it turned out to be the last he wrote for the Impressions. Richard and Arthur felt that history was repeating itself, since by now they'd had no big hits for almost a year. Curtis was homesick and wanted to move operations back to Chicago but the Brooks felt that the group would do better based in New York. Opinions polarized and uneasy divisions within the Impressions split the group into two factions. So it was that, in the autumn of 1962, Curtis, Sam and Fred relocated to Chicago and Richard and Arthur Brooks remained in New York where they created their own short-lived version of the Impressions. They recorded a single for the New York-based Gramercy Records under that name. Richard sang lead on two of his own songs 'Don't Leave Me' and 'I Need Your Love' (yet again), but this release on the Swirl label could not create the attention that the real Impressions demanded and the single quickly sank into the obscurity of collectable status. Though this record was inconsequential commercially, it did create a rift between the Brooks and the other Impressions that was never really completely repaired.

To many people, Mayfield's move back up north seemed a bit risky because the Impressions' resurgence with 'Gypsy Woman' had come out of New York. Although Curtis appeared to have temporarily lost his hit formula, he had made a couple of promising records ('We Girls' and 'Behind Curtains') with Jan Bradley for Formal on his return visits to Chicago earlier in '62. Jan's third Mayfield single 'Mama Didn't Lie' caused a lot of interest in Chicago and Detroit in late '62 and, when Chess picked up the Formal masters, it became a nationwide smash by February '63 (#14 on the Hot 100/8 R&B). This bought Mayfield back home with a bang but Jan's move to Chess effectively ended their association because of previous royalty disputes with the label, so Curtis declined any further involvement.

From the early 1960s, Curtis Mayfield began to extend his role of singer/songwriter to that of arranger/producer. After he began getting hits with Jerry and the Impressions, lots of artists began to want his songs (and the sound of his guitar) so he wrote words and music, coached the artists and was often at the sessions when they cut the records. The more studio time he got the more he began to produce and arrange. As his reputation grew, many opportunities came his way to record his songs with a wide variety of vocal groups and singers on the Chicago scene and in New York. The next three years (1962–5) would see Curtis collaborating with a number of different artists and labels to produce a string of hits.

First in line was famed Chicago producer Carl Davis, who was in the process of rebuilding the OKeh label and offered Curtis a freelance production deal. Davis re-acquainted him with Johnny Pate, who he had first worked with on the 'For Your Precious Love' session and pretty soon it became evident that the teaming of Mayfield and Pate was a masterstroke. Johnny Pate, a flautist and bass player turned arranger had been a regular on the jazz club scene with his trio in the Chicago of the '40s, where he worked alongside Coleridge Davis and Stuff Smith. Though Johnny was 20 years Mayfield's senior, their partnership at OKeh worked well and, by January '63, he began arranging the Impressions' sessions. Over the next five years, this production team would be responsible for all the Impressions' records and between them they created ten Top 40 hit singles and nine of their albums hit the Billboard LP chart.

Carl Davis worked closely with Mayfield and Pate at OKeh and, between 1963 and '66, these collective talents brought about a creative rebirth of the label under his guidance and direction. The very first OKeh hit that the team produced was 'The Monkey Time' for Major Lance, which also became his biggest career hit when it scored #8 pop/2 R&B in August '63. The record was immense and it created a dance craze that in America came close to rivalling the Twist, spawning even more Monkey hit records for the likes of the Miracles and Rufus Thomas among many others. It was phenomenally successful but, more importantly, it was a milestone because it was the very first to use what was later to be become known as the 'Chicago sound' – a big band brass arrangement with heavy bass lines and strings, Mayfield's guitar as rhythm and the Impressions on backing vocals. With Major, the Mayfield sound was almost total and, at the time, some said that his records and those of the Impressions were almost indistinguishable. Even if this observation were true, it was hardly surprising given that the only difference on these recording sessions was the lead singer.

Meanwhile, Curtis did not neglect his work with the Impressions. There had been a nine-month break between their last New York and first Chicago session and, rather surprisingly, it did not provide a hit single. 'Sad, Sad Boy and Girl' flopped and the B-side 'Twist and Limbo' was a rather pathetic attempt to trawl sales on Chubby Checker's dance hit 'Limbo Rock' (which had topped both pop and R&B charts at the end of '62). But by the next session, on 21 August '63, the trio had moved up a gear. 'It's All Right' hit #4 pop and #1 on the R&B charts – it was a massive hit single for the Impressions, their biggest to date and it established a style that made them one of the most influential and successful soul vocal groups of the '60s. The tight but easy Pate arrangement coupled with their confident vocalizing appealed to listeners and dancers alike. The horn arrangement, a suggestion of Mayfield's, took its inspiration from a Bobby Bland single but the idea for the song itself had come from a conversation between Curtis and Fred one night when the Impressions were on tour in Nashville. Mayfield was effusively expounding some ideas and future plans and Cash was interjecting from time to time and concurred with 'Right' and 'Well that's alright' – suddenly

Curtis had a hook line, 'Say It's Alright'. The next evening, as they sat in the car between shows, he played Sam and Fred the whole song.

They cut this historic track at Universal Studios in Chicago just two months after Curtis' hit production of Major Lance's 'The Monkey Time', which was still riding high on the charts. All the vital elements came together and this modern classic bought the Impressions back even stronger than before. They worked better as a trio, their personas were sharper and Mayfield had finally hit a stride that would take them all to another level both artistically and commercially. ABC stopped pressing *The Impressions* (ABC 450) album and replaced 'Can't You See' with the current hit (though some early versions, now highly collectable, were released). The *It's All Right* album sold well and was placed at #43 on the Billboard album by late summer of '63. It was largely a collection of songs recorded in New York between July '61 and March '62. The album further established Mayfield as a writer and producer, bringing him even more work via his publishing company Curtom, through which he controlled his own sessions and the royalties due. This arrangement still allowed Curtis to follow his freelance activities unhindered. In addition to the often-covered 'Gypsy Woman', (the most successful version by Brian Hyland earned a gold disc when it reached #3 on the pop chart in October 1970) two other tracks from the album, 'Little Young Lover' and 'It's All Right' were also recorded later many times by other artists.

Ever the opportunist, Calvin Carter compiled an album entitled *For Your Precious Love* (VJ 1075) and issued it on Vee-Jay in '63 to capitalize on the huge success of *It's All Right*. Carter had re-issued other VJ singles of the Impressions since their 'Gypsy Woman' hit but none of them had made the charts. It was Jerry Butler and the Impressions' only album. An even mixture of singles and unreleased cuts were featured: 'Young Lover' the other half of Mayfield's 'Little Young Lover', 'Let Me Know' a doo wop-flavoured Mayfield ballad, plus 'Don't Drive Me Away' a Pop Staples ballad with lead by Jerry Butler. The album also contains the previously unreleased 'Believe In Me' a Richard Brooks-led gospel plea that possibly echoed his inner turmoil at that time it was cut. The final track, 'A Long Time Ago', blends the lead of Curtis harmoniously with the bass of Sam Gooden. Later UK albums on DJM (Dick James

Music) and Charly included another five songs but the most complete collection was issued in '94 as *The Impressions, Their Complete Vee-Jay Recordings* (NVD2-719) by the briefly reactivated VJ. This contains an alternative take of 'Lonely One', which features another great lead vocal from Gooden and 'Give Me Your Love', an excellent Butler lead song written by Richard and previously only available as a solo Butler B-side. This was recorded again by the Impressions in March 1962.

Mayfield's next hit came with Major Lance and 'Hey Little Girl', which went to #13 pop/12 R&B in November and then the vaguely mystical 'Um Um Um Um Um Um', which scored even higher on both charts (#5 R&B /Hot pop) in January '64, bringing Lance international recognition. Even though the UK hit went to a lacklustre cover by Wayne Fontana and the Mindbenders (#5 UK pop in October '64), Major still achieved #40 UK pop with his original version, his only British pop hit. It was this memorable record that placed him at the forefront of the UK '60s soul boom. Lance and Mayfield's roots went back to their schooldays at Wells High, where their paths often crossed. Curtis wrote and produced 'I've Got A Girl', Major's first record for Mercury in '59 and the Impressions provided the backing vocals, (as they did on most of his early records) but this single only achieved local hit status. The Impressions, with Curtis on lead, had recorded it themselves a couple of years earlier for the demo tape that eventually got them their deals with Bandera and Vee-Jay.

At the same time, 'Talking About My Baby' maintained the Impressions' hot streak when it hit #12 on both charts in January '64, where it nestled right alongside 'Um 6'. The smooth vocal interplay between Mayfield, Cash and Gooden was so easy on the ear that listeners slipped subconsciously into the classic format they had created. The Impressions projected an air of stylish confidence that set an uptone making this and their other singles of this era very enjoyable listening. The title seemed comfortable, sandwiched between the Beatles 'I Wanna Hold Your Hand' and 'I Saw Her Standing There' on the Top 20 of the day.

The Beatles took the American charts by storm at the beginning of '64, just prior to their incredibly successful US tour that began that February. Despite the 'British invasion', the Impressions managed to maintain their string of hits. 'I'm So Proud' came next and it went to #12 pop/14 R&B. This tender ballad faired well on the rock-oriented chart of the time. ABC released the trio's second album *Never Ending Impressions* (ABC 468) in May '64, which contained 12 potent tracks, many strong enough to be singles. 'Sister Love', 'That's What Love Will Do' and 'Girl You Don't Know Me' could all have provided big hits for the Impressions but surprisingly none of them were issued by ABC as singles. The commercial potential of 'Girl You Don't Know Me' did not go unnoticed by Don Julian (lead singer of Los Angeles group the Larks) however, who wrote alternate lyrics and turned it into a Top 10 hit for himself as 'The Jerk' in January '65 on Money Records.

During this period, Mayfield wrote and produced for Okeh and ABC in tandem, scoring hits all round. Perhaps the OKeh artist to benefit most from his encouragement and tutelage (though not commercially) was the very young and extremely talented Billy Butler (Jerry's younger brother). Jerry and Curtis were both of major influence in Billy's early development as a singer/songwriter. Billy said in '72, 'Curtis taught me the very first things about the guitar. I guess we were the two closest guitar players in the city at one time, having that type of feeling for the instrument. Since then, I've tried to broaden my thing a little but it's still basically Curtis orientated.' Mayfield supervized and Carl Davis produced Billy's very first session at OKeh on 8 May '63, and they co-wrote 'Found True Love', which was arranged by Johnny Pate.

Chart action wasn't any friend to Billy Butler – a series of badly timed events dogged progress throughout his singing career but thankfully he persisted long enough to produce many beautiful love songs and some of the greatest 'uptown soul' of all time. Their work was not only confined to the studio, as all of them toured together: Curtis and the Impressions, Jerry, Billy and The Chanters plus Gene Chandler, The Vibrations and The Drifters were all on the road in one package. It was in such illustrious company that Billy got his start at that time. He wrote one of his finest songs 'I Stand Accused', which co-author and elder brother Jerry recorded and hit the charts with in August '64. Curtis provided Billy with songs like 'Nevertheless', 'You're Gonna Be Sorry', 'Does It Matter' and 'I'm Just A Man' for the early OKeh sessions, most of which he played and sang on as well. But, it was a reworking of the Impressions' 'I Can't Work No Longer' gave Billy Butler his biggest chart success, when it hit #6 R&B in June '65. An early version of 'Gotta Get Away' (that the Impressions cut later) didn't catch on, but the insistently uptempo 'Right Track' made #24 R&B in July '66 after which Billy parted company with OKeh and the Chanters to pursue a solo career with Carl Davis at Brunswick.

Another of Curtis' associations that brought about a number of hits between 1963 and '65 was with Gene Chandler. 'Duke Of Earl' had been a huge hit for Gene at the beginning of '62 when it topped both R&B and the Hot 100 charts but he had been unable to provide himself with a big enough follow-up hit to fully capitalize on his initial success. So in early '63 he went in search of a different sound and found it with Mayfield. Chandler recorded a dozen or more of Curtis' songs and most of them hit the R&B chart. The first 'Rainbow' (#11 R&B/47 pop), became Gene's theme song (it was recorded by him again as 'Rainbow '65' bringing him even bigger success when it went to #2 R&B). He followed up with 'Man's Temptation' six months later that went to #17 R&B/71 pop and was his last hit for Vee-Jay. The Mayfield/Chandler combination struck gold again with 'Just Be True' in July '64 when the record notched up another Top 20 R&B/pop hit, this time for Ewart Abner's Constellation Records. 'What Now' made the Top 40 in January '65, hotly pursued by 'You Can't Hurt Me No More' in March and 'Nothing Can Stop Me' (probably his most famous record in the UK) made #18 pop/ 2 R&B the following month, all on Constellation Records.

Curtis also worked briefly with Walter Jackson, who had to wait for Mayfield's 'It's All Over' to break in November '64 before the hits started to happen for him. Jackson had recorded 'That's What Mama Say', a sequel to Jan Bradley's earlier hit 'Mama Didn't Lie' but, great as it was, it didn't chart. During their short working relationship both artists developed much mutual respect and when interviewed in '72, Curtis said, 'I met Walter in New York a few weeks ago and he's got a few hang-ups with his career at the moment. It's such a pity as he has exceptional talent and ability but in recent times he's had a bad deal. Nobody builds a song quite the way Walter does.' Jackson had been discovered by Carl Davis performing in Detroit but despite cutting several great records together, it took Mayfield's spark to ignite Walter's earliest chart success.

In little over a year, since the spring of '63 Curtis had set Chicago and the rest of America alight with a string of big hits. This level of continuous success had a very positive influence on his confidence and by March '64 Mayfield was ready to make his next creative leap. The Impressions' 'Keep On Pushing' was a heavily gospel-influenced song, which became a milestone in the lyrical development of Curtis Mayfield. It went to #10 in June '64 on both charts and provided the Impressions their third Top 20 pop hit of the year. The song lent lyrical and spiritual support to the civil rights movement, which was then gathering momentum behind its most charismatic leader Martin Luther King. Mayfield's lyrics embraced a much wider audience, however, who could equally apply them to the everyday struggle in their own lives. 'Keep On Pushing' struck a universal chord within a generation. It was the very first of his message songs and it provided him with a new direction where he could further explore, create and express his ideas and opinions.

The Impressions still had two more Top 20 hits to come in the remaining months of '64. 'You Must Believe Me' (which had more than an echo of 'It's All Right' about it) hit #15 pop/15 R&B in September. 'Amen' climbed to #7 pop in December and this gospel-inspired hit kept them high on the charts into the New Year. Thus far, 1964 had been a great year for Curtis, Sam and Fred with five hit singles and two hit albums that had sold very well, reaching #43 and #52 respectively on the album charts. But the Impressions hit the peak of their commercial popularity in the summer of '64 when they released their third album, *Keep On Pushing* (ABC 493). It contained 11 hot Mayfield songs plus 'Amen', which although not his song was soon very much associated with the Impressions.

In addition to the singles, the album contained 'Dedicate My Song', 'I Made A Mistake' and 'I've Been Trying', arguably Mayfield's finest love song. 'I've Been Trying' is a perfect record. Previously cut by Jerry Butler, and by many others since, it embodies the essence of the Mayfield ballad and though often imitated, nothing comes close to the Impressions' original: it is thought by many to be their finest record. 'Talking About

My Baby' portrayed the trio at their coolest and was also included on the album along with 'Long, Long Winter' (which did well on the R&B chart of late '64). *Keep On Pushing* was the Impressions' biggest album and took them into the Top 10, where it peaked at #8 on the Billboard pop LP charts in August '64 and #4 R&B over the same period.

Christmas 1964 saw Curtis and the Impressions celebrate their most successful year in the music business so far as they had earned constant chart and media exposure. No one could have predicted that the new year would bring them even greater achievements. In 1965 the Impressions would score eight hits on the R&B singles chart, three of them reaching the Top 30 pop. In terms of best-selling singles it was to be their most successful year. 'People Get Ready' continued the gospel theme when it hit the charts at #14 pop/3 R&B in March and also became the title of their fourth album.

People Get Ready contained 12 Mayfield songs, mostly soulful ballads. When interviewed at the time Curtis observed, 'My experience has shown that the group does better with originals. I think this is because my own sincerity and emotion, which have gone into the song, are reflected in our performance of it.' 'People Get Ready' illustrates this statement perfectly: a slow tempo ballad with all three Impressions voices against the backdrop of Pate's superbly controlled arrangement and Mayfield's distinctive guitar work produced a powerful and confident message. It became one of his most celebrated and, in the intervening years, recorded songs. It was soon taken up as a slogan for the civil rights movement and was also used by other oppressed minority groups.

The song itself has heavy gospel overtones and, like 'Keep On Pushing', the lyrics expand the song's central theme: it is a completely open invitation to all, with no conditions, no religious or racial barriers. Mayfield had again added his social voice to the poetry of his love sonnets, cautiously at first, but also with growing confidence and self-assurance. He had created the perfect musical set-up and at that time the combined talents of the group (Johnny Pate, the musicians and engineers in Chicago) couldn't miss.

This success inspired Mayfield even more and his songwriting reached prolific proportions. The creative process was so well tuned that in a series of long sessions the team recorded near complete albums. On 26 October '64 they recorded eight finished songs to complete the *People Get Ready* (ABC 505) album. All 12 tracks on the fourth album are Mayfield songs. While 'Woman's Got Soul', their hit single of the time, was a smoothly hip mirror of the moment, generally the album reflects a rear-view glance both in the choice of subject matter and the inclusion of older material. 'Emotions' is a reworking of an earlier song recorded in March '62 at their last New York session (the original cut first found UK release with the *Right On Time* album on Charly in '83). 'Can't Work No Longer' a #6 R&B hit for Billy Butler in June '65 was also retrieved from that same Impressions session for this album. The quintet's vocal treatment and Roy Glover's arrangement both sound curiously dated (but nevertheless enjoyable) when compared to the other tracks recorded at the time.

The contemporary songs yielded an even mixture of ballads and uptempo sides like 'I've Found That I've Lost' and 'We're In Love'. *People Get Ready* climbed to #23 on Billboard's album chart (#1 R&B) in March '65. This collection of distinctive and original music gave the Impressions their second biggest seller of all time. Had the album sleeve been a little more contemporary it would have outsold its predecessor. The album's release was followed by two months of touring and constant media exposure after which ABC issued a *Greatest Hits* (ABC 515) album and this too went to the top of the R&B album charts.

During this period, the Impressions also spent a good deal of time out on the road touring America. In the early days they played several shows a day travelling by coach or car between gigs – all three Impressions hated flying. Things had loosened up a bit in some parts of the country but they still had to tolerate some restrictions in a few locations and sometimes it got to be a bit of a grind. One destination the group always enjoyed playing, however, was Jamaica. Here the audiences were different, enthusiastic, colourful and the local music, culture and feel of the place was intoxicating. Curtis and the Impressions were particularly popular there. Mayfield was revered as a leading voice in the struggle for civil rights and his songs of conscience were very influential in the development of the attitudes expressed by the upcoming new musical generation there, which included Bob Marley and the Wailers, Prince Buster, Jimmy Cliff and many others.

Curtis Mayfield must have been the busiest man in town, rarely out of the studio. It was becoming difficult for him to find enough time to write, tour and promote the Impressions recordings as well as all his other writing and production commitments, his workload was approaching critical mass. Mayfield songs packed the US singles charts as Jerry, Gene, Major, Billy and the Impressions yo-yoed past each other all year long. 'Sometimes I Wonder', 'Good Times', 'You Can't Hurt Me No More', 'I Can't Work No Longer', 'Rainbow '65' and other Curtis titles kept labels like Constellation, Vee-Jay and OKeh on the R&B charts.

In addition, his sound influenced that of his contemporaries. During the early '60s, groups like The Van Dykes, The Esquires and The Radiants showed considerable Mayfield influence, some quite obscure records from Johnny and the Expressions and Willie Cooper and the Webs also filched the sound. Many of these groups evolved a completely different sound later on, but like the Beatles, Mayfield had created such a uniquely infectious style that for a while everybody wanted to try it on.

Mayfield stopped writing and producing for OKeh in mid '65 and began to refocus on the Impressions. It occurred to him that it would be better business sense to sign artists himself and create a roster of his own. The past three years had been an incredibly creative and commercially successful period. Not only had Curtis firmly established himself as a consistently brilliant independent writer/producer, providing a bonanza of hits for other Chicago artists, he had re-invented the Impressions and put them back on track commercially, where they would remain for another ten years. He had produced a truly amazing body of work and it was these resultant hits that were among the records most influential in redefining 'Chicago soul'. The Mayfield sound did for Chicago what Tamla Motown was doing for Detroit and Stax was about to do for Memphis. All this and he was still just 23 years old.

4 Windy C, Mayfield And *We're A Winner*

Following the success of their albums *Keep on Pushing* and *People Get Ready*, the Impressions had a series of singles that did not match up to their previous form. 'Meeting Over Yonder' went to #12 on the US R&B chart in August giving them their fourth hit single of '65 but failed to make the pop Top 40 by eight places. This was a return to the gospel anthem, reinforcing but not converting any new fans. Their next single 'I Need You' and flipside 'Never Could You Be' both made Top 40 R&B between October and December of '65 but split sales prevented the record hitting the Top 40 pop chart at all. There was no clear A-side, with both songs having a similar tempo and sentiment, and so they received divided airplay and, for the first time in two years, a single missed its target. Instead of taking stock and making the necessary adjustments, ABC rushed out a follow-up with all the same characteristics. 'Just One Kiss From You' was another beautiful Mayfield ballad, but not single material and it became the first Impressions single to miss the charts in two years.

Soon after recording two of the biggest albums of their careers it seemed, from outward appearances that Curtis Mayfield and the Impressions were going through a period of reflection, of taking stock. In fact, Curtis was experiencing an intensely creative period, developing projects that would evolve into his first two record labels Windy C and Mayfield, forerunners of his most successful venture Curtom, which was still three years further down the line.

One By One (ABC 523), their next album was issued in early '66 and uncharacteristically contained only three Mayfield songs out of 12. At the time, this album was seen as something of a backward step for the

Impressions, who had created a reputation for music that was both stylish and up to the minute. Now with the passage of 30 or more years, the album reflects some interesting influences and can be judged with less of an emotional perspective. 'Twilight Time' the opening track, was one of two Platters' hits that was effectively restyled for this album. It was also used as a B-side of 'Just One Kiss From You'. Sam Gooden took the lead on 'I Wanna Be Around' the song previously made famous by crooner Tony Bennett but his rich baritone could still not make the song any more palatable. 'Nature Boy' had been a huge R&B hit for Nat King Cole in May '48 and went Top 40 for Bobby Darin in '61. The Impressions' version, with Mayfield lead, gives the song yet another lease of life and it benefits immensely from Johnny Pate's sumptuous arrangement.

Nat King Cole had been one of the biggest black solo singing stars of all time. After crossing over from jazz to pop, he began to have Top 40 hits on Capitol from early '55 right up until his death in '65. His highly consistent success rate also made him a TV star (he was the first black artist to have his own show) and movie star: this kind of exposure elevated him to megastar status with black America. Obviously his influence also touched The Impressions, who cut three of the songs associated with him on this album, 'Answer Me, Oh My Love' and 'Mona Lisa' being the other two. 'Falling In Love With You' and 'Lonely Man', the other two Mayfield songs, were again led by him and seemed to be in an earlier Impressions style, which they were slowly moving away from, but which fitted perfectly into this album's mood. Curtis also took the lead for 'I Want To Be With You' and 'Without A Song'. Both were beautifully executed but Pate's arrangements were perhaps becoming a bit predictable, though still technically excellent. The energetic version of 'It's Not Unusual' has the trio demonstrating their great vocal technique once again but was rather a surprising choice of material. Fred Cash took the lead for the second Platters track 'My Prayer' but unfortunately he was just a bit out of his depth and this remains *One By One's* least enjoyable track.

The Mayfield/Pate partnership had developed a revolutionary style that became a cornerstone of the 'Chicago sound'. The combination of the songwriting style, the orchestral arrangements and funky production had not been put together like this before. This format was now used in the restyling of established standards and, in some cases, this was an unflattering fit. For this kind of album to really succeed, it needed a much more flexible concept, with experimental arrangements and production. The group's version of 'Let It Be Me' for instance, gives an indication of brighter possibilities. This was the first time that the partnership showed any signs of disharmony. Curtis was already respected by many as an innovator and a poet with philosophical aspirations. His fans expected more than lukewarm versions of other people's hits from the Impressions, no matter how well performed or technically perfect they were. Also, the whole idea of a *One By One* album was that it gave all group members a chance to sing lead. Sam and Fred, both great singers in their own right, only got one lead each whilst Curtis took the other ten, and it might have been a little more interesting to see what they could have made of some of the material. Atco Records had released a *One By One* album by the Coasters back in 1960, which featured three lead tracks from each of their individual members and, while it was no raving success either, it did give an in-depth portrait of the group.

Although it was not uncommon for the Impressions to trade vocal leads, Mayfield's was the lead voice that most fans wanted to hear. But not this time, however. The public obviously did not share the group's taste for nostalgia. Back in the mid 1960s, this kind of showcase had been the object of many vocal groups' aspirations. It had become an accepted format, like the 'The Two Sides Of...' or 'The Many Sides Of...', a title that immediately indicated that here was a successful group with an album of standards presented in their own style. To groups like the Impressions this kind of material represented the hallmark of the established artist and it was generally thought by the major record companies that such collections would get groups 'over the hump' and expose them to a wider (and whiter) audience. But times had changed and things were no longer quite that simple.

When released in early '66 *One By One* became the first Impressions ABC album not to enter the Top 100 list. Even with a different title and a slicker sleeve, it probably would not have become a hit, but it might have gone over a lot better. In addition, because the album was considered a commercial flop in America (#104 in September '65) it did not gain a UK release and was not re-pressed by ABC, so copies became very rare. Until recently it has remained virtually unobtainable on vinyl anywhere, though a Canadian re-issue on Reo did provide a second chance for avid collectors to obtain a copy. The master tapes lay buried in the MCA vaults for many years until after several attempts they were finally unearthed by Kent for their first excursion on to CD in '98.

Rather than look for another single from the *One by One* source, Mayfield dipped his pen in the Motown fountain to restore the Impressions to the singles charts by creating the uncharacteristic 'You Been Cheatin'', which put them back on top when it went to #12 R&B/33 pop in December '65 and carried them into '66 on the crest of a new wave. Curtis had once again created the right momentum to please their public. ABC Records however, seemed oblivious to this positive change of direction and issued 'Since I Lost The One I Love'/'Falling In Love With You', two Mayfield ballads, as their next single, which missed the charts once again. In the UK, HMV had issued every single since 'It's All Right' but they sensibly coupled 'Just One Kiss From You' with 'You Been Cheatin'' and it secured better soul single sales. Though the Impressions' records didn't hit the pop charts, they sold consistently well enough to soul fans to guarantee UK issue but confidence was not as rock solid as it had been, as sales began to fluctuate. 'Too Slow' came next in mid '66 and provided the second flop in a row. It took 'Can't Satisfy' the second Motown-flavoured single to restore them to #12 on the US R&B chart in August '66.

This evolution of the Impressions' vocal and musical style was shaped and guided by Curtis Mayfield, as it was he who created the lyrics and music for their songs. *Ridin' High* (ABC 545), their next album, was written and recorded at roughly the same time as their previous set but this time reflected the progressive mood Curtis, Sam and Fred were currently enjoying, despite their blip on the charts. It went some way to restoring the Impressions to the charts when it went to #79 on the pop album chart in March '66.

'Too Slow', 'Ridin' High' and the superb 'Right On Time' were the contemporary tracks and reflected where the Impressions were at, right then. 'Too Slow' was wrongly chosen as the single and flopped. The more positive 'Right On Time' would have been a much more appropriate choice. This time, ten of the 11 tracks were from Curtis' pen but some of the songs had been used before by Jerry and Billy Butler, Major Lance, Gene Chandler etc. In 1990 Curtis recalled, 'I used to get some flack from the fellas [Sam and Fred] because even before we had any hits as the Impressions, I had written many songs for other artists and some like "Monkey Time" had become big hits and this upset the fellas because we didn't do it. But we did cut some of those songs as album tracks later on.'

The exquisite 'No One Else' would be recorded a number of times later, notably by June Conquest and Holly Maxwell. The song listed as 'I Need A Love' was in fact 'I Need You' and had been used as a single a year earlier and scored #26 R&B/64 pop on the charts. These two songs created some confusion at ABC, who supplied the previously unreleased 'I Need A Love' by mistake to the UK Stateside label, who were delighted to use the track on their second *Big Sixteen* compilation. It still remains unreleased in America. the Impressions turned in excellent versions of 'Gotta Get Away' and 'I Need To Belong To Someone' (which they remade with Leroy Hutson singing lead in '72). 'Man's Temptation' on which they managed to top Gene Chandler's earlier version and 'I'm A Tellin' You', a hit written for Jerry back in '61, are also up to scratch and this time are handled by Sam and Fred. Another song – a huge hit for Butler in duet with Betty Everett – was the evergreen standard 'Let It Be Me', which now took on a completely refreshing style and arrangement with plenty of vocal group involvement. When it came time to release *Ridin' High* (CLP 3548) in Britain, HMV removed two tracks and added five for the UK version of this album in line with the previous British releases.

Aside from his work with the Impressions during this period, Curtis Mayfield was also planning to launch his own label. He had witnessed the success that label mate Ray Charles was having with his label, Tangerine, and so Curtis had been making his own preparations with Windy C Records, the first of his independent labels, which he launched in April '66. This move further expanded his operations through

Curtom Publishing and created a base to sign new artists who he could write and produce for as an independent.

Windy C (distributed by Cameo Parkway Records Inc) virtually became a showcase for new discovery the Five Stairsteps. The group consisted of the Burke family, four brothers and sister, Alohe. The brothers Burke were Clarence Jr (lead tenor and guitar), James (first tenor), Dennis (baritone) and Kenneth (second tenor and bassman extraordinaire).

The Stairsteps' story began in '58 when Clarence Burke Senior (Papa Stairstep) who was a detective on the Chicago police force, began to organize his children into a vocal group. He managed and tutored the group through a number of amateur talent contests, competitions and live appearances at local Chicago venues. They won a major talent contest at the Regal Theatre in '65, and happily, Fred Cash and Curtis Mayfield were conveniently on hand to discover them. The Five Stairsteps' reward was a contract with Windy C records and their first single hit the R&B charts at #16 in May '66 entitled 'You Waited Too Long' (WC-601). The R&B sales did not translate to pop successfully and the single only bubbled low on the Hot 100 at #94. Their second single 'World Of Fantasy' (WC-602) did rather better in August '66 when it went to #12 R&B and #49 pop and became the best-selling Windy C single. All The Stairsteps' Windy C singles were hits on the US R&B chart and most featured the excellent tenor voice of Clarence Burke Jr, who also co-wrote most of the songs. Curtis Mayfield wrote the first B-side 'Don't Waste Your Time', which featured Dennis Burke on lead. 'Behind Curtains' was also an original that was first cut by Curtis with Jan Bradley for Nite Owl. Mayfield produced and Johnny Pate arranged all the Windy C sessions. The third Stairsteps' single 'Come Back' (WC-603) kept ringing up the hits when it registered at #15 R&B/61 pop singles in November '66 and 'Danger She's A Stranger' (WC-604) started '67 with a bang for this exciting young group when it scored a healthy #16 US R&B hit.

Their next single, 'Ain't Gonna Rest' (WC-605), represented a slight stylistic shift for the Five Stairsteps. The earlier R&B hits were mainly ballads and this was an attempt to cross over to pop with a more uptempo dance number. It did not sell as well as their earlier singles but reached #37 R&B/87 pop in April '67. Unhappy at this dip Windy C quickly issued 'Ooh Baby Baby' (WC-607) a cover of the Smokey Robinson and The Miracles' classic but that didn't do much better, peaking at #34 R&B two months later. The Five Stairsteps were the first family of soul, but they didn't cross over as successfully to the pop chart as the Impressions had. 'World Of Fantasy' did best when it just made the pop Top 50 but, in the main, their singles were not dance oriented at that time and this denied them even greater success.

These singles were put together to make up the only Windy C album entitled *Five Stairsteps* (WC 6008), which earned them big R&B sales when it went to #8 on the R&B albums chart in March '67. By mid '67 interest in The Five Stairsteps' singles was beginning to wane and 'Change Of Pace' (WC-608) made no impact at all on either chart. Mayfield wound up the Windy C in anticipation of the Curtom Records launch, but signed the Five Stairsteps to the new label where they continued to collaborate with Mayfield (see Chapter 5). In addition to their R&B chart success, the Five Stairsteps, during their spell with Windy C, won much recognition for their mellow performances when New York DJs voted them the most promising vocal group in '66, and they received the NATRA (National Association of Teenage Recording Artists) award for outstanding R&B group for 1967.

The only other record issued on Windy C, 'Take Care'/'All I Need' (WC-606) by June Conquest, did not make any impact on the charts. June of whom Curtis later said, 'June had just a couple of singles with us, she then suffered a period of bad health, which lasted for quite a long time. We tried a duet with Donny [Hathaway] and June together on Curtom [see Chapter 5, Curtom Records] but it didn't happen so we let her go.'

Running concurrently with Windy C was Curtis' second label, Mayfield Records (distributed by Calla Records), which was was launched in mid '66. Once again, it mainly showcased another group, the Fascinations. This stylish bouffant-haired female quartet hailed from Detroit and had a similar look to the Ronettes but a very different sound. the Fascinations were Shirley Walker, Bernadine (Boswell) Smith, her sister Joanne (Boswell) Levell and Fern Bledsoe, who had early Motown connections. Sam Gooden and Fred Cash had discovered the girls in '62 and took them to Curtis Mayfield. Nothing materialized on record until May '63, however, when Curtis, through his independent production deal with ABC, produced 'Mama Didn't Lie'/'Someone Like You' and it was issued on ABC. Jan Bradley had recorded 'Mama' a few months earlier, so in early '63 both versions competed for a short time before Bradley's version won out and became the national hit. The Fasinations' 'Tears In My Eyes'/'You're Gonna Be Sorry' followed on but didn't capture much public attention. They remained in limbo for three years before (with a 'c' added to their name) their third single '(Say It Isn't So) Say You'll Never Go' (M-7711). It hit the R&B charts at #47 in September '66 but the single created little pop interest.

But they came bouncing back with their career hit 'Girls Are Out To Get You' (M-7714), which went to #13 R&B/92 pop in January '67. When interviewed in '72 Curtis remarked, 'Ah, my Fascinations. They were a beautiful group but I can't remember all their names. Shirley Walker was lead and Joanne – I don't know, me and my memory will have to get together. I'm very pleased by the success that they are having with "Girls Are Out To Get You" in your charts now.' ('Girls...' had only managed a low Hot 100 hit in America but six years later and on the third time of UK release, it was a sizeable soul hit and went to #32 on the pop charts in July '71.)

the Fascinations' next single with Mayfield, 'I Can't Stay Away From You' (M-7716), followed in July '67 and registered Top 50 R&B but 'Hold On' (M-7718) made no headway at all. A master bought in New York and featuring Tony Foxx titled 'ESP' was released as (M-7715) and suffered much the same fate. 'Just Another Reason' (M-7719) was later re-cut by June & Donny but again produced low sales for the Fascinations and was the last Mayfield single to be issued. Almost all Mayfield's releases were written and produced by Curtis who co-wrote a couple of the B-sides with Guy Draper. In the UK, soul fans found these records hard to come by.

The other single released on the Mayfield label of great interest was 'I've Been Trying' (M-7712) by the Mayfield Singers who consisted of Leroy Hutson, Donny Hathaway, Guy Draper, perhaps Curtis himself plus three other unknown voices, all students at Howard University. The record features several leads as they dip in and out of this emotionally charged version of the Mayfield classic, to which he also lends the beautiful sound of his guitar. This great single was coupled with 'If', a Guy Draper song that again features the shared leads of the Howard fraternity. It is backed up by a cinemascope production from Johnny Pate who uses an effective sample of a well-known western movie theme inside his dramatic arrangement.

Numerically, the label listing shows nine releases but, so far, research has not revealed the missing two. Unissued tracks include a second single 'Little Bird'/'Don't Start Now' by the Mayfield Singers, which was cut in '67 and may have been intended as M-7717. 'Trusting In You'/'Crazy' by the Fascinations was also unreleased at the time but in '97 Tony Rounce of Sequel Records, put all the original Mayfield label tracks together on one CD for the UK market, which included all the previously unreleased material plus some unheard cuts by the Mayfield Players.

The Mayfield tracks were cut in Chicago, probably at RCA studios, but right from the start Mayfield and Pate maintained a Detroit sound for the Fascinations (at least on the uptempo sides). This provided them with R&B chart hits and Chicago sales but, with the exception of 'Girls Are Out To Get You', they could not achieve any crossover into pop.

When Curtis started Curtom Records, his most successful label venture, Mayfield Records hicupped temporarily and then disappeared. No Mayfield album was issued in America and none of the records had any real pop chart success bar the one above. Whether this was due to poor distribution, bad timing or lack of airplay is open to conjecture. The quality of Mayfield product was always high and the performances were great.

Although June and the Stairsteps moved over to Curtom, the Fascinations weren't so lucky. They later recorded their own version of

'I've Been Trying' in Philadelphia but not long afterwards they splintered to non-musical pursuits. Due to rekindled UK interest the girls reformed again in '72 for a European tour that went off successfully and inspired them to try again at home. They persevered for a short period but, due to lack of interest, the Fascinations finally stepped out of the limelight completely in the early 1970s.

As well as working on these two record labels, Curtis continued to produce music with the Impressions. The singles that were being released by ABC slowed down, once again falling out of step with Impressions' fans. In contrast to '65 when they had nine singles in the R&B chart, in '66 only one of their singles, 'Can't Satisfy', charted. Their fans wanted uptempo singles at that time. Mayfield's ballads were album material and that's the way they liked it. Whether ABC's reshuffle or Curtis Mayfield's external projects were the reason for the inattention to the effective marketing of Impressions' product at this time can only be speculated at but, by Christmas of 1966, the group's albums were selling better than their singles.

In the late summer of '67 ABC released the Impressions seventh album *The Fabulous Impressions* (ABC 606), which marked a return to a style that had previously supplied them with their biggest hits. The opening track 'You Always Hurt Me' was their most recent hit single – a #20 R&B/ 96 pop in March '67. It was the third semi-Motown-style Impressions single that Curtis had written in his bid to keep the trio on the charts, while his own unique style seemed temporarily out of fashion with American record buyers.

'It's All Over' had originally been written for Walter Jackson three years earlier, providing his début hit single (see Chapter 3, 'Gypsy Woman', ABC and OKeh). The Impressions' version with Curtis taking lead is a superb rendition of this classic song and one that Sam and Fred had always wanted to cut. 'Little Girl' features the dark brown lead of Sam Gooden for which this album is something of a showcase, in as much as he is featured lead as often as Curtis. It was used in America as the flipside to 'You Always Hurt Me'. Sam had been the lead singer with the Roosters and it is no surprise that his vocal approach and timbre have often been compared to that of Jerry Butler, to which there are some superficial similarities.

'100lbs Of Clay' is the only non-Mayfield song on this album and is, of course, a restyled version of the Gene McDaniels' hit of '61. The treatment borders on novelty and it may have been a late idea for the *One By One* album. 'Love's A Comin'' sounds like another old song, which may have been written with Butler in mind. The group, with Gooden taking lead, supply an infectious rendition that was used as a single coupled with the rare 'Wade In The Water' in late '66, but bombed. Johnny Pate provides an insistent arrangement/production for the uptempo 'You Ought To Be In Heaven' which in better times might have provided another single. 'I Can't Stay Away From You' was an Impressions single, released soon after 'You Got Me Runnin'' had disappointingly peaked at #50 R&B just as this album was issued. It had just been recorded with the Fascinations and went to #49 R&B in July '67, but Curtis, Sam and Fred's version did better reaching #39 R&B/80 pop two months later.

Gooden provides lead on the excellent 'Aware Of Love' that Curtis wrote for Jerry Butler in '61 while they travelled together on a lengthy US tour. 'Isle Of Sirens' also comes from that period and was previously cut by Jerry but this time the group provide the perfect treatment as they relate a Mayfield storyline akin to Greek mythology, in which their crew are dashed on the rocky shores of romance. 'I'm Still Waiting' is a pleading yet powerful Mayfield ballad of the kind that Curtis built his early reputation for songwriting and production on. 'She Don't Love Me' almost follows on from the last track in realization and it builds into a great ballad as they step out of the format and the arrangement takes on unexpected directions with superb vocal interchange by the trio. This great track is one of the lesser-known Mayfield gems.

So once again Curtis and the team supplied a pot-pourri of new songs and old, recorded in Chicago over the previous 18 months. This time the consistency was perfection and an improvement on the past two albums. While the sleeve was OK, it did not really do this collection justice and, once again, appropriate sales were not forthcoming. It was released unchanged in the UK at a later date (CLP 3631) where it sold steadily but didn't chart.

In November '67 Curtis, Sam and Fred regrouped for a final push on their ABC contract that was due to finish in the following year. Two days in the studio produced ten songs and one track in particular was to provide their next big hit single and the title of their following smash album, *We're A Winner* (ABC 635). The sentiments clearly expressed in 'We're A Winner' struck just the right chord for so many people at the time that the record went to #1 R&B/14 pop in January '68 and became the Impressions' biggest hit for five years. A new surge of interest put them back in the media spotlight once again. At the time Curtis had this to say: '"We're A Winner" is a song with a message, a message to all, and yet basically to the black masses of people. It is an inspiring song, I believe, everybody every once in a while should sing in terms of trying to keep the movements going, even though sometimes things are tough. Things move slowly sometimes but with the movement we truly are a "Winner".'

'We're A Winner' is another slice of the Mayfield social philosophy that echoes through quite a few of his songs, two of which nearly appear as lines in the lyrics. 'Keep On Pushin'' that he had already used and 'Moving On Up' that would roll on to reappear later. The song is truly inspirational and though it echoes black pride, it also articulates the voice of oppressed people everywhere. The production team provided perfection and public reaction was suitably appreciative. Despite some moves from the right to ban the record and some restriction on airplay, the song's success proved unstoppable. Recorded just three months before the assassination of Martin Luther King, 'We're A Winner' confidently showed the direction for civil rights to proceed. But after King's death the movement was shattered by the shockwaves that ensued and is still only now slowly re-emerging from the disarray of the past 30 years.

While the first cut on this album articulates the social conscience of young black America, the rest of the tracks examine that other great liberation, true love. 'Moonlight Shadows' is a poetic sonnet and well-placed reminder that the Impressions were and remain unmatched vocally and technically when it comes to the rendition of Mayfield's love songs. The trio really had it down and the music that Curtis and

Johnny Pate created is still unsurpassed. Fred Cash provides the great lead on 'Let Me Tell The World' – a declaration to those who doubt and criticize when they should support and encourage. Mayfield sings lead on most of the tracks this time out but there is a lot of ensemble singing and trading of lines between the trio that makes for most enjoyable listening. The classic 'Nothing Can Stop Me' is the only song from the past, made famous by Gene Chandler in '65. Major Lance had cut it a year earlier as 'Get My Hat' but for one reason or another his version remained unissued until '95. Pate's harder arrangement suits the Impressions tight vocal routine as they deliver a superb treatment that compares favourably to the other versions mentioned. This again was one of the songs that Sam and Fred originally wanted for the group when it was written, so perhaps they had a point or two to prove.

'No One To Love' profits greatly from a looping Pate arrangement that is most effective in its support for Mayfield's lead vocal. 'Little Brown Boy' is a beautiful ballad probably written for Mayfield's eldest son Todd, who must have been around ten years old at the time. The powerful ballad 'I Loved And I Lost' was later chosen as a single and it hit #9 R&B and #61 pop in July '68 after the group had left ABC. 'Romancing To A Folk Song' could have been written for Chicago contemporary Terry Callier and acts as a showcase for Mayfield's beautifully understated guitar work, which is particularly evident on this album. As it draws to a close, one becomes aware of the high level of perfection that this team had reached, it seemed that they were at the pinnacle of their powers and that there was musically little beyond their ability, should they decide to pursue it. Also on this album was the Impressions' version of 'Up Up And Away', the Jim Webb song made famous by 5th Dimension. It was rather surprisingly not an R&B hit in America but had hit #7 on the pop charts a year earlier.

When the album was released it topped the soul charts and went to #35 on Billboard's album chart in March '68 becoming their third-largest career album. When released in the UK by Stateside four months later it had not only grown in reputation but volume, as they added four bonus tracks making a total of 14. Though big with soul fans, the album did not cross over here and sell as well as it deserved to but has over the years grown to classic status. The follow-up single to 'We're A Winner' was the somewhat incestuous 'We're Rolling On' Parts 1 & 2, which hit #17 R&B and #59 pop in May and trawled in the wake of 'Winner'. It signalled Mayfield's and the Impressions' imminent departure on completion of their ABC recording contract.

ABC had been very good for the Impressions, especially in the early years. They had recorded 22 single hits on the national R&B chart and a dozen albums on the LP chart in an unusually successful run for a black group with a major label. After their move to Curtom, ABC issued *Best Of The Impressions* (ABC/S 654) a fairly predictable collection of 11 songs, which attempted to chronicle the Impressions' output during the past five years. *The Versatile Impressions* (ABC/S 668) a patchy ten-track album followed on in late '68. This album was also later re-issued by Pickwick (SPC 3554) with one track 'Just Before Sunrise' omitted.

In an interview in 2001, Sam Gooden revealed, 'I remember ABC told us that we owed them an album just as we were about to leave them for our own company, so we said, "right!" And we went into the studio and put down a bunch of old songs and standards in a couple of mammoth sessions. And we ended up having a real good time doing them. ABC had enough material for two albums but they only issued *Versatile* ... – and they didn't put anything behind it, so it did nothin'.'

It was another five years before two further collections were issued in '73 *Sixteen Greatest Hits* (ABC/S 727) and a double LP *Curtis Mayfield – His Early Years With The Impressions* (ABCX 780/2), which contained 20 tracks and had two issues with different sleeves. ABC licensed 12 songs to Sire Records for their '76 compilation, *The Vintage Years* (Sire 3717-2), which contains 28 sides from Jerry Butler, the Impressions and Curtis Mayfield ranging over a 20-year period and comes in a double album format.

The Impressions' departure for horizons new marked the end of an era in their career as they were about to forsake the relative security of a major record label and embark on the journey of a lifetime alighting at the centre of Curtom, Mayfield's own independent recording company.

5 Curtom Records

Ever since he had established the Impressions, it had always been Curtis Mayfield's ambition to own, run and record for his own label. Windy C and Mayfield were tryouts for Curtom. Curtis knew that the secret of a successful independent record label is to get good partners to handle promotion, distribution, legal and other functions. He used the first two labels as a learning curve while the Impressions were still under contract to ABC. Impatient for Curtom to come on line with Buddah he released three singles locally under the logo in the Chicago area. These records were a hangover from the Windy C sessions and Mayfield wanted to clear the decks before recording his established artists, the Five Stairsteps and the Impressions, for the Buddah launch. The first of these singles was June Conquest's 'What's This I See' (8543) a Lenny Brown song that has a very similar sound to her earlier single. The flip was a restyled version of the Impressions 'No One Else'. Both tracks were produced by Mayfield and arranged by Johnny Pate. The second Curtom release 'When I Grow Old'/'Guilty' (8544) by the Symphonics became an instant rarity, big with northern collectors. The third and final issue was the Winstons' 'Amen'/'Need A Replacement' (8546) again rumoured popular in the northern venues. What happened to 8545 has not yet emerged.

None of these songs were commercially successful and the records were rare. For British collectors, only a precious few import copies reached UK shores and were generally hard to come by. The label design was black and silver and contained both Gemini and Scorpio symbols.

At the Buddah Records Annual Convention in New York on 7–9 June 1968, Neil Bogart, the label's Vice-President and General Manager announced that henceforth Buddah would distribute Curtis Mayfield's new Curtom label. Eddie Thomas (President of Curtom Inc) and Art Kass (of Buddah) signed a five-year contract. Curtom Inc had originally been formed in '61 as a music publishing company with Mayfield as Vice-President. Later it contained Mayfield's two other publishing outlets Chi-Sound (founded in '65), Camad ('68) and the Mayfield and Windy C labels.

The new label was based in Chicago at 6212 North Lincoln Avenue and was distributed through Buddah in New York. Cecil Holmes, Director of R&B for Buddah and once a member of The Solitaires vocal group, initially handled Curtom's promotion. Curtom itself projected a relaxed professional image: the label design was bright and positive with the red and black Curtom logo stretched across a red and yellow mandala in which black Gemini and Scorpio symbols appear. The background looked like a summer sunrise and tucked under the company name were the words 'We're A Winner' that stayed as part of their logo for five years. The records looked like a quality product and that soon proved to be the case. Proper attention was paid to design, marketing and promotion in all vital areas of Curtom product and this all contributed to a very successful launch of an important new and exciting independent record company.

Mayfield explained in a *Cashbox* article at the time his mixed feelings as writer/artist and producer, and the need for him to get into the studio and communicate to musicians while they created the sounds he desired. 'It's hard work running between the studio and the control room,' he said, 'and now that over the years I have found musicians who can constantly create the sound I want, I spend most of my time in the control room where I can get a better idea of what the song will sound like when it's been recorded.' He went on to explain, 'I've been blessed with very few disappointing record dates. In fact, in the eight years I've been recording, I can count the disappointing sessions on one hand.'

Curtom was more than a record label and music publishing company – it became Mayfield's creative homebase, a magnet to which he could draw many more talents to add to his own. The production company became a conduit of creative influences, some of which came and went, and others that used the opportunity to create a body of work with the label. It was a compact sphere of creative talent with Mayfield at the hub.

As early as June '68 Curtis began working with the Impressions and the Five Stairsteps in the studio on songs for the first two Curtom album projects. Early Curtom single releases were required quickly and from the first Stairsteps session 'Don't Change Your Love', written, arranged and produced by Mayfield, became the label's first single release. It was coupled with 'New Dance Craze' a track taken from their Buddah album *Family Portrait*. The A-side went into the R&B chart at #15 in August '68 and featured Clarence Burke Jr on a confident lead vocal supported by an altogether funkier sound than the earlier material. Despite their tender age, the Stairsteps had become surprisingly good musicians. 'When we were working on the *Love's Happening* album I was KO'd by Kenneth's finger work on bass, his technique was startling for one so young', Curtis said later.

Similarly, the Impressions' first RCA session yielded both sides of their first Curtom release 'Fool For You'/'I'm Loving Nothing', both produced by Mayfield and arranged by Johnny Pate. The single was a big success, hitting #2 on R&B and #22 on the pop chart in September that year. On average, the Impressions had hit the R&B chart once every three months during the past two years and, with good supervision, had switched labels without missing a beat. 'Fool For You' was often to be heard on the airwaves during the late fall of '68. The twin sirens of Mayfield's voice and Pate's arrangement combined hypnotically as the story of the singer's problematic new liaison unwound. Sam and Fred's voices feature little on the A-side. Curtis' vocal is prominent as he states 'continuously' and 'famously', the foolish predicament that he finds himself within. In contrast, 'I'm Loving Nothing' is a slow ballad with a poetic, if melancholy, recitation from Curtis recounting his lover's impassionate responses to his 'moods of fire'. This single re-positioned the Impressions – they were sharper and they were less formal but had still retained the high quality consistently shown on ABC.

Curtis worked in tandem on the Impressions and Five Stairsteps albums, which were both ready for release by November. He supplied 18 of the 20 songs needed himself and co-wrote one song 'Gone Away' with Donny Hathaway who brought 'You Want Somebody Else' with him. Curtis already knew Donny from back when the Mayfield Singers had been formed for a session on Mayfield Records. Since then he had completed his studies at Howard University in Washington DC and had worked with Guy Draper writing and producing the Unifics first records. Hathaway made valuable creative contributions to the early Curtom sessions for about a year before he was snapped up for stardom by Jerry Wexler of Atlantic Records.

The third Curtom single released was 'Stay Close To Me' by the Five Stairsteps. It didn't chart despite being a very commercial record. This song was also recorded by the Impressions at the time, and was to be found on both the Impressions' and Stairsteps' albums. The flipside was the old Impressions' song 'I Made A Mistake'. The Stairsteps fared better with more current Mayfield material. But, perhaps they would have benefited from recording some of their own material instead of re-running old Impressions songs like 'Little Young Lover', 'I'm The One Who Loves You', 'Little Boy Blue' and '…Mistake'. It's easy to see with hindsight that title track 'Love's Happening', 'Your Love Has Changed' and 'Baby Make Me Feel So Good' all suited the Stairsteps better – the last of these became their next single, which took them to #12 on R&B in February '69. The album cover for *Love's Happening* (CRS 8002) projected fun, colourfully depicting the group with Papa in a fashionable boutique – it went to #22 on R&B albums in May '69 but pop sales were disappointing.

The Impressions' next single 'This Is My Country' hit R&B Top 10 at #8 and went to #25 on the pop chart in December '68, becoming the title track of the first Curtom album, which also sold in huge quantities over that Christmas and into the new year. 'This Is My Country' and other songs like 'They Don't Know', 'Choice Of Colors', 'Mighty, Mighty (Spade And Whitey)' and 'Young Mods' Forgotten Story' were written in the aftershock of the Martin Luther King and Bobby Kennedy assassinations, which occurred just weeks apart in April and June of '68. These songs clearly articulated the outrage that the black community felt about the calculated and brutally murderous acts against two leading champions for racial harmony in the western world. They reflected with some accuracy the shattered hopes of millions worldwide, with a poetic clarity that is just as sharply in focus 35 years on. As social comment, the songs still sound fresh, maybe because the conspiracies that lie behind those tragic events have never, and will never be satisfactorily explained. The equal rights struggle continues around the planet and despite almost continuous concessions, embargoes and social unrest, seems still further from any real solution.

To Curtis Mayfield, the equal rights struggle was at the centre of his life and work and had emerged many times before in his earlier songs like 'Keep On Pushing', 'People Get Ready' and 'We're A Winner', but now the trust, generosity and optimism had given way to a sharper-edged confrontational attitude. Though 'This Is My Country' stated the obvious, it needed to be said at the time. Black pride was hurting and the message also registered with whites, whose aspirations for the social reforms that a future president like Bobby Kennedy promised to make, could have put the USA on a more enlightened path. With his death those dreams dissolved and the future for all, other than perhaps the privileged, looked dismal. The album was a well-balanced mix of love songs and social comment. The sleeve pictured the brightly attired trio set against a background of social deprivation. No punches were pulled with the visual message either: the titles were graffitied across the top of the sleeve. 'My Woman's Love' was the single's flipside and, like 'So Unusual', it's a sensitive Mayfield ballad that neatly counterbalanced the mood of disillusionment created by the message songs.

'They Don't Know' was the second 'social warning' song, in which the Impressions deliver a series of powerful messages at a medium tempo. Again the clever use of group delivery on the song, with lyrics directed at the conspirators responsible and those that concealed the truth about the recent atrocities, clearly lays out the reasons why 'They Don't Know'. Mayfield expertly weaves a series of concise statements together to great effect. Lines like, 'We cannot let our people be until we're all out of poverty,' and, 'Never think we have no one to lead us,' articulated the reactions of many to the situation and sharply reflected the social mood of that time. Most of the arrangements on the first Curtom album were the work of Johnny Pate who tuned in with his usual high-grade sound, but Donny Hathaway also made valuable contributions. He provided the arrangements for 'You Want Somebody Else' and 'Gone Away', both of which he co-wrote. These Mayfield/ Hathaway collaborations provided the album with the two love song highlights.

'You Want Somebody Else' featured prominent drums beating out a constant midtempo behind a less brassy orchestration and occasional bells to good effect. The Impressions' voices rise and fall as Curtis complains of being short-changed in an affair with a lady who regularly out-manoeuvres his attempts to exclusively control her affections. He knows he's losing but he won't let go. The album highlight is 'Gone Away', a sensational ballad perfectly created and delivered by Mayfield, Hathaway and the Impressions. The musical and vocal arrangements blend superbly as Curtis soulfully relates a poetic lyric and delivers a familiar story of love lost with a perfect mixture of resignation and sincerity in his voice. Sam and Fred supply sensitive vocal understatement, which is enriched by a wonderfully inventive arrangement. The break is inspirational and sets up the last verse perfectly. Donny tops it all off with strategically sprinkled bells for extra sparkle. Between them they created a definitive groove soul ballad. It was a truly unrepeatable combination as Roberta Flack found to her cost when she attempted a lacklustre version some years later.

Over the course of '69, Curtom released singles and albums by a range of different artists. As well as co-writing with Curtis on early Curtom sessions, Donny Hathaway also released his own material. His first single 'I Thank You Baby' came from further collaboration with Curtis who wrote and co-produced the song for a Donny and June Conquest duet, released first in '69, passing the arrangements to Hathaway. The B-side, 'What's This I See', was an uptempo item featuring a June Conquest lead vocal with Mayfield in support. The record went to #45 R&B in February '69 and Curtom re-issued it in '72 to ride on the back of Donny's then solo Atco success. This time it was coupled with 'Just Another Reason', which sounds so good, it could have been the A-side and was an excellent reworking of the Fascinations' earlier version. The vocals work well off each other, Hathaway's arrangement and Mayfield's production blend beautifully. This time it registered a tad higher up at #41 R&B and garnered low pop success at #94 in June '72.

Originally the duet was intended for June and LC Cooke but when Cooke failed to sign with Curtom, Donny stepped in at the last moment.

The next artists to release on the Curtom label were Baby Huey and the Babysitters, who had amassed a large cult following due mainly to their exciting stage performances in New York, Paris and Chicago. The Babysitters came together in Richmond, Indiana when they were formed by keyboard player Melvin 'Deacon' Jones in mid '67 and began to work locally in clubs and bars. Though they toured extensively throughout the States, it was some time before they caught the attention of Curtom through their high profile performances at a small Chicago club called the 'Thumbs Up'. Curtis Mayfield captured some of the atmosphere that Baby Huey generated on stage with the first single 'Mighty Mighty' Pts 1 and 2. This song had just been recorded by the Impressions as part of their next album. Though the record didn't chart nationally it sold well in Chicago and Baby Huey, also known as James T Ramey (who weighed in at between 160–280kg/350–400lbs), became a hot item. The band was booked solid with club dates and TV for the next year but a rift suddenly opened up in '69 and the Babysitters and Huey parted company. Marv Stuart took some of the band members and added Chaka Khan to form Goliath, and the others, including Deacon, joined the Impressions road band. Incidentally it was Curtis who dubbed Melvin 'Deacon' one night when introducing the band to their audience, and it stuck.

Another artist to work with Curtis during this period was Holly Maxwell. She cut 'Suffer'/'No One Else' on Curtom but, despite the excellent Mayfield production treatment, it didn't sell. Holly sang both sides of this great single superbly but due to its lack of success soon left Curtom for the Slim Whit label where she stayed briefly to record 'Never Love Again' amongst other fine tracks.

Other departing artists, the Five Stairsteps returned to the parent label Buddah towards the end of '69. Of their five Curtom singles, four had reached Top 40 R&B but their album had only sold well to R&B fans and had not crossed over to pop as well as expected. Curtis, who considered The Stairsteps 'elegantly talented', later said 'Curtom suited the Stairsteps at first, but they are creative people and they have plans and desires of their own, still they are with the same company and we are in regular contact.' The Stairsteps were ripe for success, they fizzed with talent, and by rights it should have happened bigger with Curtom but somehow it didn't.

The Impressions had also continued to release singles during this period with a high-level of success. 'My Deceiving Heart' hit the mid 20s on the R&B chart in March '69 and 'Seven Years' went to #15 R&B. It also sold a little better on the Hot 100 where it went to #84 in April '69. 'Choice Of Colors' was chosen as the Impressions next single and was a huge hit for them in June '69 when it topped the R&B charts and rose to #21 pop. Its success boosted the sales of the group's second Curtom album *Young Mods' Forgotten Story* (CRS 8003) in May '69, which features ten tracks all written by Curtis Mayfield who produced and used arrangements by Donny Hathaway and Johnny Pate. The album was once again an agreeable blend of social-oriented message songs and love songs. It came inside a moody cover showing the Impressions photographed on and around the 125th Street Railway Station. It begins with the title track; a song that examines what the aftermath of the King/Kennedy assassinations did to establish the attitude changes in the black and liberal sections of society at the time.

Curtis uses the 'so-called right of his opinion' to explain how the young Mods know why and who, despite the wide confusion and deception at the centre of these conspiracies. Pate's arrangement perfectly highlights Mayfield's observations that give way to the less judgmental lyrics expressed in 'Choice Of Colors', the second track. This song quickly grew to the status of other Mayfield classics to become one of the most important racial harmony songs ever written. The lyric asks big questions and offers wise solutions when it states, 'people must prove to the people, a better day is coming, for you and for me. With just a little bit more education and love for our nation, we'll make a better society.' The Impressions trade lines from the master's poetry to superb effect as they urge the listener to consider weighty social issues and ponder the implications of ignorance and non-involvement. 'Choice Of Colors' also touches on the fundamental mistake that the West has made by allowing successive conservative administrations to politicize education instead of ensuring provision as a free right for all. Jerry Butler later compared this song to the poetry of Longfellow and it is certain to be one of the most admired and remembered Mayfield lyrics of all time.

'The Girl I Find' is another great Mayfield love song. Curtis' apprehensive vocal drifts poetically through a sensitive Hathaway arrangement, which includes a fascinating background of what sounds like purring cicadas or petting doves. 'Wherever You Leadeth Me' became the Impressions' next single and crept into the R&B Top 40 in January 1970. It exercised an established Impressions format and rolls comfortably along on the crest of Pate's easy arrangement using language and phrasing that are reminiscent of their earlier records. 'My Deceiving Heart' rounds off perfectly the first side of this great album. Curtis' vocal woefully regrets a recent misdemeanour that has cost him a much-valued relationship. It's a very soulful reflection of better times. 'Seven Years' is sung in a different, more critical mood and looks at the other side of a break up. The Impressions wail behind Mayfield's assertive lead that pulls no punches. As the Mayfield focus moves more positively to the future and a new romantic beginning, 'Loves Miracle' examines the wonder and elation of such a transition. 'Jealous Man' deals with new ground rules and suspicion but 'Soulful Love' probably captures the mood at its peak for in 'Who can define soulful love?' Curtis defines as he sings and plays a subtle guitar that weaves in and out of yet another superb arrangement.

The final track 'Mighty Mighty (Spade And Whitey)' was previously released as a flipside to 'Choice of Colors'. It's a warning song that was heeded by many but ignored by many more. It contains several powerful messages like 'We're killing off our leaders don't matter none black nor white, we all know it's wrong but we're gonna fight to make it right'. The song has the party atmosphere of 'We're A Winner' but the messages are more sharply defined: 'give this some thought, in stupidness we've all been caught.' Mayfield has the solution in this song's title. There can be no real progress without integration, equality and common purpose and while governments encourage and reinforce the deep divisions in society created by prejudice and ignorance, there is no way forward for western social consciousness. Between them, Curtis, Sam, Fred, Johnny and Donny in a few short months, created the Impressions two finest albums. They both became and remain milestones in the development of popular music. Mayfield's telling of the socially aware love story deeply affected all who could not compartmentalize their lives into the 'them and us' philosophy of the political right.

Seven of the tracks on *Young Mods'*... were released as singles or B-sides. Singles still played a very important role in the marketing of Curtom product and in those first two or three years the company had almost continuous success on both R&B and pop charts in America. Mayfield and Eddie Thomas experimented in 1970 when they bought a number of completed masters for release on their label in an attempt to broaden the appeal of their roster. However, this experiment was commercially unsuccessful when 'Mix It Up' by the Stridells didn't register and Freddy Waters 'Singing A New Song' didn't either. Freddy had two minor hits later on October and Kari Records in '77 and '81.

Around this time, the Impressions gave a revealing interview with *Rolling Stone*, top American rock monthly, who published a three-page article about them in their 16 January 1970 issue. The article, written by Michael Alexander, was taken from several interviews made over a few days stay at the San Francisco Hilton with the Impressions when they headlined at Fillmore West and again later in LA. The trio were booked to play three nights at the Fillmore and four nights at Basin Street. Alexander turned in an objective and fascinating piece, interviewing each member of the Impressions in turn, as he accompanied them on an excursion shopping for clothes, attended a probing interview with Radio station KDIA and a taping session for an *American Bandstand* segment – where he observed four complete changes of wardrobe.

Fred Cash, who was the first Michael interviewed, stated that he was completely at home with hotel life and expressed a preference for spending time in his room with the TV or radio playing and ordering anything he wanted on room service. He even took most of his meals there. He confided to Alexander that he found touring a lot easier these days, unlike three years back when they were playing the theatre circuit, performing four sometimes five shows daily. Now they only toured six months of the year, which left time for other pursuits – in Fred's case this was a chain of beauty salons.

Cash further related the tragic story of how the Impressions' road band were killed in a horrific car wreck while on tour in Atlanta early in '69. He spoke about the ordeal of making the identifications and the difficulties in building and rehearsing a new band. All three Impressions hated flying so they drove everywhere, unless it was impossible to do so. These flying phobias prevented them from making earlier European appearances. So UK audiences never got the chance to see the Impressions on tour while Curtis fronted the group.

Alexander spent less column inches on Sam Gooden, who he described as the 'handsome Impression'. Sam had always been obsessed with sports and was trying to book a seat at the Fox Warfield to see his buddy Joe Frazier fight Jerry Quarry on closed circuit TV. Sam confessed to being more nervous at a fight than when he performed on stage.

Inevitably, the article made a more detailed exploration of Curtis Mayfield his music, ideas and opinions. Alexander travelled with them down to Los Angeles for more TV, Radio spots and concerts at the Troubadour and Hollywood Palladium. He visited Curtis at the Century Plaza who talked about writing songs and how he would like to extend his writing to stories and in other directions. Mayfield reminisced about the early days and how he spent his 15th birthday playing the Apollo, the reasons for his lack of academic achievement and how 12 years on the road wears a man down. But again, no matter how problematic that this life was, it was also addictive and very rewarding. Alexander concluded, 'He is writing the songs of the up-and-coming black middle class. The songs of aspirations. A good home, a nice car, decent neighbors, money, educated kids, travel, security. You can't knock it until you've had the opportunity to reject it, which is what the White Political Conscience at the Fillmore didn't understand. Curtis Mayfield is 26 years old.'

The two Curtom 'non' hits of considerable interest from this period were by Moses Dillard and the Tex Town Display. 'I've Got To Find a Way' was released first and featured three lead voices, Moses, Peabo Bryson (on his recording début) and Bill Wilson. The song runs for seven minutes and so covered both sides of the single. It was produced by Moses and arranged by R Kinder: between them they created a sound not unlike earlier Mala/Bell records where the band had previously worked with Papa Don Schroeder in '67. The sound is infectious with a slow loping beat behind the trio as they take it in turns to bear their souls and 'try to find a way'. The second single, released a few months later was 'Our Love Is True', in a very similar mood and style with switching lead vocals. It was almost as good but neither track found a commercial market and the two records became collectables instead of the hits they deserved to be.

Another old associate of Curtis' who signed to Curtom in 1970 after a brief stay at Dakar was Major Lance who recorded two singles. The first, 'Stay Away From Me', gave him his biggest hit since 'Sometimes I Wonder' five years earlier when it reached #13 R&B in July that year. It was typical Mayfield fare and suited Major down to the ground. The B-side was the old Mayfield standby, 'Gypsy Woman' that had recently been re-recorded by the Impressions for their new album project *Best Impressions* and was made up of new versions of some of their old standards plus current Curtom product. The Major's version rates well amongst many other fine interpretations of this classic song, but somehow the follow-up 'Must Be Love Coming Down', which was good enough to capitalize on the last hit, struggled to peak at #31 R&B.

The Impressions' popularity at the time was revealed in the *Blues & Soul* Readers Annual Polls '69, which were published in the magazine's 30 March '70 issue. They proclaimed Jerry Butler the new 'king' of soul. Butler who had just arrived for a UK tour and was currently riding high on the UK soul singles and album charts had pipped Otis Redding and Marvin Gaye to the top. The female honours went to Aretha Franklin (#2 Gladys Knight, #3 Nina Simone) and the group section was topped by the Temptations with the Impressions at #2. Readers voted 'Choice Of Colors' (the Impressions) top single '...Grapevine' (Marvin Gaye) was #2 and 'Can I Change My Mind' (Tyrone Davis) took the #3 spot just edging out 'Only The Strong Survive' by Jerry Butler. London and the UK were treated to a number of highflying soul stars that came here on tour including Aretha Franklin (in June), Ben E King (May), Wilson Pickett (September). Motown also kept a high UK profile with appearances from Stevie Wonder (at the Talk Of The Town) the Four Tops, Jimmy Ruffin, Marv Johnson and Edwin Starr.

During the spring of 1970 Curtis Mayfield began to make a number of changes at Curtom. He bought in Marv Stuart who he had met in the past year while working with Baby Huey. Marv owned the Thumbs Up nightclub, managed a couple of bands and worked for a booking agency on Chicago's southside. Curtis and Marv became friends over the next six months and Mayfield invited Stuart to manage the Impressions, as Eddie Thomas wanted to concentrate on Curtom's promotional business. Mayfield still harboured the desire to make Curtom as important to Chicago as Motown was to Detroit or the Gamble/Huff labels were to Philadelphia. What he had achieved so far was some way towards that target but things were not happening soon or big enough. He wanted to grow faster and reach more people.

The Impressions' next album in February 1970, *Curtis, Sam & Fred, The Best Impressions* (CRS 8004), featured a dozen tracks, seven of which were new hits and five – 'Amen', 'Keep On Pushin'', 'Gypsy Woman', 'I'm So Proud' and 'I've Been Trying' – were freshly recorded versions of long-established Impressions classics. All of the songs were part of their continuing repertoire. 'Amen', the group had made their own and was a firm favourite with the fans at concerts and clubs universally. Wisely Mayfield (and Pate) purchased the song from its original author and it is their names that appear as the writers' credits from that time onwards. The album had an aura of reflection, a kind of taking stock. After much discussion and deliberation, Mayfield was about to make his own bid for a solo career.

'Amen' (1970) was released as a single in December '69 and had only medium chart success whilst the flipside 'Wherever She Leadeth Me' did rather better hitting #31 R&B the following January. In the UK the *Best Impressions* album was simply retitled *Amen* when it was released the following October. Mayfield's work with the Impressions was not over, however, as he fronted, wrote and produced the next album *Check Out Your Mind* (CRS 8006) while also producing his first solo album *CURTIS* in tandem. Some of the tracks could have been used on either album.

This era of change brought creative and musical innovation also. Riley Hampton had gained much experience arranging in Chicago and New York for just about everyone since he and Curtis had last worked together on the Impressions' Bandera session in '57, when they cut 'Listen'. Riley teamed up with Gary Slabo to supply all the arrangements for both albums that were recorded during the spring and early summer of 1970.

This period of change seemed to inspire Mayfield with a twist that reflected itself in some of the most sensational music that he had recorded so far. 'Check Out Your Mind' and 'Can't You See' the first two album tracks gave the Impressions their next single, which hit R&B at #3 and by May had reached Top 30 pop. The chant, 'Why don't you check out your mind, been with you all the time' clicked with listeners and movers alike. The sound was subtly infectious with the wah wah guitar weaving in and out of heaving bass on top of endlessly shifting layers of percussion and strings. Mayfield's relaxed vocal slips along as he exchanges vocal lines with Sam and Fred. Heavy echo is used to create fluid effects on vocal and sound to produce a stunning impact. It was another magic step that surprised many with its inventiveness and powerful delivery. For 'Check Out Your Mind' Curtis paints in bold strokes urging self-reflection and personal honesty over denial and greed. 'Can't You See' bought us all back to earth as the group manage to improve on the original cut made nine years earlier with a beautiful reworking of a song that now added Jerry Butler to its writing credits.

The third track 'You're Really Something Sadie' describes how Sadie dances supreme and moves singers to respond. Aimed at the dance market, the Impressions turned in their usual high performance. Obviously not considered strong enough for single release 'Do You Want To Win' again relies rather too much on a great arrangement, as does 'Only You'. These three songs sound like they had been in Mayfield's kit bag for a while and were perhaps a little pale compared to other tracks on this album. 'You'll Always Be Mine' is more reminiscent of earlier material, with a softer sound than before. 'Baby Turn On To Me' was the obvious follow-up single. It has all the attractive characteristics of 'Check Out....' but did not move the pop audience as much as it might have done and went to #6 R&B in September 1970. 'Madame Mary' conjures up images of a gypsy surrounded by bubbling cauldrons, mixing love potions and laying on spells. Mayfield slips us the storyline with consummate ease and the rest of the guys provide great funky support. It was previously a single for the Stairsteps as was 'We Must Be In Love' but the Impressions sharpened the commercial edge on both tracks. The chant borders on irritation but great performance wins over in the end.

The final track 'Say You Love Me' had already been a hit single and an album track. Stylistically it looks back but hits the spot with its sincerity and impeccable arrangement. *Check Out Your Mind* received critical acclaim across the planet when released by Curtom in September 1970. *Blues & Soul* Editor John E Abbey in the March issue of '71 claimed that it was 'Curtis' most creative work with the group' and despite the top-of-the-market price (£2.15 in those days), Abbey urged instant acquisition declaring confidently, 'A tremendous album that is loaded with creativity.'

The album sold well and by November had peaked at #13 on the R&B album chart but the pop sales were disappointing. It would have done much better had *CURTIS* not been issued at the same time. When both albums were released in the UK six months later, it was a similar story with the Impressions album settling at #12 R&B and *CURTIS* doing much better.

For Mayfield, *Check Out Your Mind* was a perfect swansong with the Impressions. When interviewed in '84, he said, 'Leaving the Impressions was a lot like leaving home. We were together for 14 years but when the time is right, you have to go. You need to make it on your own – for yourself.' For the Impressions the future must have looked a little less certain and despite Mayfield's assurances that, 'We will all still be working closely together,' the thought of Sam and Fred supporting anyone other than Curtis must to them have seemed a pretty daunting prospect.

Just before Curtis released his first solo album, James T Ramey better known to soul fans as Baby Huey died of a drug overdose in October 1970. Marv Stuart, Ramey's manager, began work with Curtis on the construction of a memorial album to be called *The Baby Huey Story – The Living Legend* (CRS 8007). For this album, they used the previous single 'Mighty Mighty Children' and seven other tracks, three of them instrumentals, from the two sessions that the Babysitters had cut for them. Curtom released 'Listen To Me'/'Hard Times' as a single in the spring of '71 and Curtis also put out 'Mighty Mighty Spade And Whitey'

(CR-1963), culled from his upcoming *CURTIS/LIVE* album as a mark of respect perhaps. Neither single charted but the Baby Huey album, released in March that year, climbed to #22 R&B by May but only managed bubble-under business outside America. Inevitably with so little to work with, this selection came over a little patchy. Baby Huey's potential was clear for all to hear though and the Babysitters were on top of the sound. Mayfield produced and had successfully shared some arrangements with Ramey but there were still a lot of loose ends and unfinished tracks that Curtis had to complete after Huey's death.

Curtis edited the first single down from 5 minutes to 2.45 and added two other Mayfield originals 'Hard Times' and 'Running' a rearrangement of the old Impressions hit 'You Got Me Running'. James T wrote 'Mama Get Yourself Together' and 'One Dragon Two Dragon', both instrumental cuts. The album gives an indication of just how the band's stage show must have sounded, the medium on which they had built their short but solid reputation. Huey adds another slant to Sam Cooke's 'Change Is Gonna Come' with monologue, and the track runs for 9.5 minutes. 'Listen To Me' is delivered with energy and should have been a hit single. Also included was a slightly different version of 'Mighty', an original interpretation of 'Hard Times' and an interesting slant on 'California Dreaming'. When released in the UK two months later the album bubbled under briefly, but then dropped out of sight. Baby Huey's talent, originality and innate inventiveness can only be glimpsed at. These talents glimmer briefly on this album that Mayfield pulled together in faultless production. It's impossible to say whether Huey's talent would have ripened or faded but it's all we have to go by and stands as a memorial to Baby Huey, James T Ramey, aged 26. Unidisc transferred the album to CD in '93 for Canada and in May '99 Sequel re-issued *The Baby Huey Story* on CD in the UK, with two bonus tracks added.

It was in September 1970 that Curtis' first solo album, the aforementioned *CURTIS* (CRS 8005), was released. It became a monster and instantly endorsed his decision to go it alone. '(Don't Worry) If There's A Hell Below We're All Gonna Go' was chosen as the single and reached #3 R&B and #67 pop by November. It achieved remarkably similar success in the UK two months later and quickly became a hit worldwide despite the contentious subject matter and hard-hitting criticisms of American society expressed in the lyrics. From the intro, the atmosphere Mayfield, Riley Hampton and Gary Slabo create is supercharged. As the lyric is laid out, Curtis climbs once again to the apex of soulful debate when he talks directly to 'Educated fools from uneducated schools'. Crystal observations of survival under the Nixon administration are sung to a hypnotic bass line that weaves in and out of a fascinating cacophony of riveting musical power. It is one of his most forceful prediction songs and it was a very brave début single, a decision that paid off handsomely.

The second track 'The Other Side Of Town' tells something of what it's really like to live in the ghetto, where the sun of opportunity never shines and the depression's not only in the weather. 'The Makings Of You' returns to the love song and an appreciation from a lover's perspective. Aretha Franklin also did a fine version of this one 24 years later on the *Tribute To Curtis* album. The song deals with the subject that the love of mankind should reflect but rarely does. 'We People Who Are Darker Than Blue' talks straight to the black community about the need for desegregation. Mayfield's mixture of eloquent poetry and soul funk make this another essential track. The piece starts and ends slowly with an uptempo centre section. The song, amongst Mayfield's best, is on a par with 'Strange Fruit' the Billie Holiday classic. An alternative experimental cut made at this time, also reappeared after much restyling on the amazing *New World Order* album in '96 (see Chapter 12).

'Move On Up' is Curtis' best-known European hit, featuring a text aimed at the young, who in the UK took it to their hearts, helping it to the top of the soul charts in the early months of '71. The single was edited down from 8.55 minutes to 2.53. In the years since, through constant advertising and TV documentary usage, the song has been subsumed into evergreen popularity here in the UK but in America it went missing. Despite attempts to re-release the single in the USA after its big UK success, it again floundered. This timeless message of encouragement in self belief has a driving groove that lifts us on and up towards our destination... In 'Miss Black America' Curtis examines the views and aspirations of the young black American female through his daughter

Sharon's eyes, whose voice introduces the track. 'Wild And Free' expresses a celebration of change for the better, the natural development that should theoretically lead to real freedom for all. It clearly depicts the struggle, the pain and strife of constantly living with the reality, while still clinging to the hope of a brighter future. The song was later picked up and recorded by Major Lance more than once. The final cut 'Give It Up' relates the disappointments of coping with a marriage breakdown, the unfulfilled expectations and the knock-on effects of incompatibility and indifference. It was one of the final tracks to feature the voices of Curtis, Sam and Fred together (along with 'Miss Black America').

CURTIS received critical acclaim – John E Abbey of *Blues & Soul* observed, 'This album is soul perfection personified,' and he further predicted, 'An incredible album that, on merit, will stay No 1 until the end of the year.' Not quite – but close. *CURTIS* hit the top a month later in April '71 where it stayed for three months before being replaced by Marvin Gaye's *What's Goin' On*. (In the past, Curtis was quite often wrongly criticized of being influenced by this album but, if anything, the reverse is true.) It returned to #1 in August due to a renewed interest created with the release of *CURTIS/LIVE* and stayed close to the top for the rest of the year. It also managed to cross over successfully, reaching #19 on the US pop album charts, propelling Mayfield en route to solo stardom.

Curtom's good design and marketing approach also added much to the visual impact of the album. In America it was released in an excellent gatefold sleeve, designed and photographed by Bob Cato. It pictured Curtis relaxing with his children and their friends, enjoying the sunshine in parkland. Mayfield projects a comfortable image in his casual yellow outfit, Indian shirt and beads, a scene that visually reinforced his message of peace and love at the time. The album quickly became Curtom's biggest success so far. He enjoyed months of continuous high media profile and this kind of popularity demanded that he evacuate the studio to begin preparations for a worldwide tour.

Curtis pulled a quintet of musicians together to create a solid unit of support with which he could tour and record. The band consisted of Craig McMullen and Tyrone McCullen on guitar and drums, to which he added the already proven talents of percussionist Henry Gibson and bassman Joseph 'Lucky' Scott. After a short rehearsal time, Curtis and band debuted at New York's Bitter End, in late January '71. Buddah Records had the foresight to record those first four appearances at the club and an edited version of these became his second album *CURTIS/LIVE* (CRS 8008). Mayfield produced a superb live album, which enabled him to establish his pedigree with a new audience while also satisfying confirmed fans with a fresh cocktail of small club intimacy. He edited the tapes and used Eddy Kramer to engineer at Electric Ladyland Studios just around the corner from the club. Tom Flye at Record Plant, New York City, did final mixing and the package was ready to go.

'Mighty Mighty (Spade & Whitey)' was chosen as the opening track and Curtis delivered an updated version of the Impressions song with lyrical changes and a small group treatment that was very effective on the day. His comments between tracks to the mixed race Greenwich Village audience were, 'We can do everything but get along', the theme of which he developed in the next number, 'I Plan To Stay A Believer' – a song that touches on the Native American experience and proffers a practical solution when Curtis proposes black renewal through self-help. On this subject Curtis was later to say, 'Everybody has their opinions on the racial issue and there'll be opposition, whatever we decided to do. But we must unite, educate and become stronger. There are 22 million black people in America today and if only half of them earn enough say, to donate 10 dollars a year to one central fund, we could clear away a lot of problems in the ghetto.'

The Impressions anthem 'We're a Winner' follows in a relaxed version within which Curtis relates a little of the song's contentious history. He amplifies further upon this with an updated lyric that engages full enthusiasm from the small audience who concur that, 'The black boy has dried his eye.' It dovetails neatly into the only non-Mayfield tune in the set, 'We've Only Just Begun', a song that allows the band to ease off the social gas a touch. Curtis exploits the duality of the lyrics a little in his interpretation of Paul Williams' words that didn't come over in the Carpenters' original version. The band rolls on into 'People Get Ready', another crafted version of the Mayfield classic, much admired and recorded by countless other artists like Rod Stewart, Dionne Warwick, Bob Marley. 'Stare And Stare' is another curious Mayfield song that was often featured in his live shows but wasn't recut for a studio album and therefore remains something of a rarity. It neatly parallels a city bus ride with any man's journey through contemporary urban life. Good interaction with the audience demonstrates clearly why the song was rightly included on this set. Curtis finishes with a good-natured dig at the audience by repeating the title , 'Stare and Stare folks – Keep It Up'. 'Check Out Your Mind', another Impressions hit, superbly reworked for the current line-up, doesn't really deserve comparison to the original any more than 'Gypsy Woman', the following track, does. These versions work well as sketches, reminders of earlier brilliance, and lyrically they stand up to the simplicity of unplugged reinterpretation but sensibly Curtis does not attempt to reconstruct the original records. 'The Makings Of You' taken from the hit album of the time brings into focus the Mayfield of that time, then looking forward to a celebrated solo career. Curtis took the opportunity to introduce the band before continuing with more of his contemporary material – 'We People Who Are Darker Than Blue' followed by 'If There's A Hell Below', his then-current gold single. This version ran to over nine minutes within which once again the audience hit another peak of enthusiasm. The live set concludes with 'Stone Junkie', a song used on many shows but still another Mayfield rarity on record. This is a pity because the song's message conveys much as it underlines the inactivity bought about by domestic drug abuse, a theme developed and discussed in depth by Mayfield a year or so later in *Superfly*.

Curtom released the album in May '71 and it quickly climbed to #3 soul/21 pop album charts that same month and it mirrored this success when it was issued in the UK two months later. In general, live albums sold less than their studio counterparts. However, due to Mayfield's popularity, good timing and clever marketing, Curtom were able to capitalize and create another big hit album against those general trends. In addition, its popularity exposed new versions of his current hits, and the knock-on effect sold more of the *CURTIS* album and the 'If There's A Hell Below' single, pushing them back up the charts. This, in turn, established the necessity for a tour big enough to satisfy the rapidly growing interest *CURTIS/LIVE* now created.

Curtis and his new band began to appear at venues large and small right across America. Many more people became aware of his poetry, some for the first time, others reacquainting themselves with the many great lines from his songs, which have long since become absorbed into the parlance of the streetwise: 'We're A Winner', 'Keep On Pushing', 'People Get Ready' and 'Move On Up'. Because of his commitments to record production, songwriting, the movies, etc, Curtis could not just drop everything or pass it on to somebody else to finish, so his live appearances at first were somewhat chequered, a few days here, a week there. So it was with his first solo tour to the UK in June '71. Word got around that 'the man' would tour the UK during that summer, but to the amazement of thousands anxious to buy tickets, Curtis came and went within a few days. He only appeared live at exclusive venues – The Speakeasy plus a couple of US airbases. The music press was barraged with mail from disappointed fans who had to settle for the BBC TV's *Top of the Pops* appearance when Curtis sang two tracks from the début album. Few could have really appreciated the incredible schedule that Mayfield must have been operating under at that time. But they were all to regain their perspective when *CURTIS/LIVE* became available later that month in the UK and was bought in such great numbers that it reached #3 on the soul album charts by August.

Mayfield returned to Chicago during the autumn to honour his engagements and, most importantly, to begin work on his next album *Roots* (CRS 8009). This time he used the road band as the nucleus of the orchestra and called in the regular support arrangers, Riley Hampton and Johnny Pate plus engineer Roger Anfinsen. The package was ready and released by Curtom in October '71. 'Get Down' introduces the album with breathless female sighs leading us into mode clubland, the funky groove, where Curtis lets the light fall on his natural mood. As a single, it had hit #13 R&B/69 pop the previous year; this extended version was big in the clubs and received frequent airplay. The inspirational 'Keep On Keeping On' is yet another Mayfield classic. The theme is education and outlines a responsibility to teach your children well, to get through to them with the important and relevant knowledge, and affect lasting change for the better in future generations. The song advocates self-improvement and the general well being that can be gained from not giving up, even if the odds seem impossible. It still remains one of Mayfield's most positive songs. But the majority of the record-buying public at the time, while pleased to buy his love songs and dig his funky grooves, were apparently tiring of his preachier stuff, at least as singles.

'Beautiful Brother Of Mine' had flopped as a single and 'We Got To Have Peace' had only a slight return, reaching #32 R&B/115 pop in February '72. 'Underground' came next on the album but was destined later only as an edited flipside (twice). Here, Curtis talks pollution, taking us on a journey below the planet's surface in a prediction scenario of what could happen if the powerful industrial conglomerates continue down their destructive path. Thirty or more years later we are way further down that road to ruin. With 'We Got To Have Peace' Curtis once again raises his eyes to an international perspective of world peace. Unfortunately it seems still to be in the interests of the power brokers and international arms dealers to keep the rest of world from making that choice. Equality of choice and opportunity are great ideals for us all to aspire to, but in the years since Mayfield wrote songs like this, the oil wars and industrial pollution have added great damage to the environment – long past critical point – and peace plans have become deeply cynical and manipulative events in the view of ordinary people. Nevertheless, his message songs still ring true today and sadly, will probably be even more relevant tomorrow. 'Beautiful Brother Of Mine' made little impact as a single in the US but was popular in Europe as part of a maxi single combined with 'Give It Up' and 'Move On Up'. It went to the top of the European charts with a few exceptions and received a lot of exposure on radio due to its integrational theme.

Curtis wrote the next cut 'Now You're Gone' with Joseph Scott, his long-time associate and now band member/musical director. An insistent lengthy drum intro takes us into a moody torch song, in some ways slightly reminiscent of Pate and Mayfield's earlier work with the Impressions on ABC as Curtis mourns the loss of his lover and soulmate. It takes us to the final album track 'Love To Keep You In My Mind' and, once again, celebrates that loving feeling present in so many of his fine songs. The sympathetic arrangement captures the light high of the lyric and transports us to a relaxed and thoughtful exit. Although Mayfield's single sales had taken a dip in America, they still sold well in the UK and Europe. 'We Got To Have Peace' hit #9 on the UK soul charts in December '71 and was followed by 'Move On Up', his biggest European hit. Curtom released *Roots* in time for Christmas '71.

The original album sleeve folded out elaborately to reveal song lyrics and an astrological calendar that could detach, still leaving a complete sleeve for the album. It was designed to guarantee maximum sales over the holiday period, but cute as the package was there were two fundamental flaws in its structure – the cover picture and the title. The choice of *Roots* as a title for this album just doesn't make sense. The album is not reflective and as for a visual pun of Curtis and the tree, it's a bad joke. While technically good, Gil Ross' portrait of Curtis doesn't capture the spirit of his subject. Instead Mayfield looks posed, uncomfortable and a little unhappy to be there. In an interview at the time Curtis said, 'I believe my vocal is stronger and certainly that the material is better than anything I've written.' He admitted though that he was unhappy with the *Roots* title, 'I must admit I wanted to change the name at the last minute but Buddah had already printed 50,000 sleeves, so I was too late.' The album sold well enough to hit the Top 50 pop charts at #40, some 20 places below the previous two. R&B sales reflected better when *Roots* went to #4 a month later though, but an album of such ingenuity and beauty really deserved better initial success. Meanwhile, Curtis and the band returned to a demanding tour schedule.

Curtis and the Experience's début European tour opened at the Rainbow in London on Sunday 23 January '72. This concert was fraught with problems, however. Bloodstone, the support band went on over an hour late and performed to an indifferent audience, at well below their best. After a short interval the audience began to settle down in anticipation of what was to come. The quintet opened with 'Check Out Your Mind'. Mayfield, clad in a navy suede outfit with knee high black boots, clutched a large white Fender that seemed to accentuate his diminutive build. Any visual imbalance was redressed the moment that he and the band began to play. The two guitars made their way through a funky rearrangement beautifully. They continued the same groove through the second tune 'Inner City Blues' using Henry Gibson to great effect. The problems with the PA stuttered at first and then went out on a whole section of the audience. Despite insistent prompting from Curtis, engineers seemed unable to put things right. The mikes were set too low and Craig McMullen had a number of technical problems with his guitar.

Nevertheless the band played on through 'Mighty Mighty ...' and 'We've Only Just Begun' before the frustrated singer made a public appeal for, 'Someone to turn up the sound level'. It seemed to improve for a short while with 'Move On Up' and 'Keep On Keeping On' receiving riotous responses from the audience. During the quieter passages of 'Gypsy Woman' and 'Stone Junkie', the volume plummeted again and 'Stare And Stare' became inaudible, bringing loud appeals from both audience and band. Curtis abruptly terminated the show with a truncated medley of 'Beautiful Brother', 'Hell Below' and 'We Gotta Have Peace'. His disappointment was obvious, as was that of the crowd, and the group walked off stage. Mayfield returned briefly not to encore but to apologize for 'the inadequate acoustics'. While gremlins had helped to make the experience less than great, it gave British fans a tantalizing first glimpse of *CURTIS/LIVE*. The remainder of the tour went without a hitch and gave Mayfield the opportunity to begin the affinity that he quickly built and positively fostered with UK and European audiences throughout the following 18 years.

Most of the British music press carried features and interviews with Curtis while he and the band were on tour. Since Mayfield's big success with *CURTIS*, he had crossed over from the specialist magazines audiences catered for by *Blues & Soul* and others who had long followed his career with interest, to the mainstream that read *NME, Melody Maker* and *Record Mirror*. Predictably, the features tended to concentrate on his colourful past but some interviews carried quotes and observations of interest to the converted. When interviewed at the Churchill Hotel between gigs and quizzed about his changing audience, Curtis said, 'I think my music is aimed at a general audience. However, at home, the biggest concerns that I express are mainly those of the black community. The community in which I grew up. But those concerns are not just black problems, no; most of my songs are songs that I'm sure relate to the majority of people's everyday life. But attitudes in the world are constantly changing. The subjects and moods of my songs reflect what concerns me, what I am currently thinking about. My songs attempt to break it down – communicate my theories to people of all kinds. I'm very happy if my songs hit home with a wider audience – as they seem to be doing right now.' When questioned about his departure from the Impressions, he stated, 'Well, running Curtom takes a lot of my time. I spend many hours in the studio producing, arranging, recording other artists and then there is all the administration and publicity, etc. I found it impossible to get away to spend any time on the road. I was always hanging the fellas up. So I decided to quit and find a replacement who could concentrate more on getting behind the Impressions records, leaving me free to write and produce them as always. I think it's the right time for all of us. As it worked out though, my first album took off in a big way so I had to get a group together and go back on the road myself.'

Curtis' level of success with the record-buying public was not matched by some of the other artists on the label. Curtom released two more albums at the end of '71, both aimed at the pop market. *Patti Miller* (CRS 8010) and *Ruby Jones* (CRS 8011), but both missed their target. Marv Stuart and the newly appointed Richard Tufo produced the Ruby Jones album. Richard was to become an important influence at Curtom after this inauspicious start. He had been approached by Stuart to participate in the Ruby Jones project and stayed on at Curtom working as arranger/producer on many in-house projects.

Ruby Jones were a quintet fashioned in the image of Janis Joplin and the Big Brother Holding Company. Marv Stuart signed them to Curtom and issued '46th Street', written by the in-group poet Frank Smith in early '72. Ruby's vocals turn us over providing a catchy if uneven ride from the group with big band accompaniment. 'You Better Run', a Young Rascals song, was issued as their second Curtom single but made no bigger commercial impact than their first, though it turns out to be a pretty good midtempo ballad that, with more airplay, could also have taken off. On reflection, they might have been better advised to push the B-side,

Mayfield's pre-*Superfly* drug alert 'Stone Junkie', which has emerged over the years as their most popular record. Frantic drumming drives this track that is an almost unrecognizable version of a song that had up until then only been heard on the *CURTIS/LIVE* album. None of their records found UK release until Sequel issued the album on CD in 2000 as *Stone Junkie* (NEMCD 367). Curtom dropped Ruby Jones and from this point on concentrated on what they did best – soulful music.

In addition to work at Curtom, Curtis also had a finger in a number of other musical pies. Curtis Mayfield and Eddie Thomas both had independent production deals with Scepter/Wand in the early 1970s who also distributed their short-lived Mad Tad label that managed only two single releases. While Mayfield struggled producing Patti Miller, Thomas did better with Nolan Chance cutting 'Sara Lee' (which incidentally was also recorded by the Independents for Wand a little later). Curtis cut some excellent sides with Patti Jo for Scepter in late '72. 'Make Me Believe In You' and 'Ain't No Love Lost'/'Stay Away From Me' both found single release but rather surprisingly managed no chart success. Scepter put the two A-sides through 'A Tom Moulton Mix' for inclusion on their *Disco Gold* album in '75 that also featured tracks by Ultra High Frequency, the Independents and Clara Lewis. This album was released in the UK on CD by Sequel in July 2000. During this period Curtis also produced for Buddah, where he had major success with Barbara Mason and Gladys Knight.

While Mayfield and his team had already scored a number of significant hits on Curtom, too many good records and artists' aspirations were falling by the wayside. Already Mayfield was beginning to spread himself a little too thinly. What Curtom needed were more artists like Mayfield himself – that is to say artists who able to write, produce and arrange for the talent on roster who were standing in line awaiting creative direction. Leroy Hutson would soon stand in to supply just this kind of service.

6 Times Have Changed

Curtom Records went through some major changes in late '71 and early '72. Eddie Thomas who had been Mayfield's manager and partner of 14 years decided to sell out his interest in the company to Marv Stuart. Stuart persuaded Mayfield, who had by then become his own hottest act, to cut down the roster at Curtom and concentrate on those who had been making hits. Some artists had already left – The Stairsteps, June Conquest, Holly Maxwell, Major Lance and Donny Hathaway had all moved onto other options. The label didn't look for any more outside product to release and for the next couple of years they concentrated on just three acts – Mayfield himself, The Impressions and Leroy Hutson.

Leroy Hutson began singing in high school with a group called the Newtoners. He stayed with them until he went to Howard University in Washington DC to study for his BM (Bachelor of Music). His roommate turned out to be Donny Hathaway and both men had met Curtis through Guy Draper back in '67 when they worked together on Mayfield Records – Curtis, Donny and Leroy got together and produced a single as the Mayfield Singers. Hutson was subsequently invited to join the Impressions and 'Love Me', the first single to feature Leroy, got a warm reception and hit #25 R&B after release in July '71.

When Mayfield produced the Impressions' next album *Times Have Changed* (CRS 8012) he used Riley Hampton, Johnny Pate and Leroy as arrangers on the different sessions that were all recorded at RCA Studios, like most of the released Curtom product had been so far. Curtis used six of his own songs and Leroy provided the seventh, 'This Love Is Real', which hit the Top 50 R&B as a single at #41 in April '72. The final track was 'Inner City Blues', which had flopped on the singles chart but was nevertheless worthy of inclusion. This song was a particular favourite with Mayfield, as was the whole of Marvin Gaye's *What's Going On* album, which had topped the R&B album charts for three months back in June to August '71. In a later interview Curtis said this about Marvin and the album: 'When I first heard *What's Going On* I felt like Marvin had said everything there was to be said. The album had such qualities and the timely release was perfect. The clarity with which he expressed himself left you wondering whether there was anything left to write about; it seemed to me that he really had said it all.' Curtis and Marvin had first met back when Gaye sang with the Moonglows who had toured with the Impressions. 'It was already clear that Marvin was destined for great things. The way he crooned a tune was magic and his natural ability with instruments, especially the drums, was something to see. I remember once backstage at a theatre in New Orleans whilst me and the guys were rehearsing, Marvin kept us all fascinated with his artistry, you could see even then that he was destined to be a star.'

During the 30 years since its release *What's Going On* has elevated itself to classic status as one of the most celebrated soul albums of all time. It was so close to Mayfield's heart because it dealt with many of the issues that had previously motivated him to write so many of his own songs. Undoubtedly Curtis' previous work with the Impressions, and now solo, had influenced Marvin on this album. Gaye had drawn these elements together into a concept package and its success elevated the work above the initial concerns and criticism expressed at the time of issue. The sad observation is that in the decades since these sociological and ecological views were articulated in the work of Gaye, Mayfield and others, the most powerful nation on earth was then and is now still unwilling to address these issues. 'Mercy Mercy Me', 'Choice of Colors', 'This Is My Country' and 'Inner City Blues' are still relevant today and continue to offer insight to the escalation of inner city violent crime and social unrest that still plagues America.

Vietnam was still in hot debate and withdrawal was high on the agenda for millions of young Americans in '71, black and white alike. Mayfield now made his opinions on this subject clear on *Times Have Changed*.

'Stop The War' sung by Fred Cash, pulled no punches. Mayfield used his familiar convention of a social gathering in the background while in the chorus the group exclaim, 'Hell no, we won't go – stop the war!' a Stokley Carmichael quotation that was quickly absorbed and used as a slogan extensively by the civil rights and anti-Vietnam movements. All three Impressions feature on this track as they do throughout the album. The title track has Hutson delivering brilliant Mayfield lyrics after a bleak howling wind of change sets up the song. Leroy asks, 'Who really cares,' as the song examines the depreciation of black social conditions. Times may have changed but the problems grind on. 'Inner City Blues' comes next and serves to underline the situation; it also links closely to Mayfield's earlier songs of sociology. Hutson's arrangement tailors the song for the Impressions perfectly and so this version really works. Their original version of 'Our Love Goes On and On' features a very effective use of vocal interchange and is superior to the later Gladys Knight hit version, that Mayfield used on the soundtrack of *Claudine* (see Chapter 9).

'Potent Love' opens with a cascading water sound effect to set the scene. It was arranged by Curtis with Johnny Pate, who together created a great medium tempo groove behind the group. The track deserved single status but strangely it was passed over and Curtom re-released 'Love Me' with a new B-side 'Need To Belong', a reworking of the much-recorded old Mayfield standby, and a big hit on the original by Jerry Butler back in '63. The Impressions turn in a fine version with a monologue by Leroy and lead vocal by Sam. 'This Love's For Real' features Hutson on his own song and arrangement. It shows all the promise of Leroy's undoubted ability in all musical areas. It's a great song delivered with sincerity and style, and it takes us perfectly to the final track, the underrated 'Love Me'. The infectious arrangement, pace and vocal treatment combined to make a potent single that fizzled out on its second release. The finished album was released in March 1972 and climbed to #17 on the R&B album chart by May '72.

Just prior to the Impressions' first British tour in July '72, Curtom released their next single, the Hutson arrangement of 'Inner City Blues'. It was so similar to the Marvin Gaye original, that when people heard it on the radio, that's what they thought they were listening to. However, very few UK fans actually got a chance to see them as they played only to US military bases. A very fortunate couple of hundred souls did catch their only public appearance at the Speakeasy in London where Leroy, Fred and Sam performed a slick set of Impressions classics plus new material with a soulful professionalism and dazzled their audience with star quality. Hutson fitted right in with Sam and Fred, almost as if he had been understudying Mayfield for years, but he also bought something special of his own to the performances. Their band, led by Deacon Jones (previously with The Babysitters), was also particularly good. When interviewed, the Impressions seemed a little embarrassed by their new single but otherwise were happy to talk. Leroy confessed that he was still rather in awe of Curtis Mayfield: 'I've always had tremendous respect for the man. He's written so many great songs over the years and he still gets better with each album. He was my hero when I was still at school – it's wonderful to work with him now.' On the subject of the split, Sam said: 'Yeah, it took a little getting used to – but everything's fine now. It got so we were getting in each other's way. Curtis works on so many other things. Sometimes it was hard for us to get together. Now we can have it both ways.'

The Topics had unwittingly toured the UK and Germany in '67 as the 'Fabulous Impressions', when a UK promoter created a stormy backlash from UK soul music fans by presenting a host of 'bogus' US groups, which also included the Drifters and the Temptations etc (with suitable prefixes). The Topics themselves, who were previously known as the Uniteds on Chess, were in fact Vaughn Curtis (lead), Charles Stodhill and Robert Lewis. As the Topics they had cut some good records on Carnival and Chadwick (available on UK Kent on two Ady Croasdell Carnival CD compilations). Vaughn went on to reform the Topics in '72 and they cut some more sides for Heavy Duty and Mercury but had no hits with their later recordings either.

Meanwhile, Curtis' solo career was flourishing. He made an appearance at the Newport Jazz Festival in July '72, which Atlantic recorded and issued as part of the album *Newport in New York '72* (ATL 40439). The two tracks that were featured, 'Stone Junkie' and 'Pusherman', were in fact recorded in Radio City Music Hall on 6 July.

This was one of three venues used by George Wein to stage the festival that year, the other two being the Philharmonic Hall and the Yankee Stadium. Other artists featured on the album included Billy Eckstine, BB King, Herbie Mann, Les McCann and Roberta Flack. The sleevenotes were split between two writers, Ira Gitler and Gary Giddins, and both supplied interesting and informative accounts of the festival, its background and current rebirth. Giddins was obviously a jazz buff and unaware of Mayfield's influential back catalogue with the Impressions, judging by his observations and report of the performance. This is not to suggest that despite his leanings Giddins' comments were in anyway anti-soul. On the contrary, he suggested that soul like jazz performers have their own tradition and artistic evolution and stated in conclusion, 'Some day they will be regarded for the validity of their great contribution, not as trivia to be compared lightly with so-called serious (read: western, white, classical) music.'

The next few months saw the construction of the Curtom 16 track Studio designed and built by Roger Anfinsen as the company went through a number of changes en route for big time success. Marv Stuart, Mayfield's new partner at Curtom, had some big ideas for the company that was inundated with offers by the time of interview in the autumn of '72. 'Curtis is working on his new album *Back To The World*, the theme is the return home of POWs from Vietnam. He's just finished a tour and is recording Patti Jo for Scepter and with Barbara Mason for Buddah. We've also just signed a new production deal for him with Linda Clifford and New World at Polydor, so Curt's pretty busy right now,' Updating other Curtom news, Marv revealed, 'We've just spent some months slimming down the roster at Curtom, so we can concentrate on promoting Curtis, the Impressions, Leroy Hutson and our newest signing, the Natural Four.'

During the late months of '72 Curtis Mayfield was riding on a high peak of popular success. The huge interest that his soundtrack hit *Superfly* (see Chapter 9) had created kept both him and Curtom in the spotlight. He was currently working on two projects in the new Curtom Studios with Rich Tufo and Roger Anfinsen. *Preacher Man* for the Impressions and *Back To The World* (CRS 8015) his next album.

Curtom released 'Future Shock' as the single follow-up to *Superfly* in July '73. It sold well, peaking at #11 R&B/39 pop but did not quite gain the public acceptance of Mayfield's previous two hit singles. It was taken from the *Back To The World* album that dealt with the highly controversial subject, amongst other subjects, of 'Vietnam at Home' as well as de-education, environmental issues, racial harmony, trust and love. 'Future Shock' as a single, was a gamble that did not entirely pay off. The subject matter was too serious to provide a huge popular hit but as an album track it was right on the money. The album begins with the title track, a few cockpit exchanges and Mayfield launches into the 'back from Vietnam' song, which highlights the humiliation and pain experienced by those unfortunate Americans who had fought and suffered on behalf of the US, only to be greeted on their return by a backlash of criticism and hostility from those whose opinions had been recently changed by America's defeat. Historically, soldiers had returned home as heroes but on this occasion they had to endure even more suffering, this time at the hands of their own people. In the post-Vietnam re-emergence, this was a warning of the deplorable blindfold politics that had successfully shifted the blame for this unpopular war and America's ultimate failure, from the politicians to the foot soldiers. Mayfield had previously touched on this subject before in '68 when in collaboration with Oscar Brown Jr he wrote 'Don't Cry My Love' but now the sentiments expressed dealt with the other end of the story.

The track 'Future Shock' connects with Alvin Toffler's penetrating bestseller of the same title published that year. Both song and book predicted a dismal future, which has since turned out to be alarmingly accurate. They both explore the environmental and social deterioration that escalated in the 30 years since they were both written. Some people never learn (and care even less) and sadly for the rest of us, it is not in their interest to do so. Curtis' poetic vocal pushed to its limits, delivers the bad news and predicts the serious consequences that are still descending on us today. The Mayfield philosophy relentlessly moves on to track three, 'Right On For Darkness', which examines the political manipulation on the educational system by which greed preserves the status quo and this provides a positive future for the privileged few, on the backs of many. The black experience then, clearly parallels the falling educational standards of all but the élite of any colour now – Right On For Darkness.

In 'Future Song' Curtis testifies to the potency of love – in relationships, the family, and by implication society in general. Love and understanding will prevail only if and when they are practised by all. Mayfield comes over as a guru, a Gandhi of soul music, and it was songs like these that earned him the tag 'Gentle genius'. On the following cut Curtis transports us back to review the world through innocent eyes with 'If I Were Only A Child Again'. If only life as a grown up provided all of us with that serene security expressed herein. As a single this track scored #22 R&B/71 pop in October '73 and was to become a constant in Mayfield's repertoire henceforth. 'Can't Say Nothin'' did better than the previous single as a Top 20 hit at #16 R&B in December but didn't cross over so well. It's a love song that encourages action in preference to conversation. The mood continues to lighten with 'Keep On Trippin'', an in-the-head song that wonders if the girl has gone with another or not. It provides perfect relief to the heavy-duty subject matter aired elsewhere on the album.

Wisely Curtom witheld the album's release for a few months while *Superfly* continued its enormously popular success, but by September '73 *Back To The World* topped the R&B LP chart and occupied #16 on Billboard's pop album chart. It soon earned another gold album for its creator despite the serious issues it touches on; perhaps the most thought-provoking of Mayfield's work is contained here. If any album established Mayfield as a serious social commentator, it was this collection. The excellent gatefold sleeve designed by Glen Christensen and illustrated by Gary Wolkowitz is a superb visual representation of the themes discussed therein. It opens to reveal Mayfield's lyrics laid out simply with good legibility and taste, the package undoubtedly enhancing sales.

Curtis was not the only potential solo artist on the label. It soon became clear that the talents of Leroy Hutson were not long to be confined by the format of the Impressions and it was no surprise when, on their return to Chicago, he began work on his first solo project. Meanwhile the core Impressions membership of Sam Gooden and Fred Cash went into the studio to record their new album *Preacher Man* (CRS 8016) as a duo. This was the first to be produced at Curtom's purpose-built studios with master engineer Roger Anfinsen (who had designed and created the new studios) at the controls. Also, it was very much Richard Tufo's baby as he wrote five of the seven songs, produced and arranged all the sessions. (Tufo had previously worked on the *Ruby Jones* album – see Chapter 5.) Mayfield was credited as production co-ordinator. From the opening notes of the album, it becomes apparent that Tufo, Cash and Gooden were making a conscious effort to present something different. Instead of struggling to find a further replacement for Mayfield, and thereby causing unwanted delays in the recording of this album, the threesome took the next positive step in the evolution of the Impressions. For the first time in the group's history, Fred Cash sang the lead throughout the album and, for the most part, he pulls it off, with the assistance of Tufo who recorded layers of background vocals, which featured Fred and Sam as well as assorted female voices. Richard's vocal arrangements are rather complex in places but never less than superb throughout.

Legend has it that the album's opening cut was not originally intended as an Impressions track, and that it came instead from a rehearsal tape that Tufo had recorded of conga player Henry Gibson. Henry, who was by now a regular in Mayfield's road band, was loosening up in the studio prior to a session and Anfinsen had already started the tapes rolling. The resultant groove owed a little to 'Freddie's Dead' and some of the other sounds from the *Superfly* album (see Chapter 9) Tufo saw the potential and wrote and recorded an arrangement around Gibson's performance. Later, when it was suggested for *Preacher Man*, Sam and Fred dubbed on the title at the end of the track, and it became 'What It Is'. The track has a fairly quiet intro, but Anfinsen soon whacks up the volume by at least a third and really gets the listeners' attention. The 'Freddie' riff rolls on into the next track, which is a strong, well-integrated piece with very bright vocalizing and arrangement. It definitely deserved a better chart fate than to miss out completely, but that's sadly and inexplicably what it did.

'Thin Line' is by far the most ambitious post-Mayfield Impressions piece of work, clocking in at over ten minutes in length and utilizing every facet of Tufo's impressive arranging skills. The track starts jazzily and builds gradually to a strong midtempo groove, all the time offering a refreshing mix of (for the time) experimental sounds and ideas and ultimately coming across like a mini soundtrack for an unmade movie. Its length gave Tufo plenty of scope to allow for undulations in the storyline and production, and it's easily the album's strongest track – a fact that didn't pass unnoticed by Curtom, who released an edited version as a 45 in July '73 in an attempt to restore the group's (temporary, as it turned out) slump in singles sales, which had been in decline since Curtis left. 'This Love's For Real' had only managed to hit #41 US R&B in April '72, and nothing had come of 'Times Have Changed', a re-release under Fred Cash's name, or the 45 of 'Preacher Man'. Sadly 'Thin Line' in its shortened format was not enough to stop the rot and it was to be a while yet before the group was deservedly restored to its former chart glory...

Of the material that Tufo did not write for this album, 'Color Us All Gray (I'm Lost)' deserves special attention. Part-written by Gene Chandler, himself briefly a Curtom act during this period with three good singles to his credit, the lyrics proffer the 'melting pot' theory as a possible solution to discrimination. It's a powerful song, which hits the mark from many directions. 'I'm Loving You' is a love song and more in an earlier Impressions style.

Tufo's arrangement on *Preacher Man* is handled impeccably if a touch elaborately in places. It was a departure from anything the Impressions had done before – a calculated move towards a new identity. Despite a little uncertainty in some of the lead vocals Fred Cash did a good job and Rich Tufo consistently demonstrated great talent in the studio. *Preacher Man* came with a distinctive sleeve – a powerful portrait of a tearful preacher is superimposed onto a Harlem street scene. The back sleeve has tastefully centred typography reversed out of a black background. Art Director Glen Christensen and photographer Joel Brodsky created a classic cover that oozed quality and style.

The finished package was released in March '73 and climbed to a healthy #24 R&B in the following month. It sold less than previous albums and this precipitated further changes for the group in both personnel and musical direction. The album stands on its own merits though. A one-off experiment that in retrospect, sparkles with mature brightness. Unfortunately for British fans, they could only buy *Preacher Man* on import, as Buddah did not release it in the UK. Mayfield's move to a solo career and stardom seemed to partially eclipse the others around him during this period. Critics and pundits tended to compare any Curtom product with the commercially successful material and so, sadly, some creative and distinctive work spluttered in Mayfield's vapour trail when it really should have received better attention and acceptance. Fortunately the passage of time allows for re-evaluation of such music, and *Preacher Man* can now be seen for what it is, a highly accomplished piece of work.

While the Impressions were finding their way as a duo, Leroy Hutson's initial solo work clearly illustrated just how talented he really was, with a stunning collection of songs impeccably written, arranged, performed and produced. His impact on the charts, however, was less than encouraging. His early singles, despite their high quality, made no chart headway. *Love Oh Love* (CRS 8017), his début album, created some interest, but only made #75 R&B in July 1973.

The other talents he added to his own on this album were arrangements from TT Washington and Rich Tufo plus Mike Hawkins who co-wrote many songs with Hutson in years of fruitful collaboration and was involved in four songs on *Love Oh Love*. The first track 'So In Love With You' inexplicably missed as a single despite Leroy's excellent vocal against a well-balanced medium tempo arrangement. The song is a perfect example of a cool soul ballad but it missed on the club circuit as well. It remains a great album track and just the right introduction to the set. 'Love Oh Love' has a more insistent tempo and Leroy's subtle vocal style begins to grow on the listener as it weaves in and out of a busy but interesting arrangement. Some of the brass lines have a jazzy flavour to them but Hutson's mix turns it into a very commercial cocktail. It is more surprising that this second single was not a much bigger hit. The third cut 'When You Smile' was arranged by TT Washington and creates a slightly different mood. Hutson's pleasant vocal starts with a spoken intro and winds its way comfortably through a slightly more pedestrian score. When Curtom released it as the third single it went to #81 R&B in October 1973. Washington and Hutson collaborated again to produce 'Getting It On', that was written for the score of the movie *The JJ Johnson Affair*. This instrumental track owes much to the earlier themes from *Shaft* and *Superfly* and merely adds to an established tradition. The soundtrack project was later aborted.

'Time Brings On A Change' is a piece of sociology that attempts to update the lower profile civil rights movement of the time. A speech extract from Martin Luther King introduces us to a discourse on the changes that recent times had made to black consciousness, an idea picked up and used many times later in the rap and hip hop music genres. The inspiration for songs like this came from the work of Mayfield and Gaye and this fits right alongside those sociological discussions. Twenty years later these same topics of 'time' and 'faith' were still being aired by Jerry Butler (Ichiban 1992) as a continuum rather than a problem that has any final solution. In the early 1970s change still implied hope and freedom. 'I'll Be There, I Still Care' returns to the subject of lost love. Leroy lays out the lyric with subtle background inter harmonies and the song is persuasive enough to affect an imminent reunion. This pleasant mood continues with 'I'm in Love With You Girl', which Curtom used as a B-side on 'Love Oh Love'. Hutson winds up the album with 'As Long As There's Love Around', which relates observations on everyday wasted opportunities and proffers love and faith whilst marking time on improvements.

Love Oh Love should have propelled Leroy Hutson to instant stardom – but it didn't. The album could not create enough sales to chart anywhere but Chicago. Public acceptance or not, Hutson was a hit with his contemporaries. During the next year he worked on several projects. He wrote and produced 'Giving Love' for the 20- strong vocal group 'Voices of East Harlem', that hit #57 R&B in June '73 on Just Sunshine Records and continued with further work for their album. He began to work with Curtom's newest additions the Natural Four whilst putting together 'The Man', his next solo album and also contributed to a TV special that featured most of the hot Curtom acts at this time.

The first highlight on the Curtom calendar in '74 came when the *Curtis In Chicago* TV special was shown across America. This TV special was an edited concert recorded by WTTW-TV in late '73, which featured most of the current Curtom roster plus Jerry Butler, Brenda Lee Eager (who had dueted with Jerry) and Phil Upchurch. The programme centred around Curtis Mayfield who was by then at the top of his profession, his solo work and his influence with the Impressions, which had in recent times paid off handsomely. Curtom further edited the soundtrack to produce the album of the same name (CRS 8018). Production credits were split between Mayfield and other Curtom staff, Rich Tufo and engineer Roger Anfinsen. The Curtom Rhythm Section plus Phil Upchurch provided all the music.

After the intro came 'Superfly', still a massive hit at the time, on which Curtis created the perfect alternative version. Jerry Butler came together with Curtis, Sam and Fred to create a great rendition of 'For Your Precious Love', which came after banter between the quartet. The group delivered a version almost faithful to the original and as close as anyone could get anytime. The first noticeable edit takes us into Impressions (Mark 3) and 'I'm So Proud' a sentimental ballad that typifies Mayfield's early work with the trio. Next came 'For Once In My Life' from the Impressions (MK6) featuring Fred, Sam and Reggie Torian, an inexplicable choice considering all of the songs at their disposal. The group takes turns on a frantic version of high-speed cabaret. Fred takes lead on 'Preacher Man' and puts events firmly back on track with a great version of their recent hit. 'If I Were Only A Child Again' taken from Mayfield's hit album *Back To The World* follows and next our host introduced long time friend and co-Chicagoan Gene Chandler, who had just signed with Curtom but reverted to his earliest hit 'Duke Of Earl' and gave a distinctive rendition encouraging the audience to join in on the 'Woo-Woo' thing at the end. Leroy Hutson was up next with a superb reading of his excellent 'Love Oh Love', which moves along at a comfortable pace as he warbles the lyric to perfection. The grand finale was inevitably 'Amen' with the complete cast involved out of the act.

This album was released in March 1974 and came in a gatefold sleeve that featured many excellent photos from the programme. It sold well to Mayfield's established fans but like the majority of 'live' albums it didn't chart but bubbled under at #135 for a couple of months. Nevertheless it provided an excellent portrait of the talent in residence at Curtom for those interested in the label's fortunes.

By the time of their next album, the line-up of the Impressions looked set to change again. They began to lay down material for what became their 15th album in late '73 and early '74, with Rich Tufo and Lowrell Simon (the latter formerly of Brunswick act, The Lost Generation) in the producers' chairs. During the *Preacher Man* sessions, Sam and Fred had taken on Reggie Torian as Leroy Hutson's replacement. Torian had been recruited by Fred Cash from a Chicago outfit, the Enchanters, and his ability to replicate Curtis' falsetto became a much-needed part of the Impressions' live shows. This brought the group back to a trio and by the time the latest round of recording got underway they had become a foursome thanks to the acquisition of the talented Ralph Johnson. 'Reggie is great at the old hits – he has a similar vocal range to Curtis. Ralph does most of the newer material.' Fred commented in an interview at the time. It had been Fred who invited Ralph to join the Impressions in late '73, after hearing some demos that he had cut the previous year.

This new injection of youthful enthusiasm gave the group a further burst of energy and provided a new wave of hits for the Impressions. In December '73 'If It's In You To Do Wrong' peaked at #26 on Billboard's R&B singles giving them their first hit in 18 months. It may have done even better had Curtom not decided to pair it with a third outing for 'Times Have Changed'! An intelligent song with a terrific arrangement from ex-Motown staffer David Van De Pitte, 'If It's In You To Do Wrong' began in midtempo mode but soon settled into a ballad groove with Ralph Johnson getting plenty of room to establish his credentials as an Impressions lead singer. Johnson's voice had a slightly harder edge to it than any of his predecessors and this gave the song an insistence that helped it re-establish the group as a force still to be reckoned with.

Other material stockpiled by Tufo and Simon for the forthcoming album was often as good. 'We Go Back A Ways' written by Lowrell and his former Lost Generation colleagues Larry Brownlee and George Davis was a pleasing ballad, while the almost northern soul-ish gallop of the unison sung 'I'll Always Be There' looked back at mid '60s Motown and forward to the mid '70s disco era in its construction and execution. Also noteworthy is 'Don't Forget What I Told You', which sounded very much like the kind of thing that future Curtom act Billy Butler and his then-group Infinity were recording around this time. It was certainly a departure for the Impressions – the background vocalizing, especially, was very untypical.

While the Simon/Tufo team and the Impressions themselves had been taking steps in the right direction, Curtom looked elsewhere for the inspiration and drive to complete this unfinished album. The '50s and '60s veteran Ed Townsend had recently become hot again thanks to his co-production of some of Marvin Gaye's 'other' great album of the era *Let's Get It On* and it was Townsend and his contemporary, the great guitarist/arranger Rene Hall (who had earned a solid reputation for his early work with Billy Ward's Dominoes and Sam Cooke) who were engaged to provide a quartet of tracks to finish the Impressions' project. Townsend and Hall pushed Ralph Johnson's tenor to an uncomfortable high at times, particularly on 'Try Me' and 'Guess What I've Got', but one song gave Ralph the chance to provide a more natural, relaxed delivery and this, together with Sam, Fred and Reggie's memorable back-up vocals and a loping groove that Townsend flew straight in from 'Let's Get It On', was all the incentive the public needed to make 'I'm A Changed Man (Finally Got Myself Together)' the hit it deserved to be.

This record was to set the style for the Impressions' next phase, giving them their 40th R&B chart entry and more importantly, their fourth R&B #1 single in April '74. (It also crossed over to the pop charts, where it peaked at a very impressive #17). Naturally it became the title track of the now-completed album (CRS 8019), which was released around the time of the single's chart decline and peaked at #22 R&B/176 pop albums, providing the group with healthy sales for six months and a positive outlook for the future. The cover pictured the quartet as losers on the front and as winners on the back, complete with all the glittering prizes: expensive cars, clothes and beautiful women. The album was also well received in Europe and relaunched the Impressions outside America, selling well on the UK soul album chart. In the following months the single went gold – more proof of its lasting popularity. Once again, the group was in great demand – and this time independently of Curtis Mayfield. Fred Cash related 'Curtis had been such a huge influence, we knew we couldn't live in his shadow forever and he wouldn't have wanted it that way either. It was rough at first but when we hit the top without him, it gave us all a lot of personal confidence'.

Immediately the Impressions began work on their next project, a movie score for *Three The Hard Way* a collaboration with Rich Tufo and Lowrell Simon as producers and writers. They were hot once again and happily rode the media-go-round as it positively exposed them through radio, TV, movies, live shows and interviews.

Leroy Hutson's second solo album was released in February '74, modestly entitled, *The Man* (CRS 8020), but it did little to enhance his commercial status. Looking back, this album needed to be much stronger with a couple of potential hit singles. Instead it came over as a collection of Hutson's samples from contemporary city soul music. While one can't blame Curtom for the hype – 'Writer! Producer! Artist! Superstar!' – the final claim was not to be because *The Man* didn't chart on pop album. The mood was light and the songs were, in the main, a little lightweight. The sessions were arranged by Jerry Long and recorded at Curtom Studios. Leroy penned five of the songs and Quenton Joseph, the session drummer, provided the other two numbers for the set. 'Can't Say Enough About Mom' finds Hutson distilling down a myriad influences to a mid Chicago/Detroit mix in his ode to mom. It's a family values song with no surprises.

'Gotta Move – Gotta Groove' is a 'musician on the road' song that meanders through situations and aspirations and takes us into 'Ella Weez' the catchiest song in the set, which, disappointingly, isn't the ode to asthmatics that the title suggests. Curtom released it as a single in June 1974 and it crept into the R&B charts at #81, the same spot as the previous single 'When You Smile'. It has a familiar, comfortable groove, which is very pleasant, but leaves the listener not entirely convinced that Ella ever got her 'fine self home'. 'Give This Love A Try' is a song that Gene Chandler must have bequeathed Leroy as he left Curtom himself, after a disappointing and uneventful year with them. It sounds like something the Chi-Lites might have done and, despite its slower tempo, had more commercial potential than any of the other cuts.

'The Ghetto' is the song that Leroy wrote with and for Donny Hathaway, which provided him with his first hit. Leroy's lacks the passion of Donny's version, which is an altogether funkier piece and has the more prominent vocal, backed up by excellent keyboards and Henry Gibson's outstanding percussion. Nevertheless, it is interesting to hear Hutson's side of the song, which is practically an instrumental with background vocals. Here, Jerry Wilson's solo sax replaces the original vocal and piano lines on Hathaway's version and sets a completely different mood. Hutson's version features percussionist Derf Raneem Reclawy (which sounds like an uncomfortable pseudonym) but he provides the perfect backbeat for 'Ghetto 2' – a different day on a different street it maybe, with less excitement, but still very well worth the trip.

'After the Fight' comes next and has Leroy trying on Philly sound for size. It ends up as a mixture of O'Jays-Gamble-Huff, punctuated with Kung Fu 'Huhs' and diverts the listener from serious attention to the lyrics, which might be interesting. 'Could This Be Love', Leroy's own song suffers from a UK mid '60s post-Motown treatment. It is a worn out imitation unworthy of such a talent – or is it intended as a spoof Four Tops homage? It demonstrates all the clichés to distraction and leaves us with the final track 'Dudley Do-Right', which strays into novelty with horse snorts 'n' all. The album was beautifully and tastefully packaged, and it had healthy sales on R'n'B but failed to excite the record-buying public.

At this time, Curtom began to wind down its US distribution deal with Buddah, which ran until the end of '74. They released five more *Epilog* albums, which were prefixed CRS 8600–8604. The first issue on the *Epilog* series was the first Curtom album by The Natural Four, who were originally formed by their leader Chris James in San Francisco during '67. They cut a single 'I Thought You Were Mine'/'12 Months of the Year' on the obscure Boola-Boola label the following year in Oakland. Commercially the record meant nothing but it created enough interest for ABC to pick them up in '69 where they put together an album with producer Willie Hoskins at Sierra Sound Labs in Berkeley. 'Why Should We Stop Now' was the strongest of their four singles at ABC when in March '69 it peaked at #31 R&B but their reworked uptempo version of 'I Thought You Were Mine' is thought by many to be their best record from that period. During their first West Coast phase, The Natural Four consisted of James, Allen Richardson, John January and Al Bowden.

They were signed to Chess Records in '71 where they cut six sides with Ron Carson, but only one single, 'The Devil Made Me Do It', was released. It created a good club reaction but didn't chart. When Chris James (aka Ollan Christopher) reformed the Natural Four in '72 with Steve Striplin, Darryl Cannardy and Delmos Whitley, they performed at a concert in Oakland and began getting local gigs. 'Our introduction to Curtom was through a friend of ours named Wally Cox, who was also a friend of Curtis. Wally told Curtis about us. Marv and Curtis talked about Curtis coming to California to do several gigs. Marv came out early to secure the gigs and also audition us at the same time. We were supposed to sing one or two songs but we ended up doing a half-hour show with choreography. Marv liked us and told Curtis about us. When Curtis came out he saw our group. Within a month's time we were signed with Curtom Records,' James said in January 2000.

Their first Curtom single 'Things Will Be Better Tomorrow' was produced by Rich Tufo but due to radio interest in the B-side 'Eddie You Should Know Better', a song from the *Superfly* movie, Curtom switched it from B- to A-side and re-pressed it with 'Try Love Again' but unfortunately it was too late for any chart action. Their next teaming was with Leroy Hutson and 'bingo' it gave them their biggest hit with 'Can This Be Real', which scored on both charts at #10 R&B/31 pop in November '73. They began work on their first Curtom album *Natural Four* (CRS 8600) immediately and it was ready for release by April '74. Leroy co-wrote six of the nine tracks, which he also arranged and produced while Rich Tufo co-produced the remaining three with Lowrell Simon. Therefore, the album comes over less well-integrated than it might have been and the group bears little resemblance to their previous recordings, which is hardly surprising. Initial reactions were that they seemed more comfortable with the Hutson material – these were generally positive love songs, which were beautifully performed and produced. 'Can This Be Real' is a superb record, everything is right on the groove. It's hard to understand why it did not cross over to an even greater extent. Easy-on-the-ear vocals by Delmos Whitley and a delightful arrangement with a great jazzy sax solo all contributed to keeping this single on the chart for four months.

Chris James leads on 'You Bring Out The Best In Me', which is much more immediately commercial and typical Chicago soul/pop of the era. It was used later as a single and charted #20 R&B in July '74 and also became another northern soul favourite. 'Try Love Again' keeps the infectious quality going with a group vocal effort like an extended chorus over a busy Hutson arrangement. 'You Keep Running Away' is a pleasant filler in a similar vein. It has a hook but no bait. Steve Striplin sings 'This Is What's Happening Now', which has a meaty lyric from Messrs Dribble and Davis and it once again explores black America's disillusionment with political and social development in general. It has a whiff of the material on *Preacher Man* via Tufo and Simon's production but has enough integrity to stand on its own. 'Love That Really Counts' returns to the melodic Hutson treatment and was used as a single in April '74 when it climbed to #23 R&B but only just crept into the Hot 100. It's a reflective piece that recounts the high value of love during the ups and downs of everyday urban life, well told by Whitley.

'Try To Smile' is a positive Simon/Brownlee song in uptempo mode and handled well by James. Had it not gone against the style of their hit, it would have made a great A-side. The style of vocalizing that N4 use had been established by others and later went on to prove lucrative for groups like Tavares. 'Love's Society' is a much more challenging song written by Joseph Scott, Leroy and Roger Anfinsen, which they jointly produced. Chris James' smooth high tenor easily relates observations in this sociological discussion piece, which centres around the problems of living life with double standards. Beautifully handled by all, it rather magnifies the professional production of 'Things Will Be Better Tomorrow' as Tufo mimics Norman Whitfield and the group lead by Chris use a Temptations format to deliver Rich's lyrics. For the listener, these similarities are rather hard to ignore. It was the first track cut with the group when they arrived at Curtom, before the influence of Hutson's songs had helped to establish their vocal approach, which was to become the central theme for their future recorded work.

Chris James said in an interview later, 'Basically what happens is songs from a number of people are submitted and we choose the best ones for the group.' Hutson and Tufo recorded separate sessions on The Natural Four's early work with the label and other Curtom backroom staff also made significant contributions, though the Natural Four were delighted with the considerable success of 'Can This Be Real', which helped to push the album to #27 on the US R&B album chart. They were unhappy about Curtom's choice for their follow-up, 'Love That Really Counts'. Of this, James said, 'The group felt that "You Bring Out The Best In Me" that came next should have followed the hit. We would have definitely been able to establish a hit pattern with that.' In retrospect it is easy to concur with James' remarks. Early in '74, the N4 were booked into a very successful week at New York's Apollo Theatre on the same bill as Funkadelic and New York City. Their schedule was solid all over the country where they toured with other acts from Curtom's roster – Mayfield, Hutson, the Impressions, etc.

Curtis continued to release solo material during this period. On the sessions that went to make up *Sweet Exorcist* (CRS 8601) Curtis used two arrangers, staffman Rich Tufo and Gil Askey, whose CV included many hits with Motown. The opening track 'Ain't Got Time' was a reworking of the Impressions' earlier single. Mayfield takes it at a slower pace on this lengthy version that is a slight re-write of the original. 'Sweet Exorcist' comes next and was chosen as the single scoring #32 R&B but found no action on the pop chart. It is a curious song that deals with a restless spiritual struggle that can only be exorcized by physical love. It also contains a reference to 'Traveling soul...', which was the name of Mayfield's grandmother's church and the reference pops up again later from time to time.

'To Be Invisible' is a remarkable song, which had also been recorded by Gladys Knight for the *Claudine* movie for which Curtis wrote the soundtrack (see Chapter 9). Mayfield's is much the better version. He accurately describes an uncaring world, which devalues the individual, while imposing the considerable constraints of class and race just for good measure. It is a delicate expression of sensitive values, which are too often contemptuously ignored. Mayfield's sad but simple solution to the problem is to become just what the establishment requires –

Invisible. The song highlights the western philosophical ideal of consistently ignoring those aspects of anything that can be perceived as a problem, as if it is not there: after all it always goes away doesn't it? Wrong – it festers and erupts later down the line (hopefully when someone else will, or more likely won't, deal with it again). 'Power To The People' touches on socialism and communism both long-feared philosophies by many Americans. In the 70s when Curtis wrote this song, that same prejudice still existed despite the number of similar songs and statements that had and were still being made. Curtis' multi-track vocal bobs on top of a busy Askey arrangement, which is a little uneven in places but bubbles along with moments that sparkle.

'Kung Fu' provided Mayfield with his next single hit when it charted #3 R&B/40 pop in June '74. The longer album track builds on previous successes and, although in America it predates the biggest hit of the genre, 'Kung Fu Fighting' by Carl Douglas, the theme was already popular via ABC/Warner's smash TV series of the time *Kung Fu*, which starred David Carradine as Grasshopper. In addition, the fact that Bruce Lee had died the previous year had turned his final movie *Enter the Dragon* into a long-running success. The single had more dance appeal than others of late and sold well in the UK when released that September. 'Suffer' is another reworking of an earlier song written with Donny Hathaway back in '69 for Holly Maxwell. Curtis delivers a less intense reading of the lyric but still retains enough tension in his delivery to achieve conviction. Gil Askey's low-key arrangement perfectly echoes Hathaway's earlier treatment. 'Make Me Believe In You' has Curtis laying it down to an upbeat Rich Tufo arrangement while insisting on 100 per cent proof from his new love. Mayfield's brilliant original production of this song for Patti Jo on Scepter had flopped the previous year. His dreamy guitar beautifully weaves its way through long instrumental passages to its satisfactory destination. Curtom tried to repeat the success of *Back To The World's* great sleeve but Bill Ronald's design/illustration for *Sweet Exorcist* fell woefully short of the mark. The treatment was naïve and badly misrepresented this fine collection of songs. They would have done much better using the portrait of Curtis that was tucked away on the back of the sleeve. The album sold well and went to #5 R&B in May

'74 but pop sales dropped off to #39 and the album really should have had more success. The music is more accessible than its predecessor and 'Kung Fu' had been Mayfield's biggest single in nearly two years.

The penultimate album released from the Curtom/Buddah partnership was a departure for them and featured a collection of folk-pop songs written, in the main, and performed by Bobby Whiteside under the title of *Bittersweet Stories* (CRS 8603). Whiteside arranged and produced the album himself at Curtom and Paragon Studios in Chicago. Since Bob Dylan's huge chart successes in the early '60s, folk had moved comfortably into the mainstream of popular music and established itself as a natural vehicle for many new and some established white singer-songwriters. Some had crossed over from rock 'n' roll and country and back again but the form has successfully persisted right through to the present. Many cities, large and small, across America had their own folk music centres and Chicago was no exception.

Across the city was a café/pub called the Earl of Old Town, which had become the northern Mecca of folk-rock. It was frequented by the resident talents of Steve Goodman, Eddie and Fred Holstein, Bonnie Koloc and Jim Post and by mid '70s had become 'the' place in Chicago to create and listen to the finest folk-rock music. The Earl consequently attracted many big stars like Kris Kristofferson and John Prine who came to visit, perform and contribute to its fame as the North American folk/rock small venue of its time. Chicago had long been a thriving musical centre for gospel, blues, jazz, R&B and now soul, folk and pop/rock carried on that tradition. *Bittersweet Stories* slots perfectly into that folk music mainstream, albeit at the pop end of the spectrum. Although some of the songs are interesting like 'Pen Of A Poet', 'Piano Man', 'Up On Living' and 'Isn't It Because You're Free', and the album has a feelgood factor in its celebration of love, rather too often it comes across as lightweight elevator music.

During the previous couple of years Jim Croce, Terry Jacks and John Denver achieved chart topping success with similar material and, of the three Curtom singles, Whiteside's 'Piano Man', had it been heard enough, could have been a chart contender to them. But for reasons of timing and opportunity it was not to be. Bobby Whiteside's music shows the many influences of Bread and Bobby Goldsboro, and his interests in choral and white church music also constructively come through. 'Pity The Poor Ghetto Child' has the added beef of the Impressions in its background. It's a comparison of lifestyle piece, which works quite well. 'Isn't It Because You're Free' comes from the pens of Cashman and West (two of Dion's old cohorts) and provides a satisfactory last mouthful from Bobby's bittersweet cocktail. It is a pleasant enough album but does not favourably compare to other contemporary folk-rock albums of that time like *Sweet Revenge* from John Prine, *You're Gonna Love Yourself In The Morning* by Bonnie Koloc, *Somebody Else's Troubles* by Steve Goodman or indeed, *Breezy Stories* from Danny O'Keefe.

The final album released by Curtom/Buddah was *Got To Find A Way* (CRS 8604), another solo Curtis outing. Again, Mayfield teamed up with Curtom staff arranger Rich Tufo, who had become his regular partner since his falling out and later litigation with Johnny Pate over *Superfly*. This team collaborated on nine complete albums and many other shared projects, during which time their understanding and appreciation for each other's considerable talents grew tremendously. Tufo provided all the arrangements for the sessions that went to make up this album. The first track 'Love Me'/'Right In The Pocket' was an extensive rewrite of the Impressions' first post-Mayfield single. It runs considerably longer than the original at 7.17 minutes but had a single edit to appear on the flipside of 'Mother's Son', which was also cut down for radio play and 45 releases. Of the two versions, the shorter is preferable listening to the long album track, which is all there, but tends to meander on occasion.

In 'So You Don't Love Me', Curtis tells one side of the break-up and his remedy for survival. When it's over, it's over. If you are free to take love, when it comes time you have to let it go, with love, and move on to find it again elsewhere, if necessary. What could be a simpler if...?'A Prayer' is the shortest track on the set and examines coping strategies for survival in the city. Curtis' vocal is beefed up with a little superfluous double tracking as he delivers the lyrics of encouragement. He concludes that in the grand scheme of things we are just people – so say a little prayer.

'Mother's Son' was the last Buddah single. It did poorly in the UK and

Europe where Mayfield's record sales were dropping off rather alarmingly. But in America it went to #15 R&B in January '75. It's the kind of record that grows on you slowly. Curtis delivers his wise advice in front of a semi-staccato arrangement while his rhythm guitar subtly threads together the lead and bass lines. While the shorter version is more potent, this time the album track loses no power from the longer telling of the tale.

'Cannot Find A Way' is an exasperated look at civil rights in a downward spiral and the state of a superpower that spent billions of dollars sending rockets to the moon (or not with Capricorn 1, but spent the dollars anyway) while so much suffering and deprivation still proliferated within its borders. Mayfield relates a personal momentary lack of faith that stands as a metaphor for the growing rejection by young blacks of their previously strong family ties and religious convictions. This led to their search for alternative philosophies in what was still to be named the 'hood' and in ganglife on the street. 'Ain't No Love Lost' (another great side, first cut with Patti Jo), the final track on the album, lifts the mood slightly as Mayfield's downbeat lyrics unfold to reveal that losing the struggle in unfaithful love isn't such a big deal after all. The ensemble bubbles along with energy and, though the material on this collection lacks the instant appeal of earlier work, with some overlong versions and fewer songs, the album peaked on the pop chart in November at #76 but sold much better to black America when it climbed to #26 R&B in December '74. But pop sales of Mayfield albums had gradually been falling since *Superfly* and this unfortunately was to set the pattern for the next three years. R&B sales, however, fluctuated more in his favour. Another lacklustre sleeve could not have helped either, but this album marked the end of an era.

During this period, Buddah released *Best of Curtis Mayfield* (BDLP 4015) in the UK, a compilation that featured two tracks from each of the six albums released so far. It quickly climbed into the lower 20's on the UK soul album charts in February '75, but it seems that relatively few copies were pressed and it soon became something of a collector's item. Most copies probably sold to general interest fans, as most soul fans would have bought his albums in large numbers already.

As well as Curtom Records, Mayfield also founded another production company in late '73. When Mayfield (Gemini) and Marv Stuart (Virgo) first founded Gemigo, press reports predicted projects with Leo Graham, Linda Clifford, The Jones Girls, Rasputin's Stash and Chuck Ray. The record label was launched a year later just before Curtom changed distributors. The first four singles (100 series) were independently distributed. The initial release 'Bumpin'' was written, produced and performed by Leroy Hutson and songwriting partner Mike Hawkins under their Groundhog moniker, which cloaked another side of their musical personas. It's a funk/dance semi-instrumental with shouted vocal instructions and caught on with US R&B fans who took it to #61 R&B in November '74. Later it was also a big northern soul favourite.

The second release was 'Reconsider', which had a 'Staxish' sound, created behind Chuck Ray by Leo Graham who wrote and produced this, his only Gemigo single. A reminiscent but very pleasant groove, this was the sort of thing that Jimmy Hughes used to do so well at Fame, which Chuck perfectly reprised this time out. But despite their efforts it did not sell well enough to chart. Issue 102 was Linda Clifford's only Gemigo side. Mayfield had written and produced 'A Long Lonely Winter' the previous year and had some low R&B success with the single, but this time 'Turn The Key Softly' stiffed for Linda and writer/producer Lowrell Simon. The final release in the first series 'It Only Hurts for A Little While' by the Notations sounded quite like departing labelmates the Natural Four. It was produced and written by Gerald Dickerson and features a fine, pleading vocal by Clifford Curry, who had spent a little time listening to Phillip Wynne sometime in the past but had some inflections of his own that are well worth contemplation. It became Gemigo's biggest hit when it reached #27 R&B in March '75. The flipside 'Superpeople' is an uptempo groove inspired by Mayfield's 'Superfly' and 'Mighty, Mighty', which created some independent interest of its own and was produced by Dickerson, Emmett Gardner and Rich Tufo. When Curtom moved over to Warner Brothers for distribution, Gemigo did also and relaunched with the 500 series.

Another band that signed to Gemigo at around this time was Stash (aka R Stash and Rasputin's Stash). They were a self-contained Chicago group led by Martin Dumas Jr and comprising Paul Coleman, Ernest

Donaldson and Bruce Butler, who had already cut an album for Cotillion (9046) in '71. At that time, Rasputin's Stash were an eight-piece band forged from seasoned session men who'd played on a number of soul sessions dating back to the mid '60s. They were signed to Gemigo as a quartet and their second album *Rasputin's Stash* (Gemigo GMS 1000) was released in '74, just prior to the switch to Warner. The album was self written and produced with some assistance from Joseph Scott with string arrangements by Rich Tufo. Stash were a groove/funk outfit, which bore some similarities to Kool & the Gang and groups of that ilk. Their Gemigo album later became quite a collectable in London. Stash later moved over to Curtom where they had two more singles 'Dance With Me' and 'Booty March', but these sides stiffed and a short time later the Curtom label cut back before their move to RSO.

Rasputin Stash as their name might indicate, turned in a pack of smokin' grooves for an album awash with soft drug references, which were routine in the pre-PC world of the mid '70s. Believe me these guys did inhale and, as a result, they produced some of the best-uninhibited dance/funk cuts of their era. 'Ooh Baby' was obviously intended as a single. It has a hypnotic hook guaranteed to get all that's stationary movin'. The first ballad 'I See Your Face' has Dumas and Coleman dueting in an ecstatic appreciation of physical beauty. 'The Devil Made Me Do It' is a typical Curtom funk groove issue that was also potential single material and makes more than a passing reference to Donny Hathaway's 'The Ghetto'. 'Hit It And Pass It' is a message to the Bogart smokers everywhere, to pass it on (but be careful not to pass it to the man). This track carries a government health warning. 'I Can Feel Your Jones' also uses similar references to describe the 'Jones' effect, sometimes experienced in physical exchanges and affairs of the heart. Stash ease off the grass a touch for the ballad 'You're So Special'. This is a soulful if hopeful plea to an inaccessible lady of desire. 'Middle Man' could have come from the soundtrack of 'Zappa meets Superfly' (had there been one). It's a warning to watch out for the hustlers, dealers and pimps on the street and could be extended to any of those 'legitimate' professions who shake the maximum, when supplying the minimum. 'You've Opened Up My Mind' is an appreciation of greater expectations written and sung by Dumas and Butler. Whilst the final Gemigo album track 'Givin' Way My Love' regrets love indiscretions by that woman whose freelancing activities have just recently been disclosed.

After Gemigo folded, Stash moved over to parent label Curtom for two more singles. They stuck with the funk for 'Dance With Me' a pre-disco groove that deserved a greater success both on the US charts and the northern soul circuit. On the flipside, 'Gotta Have That Thump', Dumas & Co recited their own secret recipe for the rich mixture of funk that was their groove. On their second Curtom single 'Booty March' the funkmasters sang their praises to the ultimate distraction (of which they never tired). Similar subject matter demands further deliberations on another dance anthem 'Get Down' where Stash concentrated their efforts 'to make it all real'. As an extra bonus, half a dozen previously unissued tracks by this excitingly tireless outfit were rescued from the Curtom vaults and issued in the UK on a Sequel CD (NEMCD 359) along with the two Curtom singles. None of these Curtom/Gemigo sides were originally issued in the UK and, like their name, the group's options were getting shorter. Apparently they made no more records after mid '78 but enjoyed a good reputation as live performers in the smaller venue clubs of New York and Chicago where a cult following kept them performing into the '80s.

Curtis made the most of the personnel working with him at Curtom during this period. As well as sing with the Impressions and solo, Leroy Hutson also provided arrangements for the Impressions, the Natural Four and himself and was soon to become an important producer to the company. A pattern developed where the principals would bring their individual projects to the studios and hire in the freelance services of arrangers and producers, as the sessions required them. Famed Chicago arrangers Riley Hampton and Gary Slabo were both employed this way. Mayfield, Hutson and Tufo also shared projects and by late '73 had begun to use the services of Lowrell Simon, Ed Townsend, David Van De Pitte, Rene Hall and Jerry Long. The musicians used on the sessions again depended on the producer, Leonard (Lenard) Druss later became Curtom's regular horn contractor and Sol Boblov became the strings contractor. Some of the studio musicians stayed with Curtom and appear on sessions as late as 1980.

From '71 Curtis used his road band the Experience at the centre of his rhythm section. 'Master' Henry Gibson (percussion) was used a great deal as was Craig McMullen (guitar), Tyrone McCullen (drums) and Joseph 'Lucky' Scott (bass). Phil Upchurch (guitars, bass) and Quenton Joseph (drums) were in constant use and John Howell, Howard Lepp, Loren Binford, Clifford Davis (brother of Carl) etc also turn up on album sleeves from time to time. As Hutson developed his solo career and his music clearly defined its own identity, he also developed a core of musicians for his sessions, which included some of those already mentioned plus Mike Hawkins (keyboards) and Jerry Wilson (saxes). Background singers for the Buddah sessions included the Impressions, the Natural Four, Janice Hutson and Eulaulah Hathaway. In mid '74 Gil Askey began to provide arrangements for Curtis and he was soon to make the move over from Detroit and work full time at Curtom.

During the six years that Buddah distributed Curtom Records they released 73 singles of which 41 charted US R&B, 14 hit the Top 20, and two went to #1. Curtom also released 24 albums during that period, of which 18 charted R&B, 12 in the Top 20 and three hit #1. Practically all the Curtom product that charted high on R&B also crossed over to the Hot 100 pop charts. It was an extremely successful partnership and, during this period, Curtom had attracted some of the most talented singers, musicians, writers, arrangers and producers available anywhere. Many went on to greater success like the Stairsteps, Donny Hathaway and Freddy Waters; others produced great music with little further success like Moses Dillard, Major Lance, June Conquest, Holly Maxwell, and Johnny Pate.

At Curtom, eyes were on the future and all the possibilities that a huge distributor like Warner Brothers could offer them during the next five years.

7 Curtom At Warner Bros, '75–'78

In the latter months of '74 Curtis Mayfield and Marv Stuart realised that for Curtom to grow in the way that they envisioned, it needed a stronger and more financially secure international distributor, with better Hollywood connections. They sought negotiations with the Warner Brothers conglomerate and the following year, it was this company who started to distribute Curtom, directly after their Buddah contract expired. Stuart said of the deal in late '76, 'We felt that Warner's was just the best placed company to supply the kind of set-up that Curtom needed. The working relationship that we have with them is a strong one. We still have our own independence but, as long as the business plan is sound, they will usually back us. We meet on a weekly basis to keep pace with all the projects going through, so we're all tight with what is happening'. Curtom Records signed a new distribution deal with Warner Brothers in '75 in an attempt to reposition themselves for a bigger pop market and easier access to the movie business. Initially, this move proved positive and for the first year Curtom's sales improved.

In the UK, Warner's launch of Curtom was relatively high profile. It was the first time that the Curtom label was issued under its own logo in Britain and there was an upmarket advertising push in the music press that announced the release of the first four albums. Curtis Mayfield's *There's No Place Like America Today* (which due to a contractual hangover was still issued by Buddah), Leroy Hutson's *Hutson*, the Impressions' *First Impressions* and the Natural Four's *Heaven Right Here On Earth*. In the autumn months of '75 these artists all made European and UK tours to promote this new Curtom product (with the exception of the Natural Four whose arrival did not materialize). For Curtom the scenario looked bright once again.

Curtis Mayfield's first album under the new deal was the highly acclaimed *There's No Place Like America Today* (CU 5001). Reviewers made instant comparisons to his previous classics like *CURTIS, Roots* and *Back To The World*. It was also a return to great cover art with the highly effective use of Peter Palombi's illustration. The sleeve depicts a black unemployment line in front of a huge billboard advertising the latest ('30s) white family saloon. The overall mood that pervades throughout this album transpires as 'hang on' rather than 'move up' as one by one the songs discuss and relate some of the problems that every man had to cope with at the time. The first track 'Billy Jack' is an anti-gun song, which Mayfield lays out in the form of a short story told to him by someone else. The song is simplicity itself but effective and thought provoking. He used the Curtom sidemen Henry Gibson, Phil Upchurch and Lucky Scott, plus the usual select band with arrangements by Richard Tufo, all of whom pitched in to create this classic album. 'Billy Jack' conjures up images of the many innocent victims caught in a cross fire of indecision, and their consequent loss of life in the name of liberty and freedom. In America, the single largest supplier of arms to the world, more victims pay a high price for paranoia with their lives, and every year the genocide continues to escalate. It's a situation that millions of us, all over the planet, watch spread everywhere with growing horror.

'When Seasons Change' begins with an ominous church bell ringing in the distance, to herald time and the changes that it brings. Mayfield's vocal ebbs and flows as he relates the positive and negative aspects of city life while 'stranded in someone else's neighbourhood, listening to the undertone'. The arrival of a new season usually brings with it renewal, hope and promise but his vision, more of the same abuse, suffering and denial, was unfortunately closer to the truth. 'So In Love' is a welcome ad break for romantics. It was effectively Mayfield's last single to pop chart when it reached #67 in August '75 but did rather better on the R&B chart, hitting #9 that same month. It has a comfortingly persistent heartbeat groove that moves us through a love song beautifully performed by all concerned. Curtis urges that we all keep faith with love, no matter what external pressures apply themselves to our lives. When interviewed in '75 he had this to say about the album. '*America Today* takes a hard look at some of the things that sour our life experience there, but "So In Love" shows the sweeter side of things and there is much to celebrate in America today that's good, even great. But for too many people, too often, there is still something sour waiting around the corner.' The next album track is 'Jesus' a prayer in the gospel tradition of 'People Get Ready' and 'Keep On Pushing' that proffers faith in faith. The song parallels aspects of Jesus life with those of any travelling soul constantly searching for the strength needed to pay the prices of everyday life. No matter what troubled times have loaded on his back. Mayfield's philosophy has lost some of the bite expressed in earlier songs, he sounds a little wiser and sadder now, but hasn't quite given up yet.

'Blue Monday People' cuts obliquely back to sociology as Curtis tells us that love means more than money in the everyday struggle to survive the injustices of suppression. 'Hard Times' continues in this vein and highlights the medium cool tempo of this album, as once again Mayfield takes another searching look at contemporary American culture. An edit of the album cut was used as flipside to the single, but this long version was also used on many later compilation albums and CDs. For the album's final track, the ensemble move up a gear to the positive 'Love To The People', which attempts an antidote to the problems already discussed and acts as an audio link to the cover art. Rich Tufo's cool arrangement keeps constant the mellow groove that runs right through the album. Curtis lays down his own soulful resolve not to give up, but to keep on trying. As he said after the album was released, 'Spiritual belief is a very important strength that we all need to have today, as things crumble all around us we have to have something more than just our own self image to believe in. Jesus is there for us all and I don't mind confessing that I often talk to my idea of him, seeking guidance.'

There's No Place Like America Today was released by Warner Bros under the freshly redesigned Curtom logo in June '75 and quickly rose to become a Top 10 R&B album during the following month. But it did not do well on either of the pop album charts scoring a lowly #120 in America and not appearing at all in the UK list. Warner got behind it with their PR machine but it just did not cross over. It was seen by some as too gloomy for the white palate and by others as too focussed on the black experience – it seemed to fall uncomfortably between the two perceived markets. From now onwards, with too few exceptions, his music would gradually move closer to the dance market and the dreaded disco.

Leroy Hutson's first solo album after the Warner deal was *Hutson* (CU 5002), which begins with 'All Because Of You' – a song that had the distinction of being the first single release from the Curtom/Warner alliance. It climbed to #31 R&B by February '75 with no crossover to the pop charts. It also introduced us all to Leroy's two-album self-portrait *Hutson* and *Hutson II*, which, like most of his recordings later, changed hands with collectors in the UK at vastly inflated prices. 'I Bless The Day' continues the positive enthusiasm of new-found love, present in much of Hutson's early work. A sprinkle of bells announces 'It's Different', a midtempo celebration of *la différence* and keeps the good groove going. 'Cool Out' is an instrumental track featuring a female vocal group (probably the Kitty Haywood Singers) on an MOR jazzish piece that would slot nicely into the lighter end of the Jazz FM spectrum. It was also used as a flipside to 'Can't Stay Away' his second single from this set that only managed #66 US R&B placing by September. Perhaps he might have found more success had he issued 'Lucky Fellow' that features long instrumental passages punctuated by excellent Henry Gibson percussion work and has appeared on CD collections since. 'So Much Love' though sounding a bit similar is still awaiting some more Hutson vocal overdubs but maintains a pleasantly relaxed mood.

Unlike *The Man*, this highly accomplished album showcases the excellent musicianship then employed at the Curtom Studios. At the time, Hutson's brand of mature soul was inaccurately compared to elevator music and many soul fans declined to buy it, viewing his sophisticated sound as lightweight. Today this album is much sought after by collectors. Hutson's talents as writer/arranger/musician/producer were by now beyond doubt but the music he made never really found the popular market it was designed for. Marv Stuart said of Leroy in '76, 'We at Curtom consider Leroy a major artist, he hasn't had much chart success so far but still he sold 100,000 albums last time out. We've built him to a point where he's about to break in a big way – in the very near future.' The album did well in the UK, reaching a Top 30 placing and giving Leroy his biggest album so far, which sowed the seeds of a small but enthusiastic UK cult following, which grew steadily and still lingers today.

Meanwhile, the Impressions' album sales had maintained a respectable soul chart level since Mayfield's departure but had dipped alarmingly in the pop market. In the UK, *First Impressions* made further gains on their previous Buddah set *Finally Got Myself Together*, but the album's popularity had not been accurately reflected by its middling pop sales. Nevertheless it had re-established the quartet in Europe. *First Impressions* (CU 5003) was their second album with producer Ed Townsend. Butler Workshop alumni Chuck Jackson and Marvin Yancy also added their creative production and songwriting skills, which honed the commercial edge to this album. Once again, the arrangements were split between Rene Hall and Richard Tufo. Townsend wrote all the songs with one exception. 'Sooner Or Later' begins with an introductory monologue that soon gives way to a medium tempo ballad featuring great group harmony behind a particularly fiery Ralph Johnson lead. Released as the album's first single, it deservedly barnstormed its way to #3 on the R&B chart in April '75, but its sheer soulfulness was perhaps too much for pop buyers, who could take it no higher than #68 on the Hot 100 in July. Johnson sang the majority of songs on this collection. 'Same Thing It Took' was also used as a single, but only garnered a medium R&B placing in September.

Tufo returns to 'Preacher Man' mode for 'Old Before My Time', a lament voiced by Fred Cash for a misspent youth, growing up the hard way in the windy city (which he did not actually experience first hand). This track sounds as if it could have been cut earlier circa '72, had it not been written by Townsend. For many, 'First Impressions' turned out to be the album's highlight and became their only UK pop hit single. It carried the Impressions to the very top of the UK soul singles chart in December '75 but for some inexplicable reason was not released in the US as a single until later (like Mayfield's 'Move On Up'), when it was thrown away on the flip of 'Loving Power'. Sam Gooden's bass has seldom been put to better use on an Impressions track, while Ralph, Reggie and Fred are in turn simply outstanding. For the Impressions, this classic track, at least in Europe, was to become a latter-day trademark and re-established them as a potent vocal unit. On 'Groove' Ralph enthuses the general taste for clubland and the disco lifestyle. Townsend's ode to enjoyment in public hipness, benefits from a lively Rene Hall arrangement.

Van McCoy's 'I'm So Glad' is a superficial appreciation of domestic bliss, which, despite the high quality treatment comes over less well than the best tracks featured here. 'How High Is High' is a touch repetitious but the group with Johnson out front do as well as they can with the material. Another filler is 'Why Must A Love Song Be A Sad Song', which sounds like an inferior reworking of Hutson's excellent 'Love's So Wonderful'. Poor Reggie Torian, the group's other lead, only gets this track on the whole album and does as well as he can given the mediocrity of the song. This album took a step further away from the Mayfield sound that had been the group's recorded heritage since '58. The dual leads of Johnson and Torian gave them the opportunity to broaden their horizons, while all the time retaining the ability to perform their illustrious back catalogue in fine style.

The four Impressions plus a seven-piece road band toured Europe in October '75 to promote *First Impressions*. They created an excellent live experience, but not enough UK fans were able to witness it. Fred Cash told *Melody Maker* interviewer Geoff Brown that the group was irritated about coming to the UK twice and only being booked into American airbases. 'Next time we come,' said Cash, 'we ain't comin' unless we play to the English people – it's crazy.' But nevertheless the album had good sales here, and great design by John Youssi, art direction by Jim Schubert and photography from Dennis Scott enhanced its visual appeal and provided an attractive vehicle behind which the marketing machine could really push, which no doubt contributed to the album's overall success. *First Impressions* had climbed to #11 on the R&B album chart but only managed a lowly #115 on pop. In the UK it scored #33 on the soul album chart some seven months later in February '76. It wasn't a smash, but it continued a very healthy upturn in sales for Curtom and the Impressions.

For the Natural Four, meanwhile, 'Heaven Right Here On Earth' (one of Leroy Hutson's best songs) became a disappointingly low hit when it registered at #68 on R&B singles in February '75 and actually did better in the UK. Hit or not, this is one of the N4's finest records and provided an excellent start and title track to what so far, remains their most accomplished album, *Heaven Right Here On Earth* (CU 5004). Curtom used three production teams, firstly Leroy Hutson, then Rich Tufo and Quinton Joseph, and also veteran Joseph Scott. Leroy handled his own arrangements and Tufo supplied the rest. 'Love's So Wonderful' became their next single and, though it only managed #87 R&B, remains their best record to date. Needless to say it deserved to be a much bigger hit and should have been, given the quality of the music. Hutson supplies a production that Thom Bell would have been proud of. Though it was designed for the dancefloor, the record simply got lost in the disco shuffle that was by then already dominating the charts. Nevertheless, the distinctive vocal counter harmonies of the N4 and the invisible hooks created by Hutson still reached the thousands of us who bought the album at the time and its re-issues since.

Tufo also managed to create a very infectious sound for 'Count On Me' the third track on the album with the able assistance of Lowrell Simon (and Tom Green) a good natured song that's beautifully delivered by the switching leads of the N4. Included are memorable lines like 'Let me be your Main Squeeze'. It's possible that Joe Scott wrote 'Baby Come On' with long-time collaborator Curtis Mayfield in mind, but he didn't record it. The tempo upturns once more for 'What Do You Do' on which Tufo's bright arrangement again works well. 'Give This Love A Try' a song written by Gene Chandler (and James Thompson) and already recorded by Hutson for *The Man* album, was reactivated once more here. This time Hutson tries a completely different arrangement and produces an excellent atmosphere for the group who seemed on top of their game on these sessions. The wispy lead voice of James sails smoothly through this well worked song. Rich Tufo has fun with the arrangement on 'What's Happening' a great celebratory 'new' love song delivered in an interesting high register lead by Steve Striplin, with great background work from the group.

In conclusion, Hutson returns to the beautiful mood he set at the beginning of this classic album with 'While You're Away'. The N4 demonstrate once again just how well vocally integrated they had become on this 'away at college' yarn and take us easy on out, leaving the listener up for more. This album is definitely the Natural Four at their best and provides a consistently classy groove throughout.

When it was released, it received positive reviews and sold better in the UK, where it was a Top 30 soul album during the summer months of '75. Initially, the Natural Four themselves were a little disappointed with the album. When Chris James was interviewed in '75 he said, 'We expected it to come out a little later. We felt that we needed a slightly wider choice of material, which we think would have made it a stronger album. But the public seem to think otherwise – so that makes us happy.' As far as the UK soul fans were concerned Curtom, anxious to complete for the Warner relaunch, got it right, but like their last album it only managed a middling place on the US R&B album chart in July '75.

Also in mid '75, the musical press reported rumours that the Staple Singers were about to leave the ailing Stax label to join Mayfield at Curtom. In fact, it only turned out to be a one-album deal, just prior to their signing to parent company, Warner Bros, later that year. In a production deal, Curtis was to produce their next two albums, plus one solo with lead singer, Mavis. The family group consisted of 'Pop' who also plays a very distinctive guitar, Cleotha, Pervis, Yvonne and Mavis. They were signed to United in '53, Vee-Jay in '55, Riverside in '61 and Fantasy in '62. The Staples' material was strictly gospel and it was not until they recorded 'Why Am I Treated So Bad' in '67 that any popular interest began to register. This single preceded their most successful years with Stax with whom they scored twelve big hits over a five-year period, which included their million-sellers 'If You're Ready' and 'I'll Take You There'.

Returning to Chicago in '75, they began work on the movie score album *Let's Do It Again* (see Chapter 9), which would provide them with their next gold single. But the radical shift in the lyrical content initially bothered 'Pops', who had religiously stuck to the gospel text for the past 30 odd years and was uneasy about the changes. Mayfield, who shared similar religious roots but had no such qualms, assured the group that the songs had been toned down and that they were tailor-made for the Staples. The *Let's Do It Again* album was released at the close of '75 and went to #7 on the R&B album chart in January '76 and to the very top of the pop charts. It also found soul album success in the UK where it reached #26 that same month. 'New Orleans' their next Curtom single was also a big hit and went to #4 R&B/70 pop in February '76 after which the Staples' records were released on Warner Bros.

Not all of Curtis' working relationships were as harmonious as that which he had with the Staples. According to some reports in the UK music press, Curtis Mayfield/ Curtom sued Chaka Khan for $750,000 (£45,000) in the summer months of '75. The reports at the time were sketchy as to why this lawsuit took place or as to the outcome of the action. Neither Mayfield or Khan have been very forthcoming about the details of this case in interviews that they have given since that time, so it has always remained something of a mystery. The problem that created this law suit occurred a year or so after the Curtom label had been launched, when Mayfield had signed Baby Huey and the Babysitters in '69 (see chapter 5). Shortly after signing to Curtom, Huey and the Babysitters, whose membership included Chaka, parted company. In an interview with David Nathan published by *Blues & Soul* in December '75, Chaka revealed that she had 'a disagreeable phone call with Curtis'. This was soon followed by a lawsuit for non-fulfillment of contract when she was a member of the Babysitters. At the time most UK fans were blissfully unaware of these events and it was not until Chaka's appearance on a UK TV show *Don't Forget Your Toothbrush*, announcing that she had been sued by Mayfield in a quiz about her career, that anyone was aware of it. Since that time, little mention has been made to the media by either party. So it is perhaps something that they both put behind them.

Curtom was by no means Curtis' sole occupation during this period. Gemigo, the label he had started with Marv Stuart in late '73, was relaunched by Warner. One of the main artists on this label was the Notations. 'It Only Hurts For A Little While', their début release, was the Notations' biggest hit for Gemigo when it went to #27 R&B singles in March '75 just as Curtom/Gemigo switched to Warner Bros for their distribution. So the hit had little chance to build as it might have done. The flipside 'Superpeople' provided radio programmers with a funky alternative that was very much in the 'Superfly' and 'Mighty Mighty' mode. Gemigo released 'Think Before You Stop', which should by rights have been a huge hit, it was commercial enough but perhaps the production and lead singer Clifford Curry's powerful vocal owed a little too much to Phillipe Wynne and the Detroit Spinners – it topped out at a lowly #93 R&B in August '75. Medium tempo groove 'I'm Losing' was used on the flipside but for their next session Curtom put the Notations into the hands of rising Chicago producers Charles Jackson and Marvin Yancy who created the 'It's All Right (This Feeling)'. It restored the Notations to a respectable #42 on the R&B singles chart in November '75. Principal Curtom producer Rich Tufo wrote and produced the flipside 'Since You've Been Gone', which was another Spinners pastiche, relating an agreeable plea for a lover's return. The Notations had the final words on Gemigo with 'Make Me Twice The Man' a high register ballad that despite its slow tempo and reticent charm still managed low R&B success in April '76 and proved to be a better version than the original, recorded by New York City for Chelsea three years earlier. The flipside was a rerun on the catchy 'Since You've Been Gone', which with enough exposure might have gained a wider appeal.

They released an album, *The Notations* (Gemigo GM 5501), in late 1975. Gemigo added a further four tracks to the four singles (omitting 'Superpeople' and the duplicate 'Since You've Been Gone'). 'Take It Slow' is a ballad that has Curry pleading for a more leisurely appreciation of love while 'Bills Break Up Homes' a medium pace Tufo piece, though enjoyable again owes much to the style of the Spinners. Both of the remaining tracks 'There I Go', a ballad that clicks along comfortably, and 'Make Believin', a high-register ballad, were produced by Gerald Dickerson and Emmett Gardner. This album was first issued in the UK on Curtom in May '76 – the bonus cut 'Superpeople' (a long-time collectable here) was added to the UK CD released in '97. A remastered Gemigo/Curtom album containing 11 of their finest recordings (one 'The Chopper' not issued before) was released in September '99 by Sequel for the UK as *Superpeople (NEBCD 445)* and it is still their best album to date.

Curtom had also signed the Jones Girls to Gemigo in late '73, who comprised of three sisters Shirley, Brenda and Valorie and hailed from

Detroit. Their first two singles 'If You Don't Love Me' and 'Will You Be There?' were leased to Paramount (like Linda Clifford's and the Fasination's early sides). As good as they were, these records both evaded the charts. This had been the way of things up until now for the Jones Girls. They had made many great records, at first with GM and Fortune in '68, before joining Holland-Dozier-Holland's Music Merchant for three years. Unhappily, none of these releases made any kind of commercial headway. What the Girls did manage to do, however, was to build an excellent reputation as background singers for other artists and became much sought after for both live and studio work.

They recorded an album's worth of material at Curtom in March '73 of which only two singles were released, neither of which charted. 'I Turn To You'/'Mister i' was the first in March '75 and 'Hey Lucinda'/'If You Don't Love Me No More' became their final Curtom release in September '75. By that time, due mainly to the efforts of ex-Motown and Curtom producer Gil Askey, they found a more rewarding gig – singing backup for Diana Ross and so they ended their Curtom association. The Paramount and Curtom singles plus a number of previously unissued cuts became available on UK *Sequel-NEMCD 397* in September 2000.

Another Curtom release of the period was *Now* (CU5006) in March '76. This was a solo album on Ed Townsend, perhaps in acknowledgement of his creative contributions to Curtom's roster during his brief but positive two year association with the label as writer/producer. It met with indifferent and critical reviews, some of which unkindly stated that 'vocally he simply hasn't got it anymore'. Ed wrote, produced and arranged, with the help of conspirator Rene Hall, the complete project. But it all sounds like it must have been done in a rush, because in places the tracks sound like demos for other artists, and in others the formats are too visible/audible. The songs do, however, clearly point the way contemporary music was heading, as in the near future it jettisoned lyrical content in favour of the mindless 'designed for the dancefloor' repetition. *Now* did not chart but instead became an instantly collectable oddity.

Curtom released three more albums in addition to *Now* in March '76. They were *Nightchaser* (Natural Four), *Loving Power* (Impressions) and *Feel The Spirit* (Leroy Hutson). Once again Curtom used three production teams on the Natural 4's *Nightchaser (CU 5008)* album, Hutson and Tufo were joined by Charles Jackson and Marvin Yancy. But it seems that there was a unanimous decision to go for a more commercial, disco-orientated sound on what turned out to be the N4's last stab at the charts. The 'It's The Music' title sets the tone of an album that reflects the happening sounds of the time. Unfortunately the N4 temporarily lose the identity that they had worked hard to create for themselves with their first two Curtom albums. Curtom released 'It's The Music' as a single in April '76 and it crawled to #82 R&B. 'Free' their final single registered a little higher at #71 R&B in July and when their contract expired, the Natural Four did not re-sign with Curtom due to wrangles with the label, and within the group itself. Sequel Records issued *Can This Be Real?* (NEMCD 406) in March '99 that combined all three of the Natural Four's Curtom albums plus the collectable 'Eddie You Should Know Better' single.

Not only did March '76 see the last Curtom release of N4, it also marked the last album of their longest-standing artists, the Impressions. When the *Loving Power* (CU 5009) was released in the UK, reviewers generally agreed that the Impressions had 'got it right' with this collection. As a single, the title track did good US R&B business charting at #11 in December '75. The song was written and produced by Charles Jackson and Marvin Yancy. Johnson shares the lead with Cash and Torian on a great track that was on reflection not really single material at least for the pop market. Bunny Sigler was active at Curtom for a brief period at this time and no doubt influential in the choice of their next track 'Sunshine'. Sigler and Phil Hurtt had written 'Sunshine' originally for Percy Sledge and it had also been recorded by the O'Jays a couple of years earlier, although neither version became the big hit that the song deserved. The Impressions' later version compares favourably with the O'Jays' record, as does Tufo's excellent arrangement and production. Ralph also makes a great vocal delivery but inevitably comparisons favoured the O'Jays' cut. Both versions are in danger of over singing to an overblown production but so often these dramatic illusions created by the great producers like Spector, Bacharach and Bell and others (in this case Rich Tufo) had found wide public acceptance. Nevertheless, this was to become the Impressions' final Curtom single and climbed to a healthy #36 R&B in May '76 but made no pop chart impact.

'I Can't Wait To See You', the second Jackson/Yancy production of their own song, opens with monologue from Sam and features Ralph switching verses with Fred Cash. Richard Evans supplies the inventive arrangement. Ed Townsend was credited Executive Producer and it was he who wrote and produced the remaining four tracks on the album, using the arrangements of partners Rene Hall and Rich Tufo. 'If You Have To Ask' is a fun telephone song, which borders on novelty. It features Ralph on lead cooly avoiding a direct answer to his girlfriend's pleas on the other end of the line. Great values all round, made this a strong single contender that could have really taken off. 'You Can't Be Wrong (All The Time)' is a great Townsend song and album highlight, which again features variable leads from Sam and mostly Ralph but good work all around from the quartet.

'I Wish I'd Stayed In Bed' features the fine arrangement of Rene Hall. Johnson convincingly delivers the tale of the kind of day we are all treated to from time to time and want to put behind us as soon as possible. An edited version had middling success as a UK single in the autumnal months of '76. Townsend's trademarks litter the arrangement of 'Keep On Trying', a 'they say' song that is a kind of 'I've Been Trying' sequel. Sam Gooden takes the lead and is backed by superb group work from the other Impressions.

Despite a rather ordinary sleeve the album sold well to soul fans registering at #28 on the R&B album chart and similarly #32 on the UK soul albums in the spring of '76. Shortly after its release in June, Ralph Johnson left the Impressions to create his own new group, Mystique. The remaining Impressions left Curtom seeking yet another new lead singer before signing to Atlantic subsidiary Cotillion Records of New York.

Feel The Spirit (CU 5010) was Leroy Hutson's aptly entitled fourth album that contains only seven tracks and with a couple of exceptions, has the accent right on the music. 'It's The Music' features Hutson on a multi-track vocal urging us all to 'feel the groove' on this funky alternative to the N4's disco single of the time. Leroy wrote most of the songs, shared arrangements with Richard Evans and produced this set completely. 'Feel

The Spirit', his biggest selling R&B single (#25 R&B in January '76) was an instrumental with background vocals only, none detectably by him. The album highlights include 'Lovers Holiday', which was edited for single release in May '76 and reached #68 R&B that month and 'Never Know What You Can Do', which is a 'give it a try' song, in 'Nothing Beats A Failure' mode. *Feel The Spirit* hit #19 on R&B albums in April '76 creating Leroy's biggest selling album but only scored a lowly #44 on the UK soul album charts and was less popular than the previous *Hutson (1)* set. Hutson said himself that on this album he had made attempts to reach a broader audience. He told *Blues & Soul's* US editor David Nathan in March '76, 'I'm hopeful that if this album is successful, it will open people up to what I can do – and maybe they'll go back to my previous albums.' Leroy believed that the *Hutson* and *Hutson II* albums were more the real him, but statistics indicate that the record-buying public preferred the unreal him of *Feel The Spirit*.

Three months later in June '76, Curtom released Curtis' next album *Give, Get, Take And Have* (CU 5007) the gap probably due to Mayfield's other commitments to the movies and production projects. This album contrasted sharply with the previous set and initially got a cool reception from pop pundits and fans alike. Presumably Mayfield decided, or was persuaded, that he needed to lighten up when choosing the songs for this collection. Initial core-following reaction was that it was comparatively superficial and while this is true in a couple of cases, in general it is not. As usual it was recorded at Curtom, using arrangements by Rich Tufo with all songs and production by the man himself. The opening track 'In Your Arms Again (Shake It)' was infectious enough to be a single, though not chosen as such. A hypnotic guitar line winds right through the piece, as Curtis laments on time not spent making love. He's backed up by a fine selection of musicians who provide plenty of quality accompaniment and creative flair. 'This Love Is Sweet' is a pleasant enough jingle that takes us to 'PS I Love You', which says much the same thing but better. Mayfield acknowledges a return match, like some fine wine that he's recently rediscovered but won't forget again. The song's simple but clever construction holds the attention in a relaxed mode.

Not so track four, 'Party Night', which was an indicator of an imminent nosedive into disco, a musical direction that was to influence soul music in many insidious ways. As a single it climbed to #39 R&B in November '76 but didn't make any impression on the Hot 100 where similar grooves by Earth, Wind & Fire, the Ohio Players and KC and the Sunshine Band were cramming the airwaves and jamming the dancefloors. 'Get A Little Bit' thankfully returns to the overall mood of the album, a positive medium tempo groove. 'Soul Music' is well put together and was later to prove popular with CD compilers. 'Only You Babe' was first choice from this set as a single, it hit #8 R&B in June '76 but again created no pop chart interest, which is a little surprising because it seems to have been tailored to fit right in there alongside 'I Love Music' by the O'Jays or 'Kiss And Say Goodbye' by the Manhattans. It's a catchy rather repetitive song that borders on superficial at times, but still manages to deliver a high entertainment value.

For the final track Curtis revived 'Mr Welfare Man', a song he had created two years earlier for the *Claudine* soundtrack. This excellent song explores the destructive effect on those individuals who find themselves at the mercy of the welfare state. It looks at the downside of existence while in the clutches of Mr Welfare who won't let them get up, because others want them right where they are, on the bottom.

This project shows suspicious signs of outside interference. The cover looks like lifestyle advertising and Ed Thrasher's art direction smacks of product placement. Stylish as it is, it fails to enhance Mayfield's musical content as well as it should have. Whilst the type and graphic design for the title are good, lack of attention to detail let the maximum visual impact down.

Though the music on this album is, in the main, enjoyable, it's not as easily accessible as Curtis' earlier work, even though it sounds like it has been crafted for a wider appeal. When released in June '76 it took two months to climb to a healthy #15 on the R&B album chart but could only manage #171 on Billboard's pop album listing. In the UK, most Mayfield fans were blissfully unaware that there had even been a label change. Buddah had issued both ...*America Today* and *Give, Get*... due no doubt to contractual hangovers. Whether this affected the UK sales of this album or not is impossible to say for sure but, despite the loyal fanbase Curtis enjoyed here, *Give, Get...* sold less well than any Mayfield album before it.

Since the first Warner/Curtom single had been released in February '75, the label had scored with 12 R&B placings from the first 16 issues, but only one of these singles, in the 14 month period, the Staples 'Let's Do It Again' had exceeded expectations and gone to the top of both R&B and pop single charts. Significantly, it was also the only Curtom single to have crossed over to the pop Top 40. This movie soundtrack, created by Curtis for the Staples also became a gold album. Mayfield's own *...America Today* and *Give, Get, Take And Have* were both Top 20 R&B albums. The Impressions also hit #11 and #28 with *First Impressions* and *Loving Power* and even Leroy Hutson cracked the Top 20 with *Feel The Spirit*. Not one of the remaining nine albums, including these five, sold well enough to enter the Billboard 100 pop album chart. Sales were down in America compared to the same period during Buddah's distribution, when Curtis alone had three Top 40 pop albums just prior to his career smash *Superfly*. Despite one huge success the Curtom product was not reaching its target market.

Between April '76 and January '77 there were no Curtom albums released in America except *Give, Get, Take And Have*. The company went through a metamorphosis shedding some of its core roster. The Jones Girls had recorded an album, but were gone before their second single 'Hey Lucinda' was issued in September '75. Ralph Johnson, who had sung lead on all seven Impressions hits in the past 30 months, decided that the time was right to strike out with Mystique. The remaining Impressions, Sam Gooden, who had sung on every Impressions record ever made, Fred Cash, who had joined in '58 to replace Jerry Butler, and Reggie Torian, who sang lead on the back catalogue, also quit Curtom. This was a strange move considering that Mayfield had originally built Curtom around the group, before he went solo in 1970. It was not as if their current record sales were poor either – the past three albums had all been R&B hits and had also improved their European sales. Other than Curtis himself, the Impressions were Curtom's biggest asset. This reason alone might indicate how Fred, Sam and Reggie were able to rapidly replace Ralph with Nate Evans and seek new horizons with Cotillion Records.

Outgoing with the Impressions went their producers Ed Townsend, whose *Now* album was sinking without trace and the freelance talents of Charles Jackson and Marvin Yancy who were in great demand elsewhere. Two of the Natural Fours' three albums with Curtom had also made good R&B headway but got no noteable pop response, so they also took their leave. Curtis Mayfield, Leroy Hutson and Mystique were the only Curtom artists to survive the '76 purge.

In the UK the lack of new Curtom product didn't slow down the releases as WEA took the opportunity to re-issue six of Mayfield's biggest hit albums starting with *Roots* (K 56249) and including *CURTIS, Back To The World* and *Sweet Exorcist*.

Curtis continued to work with the Staple Singers even after they had moved to parent company, Warner. They collaborated when the Staple Singers recorded their first Warner album *Pass It On* at Curtom in the autumn of 1976. The concept that Mayfield created for the album connected with the group's complete makeover in every department. Along with their new sound came a new image, new stage routines and they even streamlined their name by dropping 'Singers'. The *Pass It On* sleeve showed the leaner, hipper Staples in a series of Richard Fegly photographs acting out the album title. They looked fresh and eager, stylishly decked in Safari-style outfits that finally shook off the intentionally 'one step behind the times' image of yesterday that they had long reflected. At Curtom, Rich and Curtis laid down some sizzling tracks on love, sex and life that confirmed the Staples' change of direction. The standout tracks 'Take Your Own Time' on which Mavis vocally freefalls to an infectious dance track and 'Take This Love Of Mine' were passed over by Warner's as singles. Instead they put out the rather repetitive 'Love Me, Love Me, Love Me' which underachieved when compared to their last two Curtom hit singles – it still managed #11 R&B by November '76. 'Sweeter Than Sweet', the follow-up, featured a frantic pop/gospel vocal from Mavis over Mayfield's supercharged production, but this only managed #52 R&B and neither single created any pop interest.

This was, unfortunately for the Staples, to prove a permanent downturn in the group's future single sales on the Hot 100. Though the quality of material, performance and production values were still excellent, there were a few maybes that stopped this album from becoming a super hit. Maybe, eight tracks were too few. A couple of the songs ran themselves out and, on reflection, some edits and possibly the addition of two more songs of quality could have made the difference. Maybe their crossover from gospel cost them as many pop fans as it did hardline gospel. Whatever imponderables were responsible, a great opportunity was missed because all the right ingredients were there for big-time success. Mayfield said of the album in late '76, 'The Staples were great to work with. Mavis voice is unique – I love her voice. We all had a great time doing the sessions and I think I can say that we were all excited with the outcome at that time.'

Towards the end of '76, *Blues & Soul*, which had long time been the clarion for all that's best in sixties soul, published an excellent eight-page Curtom special after US editor David Nathan and photographer Billy Pierce had journeyed to Chicago to interview Curtis, Marv, Leroy, Ralph, Richard and new signing Billy Butler. It provided a revealing portrait of Curtom in evolution, full of promise and creativity. A group of very talented people working hard to maintain their unique musical identity and stay solvent in a marketplace that too often fell victim to the whims of fashion and hype. Unfortunately, Curtom like many other labels, large and small, was at the time being sucked ever closer towards the vortex of disco.

8 The Warner Reprise

The first album to emerge after the nine month Curtom drought was *Hutson II* (CU 5011). As usual Leroy produced, arranged and wrote most of the material himself. 'Love The Feeling' the album's opening track had an altogether harder percussive sound that created a more insistent mood, absent from much of his previous work. 'Situations' was merely a Rich Tufo instrumental filler of little consequence but 'I Do, I Do (Want To Make Love To You)' was one of the few Curtom singles to be released in the latter part of '76 and crept to #55 R&B by November, making no incursion into pop. 'I Think I'm Falling In Love' is a good uptempo item that sounds ideal Jamiroquai fodder now but its chart potential was not seen then and it was later issued as a flipside. The jazzier 'Love To Hold You Close' again influenced Jamiroquai who, of course, also borrowed extensively from Stevie as well. But here this sound grew out of the musical experimentation created by Hutson in his endeavour to broaden his own scope and range. 'Flying High' leans more toward disco monotony, swathed in nondescript thematic MOR background vocals. Distorted Hutson vocals float in and out of this forerunner to 'Killer Joe' and the like, which evolved some five years on and had much greater success for other people.

'Blackberry Jam' is reminiscent of the earlier singles under the Groundhog moniker on Gemigo. Leroy's funky but distorted vocal is too often lost in the background. It was used as his next single and only made it to #82 R&B by May '77. 'Sofunkstication' echoes the earlier movie theme work on this instrumental, which, despite its title, is less funky than the previous track. Hutson re-emerges from a three-track instrofunk interlude to a more recognizable feel-good track, which brings this album to an up conclusion. 'Don't It Make You Feel Good' should have been an A-side but again was thrown away on the flip of 'I Do, I Do'. Full of original innovation and promise as this album was, it did nothing to change the direction of Curtom's flagging commercial downturn. In the UK, Warner chose not to issue *Hutson II* and thereafter would only issue the Mayfield albums from the Curtom catalogue. No official release in this particular case led to the label's first vinyl bootleg, *Hutson's Greatest Hits*, which in later years was changing hands with collectors for unreal prices.

After leaving the Impressions, Ralph Johnson joined Mystique, which was comprised of two ex-members of Lost Generation, Fred Simon and Larry Brownlee plus Charles Fowler, a childhood friend of Ralph's from Greenville, their common hometown. The new group projected a radically different image and sound from the Impressions. They were a more dance-orientated unit, with a fashionably flamboyant image of the time. Even Ralph's lead vocals had a different hue – mellower, even set a little higher, as he shook the misleading 'Preacher Man' tag. Mayfield got behind the group for their album as Executive Producer and provided top line Chicago production and studio time, plus a rich spread of writing talent that included Gene McDaniels, Bunny Sigler, Lowrell, Jerry Butler and other talents from the Butler/Fountain Workshop.

For the *Mystique* (CU 5012) sessions, its various producers chose to record most of the rhythm tracks in Philly, LA and Chicago, the product of which provided enough tracks for at least two albums. 'If You Need', the opening track on their only album, was produced by Butler's Fountain Productions team and written by Workshop members Len Ron Hanks and Zane Grey. This uptempo track tentatively opens the Mystique portfolio. The following three tracks were produced by Philadelphia's Bunny Sigler and 'Somebody To Love' and 'Is It Really You' both make for pleasant listening – the latter was used as their second single and struggled to #77 R&B in May '77.

'What Would The World Be Without Music' chosen as Mystique's début single was a frantic cocktail of disco/funk influences of the time and even tips its hat with the occasional *Shaft*-alike riff. This one reached

#59 R&B in March '77, which is considerably better than it deserved. The following track, the predictable 'Keep On Playing The Music' could have been written as part two of the previous track. The final three cuts are all thankfully at slower tempo and therefore allow a better appreciation of Mystique's collective vocal talents. 'All Of My Life' and 'This Time I Will Be The Fool' are on a par with the work of other good soul groups of the time. They are easy on the ear and come over well with excellent production and arrangement values as well as performances. 'Fill You Up' the final cut was produced by Gene McDaniels, then based in Los Angeles. Ralph is not a petrol pump attendant at the service station of love, as the title might suggest, but along with the others in the group provides great vocalizing here and on all other slower ballads. In another era, these guys might have been contenders.

The sleeve, designed at AGI by Jim Ladwig and photographed by Richard Fegley, shows Mystique resplendent in confectionery coloured outfits and suggests a bright new beginning that unfortunately did not materialize. In general the vocal group harmonizing behind Johnson was a lighter sound but Ralph's leads still provided a more soulful touch than some of other groups that took that route. Curtom issued a post-album single, 'It Took A Woman Like You', which struggled to #71 R&B in October '77 doing a little better than their second outing. For whatever reason, Mystique just didn't click, or manage to create enough public interest to splutter on for many months. Shortly after Larry Brownlee, who had written most of their material including big hit 'Michael (The Lover)', was murdered on the Chicago streets in '78, Mystique broke up. Ralph Johnson went solo and recorded enough material for an album of his own but 'Take Me Higher', 'Some Things You Gotta Do', 'So In Love' and the other half a dozen tracks he laid down at Curtom remain as yet, unreleased. *Mystique* was re-issued in the UK by Sequel in April 2000 on *CD* (NEMCD 362) and it included ten bonus tracks, all the unissued tracks from Mystique's combined recording sessions.

Curtis' next solo outing, *Never Say You Can't Survive* (CU 5013), should have redressed the balance of Mayfield's falling sales but unhappily it didn't. Maybe some of the faithful had stopped listening, they had certainly stopped buying his music in such large quantities. All sorts of factors could have collectively had a negative impact on album sales; home taping was a rapidly growing trend at the time and created an understandable backlash from the record companies. This was unfortunate for Curtis because this album should have been a big hit for him. Had it been so, it would have rightly changed the downward slip in Curtom's fortunes. It was easily the best album that he'd recorded for many years. The production values, arrangement, musical and vocal contributions were second to none. In short it's one of Curtis Mayfield's finest albums.

'Show Me Love' as a single went to #41 R&B in April '77 with no pop chart action. It kicks off this feel-good set with style as Curtis warbles his request for demonstrable physical responses, to an exquisitely arranged musical backdrop that subtly enhances great tenor work from Sonny Seals. 'Just Want To Be With You', the flipside to the single, carries on the groove and reinforces the mood with more of the same. The tempo slows a little as we move on to 'When We're Alone' where Mayfield sings the praises of quality time together. Though some of the love songs on this set break no really new ground they have the edge of a greater conviction over those heard on the previous album. 'Never Say You Can't Survive' is a Mayfield classic with a first rate arrangement from James Mack. For some reason, it sounds like it could have been written for a movie project. However it came about, Curtis wrote yet another song that each one of us can consistently apply to our own experience. The text itself explores the struggle of establishing and maintaining one's self-confidence in the face of countless obstacles. It marvels at the special wonder of the individual and all the talents that one soul can possess. It is a truly inspirational song that too few people are aware of and stands up there alongside his other many other greats.

'I'm Gonna Win Your Love' returns to the album's central theme. Curtis sets out his promise to a funky groove as keyboards ripple at the edges of another fine Mack arrangement. 'All Night Long' continues this relaxed atmosphere, but for the first time the attention begins to wander a little. 'When You Used To Be Mine' soon snaps back though as Tufo's sharper treatment plus the great vocal exchange between Mayfield and the Kitty Haywood Singers grabs the attention. 'Sparkle', the final track, was written for the movie of the same name. Mayfield produced the original, the version for the soundtrack and also a version for Aretha Franklin. Though the three versions are all quite different, they compare quite favourably with each other. Curtis' vocal bubbles on top of the arrangement as the lyric reveals the heightened states experienced whilst in the grip of passion – 'sparkling with fire'. Whilst the lyrical content in this fine collection of love songs doesn't quite demand listeners' attention in the way that his more confrontational material does, this album sets up a relaxed mood and delivers a feel-good factor throughout. Also, this time they got the sleeve right with a tasteful combination of photography, calligraphy and design co-ordinated by Jim Ladwig.

In the UK, it was released under the Curtom logo for the first time. Warner Bros did not release a single to promote the album; in fact they released no UK singles on Mayfield during their time distributing his label and obviously considered him to be an album artist. This was just another factor that could not have helped promote album sales. One thing that Warner's did supply more regularly than previous issues were Mayfield's lyrics. A poet and songwriter of this calibre should demand this courtesy and respect for their work. Whilst economic restraints don't always allow for a gatefold cover with every album release, lyric sheet inserts were cheap and easy enough to produce, and this, for the most part, they provided.

The Impressions' new lead singer Nate Evans had been singing around town for years and had previously recorded for one or two of the smaller Chicago labels like Twinlight. He joined the group in time for their signing to Atlantic subsidiary Cotillion, where they cut a couple of Christmas songs, 'Silent Night'/'I Saw Mommy Kissing Santa Claus', which were released for the yuletide holiday. The *It's About Time* album (Cotillion SD 9912) followed in November '76 and was recorded in Hollywood, Los Angeles and Chicago by producer and ex-Invictus staffer McKinley Jackson. In addition, Jackson did some of the arrangements himself but also contracted Gil Askey, HB Barnum and Gene Page's talents for the remaining charts. Six of the eight songs were written by Mervin and Melvin Steals, the other two came from the pens of Jackson, Paul Richmond and Daryll Ellis. It was a confident re-introduction, with new lead Evans looking and sounding enough like Ralph Johnson to step into the Impressions format without missing a beat.

Evans vocal timbre was close enough to provide a convincing opening with 'In The Palm Of My Hands' that grows after a few hearings and was wrongly passed over as a single. Cotillion, in hindsight, made the wrong choices with all their Impressions singles. 'You'll Never Find' was used as their second single when it should have been the first issued. It's a great track with Evans and group all in good voice but could only crawl into the R&B charts at #99 in March of '77. 'Same Old Heartaches' is a ballad that again features Nate with tight vocal unit support. On 'I Need You' the Impressions alternate leads with some monologue on another ballad that has an uptempo change two thirds in. 'This Time' was written by McKinley and wife Shirley Jones (who sang lead with the Jones Girls) and as a single peaked at #40 R&B in November '76. It contains all the ingredients for a hit but not necessarily in the right order; either of the first two tracks work better. 'Stardust', sadly not the Hoagy Carmichael classic, sounds like a rejected theme for 'Stars In Their Eyes'. Gil Askey provides an unusual arrangement for 'I'm A Fool For Love', which is an interesting departure for the Impressions. Evans handles the jazzy slow tempo torch song, with a style that shows plenty variety and range. The final track 'What Might Have Been' is a 'It Should've Been Me' song with Nate contemplating missed opportunities from the back of the church.

It's About Time came in a sharp sleeve featuring the photography of Anthony Law and design firm Creative Direction Inc. It pictures the besuited quartet looking affluent and happy below a 'once only' Impressions logo. The Impressions went out on the road to promote the album in America but it didn't sell well enough to chart and was not released in Europe, where it might have received a better response. Shortly after release of the second single, UK press reports appeared telling of a 'near fatal' car crash that happened whilst the Impressions were touring in West Virginia. Apparently all four members had been fortunate enough to escape the wreck with little more than cuts and bruises. Cotillion released a third single 'Can't Get Along' that sold well enough to reach #42 R&B in July '77, doing almost as well as 'This Time' but that was their last single for a while.

The album was good, but with a couple of minor adjustments it could have been great. It seemed unlikely to win them any new fans and the Impressions left Cotillion in '78 after several deals and promises had fallen through including a second album, cut but not released. On their UK tour in October '78 they talked about future plans for an album with Thom Bell, that didn't materialize and some more information about the Cotillion album (SD 5203) that had been recorded and produced by Johnny Pate in Atlantic's New York Studios through the summer of '77. Review copies had been pressed but presumably the reaction had not been positive enough for Cotillion to release the album. The tracks included 'Dance', 'You're So Right For Me', 'Take My Time', 'Illusions', 'Pressure', 'Inside Out', 'Let's Talk It Over', 'Who You Been Loving' and the issued single 'Can't Get Along'. The Cotillion label had quite a lot of success on the soul charts, but seemed unable to get the absolute best out of some of the great talent that passed through their roster. Lou Johnson and Walter Jackson faired poorly and Ronnie Dyson did little better but the Impressions did manage OK for a short while. Their future records would be released much closer to home but the Impressions' chart days were behind them as far as record buyers were concerned.

The unlikely pairing of Barbara Mason and Bunny Sigler came together at Curtom in the spring of '77 and they recorded their only album *Locked In This Position* (CU 5014). Sigler came to Curtom briefly from Philadelphia International where over the past four years he had worked as a staff writer/producer supplying the Gamble/Huff roster with songs and studio skills. As a solo artist he had hit the mid R&B chart four times with uptempo dance items like 'Tossin' And Turnin'' and 'Keep Smilin'. During his passage through the Curtom environs he made useful contributions to the Impressions and Mystique recording sessions.

Barbara, also a Philadelphian, had not charted for a couple of years, since she had parted company with Buddah in '75. Her name had been linked previously with Curtom on and off for a few years, with rumours of her imminent signing on a couple of occasions. Mayfield had, of course, written and produced her comeback hit 'Give Me Your Love' (#9 R&B/31 pop) in late '72 but Mason had stayed with Buddah and scored two more big R&B hits in '75 with 'From This Woman To You' and 'Shakin' Up'. Given these two artists illustrous backgrounds *Locked In This Position* was a disappointment. A mechanical Sigler production had the duo dancing, or is that struggling in a straight jacket, for too often it sounds like they are singing in the gaps. Contributions by Tufo and most of Mystique cannot save this unremarkable recording that was cut at both Curtom and Sigma. The transplanted Phillysound, with three songs from the pen of guitarist Theodore Life, suffers massive rejection. The best tracks are 'Leaving' and 'I'm With You Now', which sounds like Bunny (aka Walter, aka Bundino Siggalucci) doing a solo take on Marvin Gaye in places and may have been added to make up the tracks. The rest is disco dross and, at the album's lowest point, is an abysmal version of the Temptations' classic 'My Girl', which was cranked up 'til it cracked up.

Meanwhile, one of Curtis' old associates, Billy Butler (Jerry's younger brother with whom he had worked while Billy was signed to OKeh Records in the early '60s) was also releasing material during this period. He had signed to Curtom in March '76 just as the exodus of the label's roster began. Since Infinity's disintegration in '74, Billy had busied himself behind the scenes at the Butler Workshop writing and producing for others. He had become Jerry's MD on the road with the Ice Man Band, fulfilling a role that others, like Mayfield and Phil Upchurch, had previously performed. Billy took a year's sabbatical in '75 and went back to college, to sharpen his musical skills in arranging and production. He wanted to acquaint himself with music industry technical advancements in the studio and to extend his already considerable knowledge. But he never stopped writing and performing when he could and later came up with 'Everything's Alright', which he cut on demo and hiked around Chicago. The opportunities in town had been steadily shrinking and after quite a few rejections he reconnected with Curtis, who couldn't see much merit in the song he heard but nevertheless took Billy on knowing his proven talents could easily fulfill both of their expectations. Billy was interviewed by David Nathan for *Blues & Soul* mid way through recording his only album for the label and was naturally enthusiastic about his future with Curtom. When asked what his main ambition and aim for the future was Billy replied, 'To really perform and put out some good records. I could say I want to be rich but then who doesn't? But I don't think material things alone will satisfy me because I've already been through some of that. I'm looking to produce other people too, but I don't have any immediate plans in that direction.' When asked about Chicago in general he added, 'I feel a lot of things are happening, especially at Curtom. I think the company's just beginning to reach its peak as a growing company. And I'm glad to be part of it.'

Billy had not had any new records issued for three years but, during that period, due to fermenting northern soul interest, Epic re-released 'Right Track' in the UK and it went to #22 on the soul singles chart in September '74. On the strength of this minor success, Billy toured the northern circuit a year later where he received an enthusiastic reception. On his return, he went directly to Curtom and began recording the *Sugar Candy Lady* (CU 5015) album, which he co-produced with Rufus Hill and co-wrote most of the songs for himself. Unfortunately the finished project had uneven results, the semi-disco dancefloor tracks didn't take and lacked conviction but the ballads were still up to the standard that his fans had grown to expect. The title track for instance is just well crafted plod but is followed by a good song 'I Know The Feeling Well' that was written with brother Jerry and probably originally intended for him. This beautiful ballad has Billy sounding more like the Ice Man than ever before. 'Play The Music' is, I'm sure, a sincere plea to the DJs on the club scene to give this music a fair hearing, but it panders to a scene when it should have been changing it. On 'The Saga Of Sadie Lee' Billy relates her story, which is a morality tale of prostitution and brutality.

'Feel The Magic' was the obvious single choice; it has a Phillysound intro, which moves along well, striking a pretty even chord with listeners and dancers alike. The song, written with Workshop cohort and background singer Keith Echols, is an OK midtempo item but the public didn't buy it when released by Curtom coupled with 'She's Got Me Singing' in December '76. This was Billy's only Curtom single. 'I'm Gonna Make Her Mine' is another ballad, this time with a Terry Callier treatment that is very easy on the ear. 'Alone At Last' begins as a sensitive ballad, which Billy always handles so well with his fragile vocal style and moves easily into uptempo section, which condenses the message for those suspended in dance trances but leaves the unaffected listener a little unimpressed. The final cut 'My Love For You Grows' is perhaps the most typical track on the album with Billy singing in low register.

Released in May '77, *Sugar Candy Lady* had all the benefits of recording at Curtom with the usual high quality music contributions the experience always bought from Upchurch, Scott, Tufo and Joseph plus the inspiration of Henry Gibson's percussion and Sonny Seals' sax. The string and horn arrangements were by James Mack and all these factors provided the album with a well-crafted ambience. But the final package lacked conviction, from the quick-fix sleeve to the mindless mambo of the dance tracks. It did not chart anywhere. Once again the luckless Billy Butler found himself in the right place at the wrong time.

At this stage, Curtom were in deep trouble and, in an attempt to turn things around and to restore confidence with the moneymen at Warner, they made a couple of rash decisions. Mayfield spread himself too thin on outside projects and their upcoming movie *Short Eyes* was a disaster at the box office (see Chapter 9). If the promised Mayfield–Butler teaming had happened, this album could have been great. But for reasons beyond his control Billy's last album (so far) was marginalized by events and Curtom missed another golden opportunity to create really great music. Sequel re-issued this album on CD (NEMCD 361) in the UK, which included the bonus single 'She's Got Me Singing' in September 2000.

Epic repackaged some of the best soul tracks recorded at Okeh in '82 by Carl Davis and Curtis in the early '60s. The double album featured four Billy Butler and the Chanters tracks along with other greats from Walter Jackson, Major Lance and the Opals etc. Three years later Edsel records repackaged *Right Track* to contain almost Billy's entire Okeh catalogue. The album also featured informative sleeve notes from UK soulster Clive Richardson but this excellent album has yet to make the transition to CD, though Marginal Records in Brussels, did issue an 'unofficial' compilation of Billy's Okeh sides in '97.

One of the artists who had survived the cull of 1976 was Linda Clifford. Marv Stuart discovered her, so the story goes, whilst she was performing in one of the Windy City's many cocktail lounges. He immediately saw potential and took her to Curtom where she was signed to Gemigo Productions as a solo act. Her first record 'A Long, Long

Winter' was written by Curtis (and previously recorded by the Impressions in '64) and scored by Johnny Pate. Like the early Fascinations' singles, Mayfield leased the single to Paramount and it went to #75 R&B in February '74. Curtom were in the process of setting up Gemigo Records, on which Linda's next single 'Turn The Key Softly'/'Can't Get Enough' was one of the few releases to appear. But it could not build on her earlier success. After the closure of Gemigo, Linda moved over to Curtom who repositioned her to move into the disco market.

They bought in Gil Askey, ex-Motown producer/arranger/writer to craft her first album *Linda* (CU 5016), which was released in September '77. 'From Now On', chosen as the single, was a surprisingly low hit considering its commercial potential and was the strongest track on the album. The remaining cuts were reruns of earlier hits by Rod Stewart, Al Green, Stevie Wonder and the Bee Gees but Linda's lacklustre versions took these songs no further. As a début, it was OK but really suffered from a lack of any original sparkle. One or two tracks would get some play at the discothèque but early in the evening. It crept in at #98 on the R&B album chart in September '77.

Clifford's second album *If My Friends Could See Me Now* (CU 5021) was a much better set and considered by many to be her finest album. Mayfield's involvement definitely provided another dimension; he supplied three songs that he produced, the rest he left under Gil Askey's control. 'Runaway Love' written by Askey was to become Linda's biggest single, when in May '78 it went to #3 R&B but had surprisingly low pop sales and only charted at #75. Curtom followed up with 'If My Friends Could See Me Now', a single that fell short of expectations on R&B where it settled at #68, but did better on the Hot 100 reaching #54 in August '78. Mayfield wrote 'Gypsy Broadway Lady' for Linda, which is like an updated cartoon of one of his earlier Impressions vignettes but is performed well by Clifford, who seems a much more accomplished vocalist on this album. The Jones Girls supplied great background vocals and other contributors included Keni Burke and Rich Tufo. The sleeve reflects a classy image with tasteful photography by Hauser/D'Orio. All these factors together helped create Linda's biggest album and by July '78 it had reached #22 on the album chart and #55 on R&B.

Though the distributor had changed, it was business was as usual at Curtom Studios during the Warner era. The Curtom Rhythm Section evolved to take in the talents of Gary Thompson (guitar), Floyd Morris (keyboards), Bobby Christian (percussion) and Donnelle Hagan (drums). The Kitty Haywood Singers, the Jones Girls, Arnold Blair, Fred Simon, Larry Brownlee, Mattie Butler, Denise Heard and Valerie Sams all added swell to the background vocals. Leroy Hutson used increasingly larger outfits from the 'Spirit' sessions onwards – that included Aaron Jamal and Margie Stroud (keyboards), Bill McFarland (trombone) and Tony Carpenter (percussion). In addition to the Curtom artists who recorded at the studios, Mayfield produced two albums with Aretha Franklin, two more with the Staple Singers and one with Mavis Staples. Charles 'Chuck' Jackson, Marvin Yancy, Bunny Sigler, Billy Butler and Rufus Hill all added their production skills to the company and Gil Askey came on board ostensibly to produce Linda Clifford but he also made contributions to Hutson's and Mayfield's albums. Gil also provided plenty of arrangements as did Richard Evans and Richard Rome in support of principal Curtom arranger Rich Tufo.

Sonny Seals, Jerry Wilson (saxes) and Keni Burke (bass) made frequent contributions. Natalie Cole, Aretha Franklin, Ronnie Dyson, Bunny Sigler and Barbara Mason all cut albums at Curtom and Al Green recorded overdubs at the studios. When the distribution changed to RSO the Chicago Studios were still used but the remaining Curtom roster also used other studio facilities in LA, New York and Philadelphia. Some of the Chicago musicians had changed by then but still contained Lucky Scott, Henry Gibson and Keni Burke with the addition of Fred Wesley (funky horns), Ross Traut, Tom Ferrone (guitars), Alphonso Surrett, Ricky Linton (vocals) and Bobby Eli production, plus the many others hired for individual sessions.

It was early in 1978 that Mayfield was reunited with Aretha Franklin when he produced their second album together, *Almighty Fire* (Atlantic 19161). She had previously worked with Curtis in '76 when she recorded *Sparkle* (see Chapter 9), a collection of songs that Mayfield had written for a movie score. In October '98 Aretha was voted numero uno by a panel of 180 prominent vocalists, appointed by *MOJO* magazine to find their '100 Greatest Singers Of All Time'. (Absentees from this poll included Bobby Darin, Chaka Khan, Jerry Butler, John Fogarty, Curtis Mayfield and many other greats too numerous to mention here). Back then, Aretha was simply known as the 'Queen Of Soul' who after years of gospel obscurity with Columbia had shot to prominence with her first Atlantic album *I Never Loved A Man...* in '67 and followed on with a dozen more big selling albums for Atlantic before sales began to tail off in the mid '70s.

Almighty Fire's title track provides a strong opening with freaky keyboard intro coupled with a solid Mayfield production. It's a perfect vehicle for Aretha, who sings in her best voice – head back and wailin' at the stars. As a single this track reached #12 R&B/103 in April '78. The third cut 'More Than Just A Joy' was also chosen as a single and hit #51 R&B in July '78. This kind of powerful Aretha performance has had such a disastrous influence on next generation bandsaws like Whitney, Mariah and Celine and hence the rest of us. It needed a little editing for max enjoyment, so perhaps the single edit is the best choice in this case. 'Lady, Lady' and 'I Needed You Baby' are slower, reflective ballads, which hold a fine balance between Mayfield's sensitivities and Aretha's emotional intensity, whereas 'Keep On Loving You' steps up the tempo to a gospel shout. The background vocals (delivered by the Curtom chorus and the Jones Girls) work particularly well here and contribute much elsewhere on the album. 'Close To You' is perhaps where the combined chemistry is at its most potent – this superb track emerges as one of the album highlights and is followed by another gem 'No Matter Who You Love' in which Aretha convincingly relates a tale of unbridled passion, backed up beautifully by Mayfield's guitar lines. 'This You Can Believe' explores the real things that matter to lovers and the faith required to make their dreams come true. The final track is completely different from the other cuts and features Aretha's multi-track vocal and her piano on her own song 'I'm Your Speed'. It sounds like a bonus cut and may have been added by Atlantic to fill the album out.

For those who like their soul knee-deep in gospel *Almighty Fire* certainly provides the perfect prescription. Curtis seemed unwilling (or unable) to check Aretha's vocal gymnastics and this often resulted in intensity readings that at times went right off the VU. Whilst her vocals are in the main superbly handled and make this album very enjoyable listening, she does over-elaborate from time to time. The front cover of the sleeve visually echoes this tendency but it does have a great photo of Aretha on the back.

Mayfield supplied the total service here, writing all the songs (except 'I'm Your Speed'). It was recorded at Curtom Studios using the talents in residence at the time and arranged impeccably by Rich Tufo. Underneath Aretha's awesome power the whole set oozes Mayfield's quieter presence. But this combination does take a little playing time to adjust to. The brightest moments ('Almighty Fire', 'Close To You', 'No Matter Who You Love' and 'This You Can Believe') are as good as anything else that she recorded but, in general, the pop record-buying public responded better to her earlier more structured productions like 'I Never Loved A Man', 'Respect' and 'I Say A Little Prayer'. *Almighty Fire* sold pretty well but it proved a touch rich for mainstream consumption and only reached #63 on the US LP chart in May '78. Though sadly she was not to work with Curtis again, later interviews revealed her great respect for Mayfield's talents and in '94 she cut 'The Makings Of You' for the *Tribute To Curtis Mayfield album (aka All Men Are Brothers)* released by Warner Bros. Her voice was also added to Mayfield's 'Back To Livin' Again', which is part of the superb *New World Order* album (see Chapter 12).

Leroy Hutson's sixth album *Closer To The Source* (CU 5018) was issued in April 1978. It was more collaborative than the previous five albums as here Leroy shared production and arrangement credits with Gil Askey, Bob Monaco, Tom Tom 84 and Rich Tufo. Hutson wrote only half the songs himself, along with his usual collaborators, but there was an attempt to change direction a tad, to re-align with the source of his musical roots. 'In The Mood', written by pianist James Mendell, was used as Hutson's last Warner single and despite its soulful sophistication, only managed #45 on the R&B singles chart in June '78. It is a relaxed groove that sets up the album perfectly and the following tracks don't disappoint either. 'Where Did Love Go' written, produced and arranged by Gil Askey, is a tribute to Marvin Gaye. Gil had recently spent some years working at Motown and took this opportunity for some reflection. Leroy's vocal, though less intense than Gaye's, evokes *What's Going On* a little too often, but nevertheless it is still a most enjoyable track. The song itself mourns the love culture of the late '60s, by then dissipated by grinding commercialism. 'They've Got Love' keeps the groove moving along and is another Mendell-penned song. 'Get To This (You'll Get To Me)' is the first of Hutson's own songs and he ups the tempo a shade to provide us with a closer look at his internal emotional workings.

Askey's persistent groove keeps it interesting enough and effortlessly moves things right along. The title track is all Leroy and 'Closer To The Source' reveals a positive outlook in the search for a perfect reality. Like 'Where Did Love Go' it should have been a single. It shades as the album's finest track but only just. 'Heaven Right Here On Earth' was probably cut a few months earlier with Rich Tufo handling the arrangements on Hutson's Productions Inc and compares very favourably with the Natural Four's superb version.

As the musical fashions in dancehalls and on the club scene evolved into disco, in the mid and later '70s, soul and pop merged with techno and temporarily took a creative nosedive into disco oblivion. Once it finally caught on, disco swamped the dance, R&B and pop charts and the previously established genres temporarily abandoned their game plans in an attempt to stay in touch. The disco format was one of celebration, the party and dancing all nite long, so essentially it produced more superficial records. The beats became more sophisticated but any good ideas lyrically were not developed, they just came around on repeat rather too often. Soul music up until that time had successfully evolved in many directions; a large percentage had traditionally been aimed at the dancefloor. But in nearly 20 years the lyrical and poetic development of the genre had come a long way. With very few exceptions this creative development was put on pause mode for the duration of the disco era. So, sadly, this period of soul limbo left great artists of the calibre of Mayfield, Gaye, Wonder, Butler and many others in a creative cul de sac.

Since '68 Curtom had built its reputation as a quality soul label. They attempted to broaden their roster but with little commercial success. Even after Mayfield's huge initial success as a solo performer, the label could not sign any established stars, so it could not grow in the way that it needed to. Though Curtom had earned plenty of respect from the industry, the stars of the time seemed, in general, to be looking for the financial security that they believed only a major could supply.

Sadly Warner did not bring Curtom the increased pop success that it hoped for and needed for growth. R&B sales were good (the first year) but of the 21 albums that they distributed for Curtom, the only pop album hit was *Let's Do It Again* by the Staple Singers in January '76. For the next two and a half years, not one of their 14 releases entered the Hot 100 albums, until Linda Clifford came, too late for a rescue, with *If My Friends Could See Me Now* (#22, May '78). Compared to their five years with Buddah, where they managed rather better with seven (from 23 issues) Hot 100 albums and the R&B sales were also larger, it was directly opposite to the outcome that they had intended and try as they may, Curtom could not reverse the downturn in their fortunes. After the exodus of mid '76 the label's new signings Mystique, Billy Butler, Bunny Sigler and Barbara Mason all released albums, none of which made an impact on either chart. Things were looking dismal. Mayfield had been involved in creating two more movie soundtracks but *A Piece Of The Action* by Mavis Staples could not duplicate the success of *Let's Do It Again* and the poor reception that *Short Eyes* received sealed their fate.

The Curtom singles sales also suffered similarly despite good R&B placings, with Warner the first single to register on the Hot 100 was Curtis' 'So In Love' (#68, August '75). Both Staples singles 'Let's Do It Again' and 'New Orleans' went to #1 and #70 respectively and the Impressions also had two hits with 'Sooner Or Later' and 'Same Thing It Took'. Linda Clifford, Curtom's newest star had growing R&B sales but too little, too late to impress at Warner. Linda's '...Friends...' visited at #54 and 'Runaway Love' managed #76. Of the 40 Curtom single releases, only these seven registered on the Hot 100. With Buddah 25 singles out of 77 releases crossed over to the pop charts, a ratio of 33 per cent compared to 17 per cent with Warner. If the hits were not coming as thick and fast as before, the quality of what Curtom was trying to achieve did not go entirely unappreciated. But by late '78 Curtom was looking elsewhere for a new distributor.

Due to the falling sales of Curtom product, commercial pressures became more intense, and in an attempt to reverse the downward spiral, Curtis Mayfield allowed himself to be led by current fashions in the contemporary music of the time. This situation produced his next solo album, *Do It All Night* (CU 5022), which became the final album that Warner Bros distributed for Curtom. Gil Askey, who had worked with Curtis before, was contracted in to provide disco arrangements and set the album's tone. Only a couple of the sessions were recorded in Chicago at Curtom with the team there. Most of the songs, half of them co-written by Askey and Mayfield, were recorded in Los Angeles at Wally Heider and in the Las Vegas Recording Studios. Jim Burgess mixed the dance tracks 'Do It All Night', 'No Goodbyes' and 'Party, Party' later. All the tracks were released in the US as singles, the first of which was easily the best cut of the set 'You Are, You Are'. As a single it rose to #34 R&B by April '78 and, despite its infectiously fashionable sound, did no pop chart business.

The second single 'Do It All Night' was Curtis' lowest-selling single to chart, when it only crept in at #96 R&B five months later in September. 'In Love, In Love, In Love' was Mayfield's final WB single and gained the distinction of 'no chart nowhere status' – his first complete flop for eight years. The album cover, again art directed by Ed Thrasher with design and photography from Brad Kanawyer and Claude Mougin, conveyed the glitz of 'Come Dancing', but it did not misrepresent most of the product therein. *Do It All Night* was the nadir of Curtis Mayfield's recorded work. Like his previous album, the soundtrack for *Short Eyes*, which was a far superior set, it did not make the Billboard album chart, but it did well enough with soul fans to peak at #30 R&B by August '78. Curtom UK did not release *Do It All Night* at all but instead they issued a 12in 45 special limited edition single of 'Party, Party' and 'No Goodbyes', which took many turns on the UK dancefloors and went to #65 on the pop chart in December '78.

The lack of success of the *Do It All Night* album and single of the same name sounded the death knoll for Curtom who from '79–'88 did not release any product as an independent label. Of the album, Mayfield later confessed, despite taking production credits on the sessions, 'It didn't have much to do with me, it was Marv's thing, he wanted us to have a disco hit, Linda Clifford was having some success on the dance scene, and he thought that's the way we should go. I had spread myself a little thin what with the 'Short Eyes' movie score at that time, which cost Curtom a lot. As well as many other recording and tour commitments. Looking back, I think that maybe I should have taken a break at that time and reflected on just what was going on, and not have listened so much to other people, but there were lots of pressures on all of us to turn things around.' Unfortunately for Curtis and all at Curtom, these moments of inattention were to have a damaging effect on the future of their business.

9 Mayfield At The Movies

Sidney Poitier made a 'little film that made good' entitled *Lilies of the Field* ('63) and unexpectedly his performance won him his second Berlin Film Festival award (he was the only actor in history to receive this award twice). It also won the Oscar for Best Actor for him that year, the first ever awarded to a black actor. The movie told the tale of an ex-GI handyman, who helped an order of German nuns to realize their dream of building a chapel. The movie did not mean much to white audiences in Europe or America, but it caused elation in black communities across the States. It was seen then, and is more generally recognized now, as an important breakthrough for black culture. The soundtrack was composed by Jerry Goldsmith and featured a song as its theme called 'Amen', which was performed in a commercialized version of the traditional gospel call and response style. Jester Hairston, who was acquainted with Poitier and appeared in quite a few of his later movies, rewrote the traditional version into a work song format and published the song with himself as the author. The soundtrack to Ralph Nelson's *Lilies Of The Field* was issued in America on Epic (LN 24094). It comprised 20 tracks and featured three versions of 'Amen'. A year later, in June '64, Curtis Mayfield who had seen even more potential in the song whilst watching the movie, worked out a new arrangement with Johnny Pate and recorded it with the Impressions for their then current album *Keep On Pushing* (see Chapter 3). 'Amen' was released as a single and climbed to #7 on the Hot 100 by December, giving the Impressions a big Yuletide hit that year. This anthem became so identified with the group that Mayfield bought the publishing rights from Hairston in the mid '60s and thereby forged his first tenuous link with the movies.

Curtis Mayfield's first real involvement with Hollywood came six years later in '69 through arranger and writer Mack David (elder brother of the famous lyricist Hal David). He invited Curtis to record two of the songs that he had written for use on the soundtrack for *Krakatoa, East of Java* ('69) a big budget movie being shot by Bernard Kowolski in Super Panavision for a Cinerama presentation. The movie ran into trouble at its première where it was unfavourably criticized for being too long and difficult to follow. Against his better judgment, Kowolski cut 35 minutes from the original, but it was still a flop at the box office anyway. *Krakatoa...* deserved a better fate for, while it was not a great movie and suffers from some serious continuity problems (plus hammy acting), it had some good action scenes and should really be restored to the original director's cut for its entertainment value alone. The movie, which still runs at 101 minutes, tells the tale of a bunch of fortune hunters who, due to their own bad timing, find themselves in the Indian Ocean when the Volcano Krakatoa (Krakatau), that lays west of Java as any school atlas will reveal, erupts sending a huge tidal wave on to Java causing much death and destruction, and featuring many exciting disaster scenes (given the vintage of the movie). Presumably the Impressions' songs ended up on the cutting room floor, along with the missing 35 minutes. They recorded these two tracks at RCA Studios in Chicago, on 10 April 1968, at the tail end of their ABC contract. 'Just Before Sunrise' was intended as the title song and was only released as a single that got lost in the shuffle as Curtis and the Impressions moved from ABC on to Curtom. 'East of Java' became the flipside but also found its way on to the Impressions' final ABC album *The Versatile Impressions* (see Chapter 4). Although these songs are pleasant enough, Johnny Pate's slightly clichéd arrangement merely frames Mack David's lyrics as they paint a holiday picture postcard. The record sails perilously close to kitsch, but for the Impressions' sensitive vocal treatment.

The man who in recent years has emerged as the acknowledged godfather of the black cinema is Chicagoan Melvin Van Peebles (born in 1932). His first full-length feature was *La Permission* (The Story Of A Three-Day Pass/'67). This movie won Peebles the 'Critics Choice Award' at the San Francisco Film Festival that year (they thought he was a Dutchman). At that time Van Peebles was the only black American film director. Three years later he made *Watermelon Man* ('70) for Columbia, which starred Godfrey Cambridge and was an establishment comedy about a white bigot who turns black and has to deal with the consequences. It did quite well but was not really what Peebles wanted to say. In his true maverick tradition he took any profits and credit that he had earned from *Watermelon Man* and poured them into his next movie *Sweet Sweetback's Baadasssss Song* ('71) a revolutionary story of black reprisal and survival. This time, not only did Melvin write, compose, produce, direct, edit and star in the movie but he also used a black non-union crew to shoot it, by pretending that he was making a porn flick. When it was finished, Peebles refused to submit the movie to the censors, stating that the board had no right to tell the black community what they may or may not see.

The Darius James book *That's Blaxploitation* (St Martin's Griffin '95), features the author in an interview with Peebles and suggests that ...*Baadasssss*... is an 'urban visual poem', which describes the last half of the movie to perfection. In Mark Daniel's excellent film *Runnin' Man* ('97), he called ...*Baadasssss*... 'the first revolutionary black film produced in the United States.' Although the movie is fiercely critical of white racism, it also takes side swipes at the black community's complacency, both in their religious and social attitudes, the duality and dishonesty in their dealings with the man – it even provides a slap in the face for sexy female black singers. So no one is entirely without blame. After what seems like a marathon, Sweetback hops a freight south towards the border and runs some more, this time pursued by dogs. The movie ends with the warning 'Watch Out! A Baad Asssss Nigger Is Coming Back To Collect Some Dues...', just one sentiment that sent a shockwave through white America but made Melvin a folk hero within the black communities that saw it.

Sweet Sweetback's Baadasssss Song is said to have cost $500,000 to make and its earnings were not widely publicized. But though the movie was seen by a lot of people when released in '71, uncensored and subsequently rated X, it was labelled dangerous and boycotted by the Hollywood establishment – that made it an automatic 'must see' for movie fans. It was 26 years before the movie was seen outside the US and it was the last film Peebles was to make in Hollywood.

Although *Sweet Sweetback's Baadasssss Song* stands apart from the other movies of the time both as an artistic statement and a historic document, it also set the blueprint that created a torrent of later movies, estimated at over 400, which were primarily aimed at and sold to black America, a section of the community that had previously been ignored but was now viewed as an area of rapid growth potential. These movies contributed to a genre that eventually became known as 'Blaxploitation' because, although many of them starred an all black cast, they were often produced and directed by whites, who just took any profits and had no further statements to make. Many of the 'plots' generally followed a similar format and were crammed with caricature pimps, hookers, corrupt white officials and tough uncompromising anti-heroes. Although the genre was generally dismissed by many as trashy, the philosophy that these movies projected was taken up by many young African Americans as their own, and had a far greater impact on later waves of black and white cinema than is yet generally acknowledged.

...*Baadasssss*... didn't make it to the UK or Europe, where the breakthrough came with *Shaft* in '72, the first all black movie to cross over to the mainstream audience. John Shaft was a New York detective with attitude aplenty, who for reasons of PR was quite wrongly tagged as the black James Bond by reviewers at the time. If the definition of Blaxploitation is a large cocktail of violence, drugs, sex, pimps and attitude, this movie had it all. Above all what it also had was a great soundtrack written and performed by Isaac Hayes. For *Theme from Shaft*, Hayes created an ideal mood with his deliciously tongue-in-cheek lyric and superbly infectious sound. Even though Ike was already a star after his album *Hot Buttered Soul* went platinum in '69, when interviewed in Memphis in '72 he confessed, 'I was nervous about doing it at first. I only said that I would write the score if they gave me a screen test and the director, Gordon Parks said, "Yeah, OK". So when I got back to Memphis I started work on the theme and after a couple of weeks I hadn't heard anything from the movie people, so I call them and they tell me, "Well er, we've cast it and we're shooting in New York..."

'"Oh yeah?" I said.

'"Yeah," they said, "we got Richard Roundtree."

'But I couldn't back down on the music. I was kinda tricked into it but it all came out OK.' The trick later paid off handsomely for Hayes when he was nominated for, and won, the Academy Award for his soundtrack to *Shaft*. Unexpectedly *Shaft* took $12 million at the box office in its first year and financially rescued the ailing MGM Studios.'

As a postscript to John Shaft, his spirit was reborn in a sequel starring the way too cool Samuel L Jackson who played a second generation relation of the original character with all the bad habits and more of his descendant. Now a plain clothes cop for New York's finest, *Shaft* ('00) projected all the style and slick of present day Hollywood. Director John Singleton used all the big budget special effects at his disposal in this larger than life projection of the popular black anti-hero. The original score that Isaac Hayes created in '71 was reprised and remixed.

Following in the footsteps of ...*Baadasssss*... and *Shaft* came *Superfly*, which gave Mayfield the opportunity to create his first complete movie soundtrack and proved to be the biggest album of his career. *Superfly* (CRS 8014) contains some brilliant and timeless music. 'Little Child Runnin' Wild' had been written the previous year but fitted so well to the intro of the movie that it was used there. This song dips in and out of the storyline throughout the movie and runs behind our introduction to Priest (the anti-hero drug dealer and the movie's leading man) as he symbolically sniffs coke off the cross that he wears on a chain around his neck. Curtis cut it as a demo with his new band, The Curtis Mayfield Experience, and it was this group that performed all the music for *Superfly*.

'Pusherman' the movie's strongest track, is actually performed by Curtis and band when anti-hero Priest Youngblood (played by Ron O'Neal) and his partner Eddie meet with Scatter, an old-timer who's forsaken the rackets and retired to run his club and restaurant. Julius W Harris who plays Scatter, appeared in many Blaxploitation movies but is probably best remembered for his role in the James Bond flick *Live And Let Die* and he also appeared in *Shaft's Big Score*. This track is also featured later, in director Gordon Parks Jr's (son of *Shaft* director Gordon Parks) effective stills sequence, which depicts the cocaine reaching a number of recreational fashion victims. One has to admire Mayfield's integrity in not releasing 'Pusherman' as a single, considering its hit potential, deeming that the song's message could easily have been misread as a drugs commercial by so many kids. The song graphically depicts existence within a hard drugs economy, the pressures and the temptation to escape, at least temporarily, from degradation and violence that traps and violates the individual tightly within its clutches.

'Freddie's Dead' was released in the US, as a taster to promote the movie and it was this record that grew to become Mayfield's worldwide career hit single. The vocal wasn't used on the soundtrack but the previously unissued alternate instrumental version was. Freddie, played by Charles McGregor, was a minor character hustled into the role of unwilling enforcer by events beyond his control. Mayfield saw him as a symbolically sympathetic character, who was something of an innocent and consequently dies early while attempting an escape from the 'man'. 'Junkie Chase' is an uptempo instrumental, which Mayfield's arranger and ex-partner Johnny Pate contributed to and which is used on the soundtrack to punctuate the many action scenes. 'Give Me Your Love' bubbles in undercurrent from time to time, but is featured in the soapy love scene between Priest and Georgia, his long-suffering woman, who plays second fiddle to his personal agenda, which is to make the big score and then disappear. This great medium tempo song was cut as a single, first by Barbara Mason and then by Sisters Love. It also provided the inspiration for Mary J Blige's 'I'm The Only Woman' hit in '94.

'Eddie You Should Know Better' refers to Priest's partner Eddie who got some of the best lines in the script like, 'I know it's a rotten game but it's the only game the man left us to play', which was uttered as a retort to Priest's plans of escape from the 'American Dream'. A previously unissued instrumental version was also included on the Rhino set. The Natural Four cut a great version of this song too, for Curtom, which only appeared on single in '73, after the movie's release. Mayfield introduces 'No Thing On Me' in post-vocal monologue, which was originally written for the movie's conclusion but in the end was not used as such. Instead it can be heard behind the 'other woman' scenes and spills over into Scatter's 'hot shot' departure. 'Think' another superb instrumental, marks the end of the Pate/Mayfield partnership, which had began with the Impressions ten years earlier and had created the Chicago soul sound with Carl Davis at OKeh along the way (see Chapter 3). After *Superfly*, they never worked together again and were locked in a long dispute over this album. This music is used behind the scenes of Priest as he internally hatches the sting that he's about to perpetrate. 'Superfly', the movie's final track, relates and recaps on the hero's complete story. It accompanies the scenes as Priest plays his get-out-of-the-ghetto-free card and leaves his troubles way behind.

Superfly marks the commercial highpoint of Curtis Mayfield's recording career. After the album's initial release it sold in excess of two million copies, sales that must have been significantly added to by the several re-issues since. The lasting success of the *Superfly* album, which topped both R&B and pop listings and stayed 46 weeks on the US LP charts, delayed the release of his next album *Back To The World* by at least six months. When the *Superfly* album was issued in the UK, in November '72, it went straight to #3 on the soul LP charts. The following week it climbed to the top slot and it stayed in the Top 10 albums for three months. Then instead of going down slowly, as one might suppose, it re-occupied #1 in April, by which time it had also climbed to #26 on UK pop albums. This lengthy success continued whilst it yo-yo'd in the Top 10 for a further three months and then amazingly went back to #1 for a third time in July when it finally gave way to Stevie Wonder's *Talking Book*. Though Curtis was to have many hit albums, among them other movie soundtracks, no other album would bring him the phenomenal success of *Superfly*.

During an interview in '72, Marv Stuart (Mayfield's partner/manager at Curtom) stated, 'I negotiated the deal on *Superfly* with Sig Shore Productions, it was Curtom's first movie soundtrack and it looks like it will be our biggest album so far. This success, we feel will open doors for other Curtom artists in Hollywood, all things being equal – which they are not.' Later Stuart credited *Superfly* with double platinum sales and though this figure must be close to the total sales it has not been endorsed by any chart or music reference source, at this time. Curtis was also offered the soundtrack to *Superfly TNT* the sequel but he turned it down (though he allowed some of his music to be used) and Osibisa stepped in to provide a less memorable theme and much less successful album.

It would be easy to criticize the movie for its low-budget production and Blaxploitation values but that would rather miss the point. In retrospect, it's a historical slice of sociology, for it is Mayfield's lyrics and music that carry the clear anti-drugs message. They should have acted as a warning of the impending disaster that hard drugs were about to inflict on all of western society. Despite Mayfield's efforts, on release, *Superfly* was still accused of being an advert for coke and the drug culture in general. Washington poet and radical activist Gaston Neal led pickets at theatres showing *Superfly* in '72 but in recent years he has adjusted his perspective and today he's a Mayfield fan. Despite its entertaining but showy projection of violence and overblown hipness, the movie had a serious message, which Mayfield's lyrics highlighted with credibility and plain common sense.

When *Superfly* screened at UK movie theatres in the spring of '73 it didn't cause much of a ripple, one way or another. The critics regarded it as a B-movie with an undefined audience. The term 'Blaxploitation' was yet to be coined and as one of the earliest movies in the genre, it did not create much interest here until the early '90s when Blaxploitation made its 'comeback' through UK TV, cable and video. There are many different issues of *Superfly* available on CD in the UK. Sequel released *Superfly* and *Short Eyes* together as one of their two CD budget sets in the *Double Feature* series in '98 for the UK market, and it quickly grew to become one of Sequel's best sellers of that year.

Superfly – Special Edition (R2 72836) was a superb two CD set that Rhino issued in America in '97 (and in the UK on import) to celebrate the movie's 25th anniversary. It not only featured previously unreleased music written by Mayfield for the movie (unused at the time), but also included other unheard tracks cut around that period. The last two cuts on CD one are bonus tracks of Mayfield's two big hit singles edited from the movie score but not included on the original *Superfly* issue. 'Freddie's Dead' (single edit) was Mayfield's biggest US hit (#2 R&B/4 pop in August '72) where it remained on the charts for 17 weeks earning him his first gold disc. In the UK it also had a lengthy run peaking at #13 soul in October '72. The 'Superfly' (single edit) was also a huge hit in America in November '72 (# 5 R&B/8 pop) and earned Curtis his second gold record. It was a bigger UK hit than its predecessor going to #3 soul in April '73. Neither of these two singles saw any pop chart action in the UK where Mayfield's biggest single was of course 'Move On Up'.

'Ghetto Child' is the demo previously released in the UK but not America, which grew to become 'Little Child Runnin' Wild'. The alternate version of 'Pusherman' is a very different mix from the one we are all familiar with as it features an added string section, which had been previously unheard. Also cut at the same time was a longer bonus version, which was also previously unused. The third 'Freddie's Dead' version was used in the movie as previously mentioned. All the instrumentals included here, 'Junkie Chase', 'No Thing On Me' and 'Eddie...' are not backing tracks with the vocal removed but genuine alternate versions of different length and mix. 'Militant March' a short piece of music that runs just 54 seconds was written for the soundtrack but, in the end, not required and so remains an undeveloped oddity. Curtis recorded at least two radio spots that have also been added to this collection. They were used on American radio only to announce and promote *Superfly* before the movie's release and so again, have not been heard here in the UK before. They both underline Mayfield's concern to clarify his anti-drug message to the movie's potential audience.

The 'Underground' demo was released in the UK earlier as part of Sequel's three CD set *Love, Peace, Understanding* and was recut by Curtis for his second studio album *Roots* in '71 (see Chapter 5). The alternate instrumental cut of 'Check Out Your Mind' is a very different take on the original, which Curtis recorded with the Impressions in 1970. It sounds as though it was a later studio jam, perhaps considered for use on a soundtrack and is almost unrecognizable in this form but an interesting version nevertheless.

The final track 'Curtis on Superfly' is taken from an edited interview with Mayfield in the autumn of '96 with David Dorn. Curtis relates a number of interesting observations on a range of topics, which include his influences from Henry Mancini to Ahmad Jamal. He also mentions his work with arrangers (a reference to the unnamed Mr Pate) and modestly touches on some of his achievements and the proven longevity of his music. When interviewed in '79 he had this to say about *Superfly*: 'When I first saw the movie rushes I thought it was a cocaine commercial. It was important for me to counter the visuals in depth. To go in and explain it in a way that the kids would not read it as an infomercial for drugs.' In the past few years *Superfly* and its predecessor *Shaft* have re-emerged at the very top of the Blaxploitation movie genre and have created enough interest in both the UK and the US to have prompted recent video re-issues and look like they may even make it to DVD. Charly Records issued their remodelled version of the Rhino package in the UK in '98.

Superfly's amazing success established Mayfield's reputation to deliver a hit soundtrack and other offers were soon to follow. Gladys Knight had moved over from Motown in '73 to sign with Buddah, Curtom's parent company and distributor, and the next movie that Curtis undertook was *Claudine* ('74). He produced the album at Curtom Studios where Gladys & the Pips began recording the soundtrack in late '73. It is common knowledge that Gladys Knight & the Pips had enjoyed a number of hit singles and albums since mid '61, but many people are unaware of just how successful this family group had been. Despite his own huge success, Mayfield was delighted and honoured to be working with such a big star – he had been a fan since their initial hit 'Every Beat Of My Heart' on the Chicago label Vee-Jay in May '61. After that the Pips had enjoyed 22 hit singles including five #1 R&B (19 Top 40 records) and 12 albums that had charted pop, the biggest being *Imagination*, their first for Buddah in October of the previous year, that went to #9 on the pop album chart. So both Curtis and Gladys were at their hottest when they came together over *Claudine*.

The movie starred Diahann Carroll and James Earl Jones (with a small cameo appearance by singer Adam Wade) and the storyline centres around the relationship between garbage man (Jones) and ghetto housewife (Carroll) and their combined nine children (from their previous marriages). The movie highlights the inhumanity of the system that seems to thwart them at every turn and Mayfield's opening song, the superb 'Mr Welfare Man' provides an accurate reflection of their struggle. He made lyrical and production changes to his own timeless version that he cut for the *Give, Get, Take And Have* album two years later (see chapter 7). One classic follows another here as Knight beautifully relates the heartache endured by an individual at the mercy of a society that dehumanizes to such an extent, that it seems that the only overwhelming desire left to her, is 'To Be Invisible'. Curtis also cut this classic himself later that same year, with a few changes for *Sweet Exorcist* (see Chapter 6). 'On And On' was originally penned by Mayfield for the Impressions two years earlier, and was only released as a single in the UK, culled from the *Times Have Changed* album (see Chapter 6). It was successfully remodelled for Knight whose popular vocal treatment won the group a huge hit single, that went to #2 R&B/ 5 pop in May '74 and quickly turned to gold, their fourth gold record in a row.

The second song to be skillfully restructured by Mayfield for this movie was 'The Makings Of You', which was first cut for his initial solo album *CURTIS* in 1970 (see Chapter 5). It works well enough here but should not be compared to the original that has over the years become a favourite with many Mayfield fans. The only instrumental cut, 'Claudine Theme', runs in and out behind the images throughout the movie, without demanding much attention. 'Hold On' is a ballad, which begins slowly, clicks in a third of the way through and features some subtle guitar from the master. The final cut 'Make Yours A Happy Home' was written for the upbeat ending to the movie, which was seen by some as an unsatisfactory conclusion to the story but is OK for those movie fans who prefer a happy ending.

Most reviewers do not consider this a 'Blax' movie though it deals with black issues and has an all black cast but Darius James did include it in his book *That's Blaxploitation* and gave it this five word review: 'Diahann Carroll on welfare. Right.' But despite dismissals like this, it was a popular movie, which attempted to address serious social and racial issues. It was also one of Carroll's best career performances for which she was rightly Oscar nominated as Best Actress.

The *Claudine* (Buddah 5602) album was also a big hit reaching #35 on the pop album chart in March '74 where it enjoyed a 34-week run and earned the Pips their second gold album. Richard Tufo deserves a mention for his sumptuous, big string arrangements; they complement Knight's vocal delivery of Curtis' songs perfectly. It seems peculiar that Knight and Mayfield did not follow this hit album with another collaboration, considering the success of *Claudine*. The duo worked well off each other and the combination of their talents would surely have been further mutually beneficial. Even the likelihood of a duet could have produced interesting results but sadly for Curtom this did not transpire.

Gladys Knight followed up *Claudine* two years later with her first starring role in *Pipe Dreams* to which the soundtrack has previously been wrongly credited to Mayfield (by a number of journalists), who was not involved in the project. It was, in fact, produced by Bubba Knight, Dominic Frontiere and Michael Masser. After *Claudine*, Gladys & the Pips maintained almost continuous success with Buddah until 1980, when the group joined Columbia and then MCA ('87).

Richard Tufo became the second Curtom producer to write arrange and produce a movie soundtrack in '74, this time for *Three The Hard Way*, which was directed by Gordon Parks Jr of *Superfly* fame. The Impressions, who had recently been recording with Tufo and co-producer Lowrell Simon, supplied the vocals for this project. The movie features Jim Brown an ex-football star who had appeared in many successful Hollywood movies of all kinds, Fred Williamson (who starred in tough guy black movies in the '70s and '80s), and Jim Kelly, a Karate black belt champ, who came to prominence in *Enter The Dragon* ('73) and made a number of martial arts movies. These three heroes join forces to prevent a dastardly plot by Neo Nazi, Monroe Feather (Jay Robinson), to rid the planet of the black race by poisoning the water supply with a deadly serum, to which whites are impervious (yes really!). This tedious thriller is long on action, with plenty of explosions, shoot-em-ups and combat scenes but short on (intentional) laffs – some good jokes would have made its passage that much smoother.

Neither this soundtrack or *Preacher Man* (see Chapter 6), which is the closest by way of stylistic comparison, were released in the UK – so some of the reviews that expressed disappointment at the time of its US release would have put off many potential import purchasers. 'Make A Resolution' is a good intro to the movie and sets out the trio's intentions to destroy the Nazi scourge. 'Wendy' is a ballad, with lead vocal by Reggie Torian, which centres around Brown's girlfriend played by Shelia Frazier who is abducted by the fascists to their cost. 'That's What Love Will Do' is a medium tempo song in a similar vein, this time with Ralph Johnson supplying the lead vocal. The strongest track to emerge from the movie was 'Something's Mighty, Mighty Wrong', which was chosen by Curtom as a single and went to #28 R&B in September '74 but got no pop chart action. It features Johnson on lead vocal but fell short as a follow-up to 'Finally Got Myself Together', which had topped the R&B listings five months earlier. Jim Kelly is the 'Mister Keyes' of the title, who kicks and chops his way through the 'plot' as one might expect, given his track record.

The almost choral vocal style preferred by Tufo works quite well behind the action but leaves the listener rather unimpressed when it comes to vocal expectations on the album. Female sighs and groans set the mood for 'Having A Ball', a rather unremarkable MOR ballad, and 'On The Move' has a similar groove to the earlier *Preacher Man* sessions, but both of these tracks are almost unrecognizable as Impressions' records. Ralph emerges as lead voice singing an ode to Jimmy Lait, whose character is played by Brown. 'Three The Hard Way' (Chase & Theme) is in two parts, the first an instrumental typical of the genre and the last a song of solidarity for the trio of heroes, with the lead again taken by Johnson.

The *Three The Hard Way* soundtrack (Curtom CRS 8602), though not quite up to the standard of Mayfield's current successes, was still OK but due to its non-release in the UK, both at the time and ever since, this album has become something of a rarity. It did not create any pop album chart interest in America either. The movie may have aired in Europe but will have escaped the attention of all but the most diligent fans. It was shown in London however, at the NFT, as part of the Blaxploitation season screened in August '96. Parks Jr only made a couple of movies more before he was killed in Kenya in a plane crash in 1979.

The third Curtom producer to take a crack at writing for the movies was Leroy Hutson, who worked with TT Washington on the score for a movie entitled *The JJ Johnson Affair* but this project was abandoned before its completion. Another movie that Curtom had high hopes for at the end of '74 was *Mimi* that was to star Curtis and Al Green but due to contractual obligations was first postponed to mid '75 and then the option passed.

Let's Do It Again ('74) was Curtis Mayfield's third movie score and the first for the mighty Warner Brothers, this time featuring the exquisite vocal talents of the Staple Singers. It was the second movie in a trilogy of projects that Sidney Poitier and Bill Cosby co-produced beginning with *Uptown Saturday Night* (which was successful to the tune of $8 million). The title track introduces us to the movie during the opening credits and went on to become a huge hit single for Curtom, their largest during their tenure with Warner Bros. The movie itself turns out to be a good-natured comedy that has Bill and Sid cooking up a boxing-hypnotism-bet fixing-scam, to make enough money to build a new home (and place of worship) for their brothers and sisters of the Shaka Lodge. In the process, the duo pit two rival gangs of New Orleans gangstas off each other and burn them both, before escaping back home to Atlanta. 'New Orleans' was the second Staple Singers' single from the movie, and it reached #4 R&B/70 pop in February '76. In the storyline, it runs behind the vacation that our heroes take as a cover with their wives, while they expedite their plan to snatch the cash.

Six movie months later, once the bad guys have figured it all out and located them, 'Big Mac' makes Bill and Sidney an offer they can't refuse, which involves a rerun of the original scam, this time making rival 'Biggie Smalls' the fall guy. Due to a number of screw-ups, all too tiresome to relate at this time, the duo pull a triple cross and still get home free. The music works perfectly behind the antics on screen and 'Funky Love, 'A Whole Lot Of Love' and 'I Want To Thank You' are seamlessly worked into the storyline. This movie features many famous faces including Calvin Lockheart, John Amos, Ossie Davis, Julius Harris and Billy Eckstine, but once again the real star of this movie is Mayfield's soundtrack. Curtis wrote 'Big Mac' and the haunting 'After Sex' but the final track simply entitled 'Chase', was supplied by the Curtom rhythm section. Gil Askey and Rich Tufo wrote all arrangements.

As a movie, *Let's Do It Again* did OK, but lacked the zip of *Uptown*

Saturday Night. As a soundtrack, it did much better business and became the big album for Curtom and the Staples, when it went to #20 on Billboard's album chart in November '75 and remained there for 18 weeks. When interviewed by US *Blues & Soul* Editor David Nathan in April '76, the Staples told him, 'We all felt that the material was the most commercial that we'd ever cut and although it wasn't typical Staples material, it proved that we were capable of doing whatever we're called on to do – a signal of our versatility. But the vibes throughout were so great that we just knew that the album would take off – though in all honesty, we didn't expect it to be quite the runaway success it was!'

Curtom and Curtis Mayfield were still riding high on the success of *Let's Do It Again* when they began work on their second Warner Brothers movie *Sparkle* ('76). This movie was set in the Harlem of '58 and tells the story of a group of high school kids, their bid for showbiz success and their struggle to overcome the pitfalls of the ghetto on their rocky road to fame. It centres around three teenage sisters Sparkle (Irene Cara), Sister (Lonette McKee) and Dolores (Dwan Smith) who after seeing a Brooklyn Paramount talent show, decide that they could do better and form their own quintet with two local guys. After some scene setting, up on the roof and in Levi's (Dorian Harewood) new car, where dreams are exchanged, Stix (Philip Michael Thomas) a talented writer, with Sparkle in his eye, gets to work promoting them around town. With a little rehearsal they begin singing as the 'Hearts' in a clip joint talent contest where they win the prize money with their rendition of 'Jump' and this success inspires them to keep on trying. It is Stix who has the driving ambition to succeed but he doesn't find it easy to sell the new group. Levi, impatient for the big time and not particular about how he gets there, quits to work for Satin, an underworld fixer. Stix can get no further bookings as a quartet so he steps back to become their manager and musical director and adjusts his sights to promote the trio as sex-sirens on a stick. After one brief appearance, they get a residence at Shan-Doo, a club frequented by Harlem lowlife.

Mayfield's superb 'Hooked On Your Love' is a movie highlight, which gives some clue as to what is to come. Sister and the Sisters' sexy vocal performance inspires this sinister gathering and she instantly becomes embroiled with local psychopath Satin. He introduces her to the tricks of his trade, hard drugs and physical abuse, which result in her dramatic downward spiral. But ignoring advice from her sisters and taking no heed of what Mama said, she remains under Satin's control. 'Something He Can Feel' is the next movie highlight and it emphasizes the trio's dilemma, as Mayfield's lyrics and music underscore the script. Fearing for Sister's life, Dolores drops a dime on Satin and gives the cops details of his next drugs deal. This is a disaster for Levi, who gets shot at the bust and jailed as a result. Belief goes into suspension when Satin, seeking retribution has a fist fight with Stix, from which he makes an unconvincing departure – stage left. The group shatters and Stix blows town, which leaves the girls no option but to return home to the tenement. But it is too late for Sister who cannot depart the downtown train and is glimpsed singing her farewell 'Givin' Up' in a dingy blues club – cut to Sparkle's tearful funeral dedication 'Lead Me On'. After these events the characters (and the movie) never really seem to recover. Dolores delivers a 'for what' eulogy on domestic black liberation and departs, leaving Sparkle, who has lost her sister, career and man in one fell swoop, to contemplate her lot. She does, however, eventually listen to Mama and yields to Stix (who has returned to work at a record company) and his pleas for her to give stardom one final shot (he was always primarily interested in developing her vocal talents).

Whilst some of Mayfield's score is used in background – the drug bust, prison and club scenes and liberally throughout the movie – a couple more songs would have made Sparkle's transition from nervous studio falterings to full blown star, supporting Ray Charles at Carnegie Hall, a little more convincing. To initiate these events Stix borrows $10,000 from Mama's Long Island employers, (who, surprise, surprise, turn out to be mob connected) to finance the recording of 'Look Into Your Heart' a song that takes them to the very top of the pops. When time comes for payback plus interest, the mob, smelling big money, move in, wanting a larger slice of the impending cake. This is deal that Stix naïvely refuses, busying himself with the next big event in Sparkle Williams ascent to stardom. During her Carnegie appearance, Sparkle débuts with 'Loving You Baby', intercut with Stix abduction and chastisement by a mobster heavy. He survives this ordeal to return (only slightly dishevelled) in time to see Sparkle perform their hit 'Look Into Your Heart' to an enchanted audience but even this great song cannot prevent a disappointing conclusion to this promising movie.

Sparkle, the movie, shows signs of outside interference and the consequent editing at times diversely affects the continuity and credibility of the storyline. It had all the right ingredients, Sam O'Steen's slick direction, good central performances and especially fine music but it lacked something and consequently did not do well on its release. Although the movie did not break any box office records *Sparkle* was one of the earliest to attempt the telling of the 'church to the charts' story from the black point of view in the pop/soul context. This was done later in other movies like *The 5 Heartbeats* ('91), *The Temptations* ('98) and in the Broadway musical *Dreamgirls* (which borrowed heavily from *Sparkle*). Incidentally the movie was produced by RSO who would distribute Curtom through their record company between '79 and '80.

Reviewer and author Donald Bogle (*Toms, Coons, Mulattoes, Mammies and Bucks*/Roundhouse Publishing '94) wrote that *Sparkle* began its career as a box-office ugly duckling but blossomed into a swanlike *Rocky Horror* hit among black highschoolers in the late '70s and early '80s – precursing Broadway hit *Dreamgirls*. It also inspired Aretha Franklin to record an album of its songs. It's easy to see why. The movie's music is by the way too cool Curtis Mayfield, who scored the first real cult film of the 1970s black America – *Superfly*.

If the movie's poor showing gave the cast a headache, then what was their response to Warner's pulling the soundtrack album and taking the unprecedented step of replacing it with a cover version by Aretha Franklin – despair one would suppose. It must have been shattering for them and possibly robbed McKee and Cara of a hit album that would have been good for both them and Curtom. Whatever Mayfield's feelings were on this question (he kept them to himself), it must have been an honour to work with Aretha Franklin, who he had first met as they had toured America early in their careers. After ten years at the top Aretha and her hit producer had fallen out of step – her most recent Atlantic album *You* had only notched #86 on the LP chart (in November '75). Franklin was desperate to turn her fortunes around and interviews at the time indicated that she too was delighted to be working with Curtis. Like the original soundtrack, her *Sparkle* was also recorded at Curtom Studios with the same musicians, orchestrations by Rich Tufo and all songs composed and produced by Curtis. The Kitty Haywood Singers supplied the excellent background vocals and the finished product was promoted by Atlantic as the soundtrack album.

Sparkle (Atlantic 18176) begins with the title track that was not actually used in the movie. It is a classic Mayfield song that he re-cut himself a year later. Aretha's version has more gospel flavour than his but both records are equally great and it confirms just what an inspired coupling this album was. 'Something He Can Feel', one of the strongest songs from the movie, became a hot single for Franklin, going to #1 R&B/28 pop where it stayed for four weeks in May '76, becoming her biggest hit for two years. En Vogue also had a huge hit with this song in September '92 as 'Giving Him Something He Can Feel' (#1 R&B/6 pop) and it's clear that they had been influenced by the *Sparkle* album, because they also cut the following track 'Hooked On Your Love' for their own *Funky Divas* album. It was passed over at the time as an A-side for Aretha due to the drug references but her powerful treatment makes it another great standout track. Atlantic did issue the equally superb 'Look Into Your Heart', which went to #10 R&B/82 pop in January '77. This was the most featured song in the movie, performed twice by Irene Cara. Aretha adds a little more intensity to Mayfield's poetic lyrics but sadly it made little impression on American pop record buyers. 'I Get High' was presumably cut from the movie for reasons as yet unrevealed. It is a commentary on the downward spiral of 'Sister' on drugs, similar in context to the bluesy 'Givin' Up' used in the movie but omitted from this album. 'Jump' became the second single to be culled from this set and reached #17 on the R&B charts in September '76 but created no pop interest at all. Aretha, not hindered by script limitations (this was performed early in the movie at the group's first appearance) was free to reinterpret, and gave it her full treatment, a right that she had always felt free to take in her musical makeovers of the past like Ben E King's 'Spanish Harlem' and 'Don't Play That Song', and Otis Redding's

'Respect'. It is a track that could stand an even heavier funk reading but both of these versions are just fine as they stand. 'Loving You Baby' rolls along comfortably with effortless expression by Franklin of the pure and simple Mayfield ballad. 'Rock With Me' was another of the songs that was either cut from, or not used in the final edit of the movie. It is a slightly coded plea to get down and boogie and provides a good high mood on which to finish the album.

As if we needed it, Mayfield proved once again that he was the ideal writer and producer for the contemporary female voice. With Aretha's powerful and distinctive vocal approach she made these great songs her own and *Sparkle* put her right back on top when it went to #18 on the US album chart in June '76. It provided her next gold album and was her biggest hit for over two years. Rhino re-issued *Sparkle* on CD in '92 after En Vogue's hit revival of Aretha's single. Both Franklin and Mayfield fans considered the album a classic. In her autobiography written with David Ritz, *From These Roots* (Villard Books '99), Aretha revealed that unknown to her, Curtis had already offered the *Sparkle* songs to her sister Carolyn and that this problem was only resolved by the intervention of their father the Rev C L Franklin. The final results of the Curtis/Aretha sessions produced one of her favourite albums. She considers *Sparkle* and *Almighty Fire* (see Chapter 8), the two albums made with Mayfield, who she calls 'The black Bach', highlights in her career.

However, not all of Curtis' soundtracks found the same level of success. His next project, *Short Eyes* (aka Slammer, '77), is a serious movie based on a serious play, written by Miguel Pinero, which deals with child abuse, a subject that because of its sensitivity has perhaps excluded this movie from a more general appreciation. The storyline of the movie though told in a prison setting, parallels the rush to judgment of the moral majority in cases like this, which have been highlighted in recent years by the media who sometimes seem locked on to paedophilia in some sad 'ratings booster' fascination, without ever finding anything constructive to say.

As a movie *Short Eyes* is an uncompromisingly realistic and powerful story, shot in a NYC men's detention house known as the Tombs. 'Do Do Wap Is Strong In Here' is probably the best-known song from this movie. It was a US Top 30 R&B hit single for Curtis in October '77, right after the movie's American début. The album was cut in Chicago at Curtom Studios and employed the talents of Richard Tufo as arranger for the by then famous Curtom house band. They provide their usual excellent support for Mayfield as he winds his way through the remaining seven songs on the album. The second cut is 'Back Against The Wall' an atmospheric piece that relates the hopeless desperation of long-term incarceration. 'Need Someone To Love' is an interesting re-write of 'I Can't Wait No Longer' previously recorded by the Impressions and Billy Butler and a very popular song in Jamaica. The more frantic 'A Heavy Dude' and the title track 'Short Eyes'/'Freak, Freak, Free, Free, Free' relate the storyline of the movie, which revolves around the star Bruce Davison, who plays a child molester on the wrong end of rough justice. 'Freak, Free...' is the instrumental second part of the song. 'Break It Down' tells of the deprivation of life in a jar and is the only non-Mayfield song. 'Another Fool In Love' has a universally applicable theme whether inside or outside and 'Father Confessor' instrumentally brings the album to its conclusion.

As an album *Short Eyes* (CU 5017) was the first Curtis Mayfield album to fail on the charts. Like the movie, it completely missed its audience and this was nothing short of a disaster for Curtom and Mayfield, who had not only appeared in his first dramatic role (as Pappy) but had invested a large amount of money, time and energy into the project. Tex Mex rock and roller Freddy Fender also had a small part in this movie and there had been some press speculation of a spin off project with Curtis writing and Freddy recording some of his songs but if their coming together did transpire, it has yet to make an impression on the rest of us.

Meanwhile, such was the success of First Artists production of *Let's Do It Again* that Cosby and Poitier looked around for another vehicle to complete their movie trilogy partnership and came up with *A Piece Of The Action* ('77). They put together a good cast that included James Earl Jones, Denise Nicholas, Hope Clark, Tracy Reed, Titos Vandis and Ja'net Dubois. Using much the same format as previously employed, Bill and Sidney played a pair of wealthy thieves who are blackmailed by James Earl Jones, a retired cop, into making active contributions to a community centre for ghetto kids, detained there by the juvenile court. Though well intentioned, the movie's overall sociological message is blunted by an attempt to make it broader entertainment. Despite the engaging performances all around, today this movie (in this form) would have gone straight to video. It has been screened on TV less than the others and is consequentially the least memorable of the trilogy. Mayfield produced and wrote the soundtrack for *A Piece Of The Action* (CU 5019), which was recorded as usual at Curtom with the regular studio support of Rich Tufo, Quinton Joseph, Henry Gibson and Gary Thompson plus the added talents of Keni Burke and Gil Askey. Mavis Staples supplied all the vocals on these sessions.

'Chocolate City' the soundtrack's opening cut, is an upbeat side that Mayfield co-wrote with Tufo, Burke, Joseph and Gibson, using Curtom background singers to provide the support that the Staples would normally supply. The song's lyrics explore the limited possibilities for kids growing up in the 'modified ghetto' of the era that was imperceptibly better than before or since. 'Of Whom Shall I Be Afraid' is a sensitive question that Curtis poses and trawls his own childhood memories in an attempt to answer. The ballad is beautifully handled by Mavis, whose vocal treatment matches the mood perfectly. Deeper issues are again touched on with 'Orientation' a midtempo song that the movie itself doesn't fully explore. The only single taken from this album was the title track 'A Piece Of The Action', which only went to #47 R&B in November '77 and did not manage to break the album/movie to a wider pop audience. It was not as immediately commercial as the Staples' *Let's Do It Again* singles, though it is still the most accessible song in this set. Written for the love scenes 'Good Lovin' Daddy' and "Til Blossoms Bloom' are ballads pleading for longterm attention, the latter co-written with Gil Askey. The abstract lyrics and controlled electric distortion of 'Koochie, Koochie, Koochie' provide some interest but the film's only instrumental 'Getting Deeper' works best in the movie. The soundtrack content is more serious than that of the movie and may have been 'lightened up' and consequently fell short of its expectations.

The Blaxploitation genre had run its course by the end of the '70s, at least as far as mainstream interest was concerned. The next black new wave in American cinema emerged seven years later, with directors Spike Lee, the brothers Wayans and Robert Townsend at the helm. In contrast to Blax, this new genre attempted to articulate a more mature view of the black American experience and its aspirations. By the '90s, black cinema had grown in popularity to a point where it paralleled and then moved to the centre of mainstream interest, discussing and examining its cultural achievements and contributions to all aspects of life and art, while at the same time providing real glimpses of the black American experience in the ghetto/hood.

Keenen Ivory Wayans made a movie that was to draw a line under Blaxploitation, *I'm Gonna Git U Sucka* ('88) that was, some say, a belated but merciless and complete send up of the genre. Wayans wrote, directed and starred in this enjoyable spoof and the soundtrack was co-ordinated by David Michael Frank, with one track from Curtis. The action takes place in 'Any Ghetto USA' where Sergeant Jack Spade returns from the army only to learn that his younger brother 'Dune Bug' had OG'd (the shame of it) and vows revenge on the perpetrator Mr Big (John Vernon). Brother Damon (Lenny) and George James play Mr B's incompetent heavies, who turn up at the Spade household demanding the $5000 that the crime boss insists they now owe him. But Mama (Ja'net Dubois) kicks butt when they try to take daughter-in-law Cheryl, in part payment. This is serial runnin' gags and Wayans leaves no cliché unturned, whilst he recruits John Slade (Bernie Casey), Slam (Jim Brown), Hammer (Ike Hayes) and Kung Fu Joe (Steve James in a hilarious spoof Jim Kelly role). The movie is awash with machismo, attitude and blackness references, bad stunt doubles, the love/veg generation, pimp duds and 'nuff guns. Mayfield's only musical contribution, 'He's A Fly Guy', runs behind Antonio Fargas' (Fly Guy) amusing exit from the slammer, complete with aquarium heels. Needless to say, the five heroes go up against Mr B with rather predictable but nevertheless comic results. There are special appearances from Jester Hairston, Clu Gulager, Fishbone, BDP and the family Wayans, who all make positive contributions to this enjoyable movie. This movie was also significant because it changed established perceptions of the Blaxploitation genre and it provided a much broader and less threatening persona that allowed the considerable back catalogue to be represented with an emphasis on the humour both intentional and otherwise.

The soundtrack album to *I'm Gonna Git You Sucka* (Arista AL 8574) credits Keenen Ivory Wayans as Executive Producer. Mayfield spoke about his contribution to the soundtrack on his UK summer tour in '88, it sounded like a large project when he said: 'We're also preparing a new movie score, which, I believe, will star Jim Brown and Ike Hayes called "I Mo Git U Sucka". It's a very funny satire in the style of *Airplane* and is an Ivory Wayans production.' Curtis cut 'He's A Fly Guy' with Fishbone at Curtom Studios in Atlanta and he co-produced it with David Kahne. Two years later he issued an alternative version that he had re-cut for his *Take It To The Streets* album (see Chapter 11), which also included his version of 'I Mo Git U Sucka' and gave him writer's credits, instead of N Whitfield/W Bryant II, who had 'allegedly' written the Gap Band's version, used in the movie.

Curtis's last soundtrack was the sequel to his greatest success, *Superfly*. The bang-bang start to *The Return Of Superfly* ('90) via the streets of New York City and the brutal murder of Priest's ex-partner Eddie are our introduction to this movie. Sensibly, Mayfield resisted the temptation to write 'Eddie's Dead' and instead opens up with the title song, which he cut with Mr Constantly Cool, rapper Ice-T, 'Superfly 1990'. We catch our first glimpse of Priest (this time played by Nathan Purdee) at the airport, tangled up in customs. This time our hero is offered a shitty deal by 'the man' before he gets out of the air terminal. We see a more laid back, mature Priest, now the owner of a legitimate business in Paris, who has been lured back to the jungle of the New York streets to enact one final ritual – revenge.

Samuel L Jackson makes an all too brief appearance as Cabot but is wasted as an early victim, in the senseless slaughter that drugs enforcers (this time it's crack) inflict in their search for the elusive Priest. This movie is a predictable cocktail of bent cops and councillors, hookers and heavies and though director Sig Shore took much from the original movie, he added little to make this saga any easier to swallow – 18 years down the line. Anyhow, Priest with the help of Willie 'Nitro' Green (Tico Wells) sets about taking down drugs czar Hector's operation. Eventually after mucho boom-boom, to which Curtis wrote the appropriate 'Showdown' that fits perfectly into the mayhem, Priest's quest is complete. He makes a hasty exit, with lady Francine (Margaret Avery) back to the relative sanity of Paris to the strains of 'For The Love Of You', a simple Mayfield ballad that takes us through rather more of the end titles, than we perhaps would normally have endured.

The album *Return Of Superfly* (Capitol CDP 79 42442) was released shortly after his tragic accident in August 1990. 'Superfly 1990' was the first track, performed by Curtis and Ice-T in a great duet. Mayfield's lyric fills out the flesh of Priest's character, as the duo's contrasting vocal techniques interplay perfectly and the two sides of our hero's persona are revealed. Synthetic sirens hang in the air, creating an atmosphere of tension and expectation and the guitar licks (courtesy of Lenny Kravitz, who also takes a production credit) add an extra bonus. The clear sincerity of Mayfield's lead vocal is the perfect counter to Ice-T's cynicism from the shadows. It is Curtis back to his best, performed with a confidence and an urgency that had been missing for some time.

After a lengthy break from recording, Curtis had relaunched Curtom and found his musical feet once more. There are a host of mixes and versions of this song, but just two were used in the movie, the title track and the instrumental 'hip hop' version. As a single, the song was released in the UK on 7in and 12in vinyl and also as a CD single 'Superfly 1990' (CDCL 586), with four different mixes. This single accentuates the technical changes that Mayfield had been evolving through since getting back into the Curtom Studios in '88. It's hard to keep up with the variety of different mixes, but there is something unique about each one of them. 'The Mantronix Mix' features a rap chorus, with some alternate lyrics for Ice-T, as he puts the retribution to the reason of Mayfield's original vocal track. The 'Fly Mix' is more frantic with insistent percussion and scratch but the 'Bonus Mix' (not issued on the 12in), even without vocals, is a great piece of entertaining afterthought, with additional production and mixing by Bilal Bashir. Though Mayfield was rightly credited with the theme for this soundtrack, other music was recorded, produced and used without his influence. The album features Rap music from Easy Street, Tone Loc, Mellow Man Ace, CPO and Def Jef. These contributions work better with the action scenes but tend to distract from the dialogue (such as it is), when used as a theme.

An unexpected highlight is the Uzi Bros 'There's A Riot Jump Off', that uses Coasters' samples (taken from their 'Riot In Cell Block #9', recorded in LA as the Robins in '54) as its inspiration and is the best of the rap trax, with great production by Will Griffin. Mayfield's 'Showdown', which accompanies the explosive interlude, has a rap flavour to it, with a great synthesizer/horns sound. Taken out of context this cut can be heard as a warning song, given the writer's track record. 'Forbidden' features plenty of creative percussion (echoes of Master Henry Gibson) and its hypnotic groove brings jungle beats to the traffic sound and tempo of the inner city. 'For The Love Of You' is a ballad that Curtis might have written at any time in the past 20 years, for any of his albums, but for the production – which is where all the changes come. Presumably all the Mayfield tracks were cut and mixed at Curtom Studios in Atlanta, before reaching Tim Devine and Morey Alexander who took Executive Production credits for the soundtrack. Had the *Return Of Superfly* been a better movie, this album could have been a big hit for all those concerned and, with more exposure, the music that had developed in all kinds of positive directions could have found a more appreciative audience. As things stand now, it will unfortunately always be compared with Mayfield's original *Superfly* score that as a classic will generally be preferred.

Almost all of the movies that Curtis Mayfield wrote a soundtrack for fall into the generally accepted category of 'Blaxploitation', a term that was coined after the period during which they were made ('71–'79). There are many writers, actors and directors who feel that this term, as a description of a black film movement is dismissive, derisory and inappropriate. It is their opinion that the term doesn't accurately describe the number of films (estimates vary between 200 and 400) made on a wide variety of subjects by all the major Hollywood studios, with enough breath or clarity. There have been reports of bitterness of any involvement from leading figures like the star of *Superfly* Ron O' Neal (a classically trained actor) who has stated that he is ashamed of this work, which he wants no further associations with and that Blaxploitation wrecked his acting career. It seems even he misunderstood the anti-drugs messages in *Superfly* and what a forceful indictment of the hard drugs lifestyle it really was. The highly respected American movie reviewer Leonard Maltin calls the film 'Morally dubious' and there were many other reviewers and critics that had a lot worse things to say. *Superfly* will always be a source of argument and conflicting opinions, that as time goes by can only strengthen the anti-drug lobby through Mayfield's song lyrics and their reinterpretations.

Tim Gordon of *The Entertainment Show* on the WOL-AM Newstalk Network, Washington, hosted a radio discussion show that dealt with the Blaxploitation issue in the autumn of '98, as part of the launch of the latest book on the subject *What It Is...What It Was!* (by Gerald and Diana Martinez and Andres Chavez). This excellent book makes full use of the poster art of the period (from the collection of Ron Finley) in its large format to describe and discuss the black film explosion of the '70s. One prominent phone-in guest was Gerry Martinez, publisher/designer of Rolling Thunder Books (published through Miramax and Hyperion) who made significant graphic contributions to movies like *Pulp Fiction* and *Jackie Brown*. Another phone-in guest was co-author Andres Chavez. Chavez mooted that the civil rights movement of the '60s and '70s developed an appetite amongst the black communities in America for heroes of their own. Martinez talked about the power that these black heroes displayed as being symbolic of the individual empowerment that they represented in the eyes of their black audience. Everybody has their opinions and whatever they are it would be foolish to try to change a logo that has already been sold.

So what exactly was a Blaxploitation movie and what wasn't – and do all black movies made in the '70s automatically fall into this category and does anybody connected to the movie/music business really care as long as there is money to be made...? Was Blaxploitation really a film movement, or was this work the result of yet another update of the 'budget line' movies format, devised by the Hollywood studios to create cheap B-movies and shorts that were used to garnish the main features of the time? Similar to the low budget formats that created the 'Exploitation' movies of the '30s, the 'Hard Boiled Detective' movies of the '40s, the 'Noir' cheapies of the '50s and the 'Spaghetti Westerns' of the '60s. Wasn't it the style and spirit of these movie genres that also created their cult followings? In most cases, the music created for these formats also played a big part in their popularity. Would it be cynical to suggest that 'Blaxploitation' was just another phony classification dreamed up by some hack to repackage a group of movies to a wider audience through cable TV and video?

The discussion of the Blaxploitation genre above has only superficially touched on the history of the black cinema. There are far too many actors, directors and writers who deserve a more detailed exploration than this opportunity allows. For those interested in further and more detailed reading on the subject I recommend – Darius James' book *That's Blaxploitation* (St Martin's Griffin '95), *What It Is... What It Was!* written by Gerald and Diana Martinez and Andres Chavez (Rolling Thunder Books '98), Donald Bogle's *Toms, Coons, Mulattoes, Mammies and Bucks* (Roundhouse Publishing '94) *Black Hollywood* by Gary Null (Citadel Press '93) and *Jazz In The Movies* by David Meeker (Talisman '81).

Although Curtis did not produce any more soundtracks, his songs still feature regularly in movies. A number of his songs were used in Spike Lee's *Get On The Bus* ('96), which was made to highlight and celebrate the 'Million Man March' that took place in Washington on 16 October '95. The movie tells the stories of a small group of West Coast black men who fate brings together on a bus ride from south central LA to the capital. *Get On The Bus* was released through Columbia in '96. It was a '15 Black Man Production' who included Wesley Snipes, Danny Glover and Will Smith amongst their number. The original score was written and conducted by Terence Blanchard and produced with Alex Steyermark. The soundtrack album *Get On The Bus* (Interscope IND 90089) featured 'Put Your Heart On The Line' by Michael Jackson and the great James Brown track 'Papa Don't Take No Mess' plus music from Stricktly Difficult, D'Angelo, Maryon Davis, Blackstreet, Guru, Earth, Wind and Fire, Stevie Wonder and God's Property. One of the tracks added late to the project was Curtis Mayfield's 'New World Order', which was released at the time of the movie's completion. Some of his other great civil rights songs had already been included in the movie like 'People Get Ready', 'We're A Winner' and 'Keep On Pushing' but were not used on the album.

Curtis' music has been used on the soundtrack of countless movies other than those already mentioned. 'Pusherman' was used in *Armageddon* ('98) and on the *Crooklyn* ('94) soundtrack. 'Move On Up' turned up in *The Pallbearer* ('96), *Bend It Like Beckham* ('02) and 'If There's A Hell Below', 'Right On For Darkness', 'We People Darker Than Blue' (Live version), 'Keep On Pushing', and 'I Want To Go Back' were used for *Dead Presidents* ('95). His songs also turned up in *Superfly TNT* ('73), *Hairspray* ('88), *Cable Guy* ('96), *Eve's Bayou* ('97), *Friday-Old School* ('95), *Mod Squad* ('99) and are included in many other movies as a matter of routine, and this practice is still ongoing. Documentary and TV programs like *Channels of Resistance* (Noam Chomsky) featured 'People Get Ready' on the soundtrack, *Architecture of the Imagination* used 'Keep On Pushing' and the Muhammad Ali documentary *When Harry Met Ali* featured 'Right On For Darkness' and 'Hard Times'. 'Here But I'm Gone' bubbled under the opening titles of the US TV series *New York Undercover* ('The Reaper' episode). Mayfield's best-known UK anthem 'Move On Up' was the theme to a series of Thames Ford Dealers TV commercials in the early '90s. This song title was also used as a strap line in MVC's 'Motown 40' press ad campaign. Mayfield's music is everywhere and often where you least expect to hear it.

With the ongrowing interest in Blaxploitation many more of the soul soundtracks gradually became available in the UK. Of the movies that Curtis Mayfield has been involved with, only a few are available here. *Superfly* (Warner Bros SO11138) '96, *Return Of Superfly* (VIA 7522) '92, *I'm Gonna Git U Sucka* (PEV 99699) '89, and *Get On The Bus* (CTV 25200) '96, are the easiest to obtain. *Short Eyes* was allegedly released in the UK but no details have as yet been forthcoming and a search has not yet turned up a single copy.

There are surprisingly few commercial videos that feature Curtis Mayfield or the Impressions for sale in UK Record shops or other outlets. As the video market did not develop until the early '80s it is perhaps a longshot to hope for the release of previous Curtom TV appearances like *Curtis In Chicago* ('73/WTTW-TV). Though it would surely make an excellent document of late '60s soul with virtually unseen performances from Curtis, Jerry, the Impressions (in several incarnations), Leroy Hutson, Gene Chandler and Brenda Lee Eager.

Two videos are available for keen fans. *Brothers and Sisters*, distributed by CBS/Fox Video Ltd/1980 features segments taken from a concert recorded in Chicago during (presumably) the mid '70s plus other earlier footage that looks like it might have come from several sources. Curtis Mayfield appears diminutive, in a white summer suit. He and the band give a good rendition of a 'We People Who Are Darker Than Blue'/'Give Me Your Love' medley. The 'director' intercuts Barb-B-Q and recreational scenes, as fillers while Curtis and the Experience perform their segment. The Chi-Lites, the O'Jays, Isaac Hayes, Zulema, the Jacksons, the Temptations (circa Dennis Edwards), Gladys Knight & the Pips, Marvin Gaye make appearances. Jerry Butler and Brenda Lee Eager are an interesting, though uneasy duo, with their interpretation of Bacharach's 'Close To You'. But this low budget production is disappointing and cannot really be recommended. It is something of a collectable however as it contains rare footage of Curtis performing in his mid 30s. The video highlights only one or two good performances and is badly shot, edited and produced with breathtakingly short appearances by several of the acts. There is nothing here (except for the Curtis and Jerry segments) that you haven't seen so many times before. Some of the footage looks as if it could have been shot elsewhere, then inexpertly bolted on as an afterthought. Those still interested in obtaining this video will have to go to the second hand market, as it is no longer available as new.

The second video, *Live at Ronnie Scott's* (distributed by Castle Communications plc 1988, re-issued in 2000), is an excellent reminder of Mayfield's last great '88 UK tour, shot in London at the late Ronnie Scott's Club. It is easily the best video available in the UK for anyone who wants a record of Curtis performing at his best. His support band featured Buzzy Amato (keyboards), Benny Scott (bass), Luis Stefanell (percussion), and Lee Goodness (drums), who became the successors to the original Experience (renamed Nice Ice then Ice 9), which Mayfield had put together 18 years earlier.

This line-up gave superb renditions of their current programme, which included 'Little Child Runnin' Wild', 'It's All Right', 'People Get Ready', 'Pusherman', and 'Freddie's Dead' all performed before a small but enthusiastic audience. The programme is intercut with an interview that Curtis recorded at that time and is well conducted by Mayfield buff Paul Weller. It contains interesting footage with many good shots of memorabilia, photos and album sleeves from earlier in Mayfield's career. 'Billy Jack', 'We Gotta Have Peace' and the ever-popular 'Move On Up' follow 'I'm So Proud'. The final song is the exquisite but still relatively unappreciated 'To Be Invisible', which draws a very satisfactory closure to the evening's entertainment.

This concert was also shown on UK ITV/LWT as part of Mike Mansfield's series 'Cue The Music' in '88 with some editorial differences and without the interview segments, which are only available on the Castle issue. Sequel/Sanctuary issued a repackaged video and CD of this concert in September 2000 with a host of previously unseen photos taken at the gig, the interview with Paul Weller and notes by Peter Doggett and Rob Lemkin Producer/ Director of the video.

Rumour has it that there are a number of bootleg tapes available in the States but these have presumably not made it to the UK due to the format incompatibilities with UK video recorders. Otherwise, no doubt, they would be available at markets and car boot sales up and down the country.

Curtis made two appearances in movies, once performing in *Superfly* and his acting role in *Short Eyes*. He has also made a number of interviews to camera, excerpts of which have turned up in the TV documentaries (see Chapter 12). The videos made to promote his later songs from *New World Order* were not seen in the UK and rarely if ever enter the tape loops on MTV or VH1. You might see an occasional appearance from the *Old Grey Whistle Test* or the *Superfly '90* video but airings have been rare.

10 RSO/Curtom In Decline, '79–'85

RSO began to market and distribute Curtom Records in mid '79, which moved the company into its fourth stage of evolution. Curtom had by now already discarded most of its roster and only three artists – Leroy Hutson, Linda Clifford and Curtis Mayfield – survived into the new set-up. Although the relaunch was well publicized, Curtom took a step down in profile. Their logo still appeared on the records, but smaller than the distributors' logo, and their releases also fell into the RSO numerical sequence. So it then became more difficult for all but the dedicated fans to keep track of all Curtom releases.

After the somewhat disappointing experience of the Curtom/Warner Brothers' alliance, it is easy to see why Curtis Mayfield might be sold on the RSO package. The label's impressive previous success with movies like *Saturday Night Fever* ('77) and singer-songwriters like Eric Clapton and the Bee Gees must have presented a very attractive lure. When Curtom entered the RSO story, they were not to know that spirits had already flown and that the best years were already behind them. Maybe if they had seen *Sgt Pepper's Lonely Heart Club Band*, the Bee Gees' follow-up movie in '78, alarm bells might have sounded, but bad as the movie and the music was, the soundtrack album did go platinum within a year, so any warning signs may not have been entirely clear.

'This Year, This Year' Mayfield's first RSO single seemed to predict a positive new start but in fact after some initial interest it settled at a lowly #40 R&B in March '79 and Curtis was still unable to sustain any pop chart interest. The first RSO/Curtom album issued was Linda Clifford's *Let Me Be Your Woman* (RSO 2.3902), which Gil Askey produced and arranged especially for those induced to dance the night away. Unusually, Curtom appear to have prepared two separate editions of this album. The first and most common edition was a straight-forward single disc but the second was a double album featuring a re-arranged track listing and substantially longer versions of four songs: 'Sweet Melodies', 'Don't Give It Up', 'One Of Those Songs' and 'Bridge Over Troubled Water' – the last two spread across each side of the second disc.

'Bridge Over Troubled Water' was a cranked-up version of the Paul Simon swoon classic, which scored mid 40s success on both charts as a single and sets the tone of this album. The title track 'Let Me Be Your Woman' is a ballad in which Linda pleads for a chance to prove her love. The original gatefold album cover has her bearing her breast to emphasize this point (that must have swamped her in a deluge of offers). 'Don't Give It Up' took Linda to #15 on the R&B singles chart in May '79, providing her second biggest hit. Clifford's lyric is directed at her female audience and highlights her attempts to deal with the machismo, to which she must have been constantly subjected. No doubt the song is written from personal experience but the solution is far from convincing. Curtis Mayfield's reference to 'dancing' in 'Hold Me Close' is a thinly disguised invitation to the sexual act. His wry twist on the lyric gives a whole new definition to the suspended animation of disco dancing as a solo activity and reduces the gap between dancers to that of what the next step really is, thus providing DJs with a perfect last spin of the evening.

Originally a standard ballad, 'One Of Those Songs' receives a disco makeover by Gil Askey's relentless production. The reflection is reduced to that of the moment, on repeat, just great for getting down and abandoning yourself to the beat. Linda takes a breather with 'Don't Let Me Have Another Bad Dream' her self-penned, paranoid ballad to a lover who speaks another woman's name in his sleep. The tempo eases up a notch for 'I Can't Let This Good Thing Get Away', which is an album highlight. Ms Clifford knows when she's got a good thing and here she lets us all know, just why she's not letting it go. 'Sweet Melodies' tempts most of us back on the dancefloor for a medium tempo farewell, so we can witness Curtom's Disco Queen as she dances the night away into the eventual slow fade. RSO got behind the promotion of Clifford's highly marketable image and the record-buying public reacted positively, sending the album to #17 US R&B by March, which then levelled out at a rewarding #26 pop the following month.

Linda's next album *Here's My Love* (3067) sold disappointingly despite a Harris/Tyson, Los Angeles production and topped out at #43 R&B/117 pop in December '79. Only one single, 'I Just Wanna Wanna', was released and went to #36 R&B that November. It perhaps catches the groove better than any of the other tracks of which 'Bailin' Out' gives the most valuable advice, though there is a little respite with the Mayfield-produced title track. Like most of the records made for this genre, these sides sound better on the dancefloor – they don't really pass a passive audio test in either style or content.

New Curtom signing, Gavin Christopher, also cut his disco teeth at this time and RSO issued his début album *Gavin Christopher* (3052). This dance-orientated set of self-penned and self-produced songs was cut in the main at Curtom but without the usual in-house session men. The single 'Feelin The Love', which went to #77 R&B in June '79, was produced by Bobby Eli and cut at Sigma Studios at the same session as 'What Can I Say', 'We're In Love' and 'This Side Of Heaven'. Arrangements were shared by Jump Street and Tom Tom 84 and background vocals were supplied by Ava Cherry and sister Shawn Christopher. Shawn went on to record R&B hits for Larc in '82 and '83. Of the Curtom recordings, 'Takin' Your Love Away' is an OK medium tempo ballad, with horn arrangements from Greg Adams who also provides the brassy edge to the predictable 'Dancin' Up A Storm'. Good keyboards from Gavin, who is quite an accomplished musician and solid session support from 'Tower Of Power' make the midtempo 'Lady Mysterious' quite enjoyable. 'We'll Always Be Together' is a slow growing ballad, which takes a few plays to really connect but shades as being the best track on this set. Christopher comes closest to west coast funk with 'Be Your Own Best Friend', which was his R&B blueprint for self-preservation in the music business of the time. The album didn't chart but was a bright introduction to a promising new talent.

Meanwhile, *Heartbeat* (3053), Mayfield's first album for RSO, was something of a departure in many ways. For the first time, Curtis put himself almost entirely in the hands of other producers and writers to create the project. Even though artistically *Do It All Night* had been a disaster, it was still his biggest album for three years, so the makeover continued. Mayfield retained some control as Executive Producer but he delegated three tracks to Bunny Sigler and two more to Norman Harris and Ronnie Tyson, another hot Philly production team, whilst producing just three cuts himself at Curtom. The other two studios used were Sigma Sound, Philadelphia and Kendun Recorders in Burbank. The first track 'Tell Me, Tell Me (How Ya Like To Be Loved)' though very commercial, was not used as a single. It has the irritating instant recall of a jingle and therefore could have possibly garnered some chart action. The Sigler-produced 'What Is My Woman For' is a little better with the added infectious arrangement by funkster Fred Wesley.

'Between You Baby And Me', the first commercially inspired coupling from Curtis and Linda, was the only track selected as a single and went high into the R&B charts, settling at #14 in August '79. It still rather surprisingly failed to win back Mayfield's pop following, which, by rights, it should have done. The Askey arrangement embraces the believable intimacy achieved, but the song borders on saccharine like 'I'm So Proud' and other similar vehicles of the past. 'Victory' takes us back to the music machine as Curtis sounds a touch hollow reciting the Harris/Tyson lyrics. 'Over The Hump' and 'You Better Stop' put us back in the hands of Bunny Sigler and Fred Wesley, which are a little pedestrian and are easily eclipsed by the last two tracks on the album, both Curtom productions. 'You're So Good To Me' comes out easily as the best track on this album. It is a ballad delivered in the familiar relaxed Mayfield mode and was flipside of the most recent single that deservedly earned independent airplay and was popular enough to get its own placing of #46 R&B in December '79, whilst the topside's success made it a pilot for the later Curtis/Linda duet album.

'Heartbeat' must have been considered for the next single release but was passed over in favour of 'Between You Baby And Me'. Whatever soul fans think of this set, the album's improved sales provided a welcome restoration for Curtis and provided his biggest hit for quite sometime. Whether Curtis was labouring under the illusion that he needed to stay contemporary or not, this album struck a sound commercial chord at the time on the chart. But the real Mayfield fans would have to wait until his next solo album before he was to regain his own higher level of artistry. *Heartbeat* went to #17 R&B/42 pop on the July '79 album charts and restored to Curtis some of the commercial credibility that he had been steadily losing in recent years.

Leroy Hutson also finally fell in step with the tempo of the time and place, when he recorded *Unforgettable* (3062) his only RSO album in which he went disastrously disco, trashing a Nat King Cole classic on the way. This earned an 'Unforgivable' tag from hardcore fans of the time. Yes it is the worst track on the album (and possibly Hutson's all-time worst) but '(You Put The) Funk In My Life', is a shade easier to listen to (if the engine of percussion and bass can be distanced) and also has some fun studio clichés mixed into it, yet probably didn't reach enough fans in destination clubland either. Leroy thankfully returned to his own established persona for 'Right Or Wrong', which was released as his only RSO single in November '79 and went to #47 R&B: it remains his last stateside chart entry to date. 'So Nice' and 'Lonely Without You' maintain the relaxed mood but 'More Where That Came From' is perhaps the most memorable track from the album and was used again on later Hutson compilations. The quite tastefully packaged *Unforgettable* was released in October '79 and climbed to #62 on the R&B album chart. Though generally this is seen as Hutson's worst album, there are still some highlights worth preserving, but that title track 'Unforgettable' should be wiped from the collective consciousness.

One of the bright new artists that Marv Stuart signed to Curtom during this period was Ava Cherry, who recorded her first solo album at both Curtom and Sigma Studios, in the latter months of '79. Bobby Eli produced most of *Ripe* (3072) with Curtis and Gil Askey picking up three tracks between them. Like all but one of the Curtom/RSO albums from this period, it is designed for the dancefloor but Eli does produce some listenable midtempo disco tracks and 'I Just Can't Shake The Feeling' as a single went to #79 R&B in May 1980. 'Love Is Good News' was, in fact, Ava's first Curtom single, and this Mayfield-written/produced ballad had sold well reaching #39 R&B three months earlier. The other

Curtis song featured here is the uptempo 'You Never Loved Me' on which Ava gives good voice. Considering these were among her first solo sides she comes over with assured confidence and ease with 'I'm Always Ready', 'Single Woman, Married Man', which sharply articulates stolen moments in a lonely lifestyle and 'Gimmie Your Lovin'' that moves us from statement to final demand and says it all in the title. The final track is the regrettable 'Where There's Smoke There's Fire', which is a clockwork, burnt out cliché. A track like this only fulfills the low lyrical expectations of the genre where, in far too many cases, one shallow idea on repeat seems to be all that was required. *Ripe* came in a fast sleeve with good photographs of the sexually alluring Miss Cherry taken by Stan Malinowski.

Ava, prior to this album's release, had gained some notoriety via the gutter press who trumpeted and made famous her romantic attachment with David Bowie. But as *Blues & Soul* Editor Bob Killbourn remarked in his interview on the eve of Cherry's first UK tour, 'The lady merits somewhat more than that.' She was discovered by Stevie Wonder, who used her talents at Motown until '72, when she left to join Bowie's European tour. Ava stayed with Bowie's road show for six years but also recorded with other artists like Rufus and John Lennon before joining Stomu Yamashta's Go Band as lead singer for a short period. She embarked on her quest for solo stardom initially at Curtom. Statistics reveal that *Ripe* made good chart progress and levelled off at #48 in the US R&B charts by February 1980 but it made a much bigger noise in the disco charts where it reached as high as #5. This success was no doubt instrumental in gaining Ava a nomination in *Cashbox's* 'Best New Female Category' later that year. The album when released in the UK went to #46 on the soul LP chart, only six places lower than *Heartbeat* and one above Linda Clifford's *Here's My Love*. Her solo career was off to a bright start but events behind the scenes at RSO were soon to put a dent in Ava Cherry's upward momentum.

Mayfield's next album *Something To Believe In* (3077) was recorded and produced with Gil Askey at Curtom. For established Mayfield fans this was very good news, as the essence of Curtis Mayfield was once more on the rise and this album turned out to be his best for some time.

Curtis also briefly reunited with ex-Stairstep and bassman extraordinaire Keni Burke, who had recently been trying to carve a solo career for himself despite his shaky start at Dark Horse Records. In addition to his excellent studio work on Curtom Productions during this time, Keni also collaborated with Curtis on one song for this album. 'Never Stop Loving Me' is a superb midtempo ballad, which Keni recorded himself later on RCA. *Something...* begins with 'Love Me, Love Me Now', a blatantly commercial Gil Askey production, which did big business in clubland USA but rather surprisingly peaked at #48 on the R&B chart, with no pop action in June 1980. It was Curtis strongest single since 'Only You Babe' and supplied a positive upbeat start to the album. For the second track, Mayfield reached back 26 years for a song originally recorded by Johnny Ace and revived by the Impressions in '62. This beautiful ballad 'Never Let Me Go', a song that had still lost none of its doo wop roots, remained a constant favourite with Mayfield and the other Impressions, who had featured it for many years in their stage act. 'Tripping Out' was used as a single and went to #46 R&B in September '80. Bunny Sigler wrote this love song using the parlance of the soft drug culture, which 20 years on sounds a curious mixture of quaint and hip. But it has proved popular with CD compilers in recent years. 'People Never Give Up' is a powerful reaffirmation of faith, in a similar mode to other great Mayfield songs of faith and resolve. This lesser-known anthem plumbs more personal depths and perhaps comes closest to what makes Curtis tick. It is a riveting performance, a sensitive piece of poetic insight that articulates perfectly the writer's unwavering personal resolve to overcome all obstacles with dignity and a positive attitude.

For 'It's Alright', once again Curtis used another of his vintage Impressions hits. On this version, two of the Mayfield children, Todd and Sharon, sing Fred and Sam's original parts in a style that acknowledges the song's gospel roots. The segue with 'Amen' and the call and response style used provides this track with its own historical identity and takes nothing away from the original version. 'Something To Believe In' explores the common need for faith in something or someone, which makes it all the more relevant today in these increasingly troubled times when western society seems to have substituted desire for faith. This message 'A thought that may assure in the times of self sacrifice' sadly highlights what has currently become the way of life, for even more people than it was back then, when the song was written. As with many Mayfield songs, it seems timeless and now serves to reflect the steady decline of the true democratic values in Western sociological attitudes over the past 20 years. It is an exquisite record, perfectly framed in the understated production and an almost spiritual arrangement. Like all great art, it can be heard and interpreted on several levels, the sentiments apply equally well to religious, domestic, political and romantic scenarios. This is Mayfield at the apex of his artistic powers.

Whether a different marketing and design approach could have sold this remarkable album to a wider and more responsive audience can now only be conjecture. The cover RSO used was an illustration by Ernie Barnes, whose work was also used on other albums of that period like Marvin Gaye's *I Want You*. In this case, however, it seems a particularly inappropriate choice and did nothing for the package but misrepresent it. *Something To Believe In* should have registered improved chart placings on *Heartbeat* but it sank back to #26, which were still reasonable R&B sales, but could only manage #128 on pop albums in June 80. This must have been deeply disappointing for all those concerned with the creation and production of this superb album.

Due to the R&B success of Curtis and Linda's duo hit 'Between You Baby And Me', which went to #14 on the chart in July '79, Mayfield and Clifford recorded an album together, *The Right Combination* (3084), during the following year. Between them they spun a delicious concoction of candyfloss starting off with 'Rock You To Your Socks' a track that was infectious enough to be a pop single. The magic of their combination is undeniable as they tease and flirt their good-humoured way through this album, enlisting the unwavering support of the Curtom studio talent, plus guests. A Butler Workshop team headed up by Keith Echols supplied the title song, 'Right Combination'. It's an easy-on-down ballad that rolls along effortlessly and features the subtle saxophone work of Sonny Seals. There is much spirited banter from the duo as they reflect perfectly off each other with obvious natural enjoyment, which communicates to and involves the listener.

Mayfield reaches back 16 years for 'I'm So Proud', an Impressions classic, and tries a new version for the third track. The problem with re-recording old classics (even if they are your own) is that unless you're presenting an alternative version, they rarely compare favourably with the original. Especially when that original, has already achieved its own true premier league status. Having said that, this version lacks no conviction or sincerity and is itself a pleasant listening experience.

'Ain't No Love Lost' was also done before, by Curtis (and Patti Jo) for *Sweet Exorcist*. This downside ballad seems a little misplaced within this celebration of togetherness but, that aside, as an individual piece it works really well. In the original vinyl format 'It's Lovin' Time', the only track recorded at Sigma under the control of Norman Harris, kicked off the second half. Despite disco influences, the team holds things together well and there are enjoyable moments, but this track wears least well of those included here and runs too long. 'Love's Sweet Sensation' was the second single taken from this set and climbed to #34 R&B in June 1980. It's an appealing slowish ballad, which fits right in with the album's concept. The cross talk works very well and adds spice to the positive atmosphere: it deserved to do better as a single. 'Between You Baby And Me', though it was Curtis and Linda's biggest hit single, also failed to find the pop audience it was designed for. Why this was, considering its obvious appeal, is hard to fathom. It is marginally the best song on the album. As a single it was a sizeable R&B hit in America, going to #14 R&B in August '79 but in the UK it went by virtually unnoticed, as did the album itself. 'You're So Good To Me' taken from *Heartbeat* and used as the single's flipside could easily have been recut as a duo.

The *Right Combination* was released in May '80 and went to #57 on the R&B album chart in the following month, yet despite its commercial bias it only registered at #180 on Billboard's album charts. It really deserved to be a much bigger popular hit. The album is short, only seven tracks, and leaves you wanting. It might have been considered better value had there had been a couple more tracks included. The sleeve was OK but really did not enhance the package effectively – it is too superficially clinical and misrepresents the warmth and affection of the music contained within. *Right Combination* compares favourably with

Delicious Together, the famous Jerry Butler and Betty Everett duet album. It is doubtful, however, that it will ever enjoy the kind of classic status that *Delicious…* does, though technically it is a much better album and contains excellent performances from an ensemble that includes Keni Burke, Henry Gibson and Sonny Seals.

After almost five years away from touring, Mayfield went back out on the road, but this time as a duo with Linda Clifford. Their singles had been doing quite well on the R&B charts and it was time to get behind the album. So Curtis and Linda left Chicago to headline a nationwide tour that autumn. 'We both thought that we'd give Peabo and Natalie some healthy competition,' quipped Curtis in 1980. Linda had recently married and was in the early months of her first pregnancy, but she was fully committed to the tour and to her next album. This was another big opportunity for her as Curtom had engaged soul legend Isaac Hayes to write and produce for her. She had recorded 'Red Light', a song written specifically for the forthcoming hit movie *Fame* on which RSO were releasing the soundtrack. It became her biggest career single when it went to #40 R&B and #41 pop in August '80. So naturally this cut was added to her next album, *I'm Yours* (3087). Ike provided a suitably sharp and commercial production for all the other tracks, which open with 'Shoot Your Best Shot', also a mid '40s R&B single but it made surprisingly few pop sales. The album was recorded in Atlanta and Chicago and comes over as a well-integrated set. Linda seemed in her element and technically handled most of Ike's material very well.

It was lousy luck for Linda that the events at RSO overtook *I'm Yours,* which should have become her biggest hit and perhaps could have launched her to a new level in her career. These were certainly amongst her most appealing and accessible records. It is evident that Hayes had been able to reveal a side of Linda's ability hitherto unexposed. At this point, one feels that she really could have become a contender but fate conspired that it be otherwise. Who knows what she might have accomplished in the hands of a Bacharach or Thom Bell. She cut a very good version of the Mitty Collier classic 'I Had A Talk With My Man', which was about to be released as a single when the RSO label imploded. Curtom temporarily leased its product through Capitol, who issued '…Talk With

My Man', but delays meant the single could not capitalize on the initial exposure and interest it had created. In the end it could only achieve a #53 R&B by December: it should have been a much bigger hit.

Fred Wesley also got his first and last solo hit with RSO/Curtom in June '80 when 'House Party' went to #40 on the R&B singles chart. But he was just passing through. Wesley had scored many hit singles already, for People Records between '72 and '75, the biggest being 'Do It To Death', which went right to the top and also hit #22 pop in May '73. He, like many others including Maceo Parker, had escaped the confines of James Brown's famous JBs, in the mid '70s. Wesley's talents were in much demand for session and performance and his music contributed to George Clinton's P Funk Army, the SOS Band and many others. Fred hit again with The Horny Horns on Atlantic with 'Up For The Down Stroke' in August '77, a remake of Parliament's hit single from '74. His *House Party* album was recorded and promotional copies had been pressed, but RSO/Curtom went down before it got general release, and another one bit the dust. Wesley still got plenty of work with The Horny Horns in their various guises. He teamed again with Maceo, Pee Wee Ellis and Roots Revisited, and still proved popular recording and performing in the jazz/funk venues throughout America. Wesley cut enough tracks to put together a *House Party ('93)* CD issued in the UK by Back Black Records.

In November 1980 Mayfield closed the Curtom label down, making 55 staff redundant, many of whom had been involved since the company's conception in 1968. It must have been a bleak time for all those involved. Curtis retained the Curtom publishing and production companies but sold up the studio complex in Chicago and moved most of his family and business interests to Atlanta. He had bought a house there 15 years earlier. Mayfield set about planning the construction of his new Curtom (II) studios and business suite on a site adjacent to his house, which he planned as a more compact operation in order to spend much more time with his family. Some of his older children stayed in Chicago with his ex-wife. 'I saw the situation as an ideal opportunity to unite all my business and family life in one place. One day soon I hope to reactivate Curtom Records, I still own the name and all the masters and there is some great, as yet unissued music there, that should be released,' Curtis said at the time. The Curtom roster scattered. Linda remained based in Chicago and was now represented by her husband's new Killion Management, who signed her to Capitol.

However, her album sales for *I'll Keep Loving You* were disappointing and neither of the singles charted. In later interviews Linda blamed her new company's apparent lack of promotion. Though Curtom had been unable to fully realize many of her ambitions, it had been through no lack of effort and dedication on their part. They had provided her many opportunities and great support from the best talent available anywhere – Gil Askey, Keni Burke, the Jones Girls, Isaac Hayes and of course Mayfield himself, but she had her moments and for a short period, Linda alone kept Curtom on the charts. Her best album *If My Friends Could See Me Now* went to #22 on the album chart and *Let Me Be Your Woman* did almost as well when it reached #26 in April '79. But none of the other albums that Linda recorded for Curtom, Capitol or later on Red Label made it into the Hot 100. After a couple of minor R&B hit singles, 'A Night With The Boys' and 'Sneakin' Out', record sales dwindled. Linda Clifford had everything: the talent, the voice, the looks, the hits but not it seems the luck to connect and sustain a career in the big time.

Ava Cherry also signed to Capitol and she too also watched an initially promising career slip away, when her singles and the album *Streetcar Named Desire* suffered a similar fate to Linda's. She did make a UK tour in mid '82 but her best moments were behind her on Curtom and, despite much talent and ambition, she dropped from sight, at least as a solo performer.

When Curtis moved out of Chicago, Marv Stuart stayed put but initially continued to act as Mayfield's manager. He set up Gold Coast Records with Richard Tufo who had rescued TTF, a group that he'd been working closely with since they had signed to Curtom in '79. Today, Tomorrow and Forever, who hailed originally from Florida, fall loosely into the soul/groove category. Tufo produced just three singles for them at Curtom. The biggest '(Baby) I Can't Get Over Losing You' went to #21 R&B in June '80. Shortly after Curtom's demise, Tufo produced TTFs 'Mighty Fine', which became a Top 50 R&B single for Gold Coast and led the team on to produce an album together. But they could not add to or improve upon their past success and dropped out of sight.

Mayfield soon signed to Boardwalk Records who were owned and run by Neil Bogart. Boardwalk was Bogart's newest company and had Ringo Starr, Joan Jett, Syl Johnson, Richard 'Dimples' Fields and the recently signed Invisible Man's Band, amongst its roster. Neil Bogart and Curtis had been good friends since their earliest dealings in the mid '60s when Mayfield was then looking for a distributor for Windy C, his first independent label. When Mayfield first came to Boardwalk on a three-album deal, Bogart wanted him to co-produce with Dino Fekaris, whose recent hits had included 'Reunited' with Peaches and Herb and more significantly 'I Will Survive' with Gloria Gaynor, which had gone platinum the previous year. Mayfield said later, 'At the time, I wasn't that hot, so we were looking for a recipe to bring me back. I wasn't entirely happy with the album, to tell the truth, I wanted it to be a lot funkier, but then I suppose that's what Boardwalk were trying to get away from.' Together Dino and Curtis cut the first single 'She Don't Let Nobody But Me', which also became the first cut on the album. It only grazed the Hot 100 at #103 but nevertheless was Mayfield's biggest pop hit for six years, and of course it sold much better on the R&B chart where it went to #15 in September '81. It is hard to see why the record wasn't a huge hit then – but 12 years later, Jamaican duo Chaka Demus and Pliers cover/revival of the song gave them an international hit that reached #4 on the UK pop charts in September '93. 'Toot An Toot An Toot', Mayfield's sideways look at Hollywood social attitudes, was also a medium hit as a single, going to #22 R&B in December '81. Curtis seemed less comfortable with 'Baby Doll', a Fekaris 'take me back' ballad, which lacks a little conviction. Dino also wrote the superb 'Love Is The Place' that gave them the title for the album. This song as the title suggests, celebrates being in the right place with the right person. It's a catchy midtempo foot-tapper, which could also have been a single. 'Just Ease My Mind' is a semi-country piece with a similar feel to 'Dirty Laundry' (that he was yet to cut) and reflects Mayfield's recent easing off in his personal life, and a similar theme can also be read into his 'You Mean Everything To Me'. Fekaris' next song 'You Get All My Love' also fits right in this groove too as Dino explores the other side of the 'I Will Survive' mirror, a maturing appreciation of a steady relationship. 'Come Free Your People' was Mayfield's only excursion into sociology on this album. It is a heartfelt plea against the deterioration of urban life and civil rights. Curtis' suggestions were as positive as ever, looking forward to a better future for everyone.

The photographs by Harry Langdon of Curtis in stylish white hat made an excellent sleeve for *Love Is The Place* (33239) but this desirable package did not sell as well to the pop market as anticipated. The faithful R&B fans were more enthusiastic and took it to a respectable #30 on the R&B album chart in August '81. It was not released in the UK, nor were either of the singles. But in recent years re-issues have appeared on CD both in Japan where JIMCO issued it in a great gatefold CD package and the UK where Sequel released both Boardwalk albums on one great mid-price 2fer. Shortly after the original album's release came the sudden and tragic death, from cancer, of Neil Bogart and Boardwalk fell into disarray. Mayfield had recently had a 24-track facility installed at his new studios and had already begun work on his next album *Honesty*.

Despite their difficulties, Boardwalk did manage to release *Honesty* (33256), Curtis' second album for them. The opening cut 'Hey Baby' was designed as a pop single, but it only managed a lowly #68 R&B when released in October '82. Mayfield multi-tracks his vocal in parts on the excellent 'Still Within Your Heart' – this is one of his recurring themes, which touches 'We're A Winner' territory and keeps on movin' forward. The standout track 'Dirty Laundry' has a slight country flavour to it, but the message is universal. It chronicles the by now familiar political scandals of the time and rang even truer in the UK of the mid '90s. It is another latter Mayfield classic, which should have been released as a single at the time. The team also provide a great arrangement, with a brassy Memphis Horn flavouring for 'Nobody But Me', which rolls along in a positive groove. Experimental stereo movement and sound effects make 'If You Need Me' sound like it has been recorded in an after-hours arcade, whilst the steelband-ish synthesizers and percussion give 'What You Gawn Do' an aboriginal/African/islands mood that Curtis was to revisit later for 'The Got Dang Song' in '96. The signals of change in the direction and evolution of Mayfield's musical development are also clear on 'Summer Hot', the last track he was to record for three years and also the final cut on this album. There are sounds that they created here that quantum arc between 'Get Down' and more recent Mayfield recordings for Warner Brothers.

Tufo's orchestrations and keyboards make significant contributions to this album, and also adding their talents were Joseph 'Lucky' Scott plus Curtis Mayfield III. It was highly acclaimed by the critics and unlike its predecessor found UK release, in March '83. Mayfield got behind it on the road and even made it to the UK, where he loved to tour (but for the weather, which reminded him of some of the worst meteorological aspects of the Windy City). But his stage act only featured older Curtom material and could not have helped the sales of this Epic album released at the time. In America, *Honesty* went to #34 on the R&B album chart but still managed to create insignificant pop interest. In the UK the BBC's long running rock magazine show *The Old Grey Whistle Test* featured an archive clip of Curtis singing 'Keep On Keeping On' (shot circa '72). Mayfield (clad in his camouflage outfit) and the Experience turned in a stunning performance of this classic, which sparkled alongside items from Level 42, the Go-Gos and Meatloaf with intros by Anne Nightingale. This performance has been aired a number of times since in the intervening years both on the BBC and cable TV stations.

When Curtom had closed down, Leroy Hutson had also opted for the chance to spend more time with his young family and had kept his base in Chicago. He had continued to gig and to record his own material and in the autumn of '82 he re-emerged with his new album *Paradise*, this time on *Elektra (9-60141-1)*. The album, his last to date, does not really do him justice on any level except perhaps that of technical musicianship. He had obviously missed the support of Curtom within which he had been able to create and develop a body of unique recordings, which, though they never achieved pop approval, did make their contribution to the soul music legacy of the '70s and influenced many through what exposure they had. This final album was more massage than message but it did reflect the musical state of the time, which was sadly a temporary nadir in soul music. Leroy continued to write, play and record his work for a number of years to come but few of these recordings found any general release, despite the intentions he expressed in his interview with John Abbey, for *Blues & Soul* in October '82, when he said, 'I plan to put together a band – I'll need at least eight musicians to be able to reproduce the kind of sound I want so I won't be rushing anything. I am truthfully not ready yet and I do intend to put a great deal of thought into my next album.' No new album materialized, though it may well have been cut. But Hutson had to settle instead for local hero status, though he did make some UK tours to satisfy his core of fans here.

Expansion Records also released a 12in EP *Shades Of Love* in '92, which contained three songs and a backing track, among them Bacharach's 'The Look Of Love' and two Hutson originals 'Share Your Love' and 'Show Your Love', but label information reveals no clues to the origin or date of these tracks. During the late '80s and early '90s, Leroy's records became very collectable and certain albums demanded unrealistic second hand prices. Ichiban released a 'Best of...' compilation CD entitled *There's More Where This Came From (Curtom 2004)* in '89. Since then several Japanese CD compilations have appeared, and in the UK Charly have gradually re-issued most of his albums plus a couple of compilations of their own. Sequel who obtained the UK license to issue Curtom in '96, also released two *Very Best of...* compilations on their Deep Beats label in late '97/'98 and all his albums plus a singles collection on mid-price two-CD sets throughout '99.

Since Cotillion's reluctance to release the Impressions second album, recorded for them in '77, they continued to tour America, where they were still in big demand. But their interest began to wane and after a number of recording projects had provided no hits and not many releases, they returned home once more to Chicago and to a new deal and subsequent pacting with their old ally Carl Davis' ChiSound label in late '78. They released two albums, *Come To My Party* (T-596) in 1979 and *Fan The Fire* (T-624) in 1981, but eventually ChiSound folded in January '84.

The Impressions however were far from finished. After 11 years with the group, Reggie Torian relinquished his place to Vandy ('Smokey') Hampton, who had spent the past ten years singing with the Soul Majestics and the Chi-Lites. The Impressions still found plenty of steady work on tour, playing revues and often making appearances on gospel TV. The group, which still included Sam, Fred, and Nate Evans, celebrated their silver anniversary in 1983. In the latter part of '82 on his return from a successful UK tour, Curtis, once again linked up with Jerry Butler and the Impressions to create, rehearse and celebrate their silver anniversary with a nationwide US tour (sponsored by Budweiser). According to New Yorkers Pernell Jones and Faith Aarons, who caught the tour at The Beacon Theatre, the programme ran for close to three hours with an intermission. It was staged chronologically with Butler and Mayfield performing their solo hits as well as their leads with the Impressions. In New York, the concert was well attended by an audience predominantly white (approx 60:40) and spanned right across the age groups. The performance was enthusiastically received and got standing ovations and many curtain calls.

Curtis recorded the highspots of the tour and there were rumours that he would be releasing an album of the 'Silver Anniversary Tour', as a follow-up to *We Come In Peace, With a Message of Love* on CRC (Curtom Record Company). (Unfortunately, this promising live album has not yet materialized but the tapes do exist and could still be released by Curtom in the near future).

It's been 15 years since the name of the Impressions featured on Billboard's R&B chart, apart from a solitary MCA 45 'Can't Wait Until Tomorrow', which flitted around the '90s for a fortnight before surrendering to the fast-breaking wave of hip hop and new jack swing in February '87. Sadly, times had really changed for Sam and Fred, and changing tastes forced the 'temporarily closed for business' sign to be hung on the Impressions' recording career, after nearly three decades of making incredible music. Nate had already gone and the group relocated to Atlanta, then a short time later Sam and Fred re-settled in their old hometown of Chattanooga.

And in Chicago, soul music died. Almost every record label, recording studio, venue and club that had once made Chicago one of the most important centres of soul music had changed direction, closed up or moved away from the city.

After the collapse of the Boardwalk label, Curtis Mayfield stopped recording and went into semi-retirement in Atlanta. During the next four years he made few solo appearances, but for the triumphant European tours, which began in '84. BBC2 recorded and screened a live appearance of Curtis and the Experience from his UK tour the following year. It was directed by David G Croft, featuring long established Mayfield favourites like 'Gypsy Woman', 'People Get Ready', 'Superfly', 'Freddie's Dead', 'Move On Up', 'We Gotta Have Peace' and a version of the Lionel Ritchie hit 'All Night Long'. The concert ran for about 40 minutes and was also aired on Radio 1.

Curtis tried to relaunch his recording career again in '85 with 'Baby It's You', that only scored lowish R&B success as a single and *We Come In Peace, With A Message Of Love* (CRC 2001), a Curtom (CRC – Curtom Record Company) album, distributed by the Texas-based independent Jewel-Paula-Ronn Records. This album, although it's an amalgam of tracks cut at different times, shows a further move away from the strings and brass in Mayfield's musical evolution. 'We Come In Peace' features again the familiar party backdrop, whilst Curtis goes back over well-trodden ground, this time widening the theme to include other languages and cultures, within the implied 'alien' metaphor. Lyrics and music touch on previous anthems like '…Hell Below', 'Move On Up', 'On And On' and even 'Shout', and Hank Ford's sax riffs across the background in a somewhat repetitive but nevertheless appropriate way.

'Baby It's You' is a tender ballad delivered as only he could, but was a strange choice for a single, even had he still been at the top, rather than in the marginalized position that he currently found himself. The track was edited for 7in single release but a 12in single was also issued both in America and later in the UK (November '76). For a number of reasons it was not strong enough to bring him back. For 'Bodyguard' Curtis took a track that he had recorded back in '79 for use on the *Heartbeat* album, but which had not been included. With the assistance of Barney Conway he remixed and completed the track, softening the disco-phillygroove along the way, which had originally been created by Norman Harris and Ronnie Tyson. 'Breakin' In The Streets' rolls along on an 'almost' reggae backbeat. Experiments in percussion, with good work from saxman Ford help to make this one enjoyable listening but the lyric refers to street life, rather than the sidewalk politics that the title suggests. Mayfield turns his attention to companionship for 'Everybody Needs A Friend', which is the highlight of this album. It's a ballad of encouragement and support for the times when the getting of experience and the trials of survival may seem like one and the same thing.

'This Love Is True' finds Curtis thankful for the rediscovery of emotions echoed in earlier ballads but nevertheless always relevant in matters of the heart. The track should have been used on the *Honesty* album but it was only now that he completed it for use here. Radical re-arrangement and updated news comes on a drum for a rephrasing of his perpetual classic 'We Gotta Have Peace', the final track on this set and an interesting update of the '72 original. This song is one of the finest peace anthems ever written. The original record made by Curtis for his third solo album *Roots* had disappointing sales as a pop single but in the intervening years it has grown into a classic, alongside his many others. Its philosophy urges our vigilance against the many evils of war and is a message that needs repeating every now and then, just to remind us all of the long-term sanity of peace, when stacked up against the interests of big business, arms dealers and the like. The rinky dink keyboard and drum programming give this version a curious techno quality. It provides an interesting alternative to the original, and successfully updates the song for the generations that have grown up under the threats and realities of more recent conflicts. Many wars have plagued this planet since Mayfield wrote this song more than 30 years ago and this time there seems to have been a conscious attempt to reach a younger audience, who had probably never heard the original recording.

We Come In Peace... was recorded and mixed, in the main at Curtom, Atlanta, with the help of extended family members like son Tracey, Henry Gibson and Joseph Scott and, though it charted at #39 R&B in September '85, it did not register on the US pop album chart and was not released in the UK. Given these circumstances it was no surprise that this album could not affect the lasting redux that Mayfield had planned and he stepped back into semi-retirement. He broke the silence occasionally with live appearances and a musical collaboration with UK pop group the Blow Monkeys with 'Celebrate (The Day After You)'. 'Celebrate...' was a record that the Tories pressured the BBC into 'restricted play' because it was seen as an attack on Margaret Thatcher, but despite this interference the single still reached a healthy #52 on the UK pop chart in May '87. But hit or not, Curtis was not ready to quit yet and he embarked on another European tour for the fourth successive year. This time he played a few London and more northern venues where audiences witnessed his enduring stage presence, musical growth and soulful delivery, despite three years without any record releases, let alone a hit. His whispery vocals slayed mixed-age audiences up and down the country with his established programme, tweaked on this occasion by the addition of songs like 'Trippin' Out' and a near ambient 'We Come In Peace'. It proved to anyone interested that despite a long period in the wilderness, Mayfield was not prepared to sit back entirely on his past achievements but still clearly had much more to offer in the way of new musical development. In interviews at the time he spoke enthusiastically about this his biggest European Tour yet, taking in countries not previously visited like Austria and Spain (as well as Scotland, France, Germany, Holland, Belgium, Switzerland, Denmark and Sweden). Also Curtis was looking forward to playing many of the summer festivals throughout Europe, something that he hadn't tried before. He spoke about plans to re-issue some of his past Curtom hit albums like *Superfly*, *Roots* and *CURTIS* in a 'Classics' series on CRC that had lain dormant for some time due to distribution problems, 'But Curtom is still very much alive and I have recorded some new songs in my studio at home and I plan to release a new album quite soon as well as the older albums.' He also reported a big concert, which he had recently completed in Atlanta with Jerry Butler and the Impressions when it had been declared 'Curtis Mayfield Day' by the mayor, Andrew Young, and he had been honoured on stage. He received great reviews too, while playing a number of dates down in Florida. His annual visits to Europe and the UK were still where the bulk of his current touring was done between the years of '84 to '87.

After Mayfield moved to Atlanta in '81 he recreated the Curtom Studios II on the same site as his house. Whilst construction was taking place, he used the facilities at Web IV and Axis Studios in Atlanta where the tracks cut were those for the *Honesty* album. Rich Tufo supplied orchestrations and arrangements and he also played some of the piano and clavinet parts. The other keyboards player was Theodis Rodgers Jr, Morris Jennings played drums on these sessions and saxes, and flutes were the work of Charles 'Skip' Lane. By the time they cut the *We Come In Peace...* album in '85 the studios had long been completed and they had formed a new Curtom house band including William Green on keyboards, Edward Gregory guitar, Hank Ford on saxes and Glen Davis on percussion. Curtis' son Tracey played some of the bass parts but most of this was handled by the only remaining original band member Joseph 'Lucky' Scott, though Master Henry Gibson was also present on three tracks. In addition to the new tracks, Curtis remixed and edited some of his earlier unused sides. This line-up didn't last long but Mayfield did form a new road band, Nice Ice.

11 Return Of Curtom

Due to an almost constant period of touring during the mid '80s, especially in Europe, Curtis Mayfield was now ready with a prepared programme that would relaunch his recording career and the Curtom label in 1988. Over the past year, he and the band had enjoyed an incredibly successful and lengthy European tour, which took in ten countries, numerous TV appearances and media interviews. In June, Curtis and his band were featured on the UK *Club Mix* TV series where they performed a set that included 'Freddie's Dead', 'I'm So Proud', 'What Is My Woman For' and 'We're A Winner'. He was interviewed sitting at one of the tables in the club, while segments of a short pictorial CV were dropped in behind his voice as he answered the questions put to him. When quizzed about being rediscovered by a whole new generation of music lovers his reply was 'Wonderful' and he went on to elaborate that it was a good feeling to know that he might have made some valuable contributions in his music, which hopefully could be rediscovered over and over again by music fans. Still supporting him was wonder percussionist 'Master' Henry Gibson who had played with Curtis both on record and the road over a 17-year period. He had been joined recently by Lebron Scott on bass, who had replaced his elder brother Joseph 'Lucky' Scott, Mayfield's close friend, who had been forced to quit due to poor health. On keyboards to round out the sound was Buzz Amato. The drummer Lee Goodness was the other new face who completed the quartet that now backed Curtis on this tour. For this *Club Mix* appearance, Mayfield wore knee-length black suede boots and a stone-washed denim outfit – he was relaxed and happy at the interview. When asked why he had seemingly disappeared from the public eye, Curtis explained that it was in the nature of a Gemini to appear and disappear 'and what have you'. He went on to explain that, though music was a very important part of his life, there were other considerations. He had been raising his family in Atlanta, touring writing and recording, and was currently in preparation to reactivate the Curtom label.

Mayfield hooked up with John Abbey at Ichiban Records in '88 and together they relaunched the Curtom label. Curtis embarked on yet another world tour to announce his return to recording, which bought him back to many UK venues where he received his usual enthusiastic reception from the public and music critics alike.

John Abbey had first cut his teeth as a label manager in the UK with Action (in operation between September '68 and April '74) and B&C Records. Both labels were run from offices at 37 Soho Square in London's West End. Abbey had launched Mojo by early '71, his second label and this time he achieved more consistent chart success. Contempo, John's third label started trading in early '73 extending further the format that he had created for Mojo to include northern soul. Major Lance and JJ Barnes were among the American singers who recorded here for the label.

Abbey got into the music business by creating his own magazine, *Blues & Soul*, that grew out of *Home Of The Blues*, a mimeographed fanzine, which he had begun to publish in May '66. Initially, John wrote all of the articles and reviews himself but as the magazine grew in reputation, there were no shortage of contributors. By issue #8 the *HOTB* had been transformed into a glossy, professionally printed magazine with the new, more commercial, name of *Blues & Soul* and Abbey had negotiated a nationwide UK distribution deal. Roger St Pierre's first article appeared in issue six, under the revised title, in '67. He was quickly followed by others like Dave Godin, David Nathan, Frank Elson, Ray Topping, Kurt Mohr, Peter Trickey, 'Waxie' Maxie Needham, Charles Yeats, Roy Simonds, Bob Peacock, and yours truly – I made my first contribution in January '68. *Blues & Soul's* readership steadily increased leaving all its early competition behind and in the 35 years since it first appeared, it has occupied the apex of the soul music magazine market. Abbey became Editorial Director of *B&S* and relinquished the UK editorship to Bob Killbourn in '78 when he moved to the States after the collapse of the Contempo Record label and store.

Curtis Mayfield like the Drifters, Ben E King, Major Lance, Aretha and too many others to mention, had traditionally been featured in B&S with articles regularly reporting on their career changes, both up and down. So, over the years, Abbey and Killbourn had been in ideal positions to appreciate the full compass of Mayfield's influence. As such, it was no real surprise that, once John had set up the Atlanta-based Ichiban Records and negotiated a UK outlet in late '87, he realized a long-held ambition when he signed Curtis and began issuing the Curtom masters exclusively under their own logo for the first time in ten years.

The first Curtom album that Ichiban issued was a double live set compiled from Mayfield and his new band's recent European tour (recorded in July '87) entitled *Curtis Mayfield Live in Europe* (CUR 2-2901) that was released on both vinyl and CD. The US version had a different inside sleeve from the UK issue, which contained a number of good photos taken on tour. It featured no new music from the ensemble except for the instrumental intro 'Ice 9', written by the group's keyboard player Buzz Amato and featuring great percussion work from the only original band member, Master Henry Gibson. The 12 remaining tracks consisted of lengthy versions of well established Mayfield standards like 'Back To The World', 'We've Gotta Have Peace', 'If There's A Hell Below', two songs from *Superfly* ('Pusherman' and 'Freddie's Dead') plus a number of earlier Curtis anthems ('It's Alright', 'Amen', 'Gypsy Woman' and 'People Get Ready'). No European collection would be complete without his UK signature tune 'Move On Up', which was also included plus just one non-Mayfield tune, 'We've Only Just Begun', a regular in his live performances for 18 years. The new band gave flawless and sparkling support, and had updated their sound to incorporate the keyboards into the line-up. Curtis had taken on all the lead guitar work himself. Lebron (aka Benny) Scott was the bassist and Lee Goodness provided the drumbeats. This album served as yet another reintroduction to a new generation of fans but unlike Mayfield's first live set *CURTIS/LIVE* ('71) it didn't chart in either the US or Europe. It was this line-up (with Luis Stefanell replacing Gibson) that was recorded at

Ronnie Scott's Jazz Club in London and screened on UK TV in '88 for Mike Mansfield's *Cue The Music* (see Chapter 9).

In interviews given at the time, Curtis spoke of his intentions to reassemble the essential Curtom roster, once again. He reported his signing of Major Lance and spoke about their plans to record an album together, using a mixture of Mayfield and Smokey (Robinson) songs. He spoke enthusiastically about plans to sign the Impressions, who had no record deal at that time and Leroy Hutson, who by then was allegedly living in New York City. Curtis went on to report recent negotiations with Chris James, who had reformed a new version of the Natural Four (with his son in the line-up) but admitted that so far, his efforts to locate Linda Clifford had been unsuccessful. Mayfield stressed that he would not be going back – in the musical sense – and was very enthusiastic about future developments including new artists Sugar Ray (Raymondo Thomas) and his son Tracey (Mayfield). He confessed that he was about ready to take a break from touring, that he was very happy with the Ichiban set-up and considered John Abbey a close friend. Despite all the travelling, Mayfield had managed to get back to his Atlanta Studios to cut some tracks for *I'm Gonna Get U Sucka* (see Chapter 9) and a few other new songs plus a reworking of others like 'Ain't Got No Time'.

Curtis stressed his interest in promoting young ideas. Things that were recorded years ago no longer stimulated him and he embraced what was actually happening now, in keeping with the times. He said at the time, 'The beats may be a little different but I will sing of my life and my observances today, as I did yesterday and those that know me and those that don't will be able to relate because their lives are no different from mine. Too often for the people that you are involved with in the music business the bottom line is "Can we make money" and that is not where the creative person is coming from. But on the other hand to get your message across you need commercial success, sometimes it's hard to strike the right balance'.

Ichiban continued their re-issue programme with *Superfly* (CUR 2002) that was now remastered for CD but was also released in the vinyl format as well, as were all subsequent Ichiban releases. The Curtom singles were issued on 12in and 7in vinyl and in the CD format. The first, inevitably, was 'Move On Up' coupled with 'Little Child Runnin' Wild' plus a live bonus cut of 'Move On Up' on the 12in. The second single was issued to coincide with the release of the *I'm Gonna Get U Sucka* movie in '88 and featured two songs that Curtis had written especially for the project 'He's A Fly Guy' and the title track. As popular as he was, through his many tours and high media profile, neither of these releases created any chart action in Europe or America. The next Mayfield re-issue to receive the Curtom/Ichiban makeover was *There's No Place Like America Today* (CUR 2003) and this classic received great reviews and the time was right for its remastering to CD. It sold as well as one might expect given that Mayfield fans would already have a copy and that as yet there were not enough UK fans who had invested in the CD format to positively affect sales.

Ex-Curtom label mate Leroy Hutson began his long awaited UK 'Playback Tour' in April '89. Hutson played mainly northern dates but he did appear at the Fridge, Brixton and also did a Caister Soul Weekender. Though Leroy had no recording contract at the time, Curtom hurriedly issued an excellent Best of... compilation *There's More Where This Came From* (CUR 2004), which, as well as the title track, also contained 'Lover's Holiday', 'When You Get To This' and 'All Because Of You'. The tour was very successful and he intended a return within the year but had cancelled by the spring, rescheduling the dates for a later visit. Ichiban continued to reconstruct the Curtom catalogue with three more releases in '89. First came another Mayfield classic, his best from the RSO period *Something To Believe In* (CUR 2005) followed by *Lasting Impressions* (2006) that was an amalgam of tracks from their two final Curtom albums. Their final release that year was *Linda Clifford's Greatest Hits* (2007), which contained her hit singles 'Red Light' and 'Don't Give Up'. These later albums did not appear in the UK until six months or so after their US issue. Ichiban boss John Abbey, in addition to re-establishing Curtom as well as the other Ichiban label family, had also recently been in the studio producing a new Mavis Staples album for 20th Century records entitled *Hold On To Your Dream*, which she came over to promote in September '87, just prior to her signing with Paisley Park.

Though Mayfield took a break from touring to concentrate on Curtom

The Impressions' first line-up for Vee-Jay in 1958: Jerry Butler, Sam Gooden, Arthur Brooks. Front: Richard Brooks, Curtis Mayfield (Photo credit: Calvin Carter)

Jerry Butler, pictured here in 1968, hit his creative peak while working with Gamble/Huff at Mercury (Photo credit: Yale Matheson)

Calvin Carter, pictured here in 1965, Principal Producer at Vee-Jay Records (Photo credit: Fountain Productions)

Carl Davis gave Curtis a production deal at OKeh in 1963 (Photo credit: *Blues & Soul* magazine)

Reggae star Devon Russell recorded an album of Mayfield songs in 1993 (Photo credit: Rick Davie)

Sam Gooden and Fred Cash in an uneasy reunion with Richard and Arthur Brooks at the R&B Foundation Awards in New York, 2000 (Photo by Seamus McGarvey)

The Impressions in London, 2001. Left to right: Willie Kitchens, Vandy 'Smokey' Hampton, Sam Gooden and Fred Cash (Photo by Peter Burns)

business, he did make an appearance on the US TV *Night Music* series hosted by Jools Holland & David Sanborn, which went out in America in early '89 and was later aired in the UK on VH1. Ace keyboard master George Duke and pop singer Taylor Dayne were also featured on this show. A clean-shaven Curtis performed 'Pusherman' with the Duke houseband, which included a sax solo from Sanborn. Curtis spoke briefly about the Impressions then and now and how he was looking forward to working with them again soon, before performing 'It's Alright'. Mayfield also closed the show with 'People Get Ready' in a vocal duet with Taylor, which featured all the principal guests including slide guitarist David Lindley.

At about this time, Trevor Churchill, label boss of Ace Records, came up with the idea of issuing the first UK CD on the Impressions in mid '89. Trevor and I had first combined our mutual interest in this group when I wrote the 'Curtis Mayfield Story', a series of articles that ran in *Blues & Soul* between October '68 and April '69. Churchill had just become label manager at Bell Records when I first met him and we worked together on *Bell's Cellar Of Soul Volume 2* and other Bell releases around that period. I also wrote my first sleevenotes at his request, for *Impressions Big 16 Volume 2* with John Abbey. Together, Trevor and I collated the album and then I wrote the liner notes and designed the booklet. *The Definitive Impressions* (Kent CDKEND 923) was issued in September '89 and has sold well enough (over 20,000 by February '03) to remain on catalogue ever since. After this, we laid future plans to issue all the Impressions ABC recordings, but more about this later.

At Curtom everyone prepared for what should have been a bonanza year. Curtis had completed his first new album for five years and had another mega Euro tour lined up to promote it. On 13 March '90 Mayfield flew into the UK to finalize a number of preparations for his autumn tour. He played only one London date, at the Town & Country Club in Kentish Town on the 17th and taped Andy Peebles *Soul Train* show at the BBC, which went out a few days later on the 24th. Peebles was the first to review Mayfield's upcoming new album *Take It To The Streets*. In a relaxed interview Curtis and Andy reflected on the various aspects surrounding the recording of these tracks. 'Homeless', chosen as his new single, was the next featured track. This bleak story highlights the desperate plight of the many victims of society unable to change their situation for the better. As Curtis said, 'You're only as secure as your last paycheck.' Peebles, a Mayfield fan, was enthusiastic about Curtis' many past achievements, whilst the man himself reacted in his usual modest way to the compliments showered upon him.

When quizzed about the technological changes in the music business Curtis described himself as a 'gadget man' happy to change with the times but careful to employ the best engineers to capture the sound that he desires. His updated version of 'On And On' served as an excellent audio example when compared with the Gladys Knight version recorded sixteen years earlier. Ever modest, Mayfield expressed a high regard for Gladys Knight's ability and still preferred her vocal, but this newer version (and the original by Leroy Hutson and the Impressions) are both still highly regarded and preferred within his fanbase. The conversation inevitably touched on *Superfly* and his 'six' movie scores in general. Mayfield described the process for us, how each project has its own difficulties and what starts out simple becomes hectic, once producers and the like start 'jerking you around'. Mayfield said *Superfly* was the exception – and look what he achieved with that. *I'm Gonna Git U Sucka,* on the other hand, was problematic with only two of his songs finishing up on the final cut. At the time, Curtis was still putting the finishing touches to *Superfly 1990,* his score for *The Return Of Superfly* on which he collaborated with Ice-T. He said that his children kept him in touch with current trends but described his own new respect for rap since working within the medium and how he had developed a better understanding of the rhythmic patterns involved within the genre. He described 'Do Be Down' as getting to the bottom line of our emotions. Prior to playing the track, Peebles raved about this later classic, which on reflection should have been the first single chosen from the album. In making the final selection from his huge repertoire, Mayfield said that the environment dictates and that all he does is observe and then makes adjustments to the format. This short but excellent show ended with 'I've Been Trying', Mayfield's pick from the *Definitive Impressions* CD. While he was at the BBC with Peebles he also recorded his personal choice for the 'Top 10' series, which was not aired for another two years. Also recorded by the BBC was what turned out to be Mayfield's final UK concert at the Town & Country. This was aired and issued as a CD on Windsong in '93.

Take It To The Streets (Curtom CUR 2008/CD/Tape/Vinyl) was finally released in April 1990. It featured a new band and a new sound and revealed yet another cycle in Mayfield's evolution as a singer/songwriter/arranger/producer and engineer. A broad range of collaborations, movie projects, old and new songs were featured in this marketable package. All the machinery was in place for a big push with the *Take It To The Streets* Euro tour booked for commencement in the autumn, but sadly it never happened due to his tragic accident in August 1990. The opening track, via a jaunty intro, gets straight down to business as it highlights the plight of the unwanted legions that exist at the edges of the civilized world. Mayfield's message pulls no punches and 'Homeless' is a song that sharply reflects the human anguish, suffering and rejection of being outcast by the economic requirements of a society whose values, in terms of the individual, had dropped off the scale. 'Homeless' reflects a bleak future for millions. It was issued as a 7in and 12in single in the UK but no one seriously expected it to chart either in Europe or America.

'Got To Be Real' is the first of the two Tony and Michael Brown songs on this set. It's a smouldering ballad, which makes a plea for reality within a deteriorating relationship, where faking it only makes things worse and facing up to reality is all that can save the romance. 'Do Be Down' is a sensational Mayfield later classic that instantly engages the nostalgia and crystal clarity of his earlier work with the Impressions. The string arrangement, sometimes a little reminiscent of Hathaway's early work, is now fused with the percussion and drum programming of Carlos Glover, which hones an insistent edge to this album. This beautifully poignant love song recreates the purity that can be heard in Mayfield's early ballads and for many of us this was our introduction to his eloquent work. Since then, he has engaged us all in a number of dangling conversations about love, human rights, injustice and plain common sense. His lyrics have always been thought provoking and poetic; his music has moved us both physically and spiritually. In the UK this single (in both 7 and 12in formats) came in a great full colour sleeve but did not sell anywhere as well as it deserved to. Sung with the slight resignation of a missed opportunity 'Who Was That Lady', has a hypnotic hook and easy goin' groove that rolls on as Curtis enquires after a bird who's unexpectedly flown before he had a chance to make his move.

Mayfield gives 'On And On' a complete facelift, making clever use of the percussion programming of Glover. Persistence is once again the theme, which is just one of the essential elements of his extraordinarily diverse and influential music. Curtis may have gone hi-tec but thankfully still maintained established links with his own individual and very soulful past. A heavily percussive rhythm track runs through 'He's A Fly Guy', a song that Mayfield had written for *I'm Gonna Git U Sucka*. There are plenty of throwback references to *Superfly* etc. This version was not used in the movie, which featured a recut with Curtis and Fishbone, but it would have been just perfect as it is. 'Don't Push' is where the *Take It To The Streets* title for this album comes from. 'I Mo Git U Sucka' was written by Curtis as title track for the Wayans' movie mentioned earlier. However it too was not used in this form either.

When *Take It To The Streets* was released in the UK it received very positive reviews (one reviewer compared Mayfield to Van Gogh!) as it had done earlier in America. But despite the recommendations it only reached #20 on the UK soul album chart in April '90 (and re entered the chart again in May). It did less well in the States, where it could only manage #59 US R&B. In March, the dates for Mayfield's *Take It To The Streets* Euro tour, scheduled for 20 August start in London and appearing at Bradford Festival and several UK venues/ Holland/ Sweden/ Norway/ Finland/ France were announced. Whilst still in London, Curtis was interviewed by Roger St Pierre and spoke to him about the improvements of living he had found in Atlanta as opposed to Chicago – especially the weather. He discussed the recent collaborations with Rapper Easy E and recalled recent tours that he had made with the Impressions in the autumnal months of '89, which took in Chicago, Detroit and Philadelphia. At that time he had scheduled a new Impressions album for Curtom as well as a recent re-issue and also flagged up a new Lou Pride album. He reported the progress made with his new Gospel C Records, for whom he had recently signed Kevin Yancy (younger brother of the late Marvin). He also spoke enthusiastically about plans to record a Yancy Family gospel album with Natalie Cole guesting.

It was about 9.30 on the morning of 13 August 1990 and Curtis Mayfield had just flown into New York from Long Beach, California. As he cleared arrivals at La Guardia, Curtis was met by his driver who took him directly to the hotel in New Jersey. He made a phone call to touch base with his promoter and manager/son Todd, who had intended to be there in New York to meet Curtis but was having some hang ups with his move from Chicago to Atlanta and had to cancel their meeting. Todd, who had a business degree from Morehouse College, had spent recent years working as a tax analyst in Chicago banks but he was now ready to move into the family business, Curtom Records. At this time he was midway between moving and setting up a new office in Atlanta and things were in some disarray, so for this concert he had decided to coordinate things by phone. After making some calls, Mayfield relaxed and then made preparations for his evening show. About 8.00, he took the tour van out to Queens and Wingate Field, Brooklyn. On his arrival he was rather surprised at the scale of the event, which he expected to be a lot smaller. He was greeted by event promoter Martin Markowitz, a New York state senator who annually promoted and was host to a number of R&B concerts in tribute to Martin Luther King Jr. Curtis linked up with his band, who had been watching the show from the wings – Harold Melvin and the Blue Notes had just finished their set and joined the Delfonics, the Intruders, and other acts backstage. It was about an hour into the proceedings and rapidly becoming clear that the storm (forecast earlier that day) was coming up pretty fast. Markowitz knew that if it rained he would have to stop the show, so he decided that rather than disappoint 10,000 fans, he would put on Mayfield (who was due to top the bill) right away. Markowitz reasoned that even if Curtis only performed a couple of songs and the weather broke, the audience would not be so disappointed.

Mayfield's group hurriedly set up and then ran a rapid sound check before playing the intro to *Superfly*, which was the signal for Curtis' entrance onto the stage – and then the sky fell in. A sudden freak gust of wind whipped up and in that frozen moment, as Markowitz was about to hand the microphone to Curtis, who was about 10 feet away moving towards him, the lighting tower came crashing down on to the stage. On its descent the tower narrowly missed percussionist Lee Goodness, demolishing his drum kit as it toppled downward. It struck Curtis on the neck, crushing three vertebrae in his spine, causing paralysis from the neck down. From that day until his death Curtis remained a quadriplegic, unable to move below his neck. This squall only lasted two minutes but it knocked people out of their seats, uprooted trees and propelled objects off of the stage into the audience. As Curtis lay prostrate on a stage littered with the debris of this tragedy, he drifted in and out of consciousness, as pandemonium broke loose around him. There was a crash of thunder and hard rain began to fall. Several other people were also hurt but it was Mayfield who suffered the most serious injuries. He told journalist Richard Williams in February '94, 'The next thing I knew I was lying on my back. So I must have went out for a moment. And then I discovered that neither my hands nor my arms were where I thought they were, and I couldn't move. I looked about me lying there. I saw myself totally splattered all over the stage. Then it began to rain. Big drops. I could hear people screaming and hollering. Of course, I kept my eyes open, because I thought that if I shut them, I would die.' They covered Curtis with a plastic sheet until the ambulance arrived and rushed him to the King's County Medical Centre, nearby.

In the wake of this awful tragedy there were wrangles between the Mayfield family and the Markowitz camp – allegations were made by witnesses that the lighting structure had been improperly secured and was unsafe. Markowitz denied this, citing ten years of concerts with no other incidents and he was convinced that a 'twister' like the one that hit that stage, had been an Act of God. Since the accident, he has dedicated an annual show to Mayfield. The Impressions performed there in '95 and Markowitz vowed that this annual tribute would continue until Curtis returned to his stage. He was traumatized by the accident and resented any suggestion of blame being levelled at him or his organization. Another twist in the tail to these events is that, due to a misunderstanding between Ichiban and Curtom, insurance cover had not been acquired for Curtis at this concert. It's barely conceivable that this kind of accident should happen to anyone, but particularly weird that it should happen to Mayfield, at a benefit for St Martin, way out in a Brooklyn field. It was certainly the last place that Curtis expected any kind of accident to happen to him: 'On stage was the place I felt most secure. You ride in so many planes and cars and you know you're taking a chance and then it happens where you least expect it.' This tragedy deprived us all of a great performer and virtuoso musician but it was to our collective good fortune that the poet and spiritual genius was to survive for another decade.

At first, the diagnosis and early predictions looked hopeful and bulletins suggested that a series of operations might restore Curtis back to a physical state closer to normality. In September, *Blues & Soul* revealed that, 'Curtis Mayfield remains in a critical but stable condition at the King's County Medical Centre in Brooklyn, New York, following his accident on stage when a light rack fell over in gale force conditions and landed on the singer's neck resulting in a broken neck and paralysis from the neck down. The legendary performer is expected to be moved to Shepherd's Hospital in his hometown of Atlanta, which specializes in spinal cord injuries.' Mayfield spent four months in Shepherd Spinal Centre, Atlanta before returning home to be cared for by his family.

A further *B&S* bulletin in October reported, 'Curtis has had a second bone graft operation on his neck. Curtis is now fully conscious and able to speak albeit only a few words at a time and according to sources close to the performer is "coping well" with his predicament. Some feeling has now returned to his shoulders which hopefully will "continue to improve". A benefit concert was organized recently in LA by Capitol Records who released the *Superfly 1990* album and further events are expected to be held in the future.'

A month later *B&S* told us, 'Curtis Mayfield who suffered dreadful injuries during a bizarre accident at an outdoor concert in New York last month should be able to walk once again. Surgery on the 48-year-old singer is said to have been successful and his brother [in fact, his son] Todd having visited King's County Hospital added, 'Since the spinal cord hasn't been severed, there is a chance that he can regain some movement.''

The impact of the falling structure on Mayfield's back had shattered the third, fourth and fifth vertebrae in his spine. Despite these delicate operations there was no lasting improvement in his condition.

Then, as if things were not trying enough, journalist Adam Sweeting reported that while Curtis was still in hospital, his Atlanta home burnt to the ground, heaping even more tragedy, discomfort and personal suffering on the Mayfield family. They moved to a house a few streets away and made preparations for Curtis' return from hospital. They had a special orthopaedic bed delivered, designed especially for quadriplegic cases. Once he was installed Curtis underwent a programme of physiotherapy, which would later be administered by members of the family who all became actively involved with his care and comfort.

In the remaining months of 1990 those fans who didn't follow specialist magazines or had missed the relatively few references in the UK media were blissfully unaware of Mayfield's condition. *The Streets/ Superfly 1990* Euro tour was cancelled, so Curtom were unable to maximize sales of both albums as planned – previous sales were greater when boosted by his live performances. Curtis was also unable to complete any of his ongoing or scheduled projects at Curtom or Gospel C Records, which were all suspended due to his condition.

One Curtom project that did find completion, however, was Lou Pride's album *Gone Bad* (Curtom 2009), which was issued in late 1990. Pride who had been based in Texas for the best part of 20 years had cut several good records for a number of small labels. He was constantly touring all over the southern states performing in small R&B and blues venues without making any real commercial impact with records but nevertheless gradually building a solid fanbase who would turn out with enthusiasm whenever he appeared locally. After his mother's death he returned to North Chicago, where he met Marvin Yancy who began producing tracks for his next album. Marvin died suddenly in '85 and his younger brother Kevin completed these sessions. Mayfield signed Pride to Curtom and when his album, *Gone Bad,* was eventually released it contained 'Very Special', a Yancy-produced track, alongside songs recorded in Milwaukee but the majority of the album including the title track were cut at Curtom in Atlanta. This album was highly rated on the blues circuit and gained national airplay but only with the specialist DJs, so made little mainstream impact. In the aftershock of Mayfield's untimely accident, it suffered under-promotion and sank without trace. For Pride, however, it opened a number of important doors that led to higher profile concerts and future albums with other labels.

Return Of Superfly, the long-threatened movie sequel to *Superfly* was released in America in June '90 but this unremarkable flick didn't capture the public's imagination in the way that the original had almost 20 years earlier. Both movies bore little in common except that each profited from superior Curtis Mayfield soundtracks. This time in the company of Ice-T, Easy E, Uzi Bros etc, Capitol issued the *Superfly 1990* soundtrack album in the UK prior to the movie's release. After five years without a solo studio album, the second had been released within a year but even though it was mooted as totally contemporary by the jocks and reviewers, it did not set the charts on fire the way the original *Superfly* had. Capitol issued the single in a variety of formats but it only sold well in the UK four months later, when it reached #13 on the UK soul singles chart in October. Though he didn't speak much about this project, Curtis did mention in passing that he had encountered lots of problems and it has been reported that he had not been entirely happy about doing it.

In the UK *Juke Box Jury*, a remodelled '60s TV pop chart show, reviewed the excellent video made to promote the *Superfly 1990* single. It was the first time that many fans heard the news of Curtis' awful accident when it was announced by show host Jools Holland. The stylishly shot video features Curtis (only in close up) and is cut in rhythm to the music. The camera moves swiftly between dancers, Ice-T and in amongst a number of visual devices in a perfect vehicle for this unusual duet. The panel, a little uneasy at the news, chose their comments carefully but Alan 'Fluff' Freeman, Neneh Cherry, John Fashanu, Vic Reeves and Bob Mortimer were undecided. The verdict was passed to the audience, who voted it a hit, but sadly that was not to be. Why this contemporary music performed by Curtis and Ice-T missed the market is something of a puzzle. Spike Lee's contemporary movie *Mo' Better Blues* had a soundtrack album hit at #24 UK soul albums in November '90 but then the movie was much more successful, so one served the other. It seems likely though not conclusive that if *Return Of Superfly* had been a better movie, similar or better album and single sales would have followed.

In the last month of the year Ichiban issued *Curtis Of All Time* (2.2902), in a vinyl 2LP set and CD formats, a compilation of 15 previously released Curtom songs, plus the unissued 'Tomorrow Night For Sure'. The cover states four previously unreleased recordings are included but the other three are alternatives, quite different from the original versions, but nevertheless alternatives. The final four tracks (13–16) are of most interest to the collector. The sleeve bears only perfunctory information, with no indication of any change in Mayfield's situation or update on his condition. 'Ain't No Love Lost' is a song that Curtis had tinkered with on a number of occasions and mentioned in interviews around that time – this is a tighter version with Henry Gibson's percussion more prominently featured. 'Hard Times' also seems quite different from earlier versions and runs a fraction longer. The driving dancefloor beat of 'Tomorrow Night For Sure' has the sound and feel of the RSO period and was probably recorded for *Heartbeat* or *Honesty*. 'We People Who Are Darker Than Blue' is one of the classic cuts that come from Mayfield's debut album *CURTIS*. The freeform jazz/funk treatment of this experimental new version has been cut like a live track and then remixed in the studio with sound effects added later. Once again, Gibson's percussion is prominent and the sax work of Hank Ford gives this track a similar sound to the mid '80s album *We Come In Peace*... This Ichiban compilation was a timely release but suffered from poor marketing and cover graphics and consequently did not register as well as it could have.

Bob Fisher, who founded Sequel Records in '89, was the first UK label manager to recognize the sublicensing potential of the as-yet unreleased Curtom masters, which were currently languishing in the vaults, and issued his great Stairsteps CD compilation *Comeback* (NEXCD 114) in 1990. This UK license was obtained through Buddah Records, who owned some of the tracks but had distributed Curtom when they were originally issued in the late '60s. Due to Japanese interest, Sequel repackaged this CD in '94 as the *Stairsteps Greatest Hits* (NEMCD 696). Within the 74 minute playing time, Fisher packed in 25 tracks that span the Stairsteps career between '66 and '71. 'You Waited Too Long', the group's first Windy C R&B hit introduces this fine collection. Mayfield only wrote eight of these songs but he did produce 13 before the Stairsteps moved back to Buddah where the majority of their productions were then handled by Stan Vincent and Tony Camillo. As well as containing a dozen of their hits from Windy C, Curtom and Buddah there are soul classics like 'Behind Curtains', 'Under The Spell Of Your Love', 'Stay Close To Me', 'Because I Love You' and 'Didn't It Look So Easy'. There have been other compilations of the Stairsteps catalogue (*Five Stairsteps – Collectables* COL-CD-5023 and *Ooh Child – Unidisc* BDK -5068) and although *Comeback* remains their best and most comprehensive re-issue so far, it was deleted from the catalogue in '99.

The Impressions were inducted into the Rock 'n' Roll Hall of Fame in January '91 at its sixth annual presentation ceremony and dinner. Other nominees that year included Wilson Pickett, Lavern Baker, John Lee Hooker, the Byrds and Ike & Tina Turner as well as R&B producers Ralph Bass and Dave Bartholomew with posthumous awards going to Howlin' Wolf and Jimmy Reed. Perhaps unaware of the friction between the founding members of the Impressions, the society had invited them all to the ceremony. At the pre-induction press meeting, Fred Cash and Sam Gooden clashed with Richard and Arthur Brooks and they all refused to appear with each other. On 17 January '91, New York's *Daily News* quoted Fred Cash as saying, 'They were only there for two years (actually six years), We've been with the group for 32 years and 27 albums. I think it's a shame they're being inducted and I'm very mad about it. There's no reason.' Jerry Butler countered with, 'Some of the questions about Arthur and Richard Brooks are based on their not being with the group for many of its hits. But they sang on (and wrote) "For Your Precious Love", which is the reason for all of us being here, It's right we all be here.' Of course not every Impression was there – Curtis Mayfield was still too ill to attend but spoke on a video hook-up for his acceptance. As for Leroy Hutson, Reggie Torian, Ralph Johnson, Nate Evans or Vandy Hampton, it seems that they may not have been invited, or at least they were not mentioned in press reports of the event.

Mayfield's recovery was an agonizingly slow process. Very little was written about him or his progress. In the spring of '91 whispers came from Atlanta of the death of contemporary Chicago soul music great Dee Clark aged 51, from a heart attack. UK rock monthly *VOX* reported in February '91 that an early 'tribute concert' for Curtis had not turned out as expected, stating, 'News broke recently that legal action may be taken to retrieve the five figure sum raised at an all-star benefit rap gig for the singer. A cheque from the venue – The Palace in Hollywood, California – bounced after it was deposited by the charitable organization dealing with Mayfield's hospital expenses. The Palace is now padlocked by bankruptcy trustees.' This news must have been a big disappointment to Curtom who understandably seem to have been temporarily stunned and issued no product during '91 after the public's poor response to the *Curtis Of All Time* compilation.

Generally, and not surprisingly, it was a slow year for all concerned but by mid '92 media interest was beginning to slowly build in America and David Mills wrote a four-page tribute for the *Washington Post* (2/8/92), which celebrated Mayfield's glorious past achievements and updated on his condition. He visited the Mayfields' North Atlanta house where Todd, who shared the full-time nursing duties with other members of the family, revealed the complications that plague a quadriplegic, besides the obvious ones. He explained, 'He can't regulate his body temperature very well. He usually feels real cold, even when it's blazing hot in the room and he can't regulate his blood pressure, so if he's lying down and then sits up, he gets real dizzy and faint. But most days he feels well enough to get up.' During the interview, Mills found Curtis' honest summation of the situation disarming when he told him, 'I think overall, I'm dealing with it pretty good, but you can't help but wake up every once in a while with a tear in your eye.' Mayfield related the ups and downs of his musical career from his earliest reminiscences as a child, when his experiences taught him how to speak from the heart in his songs and when habitually he turned almost everything into a song, learning rhythm from the rhymes and stories that he heard. And from there to the mixed blessings of his first movie score *Superfly*, which earned him an even measure of respect and criticism from those who did and didn't understand his motives. This was one of the earliest attempts to focus on the post-tragedy Mayfield dilemma and provided an excellent portrait of Curtis' dignified and brave struggle with his impossible situation.

My Top Ten with Curtis Mayfield was broadcast in the UK by Radio 1 on 2 August '92. The programme had been recorded over two years earlier by DJ Andy Peebles, a few weeks before Mayfield's accident. Fans were treated to a relaxed interview, which through conversation provided a better picture of some of the moments and events that had shaped Mayfield's life and had given him some of the inspiration to create his wonderful and diverse music. When Peebles quizzed him about how he had survived in the music business for so long, Curtis simply stated that for him, it had been his way of life for almost as long as he could remember – from the age of 13 it had been his profession but even earlier from quite a tender age, through the gospel years that he spent singing with the choir in his grandmother's church. That's where he got his feel for the music, where he learned how to project, harmonize and interpret 'and even a way of saying something. If you're gonna say something, have it mean something.'

As a member of the Northern Jubilee Singers, Curtis performed at churches all over the city on a regular basis and was aware of the high levels of professional pride and of the competition amongst the various local gospel groups. This was also the experience of many including the members of the Dells, who had a huge American hit twice with his first choice 'Oh What A Night' (first time in November '56 when it reached #4 US R&B and then again in August '69, when a newer version went to #1 R&B/22 pop). Record two was the Little Willie John classic 'Fever'. Mayfield had met and worked with John during his period on the road as Butler's guitarist. He picked this one out as a dedication to all the many artists that he worked with over the years, those that made it and those that didn't but nevertheless had made significant contributions to his own learning curve. The focus moved on inevitably to the influence and creative input that Mayfield had supplied to a host of great artists through his songwriting and production work. His decisions as to what to record or not with the Impressions like 'Monkey Time' or other big hits like 'Just Be True' or 'Rainbow' were discussed but Curtis maintained that, though they were his songs, they were not for him but better suited for others like Major, Gene and Jerry. This led neatly to the third choice, one of the many versions of his classic 'People Get Ready' by Jeff Beck and Rod Stewart (#49 UK pop in March '92). Peebles suggested that anthems like this might be better left alone but Mayfield countered that other soulful expressions lend a wider interpretation to any song and that this one was particularly good and provided him with further inspiration. The fourth selection was the only real surprise in the chart, Johnny Paycheck's 'Take This Job And Shove It'. Curtis said that he didn't think that there was anyone who didn't feel this way at sometime during their working life, no matter how much they enjoyed their work.

Mayfield first heard Billie Holiday's 'God Bless The Child' when he was about eight and it always stayed with him, and he said that particular treasures like this evoke so much every time that they are played. Curtis touched on the resistance from the American media that he received when 'We're A Winner', the sixth track on his chart, was first issued. It was important to him that his songs provided food for thought not only for the black community but also for all and any people who have felt oppression in their lives. Sam Cooke became an icon after his tragic murder in '64 and each one of us has their own particular favourite songs from the legacy that he left behind. Curtis' choice was Sam's matchless version of 'Summertime', the often-recorded song from *Porgy And Bess*, which has inspired countless versions since it was first recorded in the late '50s.

Chicago blues cannot be typified by just one track but Muddy Waters 'Hoochie Coochie Man' was one of the seminal songs upon which that musical legend was built. The reason he picked this track, he said was, 'Chicago will always be a blues town and as long as I can remember this gent has been around.' This music along with gospel was an influential part of the soundtrack to Mayfield's childhood. Speaking about the changes that had occurred over the years in the recording process and technological developments, Curtis said that while he embraced the changes, it was for him always important to keep a balance – a fusion of acoustic and synthesizer modules. He also expressed a growing preference for smaller more intimate gigs where he could interact with his audience. The choice of his programme on tour Mayfield said was no problem –he was fortunate in that he'd penned a number of songs that have no timescale.

After he had left the Impressions in 1970, Curtis produced their transition album *Times Have Changed*. Since the group's conception he had written 90 per cent of their recorded output but, after this album, they would cut very few Mayfield songs. So it was an unusual occurrence for them to record contemporary material but Marvin Gaye's 'Inner City Blues' was one of the few exceptions. Curtis and Marvin had crossed paths early in the Impressions career before Gaye had even embarked on any solo ambitions and was still singing with the Moonglows. He had watched and admired Marvin's development but was inspired like many others by the sheer magic of *What's Going On*, which was released shortly after his own solo début. This song in Marvin's original version was Mayfield's ninth choice. Sold on the message, treatment and delivery he remarked after listening to this track, that every statement made in the song was as relevant today as it had been then (and will continue to be for the foreseeable future). The final words were Mayfield's via the Staple Singers 'Let's Do It Again', which he had written and produced for the movie of the same name in '75. Typically this song also signalled an invitation as well as a departure.

Ichiban opened their new headquarters in Atlanta, Georgia in September '92. Long-time *B&S* columnist Roger St Pierre was invited to the grand opening at the purpose-built complex, where he was greeted by label boss John Abbey and his third wife and business partner Nina Easton. Roger was stunned by the very impressive complex that Ichiban had built for their American operation. A cluster of potential Ichiban stars came out for the informal reception, plus family and friends and assorted music biz people, who included the ex Manfred's vocalist, UK bluesman and radio DJ Paul Jones, amongst the 200 or so on the guest list. Clarence Carter, Tyrone Davis, William Bell, Ben E King, Leo Graham and even the wheelchair-bound Curtis Mayfield were in attendance to witness label founder John Abbey announce future plans for Ichiban.

He had launched the Japanese-financed Ichiban Records (Ichiban means 'Number One' in Japanese) in '85 and it grew to feature various outlets of their own like Wrap (rap, hip hop, etc,) Naked Language (alternative rock), Wild Dog (trad blues), and began to distribute a number of small independents like Wilbe (William Bell's label), Nastymix, Ultrax, SDEG, and in '88 Curtom. Shortly after establishing Ichiban, Abbey began to sign some of the greatest soul artists of all time to his label. He convinced William Bell, Clarence Carter, Tyrone Davis, Ben E King, Curtis and later Jerry Butler that Ichiban could better handle their careers. Ichiban had more than 40 acts on its roster by '92 and a further 30 in distribution. They treated Roger to an evening at one of the local R&B venues where Tyrone Davis, Ben E King, Otis Clay and others performed with the Ichiban house band (a white outfit modelled on the MGs).

Sparkle, the movie score that Curtis had recorded with Aretha Franklin was remastered for CD and re-issued by Rhino in the wake of En Vogue's #1 R&B/6 pop hit 'Giving Him Something He Can Feel' in late '92. In America MCA issued a two-CD set *The Anthology 1961–'77* by Curtis Mayfield and the Impressions, which contained 26 of the Impressions' ABC recordings, four from Curtom and 14 of Mayfield's solo sides. This was only the second Impressions' CD that MCA (US owners of the ABC catalogue) had issued so far (the *Impressions Greatest Hits* had appeared earlier in '89), though neither was released in the UK. The Ichiban re-issues of the Curtom Classics back catalogue recommenced in '92 with *Never Say You Can't Survive* (2010), which was followed by more remastered albums from the vaults such as *Give, Get, Take & Have* (2011), *CURTIS* (2012) and the Impressions *Young Mods' Forgotten Story* (2013). It was the first time that any of these fine albums had been issued on CD but not enough of Mayfield's potential audience, who already had the earlier vinyl issues, felt obligated enough to buy these issues at a time when the CD (as the preferred format) was still in transition. These days when there's a free CD given away with almost everything we perhaps forget what a struggle there was to establish the format in the first place – it was after all the first dot in the digital revolution. One UK pioneer who attempted to embrace the technology first, whilst still preserving a readership was new style magazine *Soul CD*, which carried a Mayfield feature in their first issue of November '92. Though Pete Lewis' 'Field Of Broken Dreams' didn't give us much new information and was a rerun of an interview previously published in *Voices from the Shadows* in the autumn of '88, it did serve to update the situation for UK readers and enable us to refocus on Mayfield's achievements. Also we became aware of his strength of spirit when he said, 'Maybe it's not so important to constantly be in the limelight,' and another of his statements, 'Recharge your spirit and find another way,' would take on a prophetic aspect soon to be revealed. Sadly *Soul CD* became a victim of the vinyl luddites slow to embrace technological change but when you consider that the price of your first CD purchase (even if it is a freebie) has to include the new hardware to play it on, like all of the digital formats that followed (Mini Disc and MP3, DVD etc) it was not really so surprising.

Perhaps due in part to their own internal reorganization Ichiban had been unable to release and promote Curtom product quite as well as expected but they did sublicense to the UK-based MCI, who put together an attractive 16-tracker *A Man Like Curtis* (MCI MUSCD 007), which has sold in excess of 100,000 copies since it was released and is still available today. This success was some indication as to the possibilities of the buried gold at Curtom, but too late for Ichiban, who may have issued four albums in '92 but had lost their chance to make the most of good opportunities with the catalogue and did not issue any more Curtom Records after mid '93. Reviewer Jeff Lorez, Assistant Editor at *Blues & Soul*, gave this CD a nine out of ten rating, categorizing the music as 'Essential Soul'. Also issued in the UK by Expansion Records in January '93 was the Leroy Hutson 12in EP *Shades Of Love*, which contains four tracks of the only new music issued since his Elektra album *Paradise* in '82. A demo of 'Share Your Love' had been in circulation for some months gathering northern exposure and reviewer and DJ Richard Searling considered this one of Hutson's 'best ever recordings' predicting an imminent album, which so far has not yet emerged. The music was a welcome return to the 'non disco' Hutson of old and was welcomed by his fanbase. But this kind of stuff needs growing time and plenty of exposure on radio before it can commercially take off – and that it did not receive. The EP contains an interesting deconstruction of Bacharach/David's 'Look Of Love' that was arranged – or should that be rearranged – by Steve Robinson. The similarly titled 'Show Your Love' is in the same groove as the title track, which is reprised as an instrumental with an overdubbed sax solo by Kenny Anderson.

In March, the Blues & Soul Hall Of Fame celebrated Curtis Mayfield as its featured artist with a timely three-page special by Howard Priestley. Interest was beginning to build and the following month the first tribute album *People Get Ready – A Tribute to Curtis Mayfield* was issued in the States by Shanachie. This was only available on import in the UK but received an enthusiastic half-page review by *Blues & Soul* Editor Bob Killbourn that ends with his emphatic advice 'Go Buy'. Those of us who did were pleased to learn that 50 per cent of the royalties went to the 'Curtis Mayfield Research Fund' at the 'Miami Project to Cure Paralysis' set up by The Mayfield Trust in February '91 with a cheque for $100,000. *People Get Ready* (Shanachie 9004) contains a number of Mayfield's most distinguished compositions and begins with a great rendition of 'Um, Um, Um, Um, Um, Um' by Don Covay and Angela Strehli. The excellent Covay (aided by Strehli) wraps his tonsils around the curious Um 6 and together they provide the best alternative to the Major Lance original so far. Delbert McClinton cranks up the tempo on 'He Will Break Your Heart'. He takes the Chicago/New York-based song and treats it to a Salsa dip. Jerry Butler, famous for the original hit version of this song, turned in a very different take on 'Choice Of Colors'. In the past Jerry had been very reverent about 'Choice Of Colors', the lyrics of which he has compared to the poetry of Longfellow. The rap supplied by Goldiloxx puts a very different complexion on the whole piece and broadens the appeal for a younger palate. Father and son David & Jonathon Sanborn lend their mainly instrumental version to the title track and Impressions' classic 'People Get Ready'. Angela Strehli takes 'Got A Right To Cry' back to her hometown of Austin, Texas to give it that homegrown soul flavour and Huey Lewis and the News render 'It's Alright' in acappella, as they have often done on their live shows in the past. 'We People Who Are Darker Than Blue' is a song that always invited experimentation and here Michael Hill & Vernon Reid give us a guitar heroes version of Curtis' dark classic, taking the breaks in turn. Vernon Reid had originally been inspired to play guitar after hearing Mayfield's records. Bunny Wailer, the only surviving member of the Wailers, was inspired by the Impressions' songs, many of which Bob Marley rewrote and sampled, 'I Gotta Keep On Moving' among them. Again Don Covay provides an interesting alternate to 'You Must Believe Me'. His vocal style seems particularly well suited to the reinterpretation of Mayfield songs – he should cut more. Steve Cropper and Lani Groves teamed up for 'I'm So Proud', Lani's silky voice counterpoints Cropper's brittle guitar on a highly polished version of the Mayfield perennial. 'Gypsy Woman' was the song that started it all back in '61 and Kim Wilson adds his vocal and harmonica to the long list of good versions.

This tribute album didn't receive the high-profile launch of the later Warner set when it was issued but is still very well worth acquiring. It was produced by Joe Ferry & Jon Tiven and was mainly recorded at Acme Studios in Mamaroneck, New York. 'It's Alright' was cut in Sausalito and 'I Gotta Keep On Moving' was taped in Kingston, Jamaica and then added to the album at final mix. *People Get Ready* didn't chart but sold sufficiently well to add to the swell of interest building in Mayfield and his music.

Rolling Stone published the five-page Curtis interview/bio 'A Lasting Impression' by Alan Light in late October '93. Though this interview covered the same background as many others before, it was accompanied by a graphic photograph that perhaps told us more about Mayfield's life since the accident, than any words could. Curtis was stretched out on his bed in his pyjamas, with a large wedge of foam rubber supporting his feet and a rolled towel behind his neck. His orthopedic bed was tilted down at the foot, and spread around (almost at arm's length, as if he could reach them) to his left and above his head, were a mixture of personal items – framed family photos, a chess board, gold records propped up so that he could see them. Also in view are books, newspapers, magazines and a chair just behind him, where the family members would sit and talk, read or listen to him on a regular basis. Or just sit there with him watching TV or listening to a CD. At the centre Curtis lay, his naked arms by his side, and behind spectacles his eyes strained to see out of the window to his left, from which the sunlight flooded into the room. What he was thinking we will never know.

This picture by photographer Mark Seliger and the contemporary information by Light, who found Mayfield's spirituality infectious, even inspirational, over the several days that this interview took to complete tells us more about the great man. Curtis, who spent some of the shorter sessions in a wheelchair, took his time to tell his story but, as always, he was very reluctant to complain or criticize others. When asked about his music publishing company Curtom, that he had owned since he was 19, he said, 'Some of your greatest and biggest artists, all that they ever had was the fame but they didn't have the fortune,' and later he added, 'It just wipes me out today to get a check for a song that I wrote 30 years ago. It doesn't have anything to do with the size of the check, just the idea that you got it, that it's still contributing toward your livelihood.' In response to the suggestion that some of his songs were politically charged, Curtis replied, 'No, I'm just an artist and an entertainer. I am not really a political person. I think my value was just through observances as an individual. I do take the right to make my own particular statements such as "We People Who Are Darker Than Blue" or "(Don't Worry) If There's A Hell Below We're All Gonna Go".'

Despite his complete lack of mobility, Curtis was still positive about the future, hoping for a breakthrough in technology that might set him and others with similar injuries free, but he wasn't counting on it. 'My family keeps me from being totally still by stretching my hands and legs keeping them as limber as possible. Everything is still intact,' Curtis continued. 'The character, they say, is in the head. It's not what's below my neck; it's what's above. So I hope to stay in good care and carry on. I have no pity for myself, nor do I look for it. I'm quite thankful to still be around and have such a tremendous value and volume of people who have shown me love – I'm quite thankful for that. I don't hate, I'm not bitter or anything...'

Devon Russell recorded his own tribute album of Curtis Mayfield songs entitled *Darker Than Blue* in '93; this album was licensed through his own publishing company C Sweetest Music to *Prestige Records* (CDSGPO142) who released the album (with bonus tracks) internationally in '95. Devon, was better known to reggae fans (though there is precious little about him in *Reggae – The Rough Guide*). He was born in Jonestown, Kingston on 6 August '48 and began singing with the Tartans in '65 who scored a Jamaican #1 with 'Dance All Night'. Another early hit as half of the duo Lloyd & Devon (Lloyd Robins) on Derek Morgan's Hop label called 'Red Bum Ball' was achieved in the late '60s. As a solo artist Russell created an enthusiastic following through his sellout live performances in London, Paris and all across America. His classic recordings of 'Push Push', 'My Woman's Love' and 'Jah Holds The Key' on Coxone Dodd's Studio One label further enhanced his growing reputation and great reworkings of Mayfield's 'Move On Up' and '... Darker Than Blue' (which he first recorded in the early '80s) also proved very popular. Russell developed into an excellent guitarist and songwriter and recorded albums of his own compositions like *Bible & Gun* (Black Cat '96). Though his influence was still greatest in Jamaica, he toured Geneva, Paris and London in '94 where he played to sellout audiences who flocked to his concerts and club appearances. He regarded Curtis Mayfield as the best singer/songwriter in the world and consistently performed many of his songs as part of his own ongoing repertoire. His reworkings of Impressions' songs like 'I Gotta Keep On Moving', 'Never Too Much Love', 'Songs Of Sirene' ('Isle Of Sirens'), 'I'm Still Waiting', 'Falling In Love With You' and 'Choice Of Colors' are amongst the best tracks on *Darker Than Blue*. This tribute album was created and recorded at Leggo Studios in Kingston, Jamaica with Sly Dunbar and the Fire House Crew using some previously cut tracks from Tough Going and Channel One Studios. The solo Mayfield tracks that Russell recreated for this project were 'Love To The People', 'Wild & Free', 'We People Who Are Darker Than Blue', 'Move On Up', 'The Makings Of You', and 'Give Me Your Love'. The original *Darker Than Blue* album featured ten tracks; five extra cuts were added by Prestige later. Devon did not slavishly duplicate but tastefully recreated the spirit of Mayfield's music, adding his own infectious reggae pulse and ethnic Caribbean rhythms, which lift the tempo and atmosphere of this album to that of joyous celebration. He also employs a softer vocal technique here than on most of his other records. This album is not easy to find but it's well worth the effort. Internet information reveals that *Darker Than Blue* was re-issued on House Of Reggae (2622) in June '96. Devon Russell died, a victim to cancer on 18 June '97.

The concert that Mayfield had recorded at the Town & Country club in the spring of '90 was issued on a *Windsong CD* (WINCD 052) in February '94 as *Curtis Mayfield Live in Concert*. It had been first aired on the BBC's Radio 1 *Live In Concert* shortly after it had been recorded. This was the last appearance that Curtis made in the UK before his accident five months later. The musicians backing Mayfield were the nucleus of his road band – Buzz Amato (keyboards), Lee Goodness (drums), Louis Stefanell (percussion) plus Randy Brown (bass). This talented unit with Curtis on guitar and vocal worked through the cream of his record catalogue including all the standards one had grown to expect plus great versions of 'Billy Jack', 'Homeless' and 'To Be Invisible'. This concert had received a rave review in *Blues & Soul* already and of this CD they rightly proclaimed, 'Curtis Mayfield, a living legend, never fails to deliver.'

Richard Williams (*The Independent*, Sunday 27 February '94) wrote an eloquent tribute to Mayfield around a review of the Warner album *Tribute to Curtis Mayfield* aka *All Men Are Brothers* and an interview that he had conducted at the Mayfield home in Atlanta. This was the first article to appear in the UK press that covered Mayfield's story since the accident. Richard's questions and his observations etched out a portrait of finer resolution than previous similar articles. He observed that, though he was never as imposing a figure as Marvin Gaye, James Brown or Smokey Robinson, Mayfield's quiet influence was equally profound. When asked about his early songwriting Curtis revealed, 'Everything was a song. Every conversation, every personal hurt, every observance of people in stress, happiness and love...if you could feel it, I could feel it. And I could write a song about it. If you have a good imagination, you can go quite far.' Curtis also confessed to Richard that as a businessman he was not a natural: 'I'm a creative person. And I was just too young. I didn't have the knowledge. I'm sure that for every dollar I've earned, I've probably earned someone else 10 or 20 dollars.' When he asked Curtis if he could still sing he was told, 'Not in the manner as you once knew me. I'm strongest lying down like this. I don't have a diaphragm anymore. So when I sit up I lose my voice. I have no strength, no volume, no falsetto range, and I tire very fast.' Curtis expressed his gratitude to BMI (the US song royalty collection agency) who paid him an advance against earnings each year. 'My family have been fantastic, my son here [Todd] is my legs and my arms and part of my mind as well.'

The *New York Times* reported that the Grammies honoured Curtis with a 'Living Legend Award' in March '94 and this time he was well enough to accept it in person. He was welcomed on stage by a star-studded cast of presenters including Bruce Springsteen, Bonnie Raitt, Steve Winwood and others. Springsteen made the presentation and Curtis accompanied by Jerry, Sam & Fred, gave a short acceptance speech. The enthusiastic crowd also captured on camera included Aretha and no doubt many others at that star-studded audience were there to pay homage to Mayfield. In 1995, the Grammies followed up with a 'Lifetime Achievement Award' for Curtis, adding further to his rapidly growing cache of awards.

Warner Bros issued the timely *Tribute to Curtis (aka All Men Are Brothers*, 9362-45500-2) in '94, which comprised 17 Mayfield songs recorded especially for the album, the receipts of which went towards the huge medical bills that had been piling up since his accident. Gladys Knight turned in a fine version of the Impressions' sociological milestone 'Choice Of Colors', which introduces this illustrious collection. Steve Winwood, the ex-Spencer Davis and Traffic front man came next with his version of the Impressions' '60s style-setter 'It's Alright'. Steve's vocal is good enough but the arrangement and instrumentation lack the soulful swing of the original.

For the first time since the accident, Curtis was well enough to make a contribution of his own. He cut 'Let's Do It Again' in duet with the Repercussions, which used a sample from the Staples' original. Warner shot a promotional video, part of which was shown in the UK documentary *Darker Than Blue*. A tricky intro lays in the new version to which Mayfield's soft vocal tones have been added. It doesn't have the intensity of the original but transposes a cool, relaxed and pleasant alternative mood. 'Billy Jack' the anti-gun song, written loosely in the 'Stagger Lee' tradition, is effectively restyled by Lenny Kravitz, who himself had been greatly influenced by Mayfield in his formative years and turns in an excellent version. Whitney Houston's choice of song, 'Look Into Your Heart', was first screened on the Curtis-produced soundtrack for *Sparkle*, and originally sung by Irene Cara in the film. Whitney suffers from over vocal elaboration from time to time but thankfully not here (well, not too much). Pity she didn't use the original Mayfield music track while she was at it.

The following three songs dove deep into the Impressions treasure chest and came up with a variety of interpretations. Firstly, Springsteen gives 'Gypsy Woman' a ponderous treatment, fudging some of the lyrics and stretching his vocal spectrum at times. Given that none can touch the original (many have tried with greater success) it's not bad, but it lacks one very important ingredient – conviction. Clapton, however, pulls off a creditable alternative to the Impressions '64 hit 'You Must Believe Me'. The re-arrangement works perfectly and, of course, his guitar brings with it a dimension of its own. If anyone should cut more Mayfield songs, it is Ronald Isley. His silky vocal drifts effortlessly through a near five-minute version of 'I'm So Proud'.

There's no going back for a second taste at this point because we're already into the best track on the album, 'Fool For You' by the Impressions, teamed with Branford Marsalis. Branford's stunning arrangement takes the Impressions to a whole other level. His sax break is also beautifully understated. This track sadly was not the pilot for a forthcoming album –had some executive thought it worthwhile, it could have provided some interesting results, but it will have to remain merely a testament to what could be achieved by such inspired combinations. The Impressions, still working the back pages of their catalogue in a variety of American venues, took this opportunity to demonstrate that given the right breaks, they could still really lay it down. The comparatively youthful Tevin Campbell treats the gospel anthem 'Keep On Pushin'' with plenty of respect and adds a fresh and soulful vocal of his own, that does more than just mimic the original. Aretha Franklin chose 'The Makings Of You', a song that first appeared on Mayfield's superb début album *CURTIS*. She sails a sensitive and true course with her rendition of this beautiful ballad, which makes not only an appropriate but valuable contribution to this album. Back to the hugely popular Impressions' past hits, was the route that BB King took, when he cut 'Woman's Got Soul' from '65. He uses Lucille to great effect, as he bends this version into his own fashion of the blues, a shade he's made all his own. Rod Stewart treats us to yet another of his versions of 'People Get Ready', this time not with Jeff Beck but Ronnie Wood. Ron's not as ambitious with the solos but Rod clearly has an affinity with the song, which probably ranks highest among those for which Mayfield will be remembered. Narada Michael Walden attempts to follow Curtis into the maelstrom that is 'If There's A Hell Below'. After a naff start the vocal picks it up and rolls it out with guitar wah from Vernon 'Ice' Black. It's OK but lacks any real invention and, despite insistent drumming from Walden, pales in comparison to the original. The beauty of an album like this, other than its intention, is that it introduces Curtis and his music to a host of new listeners: Winwood, Kravitz, Springsteen, Clapton and Phil Collins fans, and there's a good chance that many of those more discerning listeners will latch onto the magic of Mayfield and investigate further. Over the years, many artists have listened to and attempted to emulate 'I've Been Trying', and now Phil's name can be added to that list. It's as you might expect: competent, well produced, but given the choice, I can think of at least three or four versions I would play first. 'I'm The One Who Loves You', though not one of the Impressions' biggest hits, has stood the test of time, and Stevie Wonder performs it to fullfillingness, as only he can.

Curtis did not write 'Amen', as many people believe, but he did buy the publishing rights from Jester Hairston, who was fortunate enough to put his name to the old gospel song when it was used on the soundtrack of *Lilies Of The Field*. After it became a big hit for the Impressions in January '65, it was adopted by them as their signature tune and has stuck ever since. Elton John & Sounds Of Blackness combine to bring 'Amen' into '90s gospel and thereby provide the last word on the proceedings.

This third 'tribute' album was released and received good airplay and climbed to #19 US and #25 UK on the soul album chart in April '94. It sold better than both the Shanachie and Devon Russell sets, due to the involvement of megastars like Springsteen, Clapton, Whitney and Elton. The collection was recorded at different locations mainly in the USA, and pulled together by Executive Producer Ron Weisner, album co-ordinator Karel Hannak and mixed by Gary Katz. Katz also produced the Repercussions/Curtis version of 'Let's Do It Again' in Curtom Studios, Atlanta and River Sound, New York. Branford Marsalis produced 'Fool For You' for the Impressions, which was recorded at Signet Sound, Hollywood.

Blues & Soul Editor Bob Killbourn gave a glowing review, despite reservations about certain tracks. He was most impressed by Lenny Kravitz, the Isley Brothers and Aretha, and concluded, 'These tribute versions by a host of star attractions are meritorious in concept and deserving of your full attention.' Jeff Lorez, *B&S* American correspondent, interviewed Mayfield that same month and published 'The Spirit and the Soul', which was also based around the *Tribute* album. Curtis told him that Ron Weisner had called him for his consent to do the album and a flattered Mayfield agreed, not really thinking that stars of that magnitude would find the time to especially record his songs. It all came together easily and Weisner later reported that everyone picked their favourite song and it was the easiest project that he had ever had. When Lorenz asked Curtis if there were any surprises he said 'You Must Believe Me' by Eric Clapton and 'I'm The One Who Loves You' by Stevie Wonder. Jeff also quizzed Curtis about the attention that he received from the current music generation and he replied, 'I feel so chosen that so many rap artists have done things with my music – sampling me and what have you and I might add that one of the songs that was not included in the album because of time was Chuck D of Public Enemy doing a fantastic version of 'We're A Winner' that I hope we'll still get to hear, maybe on his own album.' Curtis did a large number of interviews to promote this album but Jeff Lorenz found a way to keep the proceedings fresh and interesting, his intelligent probings revealed a little more of Mayfield's background story, his current attitudes and opinions.

A renewed interest in Mayfield and his music began to build from '93, three tribute albums had added to that interest and on the collectors (second-hand) market his albums were fetching high prices. Articles began to appear not only in the music press but in the style mags and weekend papers.

Ichiban had introduced the Curtom label on CD to Europe for the first time in '88 but during their tenure issued few European licenses to other companies but had granted Japanese licenses to Century Records (Japan) in '91. Century issued *Give, Get, Take & Have, Never Say You Can't Survive, Heartbeat,* and *Honesty* in '91 for the Japanese market. A few legitimate Ichiban/Curtom albums, *A Man Like Curtis* and the Stairsteps *Comeback*, were swamped by an avalanche of technically inferior/imperfect CDs. After the split from Ichiban in mid '93, European import CDs of Mayfield albums began to appear in UK record shops, as it turned out without his involvement or permission. Many labels were not gaining the rights or using the Curtom master tapes as their originals. Movie Play Gold (Portugal) issued five Mayfield CDs, *CURTIS, CURTIS/LIVE, Roots, Superfly* and *Back To The World,* but none of the masters that they used came from the Curtom vaults, according to Mayfield and Curtom CEO Heiman (a closer technical examination supports these assertions). In the UK Charly Records began issuing Curtom product in '94, after striking a legitimate deal with MPG. That year Charly issued 15 Curtis albums plus four compilations, *Power To The People, Get Down To The Funky Groove, Groove On Up* and *Tripping Out.* The same year a Japanese label Jimco (under sublicenses issued by Charly International APS) also released 16 Mayfield CDs in Japan, which included *Groovy Curtis, Mellow Curtis* and *Best of Curtis.*

Flagging the imminent showing of his documentary, Caryl Phillips (a Booker Prize nominee in '94) wrote 'A tribute to a silent prophet' (*Guardian,* 11 March '95). This well researched article told us that Curtis 'Lee' Mayfield was born in Cook County Hospital Chicago, and was five years old when his father left home, leaving his family (three sons and two daughters) to a poverty line existence, often on welfare. Rootless, they were constantly on the move, Curtis attended nine different schools before high school, and the one constant in his life was his grandmother's church. Caryl wrongly diagnosed that the accident had silenced Curtis, who he called one of the great voices of oppressed America. In fact the exposure that this documentary brought to Mayfield was one of the factors that provided him with enough inspiration to try again, against all the odds. But it was a mistake to categorize Mayfield's music so narrowly; it had a far wider impact and should not be confined to stereotypical racial groupings. There was always some concern in the music biz that Mayfield's insistent speaking out against all the injustices that he encountered might be counter productive (if you are trying to sell large quantities of records to the white middle class). Phillips suggests that it was after the 'We're A Winner' debacle, that Curtis formed Curtom and became an independent maverick. Caryl concluded that only once in a generation, there comes along a writer who is so intimately connected with his audience.

Darker Than Blue was first shown on UK TV on the 21 March '95, through BBC 1's *Omnibus* series. It was written and presented by Caryl Phillips and directed by Michael Houldey. Generally, Phillips did a great job telling the Mayfield story, set against a graphically stark view of the Chicago where the singer grew up. The documentary was packed full of fascinating anecdotes from friends and collaborators Jerry Butler, Carl Davis, Fred Cash and Sam Gooden. With interesting contributions from mother Marion Mayfield and son Todd, who at the time managed all Mayfield business. In the main, both pictorial and factual research was excellent but a little misleading in a couple of places. Some of the songs, allowing for artistic license, could have been better placed. But the most glaring omission was the 'missing years' of the Impressions as a quintet. Perhaps, understandably, things had been made difficult for Phillips by the Impressions clash at the Rock & Roll Hall of Fame ceremony back in early '91, which had erupted into a stand off. Irrespective of the personal differences between these factions, historically, the Brooks Brothers played a big influential role in the early development of the Impressions. Not only were they involved in the creation of 'For Your Precious Love' but their voices made an important contribution to the group's early identity. They were with the Impressions for six years and should not have been ignored.

Despite this important omission, Caryl wove many interesting threads into the story that presented a fascinating portrait of Mayfield. His on-camera interviews with Butler, Davis, Sam & Fred, Curtis' mother Marion and, of course, Curtis himself, provided genuine evidence for his careful reconstruction of Mayfield's life and generally demonstrated the breadth of his influence. The footage shown (both past and of the time) gave us all great insight to the real Chicago, as opposed to the shiny towers of the city centre that we are so often shown. The interview with Richard Green also revealed long-suspected American social engineering over Vietnam, touched on by Curtis in songs like 'Back To The World', 'Stop The War' and 'We Got To Have Peace'. It's a touching experience to see Curtis clad in a multi-coloured broad checked shirt, propped up in his wheelchair unable to move below his neck, yet still vital and brimming with the spirit of life. Phillips use of old photos, magazines and record covers, intercut with footage shot at Wells High and other locations provide further insight into the early influences that were the background to the creation of Chicago soul. The images reinforce the story of the wilful inner city neglect that created the poverty and existence of 'the projects' like Cabrini Green. Through it all Mayfield (and many others) struggled for recognition, gradually developing his own distinctive music, a process that made him resolutely independent and self-reliant. Nobody was going to take too much advantage of Curtis. He was not going to let them steal his songs, like the generation before, or turn the Impressions into a franchise on wages, like many others had. This did not make him universally popular in the music biz but it earned him much respect for his integrity from everyone else (from those who have some interest for the rights of the individual, that is).

Modestly, Curtis claimed to be only a 'fair' businessman on camera but he was much more than that. There has been a tendency to compare Curtom, his record label, to Motown or Stax (even Atlantic) but these were much bigger labels with wider commercial opportunities. Fairer comparisons would be with T-Neck or Peoples Records, two other successful contemporary soul labels, built around one central talent (the Isley Brothers and James Brown, respectively). This would provide a less dramatic but more realistic perspective. Curtom may have been one of the greatest soul labels by reputation but not in terms of its size.

It would be difficult to ascertain just how much of Mayfield's work has been used as a teaching tool but no doubt, brighter academics have latched onto its true worth over the years. It was interesting to observe, in this documentary, that the 'Pusherman' text, so heavily criticized when *Superfly* was first issued in '72, was now understood and being used constructively in a sociology class. Almost 30 years later the school children present all agreed that things were much, much worse. More recently Chrissie Murray wrote a letter to the *Guardian* (30/12/99) highlighting that on her music-focused American Studies Course (at the Central London Polytechnic a few years earlier) a proposed list of 'serious' musicians for discussion by students as part of their course, not only included Charles Ives, Aaron Copeland, Leonard Bernstein, Philip Glass, Steve Reich, George Gershwin but also Curtis Mayfield, the only artist from the pop music field deemed significant enough to include. But she added that none of the other students seemed to know who he was.

Curtis was an artist who felt compelled to be outspoken on a number of civil rights issues (amongst many other topics) in his songs from as early as '64 but this didn't sit right not only with opposing views but with business interests that feared sponsor loss (record companies, TV and radio stations). Attempts to muzzle him failed but even those close to him were slightly embarrassed at first by all but his love songs. Curtis would ask, 'Why does it always have to be a love song?' Later as they understood the significance of these songs it would lead Carl Davis, one of the greatest Chicago record producers of all time to say, 'I think we failed to tell our kids what the real deal is out on the streets.' He went on to explain that his generation passed on existing structures but failed to fully understand the rapid deterioration of family and church values on the street. Carl was buried in some Chicago studio making many of the greatest records of all time with Jackie Wilson, Tyrone Davis, Walter Jackson etc but Curtis was still on the case. To the rap generation, Curtis is a hero, they sample and steal his music but Davis says, 'We didn't pay attention then and we lost an entire generation of kids.' As Todd revealed, Curtis likes the music of today and enjoys the fact that they incorporate his music into theirs. After all it is just the next genre after soul, reggae, rock and pop to do so.

Only a few biographical documentaries have been made about Mayfield so far and *Darker Than Blue* is the best, and no doubt since his death there will be further chances to see it in the UK on terrestrial TV (perhaps updated). At the time the *Omnibus* TV special *Darker Than Blue* was greeted with plenty of positive reaction from press and public alike. *Time Out* critic Steve Grant (21 March '95) called Curtis the black Dylan and agreed that his work finds favour with a new generation of black artists. Grant was critical of Phillips' objectivity: 'Occasionally his obvious loyalties militate against strict reportage.' But he did generally find the documentary, 'Engrossing and often moving'. *Times* reviewer David Flusfeder (18 March '95), on the other hand, found it a little pedestrian: 'middle-aged men repeating anecdotes' but was gracious enough to find Carl Davis good value. There have been a couple of repeat screenings since, on UK Arena, a cable TV station in '98 and April '99.

In the UK, Ace/Kent began to issue their Impressions 2fer series starting with *Impressions/Never Ending Impressions* (Kent CDKEND 126), the first two albums the group had recorded for ABC. Kent had earlier issued vinyl repros of the first four Impressions' ABC albums, but this time I was engaged to write biographical sleevenotes and design artwork for compact disc.

The Face in their telephone Q&A with Mayfield (June '95) had him talking about the difficulties of writing when you don't have the use of your body. As he struggled with what for most people would be an insurmountable problem, others began to find ways of working with him, accessing his stream of consciousness and found new ways to divert, trawl and develop his ideas and suggestions. One night as Curtis lay watching *The Shawshank Redemption* on TV, he connected with the story more than most of us. He saw there an added parallel of the liberation of the spirit, his spirit imprisoned in a body that doesn't function. Encouraged by the movie he began to write a song. In recent interviews he had spoken about the ideas that came to him for songs, when he said, 'I have ideas, but if you can't jot them down or get them to music they fade like dreams.' He decided not to wait for voice-activated technology but began to work with other writers, who would sit at his bedside talking about the ideas he had and adding their own. The first song that he worked on this way was to become 'Back To Livin' Again', which he wrote with Rosmary Woods.

The Washington Times announced in November '95, that Curtis had struck a deal with Warner's to cut a new album. Rumours also leaked that he was planning to record a duet with Bonnie Raitt, but that one did not materialize. The following month, Kent issued their second UK 2fer *Keep On Pushing/People Get Ready* (Kent CD KEND 130), considered by many to be the Impressions finest work. Although the interest in Curtis' earlier work with the Impressions and others had been re-issued on CD in the States, since Ichiban, Curtom had not looked for another distributor but had dealt directly with other labels to produce *Curtis Mayfield's Chicago Soul* (Legacy ZK 64770) in '95. Whilst this was a great compilation for Mayfield fans, he was not entirely happy with the deal and Curtom Classics issued two CD compilation albums of Mayfield songs independently for the American market *Curtis Mayfield* (9501) and *Living Legend* (9502), both in '95. These albums were only available in the UK on import at a few specialist stores. Curtis felt that, what with the increasing number of bogus European re-issues, significant changes had to be made and he reunited with Marv (Stuart) Heiman, (now using his full name), who was still based in Chicago and he began to run the operation from there. He legitimized the UK Charly deal until the end of that year and went looking for a new UK outlet. Charly had only issued two Curtom CDs in '95, *The Man* by Leroy Hutson and the Natural Four's début album for the label, the *Natural Four*.

In Chicago Marv Heiman assumed control of all Curtom business and began his reconstruction of the Curtom catalogue. He negotiated a deal with Warner Brothers to issue the Curtom catalogue in America through their excellent re-issue label Rhino. Curtom then approached Castle UK (parent company to Sequel) with an offer of the UK rights to re-issue the catalogue. Bob Fisher swiftly orchestrated his UK re-issue programme and through '96, Sequel released two Impressions' 2fers *This Is My Country/Young Mods' Forgotten Story* (NEMCD 782) and *Check Out Your Mind/Times Have Changed* (NEMCD 843). Charly also put out their version of *This Is My Country/Young Mods' Forgotten Story (CDGR 108)*. The first two Mayfield re-issues were *Love Is The Place/Honesty* (NEM CD 783) and a *Very Best of Curtis Mayfield* a compilation that was issued on Castle's Renaissance Collectors Series (CCSCD 806). Castle's higher profile had attracted US interest and Alliance bought into the company in late '95 and set up a US label HQ in New York. Bill Inglot at Rhino did an inventory on all the existing Curtom master tapes (including unreleased material) and Fisher planned his UK re-issue campaign.

Charly continued their re-issue program during '96 much as before with a spread of CDs across the Curtom spectrum. They issued four Curtis CDs, including a double compilation *Curtis Definitive Collection*, which followed the similar two-CD set *Changing Impressions*. Further issues came from Hutson *(Love Oh Love)*, Linda *(If My Friends Could See Me Now)* and the second Natural Four album *Heaven Right Here On Earth*. The highlight of their '96 re-issues however was a two-CD set (51 tracks) called the *Curtom Story* (CD LAB 107), which contained a 30-page booklet, compiled and annotated by Trevor Swaine.

In America, Rhino produced the most ambitious Mayfield project yet, *People Get Ready (The Curtis Mayfield Story)* (R2 72262) a three-CD box-set for the US market, which contained a luxurious 60-page booklet packed with great photos and info. This high quality package was produced by David McLees, David Nathan & Bill Inglot and designed by John McKenna. The booklet begins with a 'personal/sociopolitical' view by Wayne Edwards that reads a bit like a sociology thesis. Then comes David Nathan's historical perspective and finally Alan Warner's personal tribute (based on an interview from '94). The last ten pages of the booklet are filled with detailed track listings, discographical information and numerous credits, acknowledgements etc. As mentioned before this album is a quality item, designed for the American market where it sold for about $70. It appeared on import in larger UK record stores for around £65. Also inside the box are three CDs, the first dozen tracks are Impressions sides (eight ABC/four Curtom) and the remaining tracks are chronological Mayfield solo recordings. Many of these tracks are the edits originally released as singles but in some cases we are treated to longer album cuts. No previously unissued material was contained in this collection. In UK *Record Collector* magazine reviewer Peter Doggett a long-time Mayfield fan, described this collection as 'staggering and sometimes overwhelming' but had some reservations stating '*People Get Ready* not only breaks one of the cardinal rules of box-set compilation, by including no rare or unissued material, but it also pays more regard to chart statistics than to the music.' Doggett concludes, 'Neither long or adventurous enough to capture Curtis' breadth, *People Get Ready* is a rare disappointment from Rhino, whose box-sets usually rival anything coming out of the UK. Maybe someone on this side of the Atlantic should try their arm instead.'

One of the earliest Curtom projects Bob Fisher planned to issue in the UK was a Curtis box-set that he called me about in February '96. He had heard a rumour about some unissued Curtis tracks that I had (given to me when I had visited Curtom in late '72). This was my lucky day because I was asked to compile, notate and design the box-set. The Curtom master tapes were already in the hands of Rhino, and Bob set about making preparations to access those needed for the next set of Sequel releases. Things began well but due to changes in New York at Castle, a management shake up was about to happen, causing tremours that would reach London.

Johnny Copasetic wrote a great piece entitled 'Johnny Cool and the Isle of Sirens', an investigation of the evolutionary elements between Jamaican music and Chicago soul, in which he compared the songwriting of Mayfield to that of Prince Buster. Copasetic's interesting theories on this subject play down the real reason that Mayfield was such a big influence on Jamaican music. It was not only through his records with the Impressions but more his personal appearances there in the early '60s. At that time, the Impressions' programme included 'Minstrel And Queen', 'Gypsy Woman', 'People Get Ready' and 'Keep On Pushing' and the audience included Bob Marley and the Wailers, Prince Buster and everybody else in town. Mayfield's lyrics/music had a fundamental influence in Jamaica at the same time they did in America and Europe (to a lesser extent). Most of his 'story' songs were written at a young age when he was influenced by the images he saw and stories he heard as well as events he experienced ('At The County Fair' and 'Little Young Lover') and his understanding of the deeper ills of society had not yet entirely crystallized. 'Isle Of Sirens', central to the theme of Copasetic's rationale, was also an early composition, though the Impressions didn't cut that one until '67. Mayfield simply switched subjects from history to sociology (not politics). Even he was not to know that when the

Impressions sang 'Minstrel And Queen', the extra dimension it would have on the Jamaican perspective, or the many, many covers and versions it would inspire. 'Johnny Cool and the Isle of Sirens' appeared in *Rock File* ('72) and was later reprinted in *The Beat Goes On* (Pluto Press '96), a book in the style of the *Rock File* series edited by Charlie Gillett and Simon Frith.

Geoffrey Himes wrote 'Mayfield: Art & Soul' for the *Washington Post* towards the end of '96. After covering the usual background biographical info, Himes suggests that Mayfield seemed to disappear right off the radar screen and that he had ventured into ambitious territory, which meant that commercial radio sponsors refused to acknowledge or play his music. He also reports that Curtis used the base of Curtom to create a whole new brand of soul, through studio development. Mayfield made great demands on listeners, who, in general, want to be entertained rather than informed and tended to settle for the glossy soul of Luther Vandross, Whitney Houston and Mariah Carey. He also suggests that Curtom was under-promoted and that they bounced around between distributors. He was critical of the Rhino box-set saying that, 'Box essayist Wayne Edwards, struggles to reduce Mayfield to a political propagandist, while David Nathan settles for a dull year by year recounting of Mayfield's career.' Geoffrey also states that the solo Curtis matured to harder hitting material, after leaving the confines of the Impressions – hitting his masterpiece with *Superfly*. But Curtis counters that *Superfly*, 'didn't make enough money to be a masterpiece'. Though black America embraced the *Superfly* character as an icon, Curtis said that he had, 'Lots of problems with *Return Of Superfly* that he would rather not discuss'.

Mojo magazine published results of their '100 Greatest Guitarists Of All Time' poll in June '96. Most of the stellar guitar heroes were prominently featured but quite unexpectedly they placed Curtis Mayfield in the 25th spot. In recent interviews, Curtis had said, with a mixture of sadness and resignation, that he mourned the absence of his axe, his constant and closest companion until the accident.

It now seems that his individual, self-taught style has produced an indelible and fundamental influence on musicians of all kinds. In the VH1 *Legends* TV series (see Chapter 10) Curtis said, 'I'm sorry to say that my style of playing is probably gone forever – the tuning – I can't play it and there's no one to teach it – but there again it was a gift.' *Guitar Player* magazine (December '96) ran Jas Obrecht's 'The Messenger Returns' an article/interview with guitar god Eric Clapton, who was quoted as saying, 'Curtis changed the course of modern music. He brought a refinement, a cool to R&B with social comment leading the way for other songwriters, guitar players and singers in all fields of music. He is a great talent and inspiration to us all.'

12 New World Order

For Curtis Mayfield, the most productive and successful year since his accident was 1996. His newest album the exquisite *New World Order* was released and sold quite well in America (#24 US R&B November '96). Spike Lee was inspired enough by the title track to add it to the soundtrack of his then latest movie *Get On The Bus* (see Chapter 9). The movie also featured older Mayfield classics 'People Get Ready', 'Keep On Pushing' and 'We're A Winner'.

Initially, Curtis had serious doubts about being able to summon enough strength to even attempt the *New World Order* project. He told Vivien Goldman (*Daily Telegraph*, 25 January '97) that as he was writing 'Back To Livin' Again' it seemed to give him an inner strength. All his life, until the accident, the expression of his music had always been second nature to Mayfield, through his voice and guitar. Now he had to learn to completely rely on other musicians to realize the music evolving in his head. Curtis reported that when he first tried to sing in his studio the results were very disappointing but he soon developed a technique that enabled him to record a few lines at a time, which could be edited in the studio later. He discovered a way of getting gravity to help his lungs do the work in the studio and it was this way that Curtis evolved the system of singing, lying down at a slant (sometimes flat) on the studio floor. He recorded his voice at a slower and lower level than in the past and the results were sped up for the falsetto sections. Once it got around the industry that he was working again, Warner offered an advance on the album, other offers came in and pretty soon all kinds of people were collaborating, writing and setting up recording equipment in Mayfield's bedroom. Progress was checked and things had to stay flexible, as sometimes the efforts exhausted Curtis and he had to rest. It wasn't easy for him but he managed to tolerate it long enough to get the album completed. As he said to Chris Wells (*Echoes*, 18/1/99), 'It took all my know how and we got it done.'

The first track that Curtis actually recorded for the new album was 'New World Order' in late '95. Curtom Studios had now moved into his house and this is where all the various producers and writers co-ordinated their activities and much of the album was cut. Mayfield's son Todd, who also lived there, looked after in-house operations while Rosmary Woods and Joy Bailey were the actual album co-ordinators. Mayfield was Executive Producer and worked with the session producers as and when he could. The production of the title track was split between Mayfield, Brian Fleming, Carlos Glover and Rosmary Woods. The song itself was written by Fleming and Raimundo Thomas – they had written a couple of verses and gave it to Curtis for completion.

Now 'New World Order' is a term that's been around for quite some time and it means different things to different people. For those who feared change, even before the atrocities of 'nine/eleven', it was regarded as a threat but change is as inevitable as the future itself. For Curtis, it was about inspiration and a positive change beneficial to all; it was not about taking over the world or any kind of revolution. His concerns were, as ever, about redressing the balance of equality. A brand new day for all the people in the world – a freedom song for everyone. Curtis was ever optimistic, to him, even in his condition, the future still looked good. Writers Brian and Raimundo joined Rosmary Woods in the chorus that sang so effectively behind Curtis.

Sandra St Victor dueted with Mayfield on 'I Believe In You', which was written by Curtis and Rosmary and also cut in '95, with the same production team. It has a similar treatment and tempo to the tracks that Curtis cut with Linda Clifford on *Right Combination* back in 1980. Given how these tracks were constructed they come over as relaxed and surprisingly well-crafted records. The only other song written and recorded in '95 was 'Let's Not Forget', a collaboration between Mayfield and Arnold Hennings. This is a song of resolution, for recharging the spirit ready for the next step in the right direction. Mike Peterson and Tim Harrigan added all kinds of atmospherics, when they mixed the track at Purple Dragon Studios in Atlanta. These studios were also used in early '96 to record 'Just A Little Bit Of Love', which Mayfield wrote with Carlos Glover (and Raimundo Thomas). Glover had been significantly involved with Curtis in the recording of the 'Take It To The Streets' album in '90. Once again he provided similar skills for *New World Order*, recording, mixing and supplying drum sequencing for much of the album. Curtis trades lines with background singers Raimundo, Rosmary and Robert Scott Jr and rappers Blaise Mayfield and Lisa Coates. The track comes together as the perfect cocktail for established values, change and progress.

For 'Ms Martha' and 'Here But I'm Gone' Curtis teamed up with Organized Noize to write and perform the songs, but they were sole producers. 'Ms Martha' features the amazing Mavis Staples in duet with Mayfield, who wasn't well enough to attend the studio the day that they cut this and whose voice was added later. Mavis cut her vocal track in about an hour and a half and stunned Organized Noize with her ability and professionalism at the session. Together, they cut a beautifully relaxed groove that begins with the wah of Craig Love's guitar and moves right along. The guitar (this time by Martin Terry) also made subtle additions to 'Here But I'm Gone', a song whose lyrics rue the wasted existence of the hard drug addict.

It seems that only one song created by Curtis and co author producer Daryl Simmons 'No One Knows About A Good Thing' was used for this album. Maybe others were unfinished or just not used; without more detailed information it is hard to say. But this beautiful ballad is Daryl's only track and features his keyboards, talkbox and FX programming, all to great effect.

As part of Producer Roger Troutman's contribution to the album he wanted to record 'We People Who Are Darker Than Blue' again. Mayfield also thought it needed saying again and although he and Roger did not write any new songs, they combined to reinterpret two that Curtis had previously recorded. 'Darker...' from the *CURTIS* album had grown into one of his many well-respected tracks. Troutman and his brother

Terry, who produced both tracks, laid down the rhythm track and took it to Curtis, who then recorded his vocal track in bed on Roger's portable computer console – this was then taken away on the hard drive and the detail filled out in their own studios. What emerged was a very sophisticated collage of new sounds and FX provided by the keyboards, talkbox, bass and drum programming of Roger and some remixed sections from the original track. Their second co-production was 'It Was Love That We Needed', which was written and recorded by Curtis in '79 but not issued at the time. Troutman took this track and worked his studio magic, adding Shirley Murdock's multi-tracked vocal, which acts as a solid foundation to which Mayfield's lead is keyed.

Many of us have fond memories of 'The Girl I Find' by the Impressions ('69) – it is one of their finest records. In a telephone interview Curtis revealed, 'A few years ago, I recorded "The Girl I Find" ('87) for an Italian friend of mine. In the studio, Buzz Amato played piano and Lebron Scott played bass but as I remember, I played all the other instruments.' Curtis and Carlos took this unissued track to Doppler Studios in Atlanta and remixed it for *NWO*.

Narada Michael Walden took time out from the Arista sessions that he was recording with Soul Queen Aretha Franklin to produce 'Back To Livin' Again' for Curtis. He had previously cut 'If There's A Hell Below' for the Warner tribute album. Mayfield, who had already written the song with Rosmary Woods, got the idea after watching *The Shawshank Redemption* on TV. As he lay there Curtis identified with the movie's central character and the personal struggles that he endured, then he wrote the lyric and melody in about half an hour. It is the song from these sessions that most accurately describes the raising of Mayfield's spiritual state to a level that made this whole process possible. It was the perfect song for this situation, echoing sentiments that Mayfield had so often expressed but now had the added dimension of his current physical condition. It further emphasized his resolve to overcome all the obstacles, whatever they were and get back to what's really important. Curtis had long expressed these ideals but now his spirit had to adopt a superhuman dimension to reach the levels of expression that previously had been second nature to him. It was an astounding achievement that he ever conceived and completed these sessions at all. After Curtis and Narada had this one finished, Walden played it to Aretha, who was so impressed by what she heard, she insisted that she sing on the track and her contributions were added later.

Curtis, Narada and Rosmary combined to provide yet another classic 'The Got Dang Song' that cleverly has us singing along, before we realise the true meaning of what it is that we are singing. This is the very subject of what the song is about. It's so easy to sing along with the chorus (the general point of view) as it highlights the subconscious exclusion of things that humans often fail to confront head on. Curtis brilliantly illuminated the conditions for the many oppressed by the totem pole of their existence. Stuck in spaces of allocation when they are desperate for change and improvement. His focus falls not only on the obvious abuses of power and privilege but also on the deeply ingrained cynicism, ill-considered choices and their knock-on effects on the majority – his reference to minimum wage for instance. Once more, the poet challenges mankind's complacency and infinite ability to ignore the fundamental long-established wrongs in the world, which only serves to support their continuance.

A few words from Curtis in monologue remind us that, despite all the problems in the world today, 'Never forget the life we live is "Oh So Beautiful".' This song, written by Walden, Mayfield and Erik Hicks is the perfect choice as the final album track. It switches our focus to all that is good, as it plays out the last few minutes of this outstanding album.

You know how difficult things can be when your car won't start, how irritating when your computer or your mobile packs up, there's never a good time. The things that we use in our daily lives, rely on and take for granted – when they don't work, our response is often to curse our luck or bad fortune. After 40, when the eyesight starts to deteriorate and you catch yourself damning the tiny lettering on labels and CDs, or your hearing starts to fade and other people's mumbles wind you up. Anytime I feel like this, I think of Curtis and just how much spirit it must have taken each time he wrote or sang a line, even spoke a few words. This is one sure way of putting any inconsequential irritations into real perspective. Similarly once you begin to get over the miracle that Curtis ever managed to record this album, it is only then that you can begin to appreciate the positive, sociological poetry and the beauty of his love songs without any further reference to such considerations. It's also then that this album stands up totally on its own merits; it is a modern classic. Though I have reviewed these tracks in an approximation to the recorded sessions, the actual running order was put together with perfection. *New World Order* is certainly one of the only albums to ever be written, arranged, produced, recorded and mixed by a quadriplegic – what a marvellous achievement.

New World Order was released in America 20 September '96 and received good reviews, which instigated further media attention. Despite the coverage, sales followed Mayfield's by now established pattern, building slowly (it reached #137 pop) and topping out at #24 on R&B albums two months later. An edited version of the title track was issued in America on a CD single in October and a video was shown to promote the single's release but 'New World Order' (CD 9175682) found limited success on the singles chart where it only managed #26 R&B and did not light up the autumnal skies as predicted by many US critics and reviewers.

To coincide with the release of *New World Order* the American music TV channel VH1 aired a Curtis Mayfield documentary as part of their *Legends* series in September '96. Narrator Kris Kristofferson took us through Mayfield's formative years against a backdrop of black & white family photos and early documentary footage of the Chicago of the time. In interviews, Jerry Butler and Curtis responded to questions that set the scene and told of their combined introduction into the music business via the Impressions and Vee-Jay records. Curtis described the snowstorm that prevented their audition with Chess records and how fate led them to Vee-Jay's door and the release of their first big hit, 'For Your Precious Love'. Long unseen early TV footage showed Curtis, Sam & Fred performing 'It's Alright', 'Amen' and 'Woman's Got Soul' as the documentary traced the Impressions journey to bring a civil rights message to America via 'Keep On Pushing'.

Curtis then invited everyone on board the freedom train for 'People Get Ready' in his bid to end the apartheid that had too long plagued America and clearly shown in the accompanying footage to this great song. We were also reminded of the difficulties these crusaders for peaceful change faced, when some radio stations refused to play 'We're A Winner' but could not prevent it from becoming a hit. The Impressions can be seen performing this song on US TV in some of their earliest colour footage. After a short break of encouragement to indulge in products produced by sponsors AT&T and Plymouth cars, we were told of Mayfield's development as a freelance producer and his establishment of his own label. We see more interesting clips of the Impressions singing the remarkable 'Choice Of Colors' and 'Check Out Your Mind', which switched between two versions, the second featuring new lead voice Leroy Hutson and trace Curtis' emergence as a solo star.

Mayfield traded the compassion of his earlier work for the fire and brimstone of 'If There's A Hell Below' and the forceful message of involvement in 'We People Who Are Darker Than Blue'. From now on many of his lyrics would have a sharper edge, tempered with his ongoing philosophy of peace, reason and honesty. His excellent soundtrack *Superfly* provided an important counter to the images that the movie projected. After skipping more invitations to purchase hamburgers on the car phone, the final segment of *Legends* rather truncates Mayfield's last 28 years. We are treated to a rare clip of Curtis appearing on *Soul Train* as he lip-syncs his 'Future Shock' hit.

Through the magic of editorial cuts, we leapfrog Mayfield's five-year stint with Warner Brothers to witness his fall in popularity, unsuccessful dalliance with disco and the eventual closure of Curtom Records. Between his concerts and that of the lengthy 25th 'Silver Anniversary Tour' with the Impressions and Butler, Curtis went into a kind of semi-retirement. The comeback years are sketched in with clips of the late '80s covers by Rod Stewart, Jeff Beck and En Vogue and his slight return to the movies with Fishbone in *I'm Gonna Git U Sucka* and Ice-T in *Return Of Superfly*, which provides another chance to view part of the great video made to promote *Superfly 1990*. With the reactivation of Curtom came the final album before his tragic accident, *Take It To The Streets*.

Curtis spoke in interview of the event that halted this promising comeback. But despite total physical debilitation he was back in the studio four years later to duet with the Repercussions on their reinterpretation of his 'Let's Do It Again'. Kristofferson mentioned the all-star tribute albums of Mayfield's songs and discussed the making of *New World Order*, which was in completion at the same time as this TV special. On the outro, the ever-modest Curtis said, 'I'm just me, If I'm a legend then anybody can be a legend,' and departed to the strains of 'Oh So Beautiful' the final track of his final album.

This special contained some interesting footage, clips and appearances from Marion Jackson (Mayfield's mother), Jerry and Curtis but the portrait that it conveys is only partial. It truncates his life story and 40-year career into an hour and was no doubt intended as a longer project, which has been telescoped to fit the TV schedules. I couldn't detect a directorial credit, which could indicate internal disenchantment with the final cut.

In an interview by John Leland for *Newsweek* (Music section, 14 October '96), Curtis spoke of his phantom hands, describing how he recorded his music prone, singing a few lines at a time until his breath gave out. He also recollected that he used the early limericks he remembered hearing as a child, to lay the foundations for his first songs. It became an early discipline to be able to write a few lines of poetry on any subject that caught his attention, a kind of living poetry of his reactions to the things happening to and around him.

As press reports confirmed that Spike Lee would be adding 'New World Order' to the soundtrack of his forthcoming movie *Get On The Bus* in October '96, Dove Books published *Poetic License*, a collection of Mayfield's poems and song lyrics in America. This volume had taken two years to come to fruition. It contains the lyrics to 72 of Curtis' finest songs with many illustrations by David Soto and an introduction by the man himself. Mayfield made an astute observation about his music in the introduction when he stated, 'Music lets you relate to another person and feel with them and for them. And when humans from all walks of life can experience a piece of music and feel the same way – that's soul.' Dove Audio also issued an audio book (Tape/ Dove 31490) in January '96 with narrations by Melissa Manchester, Burt Reynolds, Blair Underwood, Roy Innis, Freda Payne, Sharon Stone and Jerry Butler, which has a 90-minute running time. *Poetic License* was not published in the UK in either book or audio formats.

Mayfield, who described the relationship with his band members as to that of a marriage, lost one of his nearest and dearest friends, bassist Joseph 'Lucky' Scott in the latter months of '96. Joe, who had struggled against deteriorating health for the past couple of years, first appeared on the CURTIS/LIVE album in '71 and was an original member of the Curtis Mayfield Experience, as they were initially called. He worked closely with Curtis taking on an MD role within Mayfield's tour band but was also involved at Curtom as a writer, musician, arranger and producer. 'Lucky' was part of the Curtom House Band and recorded on many of the albums cut at the studios between '71 and '80. He cut records with Mayfield, the Impressions and Rasputin Stash. (In the past 'Lucky' has been confused with the 'other' Joe Scott who wrote 'Never Let Me Go' a song recorded by the Impressions in March '62 and reworked by Curtis later.)

In America ,'Back To Livin' Again' was nominated for a Grammy in the R&B Best Male vocalist category of '97 but was beaten out of the award by 'I Believe I Can Fly' by R Kelly. Warner had issued 'Back To Livin' Again' in the US as the third single from the NWO album but like its predecessor 'No One Knows A Good Thing', it had not made much impression on either singles chart.

As the new year came into being Warner Bros prepared to issue New World Order in the UK and Europe. Anticipating the albums release a number of articles began to appear in the UK tabloids. 'People get ready' warned Adam Sweeting in the Guardian (17 January '97), in which he reminded us that in the States relatively little attention was given by the media to his accident (even less in the UK). He also confirmed that at that time Mayfield was considered by the fashionably hip, to be a musical relic whose significance had peaked during America's radical civil conflicts of the '70s, but who had subsequently lost direction and drifted into the artistic doldrums. Adam challenges this gross over-simplification with the suggestion that this much talent was always likely to make a comeback. The report mentioned Curtis' plans for his own new rap label Conquest and also revealed how Anne Elleston (producer of BBC's Darker Than Blue) had orchestrated Mayfield's first substantial interview since the accident in '95, which not only made that documentary possible but gave momentum to all the other interviews that followed too. Curtis articulated the hope that developing technology might throw him a future lifeline. These wishes didn't materialize for one reason or another but *New World Order* was completed nevertheless. This, like many of us, Sweeting found amazing, not merely because of its existence, but because of its stunning quality, compassion, insight, optimism and Curtis' poignant dream of a better society. For those that had expected no more from Curtis after his accident Sweeting concluded that, 'with the release of *New World Order* Curtis has moved the goal posts.'

In an interview by Chris Wells ('Moving On Up', *Time Out*, 15 January '97) Curtis announced, 'I'm a 54-year-old quadriplegic and there's not too much demand for that these days.' Wells was incredulous that against all the odds Mayfield was about to release a new album. 'Curtis is quite simply an extraordinary human being,' he wrote and elaborated further in *Echoes* three days later ('New Beginnings') that he was speechless with admiration at Mayfield's triumph of hope over experience. In this telephone interview, Curtis described his recent endeavours saying, 'All people want to make better lives for themselves and their loved ones. I won't say it was easy because it wasn't.' He went on to say that he was inspired by early playbacks, which enabled him to finish the album. Wells incisive questions teased out some interesting answers and anecdotes. 'For the artist it's all about the publishing, that's where the money is. Not the live appearances, as many of the record companies in the '50s and '60s would have you believe,' Curtis said and added that he would see royalties from *New World Order* as a publisher but not as an artist – that's the way it's always been.

Vivien Goldman predicted the 'Resurrection of Mayfield' (*Daily Telegraph*, 25 January '97) and dubbed Curtis the 'message man'. She was one of those few fortunate journalists who had the opportunity to conduct a personal interview with Curtis at his Atlanta home. She described his new album's true elevation as being in the most optimistic songs such as 'Back To Livin' Again', quoting the lyrics 'Now is always the right time/With something positive in your mind/There's always someone to pull you down/Just get back up and hold your ground.' 'As I wrote it, it was giving me strength,' recalled Mayfield softly. Vivien pondered the realisation that, though Curtis was still accessible as a hero and mentor, he was lost to us as a musician and performer. His feathery falsetto survives but the magic of his uniquely concise, oblique guitar style is among the musical treasures lost. When asked how he felt able to record an album given his physical circumstances Curtis replied, 'I always need a good challenge to push me, or dare me.' Once the project was rolling Mayfield got plenty of artistic support and input from those that gathered around him. Goldman's article covers the maestro's lengthy career in a broad sweep sprinkled with her observations on how she and her family live compared to his deprived childhood. Of course it's Mayfield's quotes that give us the most insight as snatches of the transcript reveal, 'I'm not always in touch with my positivity: no one is. But I am mostly. Even if I'm angry or hurt, I like to bounce back. I usually like to keep my spirits high, and that has worked good for me.' Curtis explains between recollections of his career and childhood memories. 'I used to sleep with my guitar. I'd write five songs a night – a day. When I couldn't find answers, I would write songs. When I was heartbroken, I would write songs. It was my own way of teaching myself.' Vivien respectfully concluded that thankfully the lesson was ongoing and open to the public.

New World Order was released in the UK on 3 February '97 and while the album got its fair share of radio play at the time, it fared less well on the TV music channels. But, by the end of the month, it reached #10 on the UK soul albums chart. After all the positive critical acclaim, the many interviews, the sheer effort and unerring persistence that it must have taken Mayfield to complete this classic album, once again the pop record-buying public did not respond, recognize or reward these superhuman efforts as generously as they might have. The NWO single did not chart in the UK and neither did the three follow-ups, 'No One Knows A Good Thing', 'Back To Livin' Again' (The Walden Remix), which may have only been issued as a promotional single and 'Just A Little Bit Of Love'. Indeed, all but the first were hard to find in the UK shops.

Another fascinating TV documentary, *Record Row/The Cradle Of R&B* was screened by PBS in the US in February '97. It told the story of Chicago's famous musical mile where, from the early '50s onward, a number of independent labels made some of the greatest blues/R&B and soul records of all time. After narrator Etta James set the scene with some background information about the rapidly growing black population that created the initial demand for this music, the story began with Al Benson the city's first DJ credited with playing R&B on his radio show. There are some great 'to camera' interviews with Phil & Marshall Chess, Phil Upchurch, Carl Davis, Buddy Guy, Jerry Butler, Ewart Abner, Dick Clark, Gene Chandler, Chuck Barksdale, Fontella Bass, Billy Davis and DJs Don Cornelius, Herb Kent and Lucky Cordell. Rare photos, TV footage and recorded performances are taken from a wide variety of sources and provide an entertaining and informative narration that mainly centres on two labels, Chess and Vee-Jay records.

Excellent research provides us all with a chance to see some of the earliest TV and movie performances from Muddy Waters, Buddy Guy, Willie Dixon, Bo Diddley and Chuck Berry intercut with interviews as we learn the facts and fiction about the formation and early growth of Chess Records. Soul fans benefit from the added bonus of the VJ story, which touches on the early work of the Spaniels, Jimmy Reed, John Lee Hooker, Impressions, Dee Clark, Gene Chandler, Betty Everett and others. The interviews with Jerry Butler and Ewart Abner are particularly revealing as they explain the philosophy behind VJ, which turned it into the most successful pre-Motown black record company in America. It explores the UK connection through the Beatles and Frank Ifield and the signing of the Four Seasons, all of the elements that eventually led to the label's spectacular downfall in 1966.

Curtis Mayfield is described as the most prolific songwriter of the Chicago soul era. Jerry and Curtis discuss the Impressions' early history, the hits, disappointments and their individual influences on the Chicago scene, through Gene Chandler, Major Lance and Billy Butler etc. Mayfield tells how some of the record companies cheated so many of the artists out of their royalties in the past, which led to the formation of their own companies like Curtom and the Butler Workshop. We are treated to TV footage of the Impressions performing 'We're A Winner' and 'Choice Of Colors' as the discussion turns to the civil rights era and Mayfield's influence through his solo work and the emergence of the Chess-owned WVON black radio station.

Though this excellent documentary runs for over an hour, all too soon we reach the final segment that deals with the end of this golden era and the demise of Chess, Vee-Jay and the other independents as they were swallowed up by the white-owned majors. Record Row became a derelict wasteland. This documentary is an important and revealing piece that as yet remains to be shown in the UK, due no doubt to the attitudes of TV programmers here who consider it to be of minority interest. But the story it tells is an important chapter in the development of our musical heritage. The influence that this musical era had on all that followed should not be underestimated or ignored. Hopefully it will reach European screens at a future date.

Rhino/Curtom compilations of *The Very Best Of The Impressions* and *The Very Best of Curtis Mayfield* were issued in America. The Impressions' set comprised 16 selections – the first nine are their biggest ABC hits. Tracks ten to 13 are the Curtom hits featuring Mayfield lead and the remaining three are by Ralph Johnson. The 16-page booklet has notes by David Nathan and contains many good black and white photos of the group at various stages of their evolution. The Mayfield solo set, again with liner notes by Nathan, also has several photos but includes two colour scans taken from the *Curtis in Chicago* TV special plus three others spanning his career. The 18 tracks are a selection of his biggest Curtom hits, one with Linda Clifford. This album entered R&B album chart at #91 in March '97.

Changes at Castle Records in early '97 meant that Bob Fisher moved over to become the company's Managing Director, placing the Sequel label in the capable hands of Tony Rounce. Meanwhile at New York HQ amidst major management reorganization new kidz Alliance (recently in place) proposed a deal to negotiate the outright purchase of the Curtom catalogue. Fisher went to the New York premier of 'Get On The Bus' and the following day, at Mayfield's hotel, brokered a deal for Castle to buy the Curtom catalogue with Curtis, Marv and the Curtom lawyers. When Bob informed Curtis that Sequel had plenty of Curtom visuals, through Echo Archive, to issue the complete series of Curtom CDs, Curtis quipped, 'So – Cha'lie don't need no tapes and Sequel don't need no Artwork.'

Further senior management changes at the Castle's New York HQ, meant that after reconsideration, the Curtom deal was tossed out. This move caused Curtom to begin court proceedings against Castle in America but thankfully the companies came to an out-of-court settlement. In April '97 Fisher left Castle to set up Westside, a new label for MCI and Tony joined him there in July. During their first year, Westside issued a series of great compilations from the Philadelphia International label amongst many others plus pop and rock albums. In November '98, Kingfisher bought out MCI and over the following months cutbacks pushed Fisher out. He re-emerged a year later working his magic once more, this time with the *Connoisseur Collection*. Bob then went on to set up his own re-issue label Acrobat in 2002.

The American TV music show *Soul Train* presented Curtis with a 'Career Achievement' award on 22 March '97. Mayfield was not well enough to attend and Gladys Knight received the honour on his behalf. The later months of '97 saw a fourth Mayfield tribute album released in the UK by Trojan *I'm So Proud (CDTRL 376)*. Unlike two of the previous tribute albums, this compilation comprised previously recorded material. These 20 songs come from Curtis' early period with the Impressions including three versions of 'Queen Majesty' ('Minstrel & Queen') and two of 'Gypsy Woman/Man'. This Jamaican tribute features two great tracks by Bob Marley & the Wailers plus versions of 'Monkey Time' ('Rocksteady Time') by the Progressions, 'He Will Break Your Heart' by the Silvertones and 'Man's Temptation' by Noel 'Bunny' Brown. Liner-note writer Laurence Cane-Honeysett tells us that Curtis and the Impressions provided the model for a host of Jamaican vocalists and writers who imitated Mayfield's sweet falsetto and the Impressions' harmonies. While most of these tracks are very listenable, there are particularly good contributions from the Techniques, Jamaicans, Uniques, Gaylads, Pat Kelly, Slim Smith, Chosen Few and finally best of all Marcia Griffith's great version of 'Gypsy Man'. Mayfield's music seems particularly well suited to Jamaican hues and this album is a worthy tribute to him but it only represents a fraction of the good music that he inspired on the island. There were many more versions of his songs recorded there and hopefully future compilations will emerge.

Sequel added further to their UK Curtom catalogue in '97 with the

2fer release of the four remaining Impressions' albums *Preacher Man/Finally Got Myself Together* (NEMCD 866) and *First Impressions/Loving Power* (NEMCD 867). They also issued the Fascinations' *Girls Are Out To Getcha* (NEMCD 867) compiled from their collected Mayfield singles plus unissued tracks 'Trusting In You' (later recorded by Patti Labelle and the Bluebelles) and 'Crazy'. Bonus tracks included the long sought-after Mayfield Singers 'I've Been Trying'/'If' and although the backing tracks for their unissued follow-up single 'Don't Start Now'/'Little Bird' were included, unfortunately the vocal tracks did not surface until after this album had been issued. 'Deepbeats' the sister label to Sequel compiled two *'Best of...'* albums on *Leroy Hutson* (DEEPM 007) and *Linda Clifford* (DEEPM 008), which were also issued in mid '97.

The highlight of the Sequel/Curtom releases in '97, from my point of view, was the Curtis Mayfield three-CD box-set *Love Peace Understanding* (NXTCD 286), which was issued in May. I will be eternally grateful to Bob Fisher for giving me the opportunity to compile (with his involvement), write and design this package. It was rewarding to be able to liberate the 17 previously unissued tracks that made up most of the 'Love' CD and that otherwise may have never seen the light of day. Sequel did a first-rate job in remastering these lost tracks, which sound very good considering their origination. The 27 cuts that made up 'Peace' and 'Understanding' all came from the original Curtom master tapes, released on CD for the first time in the UK and in some cases anywhere. I was of course disappointed that this set was not generally well reviewed by the UK music press, if at all. One review that did give the box a fair hearing though was that by Peter Doggett in *Record Collector* magazine. They devoted a page to the album set, examining it in depth and generally preferring it to the Rhino box because it had not fallen back on earlier Impressions' tracks or concentrated on the hits but 'plumps for artistic integrity above record sales'. Doggett concluded *'Love, Peace, Understanding* is as timeless a record as you will ever own.' *Q Magazine* also gave the set a good review. Robert Yates was also intrigued with the 'unplugged' tracks and noted, 'If any performer was ever going to benefit from being reduced to voice and guitar, Mayfield was the one.' He also observed, 'Hearing this late, pre-accident stuff, you can't help thinking of what might have been. Mayfield's music invites no pity, though – it's always too sharp to be sentimental.' Needless to say, this set, in my opinion is the best Mayfield box produced yet and was made available to UK fans at one-third of the price of the American alternative.

Charly continued with still more UK Curtom re-issues in '97, concentrating mainly on the Leroy Hutson catalogue with *Hutson*, *Hutson II, Feel The Spirit, Closer To The Source* and a compilation *Lucky Fellow*. They also made the Notations album available and began a series of Curtom compilations *Curtom Superpeople Volume 1* and *Soul Trippin' Volume 1*, which contained a mixture of different tracks by artists associated with the label. Another good issue by Charly at this time was a 2fer of the Impressions' Chi-Sound albums *Come To My Party/Fan The Fire*, which had also not been committed to CD before. In September '97 J-Birds Records issued ex-Curtom artist Ava Cherry's mini six-track LP in the UK, which was dissed by some reviewers who said that 'Gimmie Gimmie' had already been issued a few years ago (#99 US R&B hit single on Radikal in June '93) but now the backgrounds were perceived as cheap and dated.

UK cable viewers able to access NBC in late '97 would have been able to view a 15-minute Curtis special shown in their *Music Legends* series. Presenter Jason Roberts took us through this fast-moving infomercial for Mayfield's *New World Order* album. We were shown excerpts from the making of his album shot in and around Curtom Studios, intercut with clips from the video shot to promote the 'New World Order' single. Curtis appeared in 'to camera' interviews as the background moved through a montage of stills and events that happened around that period. Spike Lee also made an appearance when they came together in Atlanta to select Mayfield's music for use in his movie *Get On The Bus* and scenes from this movie could also be glimpsed. Curtis was filmed accepting a Grammy for life achievement at the 36th Awards ceremony where, to the strains of 'People Get Ready', Bruce Springsteen, Bonnie Raitt and BB King eulogized on his achievements and influence. Mayfield recalled early reflections as 'New World Order' dipped in and out of the backdrop and black and white civil rights TV footage was shown moving us to a brief discussion of his social awareness songs. Narvada Michael Walden told of Aretha Franklin's belated involvement in 'Back To Livin' Again' that he produced at a time while he was also providing a similar service for her. Curtis talked us out with his positive attitude to the tragedy that had befallen him. His advice to anyone else who might face impossible odds was just to 'Keep On Pushing'. These scenes were some of the last footage shot of Curtis at work and the programme provided a final look at Mayfield who was clearly motivated and inspired by the events surrounding the production of this timeless album. This short document serves as a testament to the strength and depth of Mayfield's spiritual soul. To witness his resolute faith in his work to reach others with his messages of love, individual empowerment and the right to expect a better world for all, is inspirational.

Roger Semon, then Managing Director of Castle Music engaged me as a freelance consultant to relaunch the Curtom re-issue programme for Sequel in February '98, who were temporarily without a label manager. Roger wanted a new concept to remarket the catalogue. As many of Mayfield's albums were already available on the UK market in one form or another, my suggestion was that we issue as a series of two-album sets, with one bonus album free of charge. The first four albums were dubbed 'Double Feature' an idea that came from the combination of the *Superfly/Short Eyes* (NEM CD 964) soundtracks. In America, Rhino had just issued a two-CD special on *Superfly* (R2 72836) to celebrate 25 years since the movie and soundtrack's original release. This excellent package included a booklet featuring many great stills from the movie. There were 14 added tracks that included the two single mixes of the title track and 'Freddie's Dead' plus a dozen alternative cuts recorded for the movie and its promotion but not issued at the time. The Mayfield albums that were prepared for June UK release by Sequel were *CURTIS/Gotta Find A Way* (NEM CD 965), *Roots/Sweet Exorcist* (NEM CD 966) *and Back To The World/Love* (NEM CD 967). This quartet of Curtis albums received great reviews. *Blues & Soul* made *Superfly/Short Eyes* album of the month, Bill Buckley claiming, 'As Far as this year's releases go, this one is ESSENTIAL!!!' *In The Basement* Editor David Cole also highlighted the series with 'Curtis: Buy One,

Get One Free'. *Uncut* reviewer Ian MacDonald was a little less impressed; he had some reservations about the couplings but nevertheless turned in a positive critique.

Due to difficulties in locating the master tapes of the *One By One* sessions, there had been a hitch in Ace/Kent's re-issue programme of the Impressions ABC albums but at last the third 2fer was complete for issue by March '98, coupled with *Ridin' High* (CDKEND 152). The following month, this series of albums was completed with the release of *Fabulous Impressions/We're A Winner* (CDKEND 155) and eventually the objective of making all the Impressions' ABC catalogue available in the UK had been achieved to the satisfaction of all those involved. Once again, reviewers like Buckley and Cole gave positive in-depth reviews alerting collectors to the high quality of the music and the economic good sense of these Impressions' couplings, in most cases urging their imminent purchase.

Deepbeats issued a second volume *Best Of Leroy Hutson* (DEEPM 033) album in March. But Leroy had recorded little new music since '82. As mentioned before, Expansion had issued the 12in EP in '92 and one or two tracks had also found their way onto their *Soul Source* compilation CDs but nothing else had materialized. Expansion had also issued a couple of tracks by Keni Burke, who had not released any new music since the early '80s and rather unexpectedly cut an all new album *Nothin' But Love (Expansion XECD 12)* in '98 after some coercion from Ralph Tee. Three Charly/Curtom compilations found their way into the UK shops during '98. They were the follow-on volumes of *Curtom Superpeople 2* and *Soul Trippin' 2* plus their *Superfly Special Edition*, which was modelled on the Rhino package.

The making of *New World Order* and the media interest that it had created had raised Mayfield's spirits to a high. After the circus had left town, however, and the dust had settled, the grim reality of his still deteriorating health was ever present. There were rumours of preparations for a second Warner album that persisted until it was announced that the project had been cancelled due to Mayfield's inability to continue. In August '98 Curtis underwent further surgery when his right leg was amputated below the knee. Shortly afterwards it was reported that he had dipped into a state of depression and had avoided any further interviews. It was all slipping away into an agonizingly slow and irreversible decline.

Following some pre-release interest created by radio play and UK music press coverage, Terry Callier's excellent *Timepeace* album, his first for almost 20 years, was released in February '98, by UK label Talkin' Loud and it began to sell. This superb album is packed with self-penned songs on a wide variety of themes and taking in a number of different musical hues along its way. With this level of artistic expression and musicianship, it's hard to highlight tracks – they are all great in their own way. Terry makes an inspired splice between Mayfield's 'People Get Ready' and his own 'Brotherly Love' in a spiritual duet. It is a stunning album that hopefully indicates that this time hits or not – Callier is back to stay. When I see a review or press ads for Terry Callier's new album or concerts, it always reminds me that this is, but for the accident that led to his subsequent death, just what Curtis would have been doing right now – he's sadly missed even if it is only by a few thousand of us, who would try to catch his appearances in the UK whenever the opportunity presented itself. In so many ways, Curtis and Terry came, and are still coming from the same place.

The final year of the century rolled over the horizon and in March the Rock 'n' Roll Hall of Fame inducted Curtis for the second time, now as a solo artist. Curtis' wife Altheida accepted the award on his behalf from perhaps the hottest soul siren of the time, Lauryn Hill, at the 14th Annual Awards, held at the Waldorf Astoria in New York. Also honoured that night were long-term Chicagoan amigos the Staple Singers. Lauryn Hill and Curtis had recently recorded a duet 'Here But Gone' that featured on *Mod Squad movie* (Elektra 62364-2) soundtrack in '98. That same month the new look Sequel/Curtom re-issues became available in the UK, with Mayfield's classic *There's No Place Like America Today/Get, Give, Take & Have* (NEM CD 401) and his great Bitter End concerts from '71 *CURTIS/LIVE* teamed with the US TV Special *Curtis In Chicago* (NEMCD 400). Other great issues at this time were *The Baby Huey Story* (NEBCD 405) plus the superb *Can This Be Real?* (NEMCD 406), which contained all three of the Natural Four's Curtom albums plus the collectable 'Eddie You Should Know Better' single. Production of the 46-track *Curtom Chartbusters (NEECD 322)*, which featured all the biggest hits from the Curtom roster, followed on after some temporary hold-ups.

John Reed became Sequel's new label manager in July '98. He had previously worked at *Record Collector* magazine from October '89 onwards where he had shared offices with the present editor, Andy Davis. Shortly after John was in place at Sequel we met and discussed future plans for reissuing the remaining Curtom catalogue on Sequel. John wanted to ditch the conventional CD booklet for a fold out double-sided colour poster with each issue. He introduced me to designers Paul Bevoir and a team at Mc80 who between them produced the great graphics for the rest of the series, using visual research from Echo Archive and other sources as required.

UK Kent released the superb CD collection of 26 rare and unissued Impressions' tracks entitled *The Impressions – ABC Rarities* (CDKEND 170) in May '99. This album was the last chapter in a series of Impressions ABC albums issued as 2fers by Kent between 1995–99 and contained 'Can't You See', which was originally issued as the flipside to 'Grow Closer Together' in early '62. This beautiful ballad was written by Curtis Mayfield and Jerry Butler during the period when they worked together promoting Butler's early solo career. It was initially issued on the Impressions' début ABC album but withdrawn and replaced with 'It's Alright' when it became a huge hit for them in October '63 just as the first album was released. 'Love Is A Mystery' was originally issued on the live various artists compilation album *Shindig* (ABC 504), which included tracks by Tommy Roe, the Tams and Fats Domino. It was actually cut as a mono studio track in March '62 and fake applause was added later – this has now been removed restoring the track to its original condition. The lead vocal is unfamiliar but by process of elimination is probably by Arthur Brooks.

Mayfield wrote two songs entitled 'Emotions'. The first, subtitled (Won't Let Me Cry), was never issued in America but a different take to this one was released in the UK by Charly in '83 on the vinyl album *Right On Time*. The mono track issued here was recorded as take one in March

'62 and comes from the same session as 'Love Is A Mystery'. The second 'Emotions' song was recorded in '64 and appears on the *People Get Ready* album. All these early tracks were cut by the Impressions in New York between July '61 and March '62 when the group was a quintet.

The superb 'You'll Want Me Back' was cut at the 'It's Alright' session in August '63; it was issued as the mono flipside to this hit single and made its only other appearance on the UK album *Big 16 Volume 2*. This was also the fate of 'Never Too Much Love', which was flipside to 'Talkin' About My Baby' and came from their next session in November '63. 'Never Could You Be' was cut over a year later and originally issued as the flip to 'I Need You'. 'I Want To Go Back (Man Oh Man)' was co-written with Ben Krass for his group the Knights and Arthur and released as a single by Roulette in early '65. The Impressions' version appeared on the flipside of the US single 'You've Been Cheatin'' later that same year and it was also added to the UK Stateside issue of the *We're A Winner* album. 'This Must End' another beautiful Mayfield ballad (here in its original stereo mix) was the flipside to the second Detroit-flavoured hit single 'Can't Satisfy' and also found its way onto a couple of compilations but remains amongst the Impressions' great unsung gems. 'I Need A Love' (Curtis actually sings 'I'd Need Her Love') comes from the same session of October '65, which due to a mix up at ABC was sent to the UK for use on *Big 16 Volume 2* instead of 'I Need You'. That was the only time it was issued anywhere up until now. ABC did publish the title on a couple of occasions but in each case the track that they used was 'I Need You'.

'You Got Me Runnin'' was an A-side in the States but made little chart impact and so was not issued as such in the UK but instead was coupled with 'We're A Winner'. However, it did appear later on a couple of UK albums, but was, as it is here, only ever issued in mono. 'We're Rolling On' (Pts 1&2) was written to follow the huge hit and civil rights anthem 'We're A Winner' and went to #17 R&B/#59 pop in May '68 just as Mayfield and the Impressions were leaving ABC for Curtom Records. Stateside did not release the single in the UK but they did include it on *Big 16 Volume 2*.

After the Impressions had left and were having hits on Curtom, ABC issued two more singles but without the group to promote them, they fell fallow on the charts. 'Don't Cry My Love' is a superb anti-war song co-written with jazz performer Oscar Brown Jr, which deserved to do much better. As a single it registered #44 R&B/71 pop in December '68 and ABC included it on their final Impressions album *Versatile Impressions* (ABC/S 668), which only contained 10 tracks, all of which are included on this CD and were taken from their last three recording sessions with the label. This version of 'Don't Cry My Love' is a new stereo mix from four track.

'Just Before Sunrise' was intended as the title song to *Krakatoa-East of Java* and was released in America on a single. 'East of Java' became the flipside and together they found their way onto *Versatile ...* . Both McCartney/Lennon songs 'Yesterday' and 'Fool On The Hill' were restyled for the Impressions by Pate and Mayfield to great effect. Three of the songs on this final ABC album 'Once In A Lifetime', 'This Is The Life' and 'Oo You're A Livin' Doll' were throwbacks to the cabaret persona that the Impressions had adopted before on the *One By One* album.

Bacharach's and David's much recorded classic 'The Look Of Love' was featured in the movie *Casino Royale* ('67). The biggest hit went to Sergio Mendes & Brazil '66 but there were other notable versions by Isaac Hayes and Dusty Springfield. Johnny Pate takes his opportunity to create a suitably lush arrangement behind the Impressions, who provide the perfect vocal treatment to the song that in other hands has been subject to over elaboration. 'Sermonette' was originally an instrumental written by Julian 'Cannonball' Adderley for his quintet, that later had lyrics added by Jon Hendricks. Inevitably, this jazz-influenced piece was restyled by the Impressions to fit into their series of songs with a sociological theme, most of which were penned by Mayfield. The remaining five previously unreleased tracks comprise of three early Mayfield songs 'Thanks To You' (which he originally wrote in 1960 with Jerry Butler and was used as the flipside to 'He Will Break Your Heart'), 'Puppy Love' and 'Devil In Your Soul', which has a taste of 'Gypsy Woman' about it. The remaining two cuts are both rewrites of traditional folk/blues songs 'All Of My Trials' and 'Bring A Little Water Sylvie' ('Sylvie') the latter of which was popularized by the late great Lonnie Donegan during the UK Skiffle boom of the mid '50s. Curtis wrote some new lyrics and completely re-arranged both of these songs to fit the Impressions' style. It seems inconceivable that they were passed over in favour of some other songs that were used on *Versatile...*, perhaps they were earmarked for a future project that never materialized but whatever happened then, it is our good fortune that Kent was finally able to issue them here.

Other Impressions' rarities that did not make it to this CD were 'Rainbow' (13082), which Gene Chandler cited as his favourite Mayfield song and 'What Now' (13083), which also provided him with a big hit. These two songs were recorded by the Impressions in February '66 but, according to US sources at Universal, have since been destroyed. 'Wade In The Water' is part of the as yet unissued *Live at the Club Chicago* album, which was recorded in three sessions on 2 September 1966. This track was issued by ABC as the flip to 'Love's A Comin'' three months later but didn't make it to the UK and still remains a rare item. These precious tracks had, at last, been unearthed like ammonites in vinyl from the ABC vaults due to long hours of persistent research by Roger Armstrong and Alec Palao, with coaxing by Trevor Churchill. They are all the remaining rare and unissued recordings by Curtis Mayfield and the Impressions and, according to US information, there are no further unissued Impressions masters left in existence, except for the *Live* album that Kent is considering for release at a later date.

Westside who had been issuing an excellent series of CDs on Chicago artists amongst many others, re-issued the Impressions ChiSound 2fer *Come To My Party/Fan The Fire* (WESM 582) and two Walter Jackson CDs *Touching The Soul* (WESA 833) and *Feeling The Song* (WESA 834) with liner notes by label manager Tony Rounce and *In The Basement* Editor David Cole. In April/May 2000 in response to customer interest in these two Jackson samplers, Westside rather surprisingly issued all six of Jackson's Carl Davis-produced albums, none of which had been available on CD anywhere before. *Feeling Good* (WESM 616), *I Want To Come Back As A Song* (WESM 617), *Good To See You* (WESM 618), *Send In The Clowns* (WESM 619), *Tell Me Where It Hurts* (WESM 620) and *A Portrait Of Walter Jackson* (WESM 621). One can only hope that other compilers follow Tony's lead and commit the OKeh albums to CD in their entirety. Walter Jackson was one of the greatest soul ballad vocalists of all time and all his catalogue should be available, including the as yet unissued Stax sessions and the lost singles on Epic, Cotillion, Wand, USA and Deb. Let's have it all.

Charlie Gillett's Radio 2 special (26 May '99) *Impressions: The Story of Curtis Mayfield*, was his own very personal and thorough appreciation of the artist's musical achievements. This radio portrait came closest to rendering a true and spiritual insight into the soulful music that Mayfield had created for himself and many others during his long and fruitful career. Charlie contacted me while doing the research for this programme and later invited my participation that I was delighted to supply. He related the stories surrounding the formation of the Impressions beginning with 'For Your Precious Love' and continued with Mayfield's first hit song 'He Will Break Your Heart' written with and for Jerry Butler during the period they performed together in '60–'61. This revealing portrait touches on the early hits written for Jan Bradley ('Mama Didn't Lie') and Major Lance ('Monkey Time') intercut with a good selection of taped interviews from Curtis. He discussed the huge influence that the Impressions created in Jamaica with their records and tours there in the early '60s, comparing three versions of 'Minstrel And Queen' ('Queen Majesty') and explored the impact on Bob Marley ('Keep On Moving') who was inspired to create his own great legacy of meaningful music from that time onward.

Gillett explored the positive aspects of Mayfield's songwriting, playing 'Choice Of Colors' and remembered his 'shock' departure from the Impressions in 1970. He highlighted the outspoken lyrics of Curtis' early solo work as we heard 'Move On Up', the record that endeared him to the UK and Europe, and how he established his popularity here with many appearances. The magic of Mayfield's live performances and the intimacy that he created with his audiences can be best experienced on the *CURTIS/LIVE* hit album that is mentioned but due to the scarcity of time is not aired. Likewise with *Superfly*, Mayfield's best-known work that introduces us to the movie soundtrack aspects of his recordings with Gladys Knight 'On And On' (*Claudine*) and the Staple Singers title track and major US hit 'Let's Do It Again'. Gillett highlights Mayfield's acknowledgement to the Caribbean rhythms in his later work on Boardwalk Records by playing 'She Don't Let Nobody But Me' the Chaka Demus and Pliers hit version of a song that he wrote and recorded with Dino Fekaris alongside 'What You Gawn Do' (which comes from the *Honesty* album).

Charlie made favourable post-accident vocal comparisons, which, despite considerable difficulty, Curtis successfully achieved on *New World Order* managing to maintain his gentle, subtle and intimate style. Curtis proved himself to be a man with a sense of purpose and destiny, living his philosophy in his final years despite the considerable hardships that he suffered and most of us can only have a fractional understanding of. Listening again to this programme as it celebrates the life, music and massive influence that Curtis Mayfield provided, it is difficult not to entertain wishes for a wider appreciation of his art. Had the tragedy of Wingate Field not taken place, Mayfield would have been an even greater force in the music of today. He may not have been on the charts but his creative and inventive talents coupled with his interest in collaborations with other artists were always going to make positive and progressive contributions. Gillett chose 'A Child With The Blues' as his outro, a song that was written and produced by Mayfield for Erykah Badu, who recorded two versions for use on the soundtrack of *Eve's Bayou*. (There were actually two different US CDs issued of this soundtrack.)

In August '99, the second wave of the year's Curtom/Sequel releases were issued in the UK. They included Leroy Hutson's complete Curtom album catalogue twinned as *Love Oh Love/ The Man* (NEMCD 441), *Hutson/Feel The Spirit* (NEMCD 442), *Hutson II/Closer To The Source* (NEMCD 443). In addition, Hutson's final album for Curtom *Unforgettable* was issued with *Lucky Fellow* a fine compilation of single edits (NEECD 318). To the Notations Gemigo album, Sequel added a previously unissued track 'The Chopper' and created *Superpeople* (NEBCD 445). All the remaining Curtis studio albums were issued as follows *Never Say You Can't Survive/Do It All Night* (NEMCD 440), *Heartbeat/Something To Believe In* (NEMCD 446), *We Come In Peace With A Message Of Love/Take It To The Streets* (NEMCD 447). *We Come In Peace...* had not made it to CD before (except in Japan) and provided another chance to listen to Mayfield '85, recorded and remixed tracks in the middle of his 'temporary retirement' from recording. Another inspired compilation was Curtis' duet album with Linda Clifford *Right Combination* with the addition of 11 bonus tracks, on which they were connected. The bonus album was the 'never issued before' *Rapping* (NEMCD 448), recorded by Mayfield for promotional purposes after his huge success with *Superfly* in '72. Topping off this feast of Curtom Gold were two new compilations of singles *Indelible Impressions* (NEECD 321) – 45 tracks containing all their Curtom hits, selected album cuts and among them a previously unissued take of 'Love Me' and single mixes not issued on CD before. Soul brother to this volume was *Move On Up – The Singles Anthology* (NEECD 320) – 39 of the very best from Curtis, containing all the biggest of his hits that time and space would allow. Even for the most casual Mayfield/Impressions fan these are the compilations to have.

There were of course many other CD compilations issued in the UK, Europe and America showcasing the Impressions and Curtis' solo work throughout the '90s. In '96 Hippo a short-term US MCA logo, issued *Further Impressions* a 14-tracker, with notes by Chicago soul specialist Robert Pruter. Pickwick issued *The Impressions featuring Curtis Mayfield* ('94) in the UK and Carlton re-issued it again in '96 with a new cover. It featured 14 Curtis-led Impressions tracks plus two solos ('Move On Up' and 'Freddie's Dead') and their UK/Curtom hit 'First Impressions' for a low mid price. Other Impressions compilations not yet mentioned were *Eagle Masters* ('97) and Music Club's *Check Out The Impressions* ('98) in the UK and *The Impressions – The Greatest Hits* featuring 16 ABC tracks issued by MCA in America in '98. There were numerous Curtis compilations issued in the UK, Europe and Japan as discussed earlier, many under the 'Greatest, Best Of' or simply 'Move On Up' titles. Hallmark offered us a dozen great tracks at budget price in '97 and Music Club issued 'Give It Up', Eagle released two compilations, one a two-CD set in their Masters series and there were 'Best Of ...' sets from Nectar and Summit, all in the same year. Delta released *Love's Sweet Sensation* in '99 and Metro issued *Beautiful Brother - The Essential* in 2000. These kind of albums are aimed at the general public not the Curtis fan or collector, they vary in price and sound quality depending on the sources used by the label concerned.

In America, Rhino/Curtom compilations (that they tagged 'Deluxe Re-issues') included a reworking of *Roots* with bonus tracks. They issued compilations of his songs around a theme *like Curtis Mayfield – Gospel* (Rhino R2 75568), gospel-inspired Mayfield songs, with and without the Impressions. The booklet, a 10-page concertina has notes by Ernest Hardy. *Love Songs ('01)* (Rhino R2 79972) provided another collection, which included four Impressions cuts and 12 ballads taken from the solo years '70–'82. They also included a number of Mayfield tracks on various artist compilations like *Chicken Soup For The Soul, Millennium Funk Party* and live tracks from the US TV series *Soul Train* '72 and '73. (Readers wanting more info check out the Rhino website at www.rhino.com).

I compiled and annotated a few myself, besides the Sequel and Kent series, the best *Move On Up – The Best Of Curtis Mayfield* (SELCD568) for Sam Szczepanski at Select who have issued and continue to issue a series of mid-price mastercuts on a wide sweep of artists. Illegible notes and a masters mix up made *Ultimate/Essential Curtis* a two-CD compilation for Recall a personal disappointment. In addition to the others already mentioned, one UK Mayfield compilation *Curtis – The Very Best Of Curtis Mayfield* was issued by Beechwood Music in '98. Beechwood got behind the album and even produced a TV commercial, which was aired on some UK cable stations using previously unseen early footage of Curtis. The album did quite well, as a result, and made a brief appearance in the lower end of the UK album chart.

Though the two compilations *Curtom Club Classics Volumes 1 & 2* were scheduled for earlier release they encountered some technical hiccups but were finally issued in the later months of '99 as *Funk-Soul Brothers & Sisters* (NEMCD 451) and *Mighty Mighty Soul* (NEMCD 402). These compilations fused together some of Curtom's best soul, dance and northern cuts with some of the rarer singles taken from Gemigo, as well as Curtom sources. Edsel (sister label to Westside) continued their fine re-issue programme of the Brunswick catalogue, with a great compilation of the Lost Generation's two albums *Sly, Slick*

& Wicked and *Young, Tough & Terrible* plus three bonus tracks that included 'You Only Get Out Of Love' (DIAB 8016). This underrated group contained some of the brightest Chicago talent of the time – Lowrell Simon and Larry Brownlee who would develop further as writers and producers themselves were then in the capable hands of Eugene Record and Richard Parker. Bill Dahl's excellent notes fill in Lost Generations' short but fruitful background as they evolved through the Chicago music scene of the early '70s.

The tragic news reached us on 26 December '99 of the death of Curtis Mayfield after his ten-year struggle against the almost total paralysis. Mayfield died at the North Fulton Regional Hospital in Roswell, GA. *Jet Magazine* (17 January '00 issue) reported that private services had recently been held for Curtis at HM Patterson & Sons Arlington Chapel in Atlanta. Attendants at the funeral service were his wife Altheida, the Mayfield family, Jerry Butler, Sam Gooden, Fred Cash, who sang an emotional and soul-stirring version of 'Amen'. Atlanta mayor Bill Campbell announced that he was honoured that Curtis allowed 'People Get Ready' to be used as Atlanta's millennium theme song. The song Campbell said 'best reflects the accomplishment of our city and the challenges of a new century.' Altheida said at a pre-funeral press conference, 'I lost my husband, the father of my children, my best friend and my soul mate. Thank God his music and his legacy will live far beyond today.' Curtis was survived by his mother Marion Jackson, two sisters Judy Mayfield and Carolyn Falls, brother Kenneth, 11 children Tiffany, Curtis, Lebrian, Cheaa, Blaise, Lena, Tracey, Curtis III, Todd, Sharon, Carolyn and seven grandchildren. The same report revealed that Warner Bros Records were organizing a public memorial for fans and admirers to be held later (no date specified).

Shortly after the Christmas celebrations, DJs in the UK and no doubt all over the globe were playing Mayfield's music in tribute to him. The obituaries too came thick and fast during the week between Christmas and new year and on into the new millennium, when the weeklies and then the monthlies finally caught up. Sometimes when you read obituaries about a person that you like, or know something about, especially if you read a lot of them, they may seem a trifle formulaic. You wonder how long they have been on file and why, though broadly accurate, only a few journalists get the details right. So it was in this case but some of the writers did make meaningful tributes, which honoured Mayfield, his music and poetry.

In the *New York Times* (27/12/99) Neil Strauss observed, 'On albums like *There's No Place Like America Today* from '75, his songs seemed to penetrate the minds of the urban hopeless and despondent, telling them to remain strong in times of poverty, unemployment and black-on-black violence.' When a *NYT* interviewer asked Curtis about the flood of recognition that he was experiencing in '96, Mayfield quoted one of his lyrics in answer 'I'm a great believer in the saying, "It might not come when you want it to, but it's right on time."'

Martin Weil of the *Washington Post* (27/12/99) said that during Curtis' early days with the Impressions, 'He was known as a man who expanded the horizons of black popular song, to speak not only of the matters of the heart but also the issues of the street.' He later included the '97 *Rolling Stone* quote 'Black music as we hear it today simply would not exist without him.'

Mike Oldfield and Dave Laing co-wrote the *Guardian* obituary (28/12/99) in which they said that Curtis 'had one of the most achingly expressive voices in black music. His high tenor delivered some of the most significant soul music of the 1960s, and then took on a grittier edge in the 1970s as he moved alongside Stevie Wonder and Marvin Gaye, in the vanguard of black musicians giving voice to social and political concern. He was also a songwriter, producer and guitarist of distinction, whose influence crossed the barriers of popular musical styles.'

The *Daily Telegraph* columnist (28/12/99) noted, 'In the mid 1960s, when other black singers stuck to love songs, Mayfield sang of black pride and gritty urban landscapes in his own words.'

Spencer Leigh made some interesting observations in the *Independent* (28/12/99) such as, 'His music was more melodic and less raucous than James Brown's and, hence less threatening to a white audience.' His conclusion made good use of a great Mavis Staples quote, 'There's a beauty about him, an angelic state. Everything he wrote had a whole lot of love.'

Barry Saunders writing for *News & Observer* North Carolina (2/1/00) wrote the most outspoken column that I read. His criticisms of Puff Daddy and the rap generation's high profile against that of really creative talent like Curtis was justified but the blame for this lack of taste cannot I feel, be laid only at their door. Hype, self-promotion and biased 'news' services are all part of the world of today. I agree that 'sampling' is another music-speak term for 'rip off' as Saunders insists but it is just another aspect of the super highway generation. Compared to most of the other Mayfield tributes that I read, Barry Saunders' unconventional obituary was refreshing and informative and, in an uncanny way, more reflective of the individuality of Curtis himself.

Blues & Soul (18/1/00) reported Curtis tributes pouring into their offices. Tony Rounce was moved to comment, 'I think that He's the most singularly important black artist ever and one of the top ten most important writers of all time.'

DJ Greg Edwards acknowledged, 'He nourished the black spirit and wasn't afraid to make us stand up and look at ourselves. He made you "Check Out Your Mind".'

Roger St Pierre wrote a respectful, factually accurate and appropriate obituary for *B&S*. He didn't gush, which would be so easy to do but did touch base with the legions of Curtis fans when he said, 'Think of Curtis, play his music and enjoy – that's the finest testament we can all pay to one of the great soul brothers.'

cdnow.com (Hank Bordowitz) published a column of biographical info using an interesting quote from Vic Steffens: 'an absolutely original, irreplaceable talent and soul. If the mantle is going to be passed to the Maxwells and Angelos... I hope they have some clue of the size of the shoes they need to fill.' AOL published a tribute by Russ Bynum of the *Associated Press*, which used a few quotes by author and music critic Nelson George but a copyright rider prevents me from reprinting any of them here so any reader interested reading further will have to surf the net.

The remaining Impressions continue to perform to this day. After the ripple of interest that the Impressions Ripete 'Something Said Love' single (their first for 12 years) caused in '89, they went into the studio with producer Jerry Michaels and cut two or three albums (30 tracks) worth of material. The group still contained the two veteran members Sam Gooden and Fred Cash with Vandy Hampton, who had been in the line-up since '82 and Ralph Johnson who had returned to replace Nate Evans. The lead vocals were shared by Vandy who took the high tenor leads and Ralph who sang on the newer songs recorded at these sessions. Twenty of these cuts were updated versions of the Impressions back catalogue, written by Curtis and re-recorded to appeal to a new generation of fans unaware of the group's long history. Johnson led the new songs like 'Draw The Line', 'In The Middle', 'Winning Combination', and 'I Can Make It Go Away' whilst Hampton handled the Mayfield songs and 'What A Feeling', 'I Found You', the single 'Something Said Love' and 'Whatever It Is'. Gooden can be heard leading on 'For Your Precious Love' and 'Find Yourself Another Girl' but as is traditional with the Impressions, the lead often swaps from verse to verse. Fred Cash also took his turn up front. None of these tracks were initially picked up and issued in America or the UK. There was a tape circulating the UK record companies in the mid '90s with 11 tracks on offer but it wasn't until the spring of 2000 that Edel Records issued *The Impressions – A tribute to the memory of Curtis Mayfield* (ED 112392/US only) and any of the above mentioned tracks were officially released. Uncredited liner notes revealed that the Impressions were about to tour South Africa and record with Eric Clapton on his next album. In July '01 Norman Jopling and Terry Chappell of Ideal Music put together *Remembering Curtis* by the Impressions for a *PIE* (265) CD, which gained UK release later in the year. This album contains 20 Mayfield songs beautifully reinterpreted by the Impressions as only they can. 'These are the Curtis songs that we've performed most over the years – in our stage act,' Sam Gooden told me in February 2001. At the moment these recordings are only available in the UK.

Juke Blues reported that the Impressions were in London in October '00 recording with Clapton. Columnist Seamus McGarvey held out little hope for fans to see them perform with Eric in the UK but added that American fans were likely to be more fortunate. As it happened, this turned out not to be the case, for Clapton engaged the Impressions to appear on his Albert Hall dates in February '01 and they joined him on a few other UK dates as well. I took this opportunity to interview the group on 11 February '01 at The Royal Garden Hotel in Kensington, London. A version of this interview was first published in *Right Track* Ace Records monthly magazine.

Despite touring here on several occasions over the years, the Impressions have never played to their UK fans. 'Except for that one time at the "Speakeasy" with Leroy back in '72, we've only performed here for the US military,' Fred Cash confirmed. So this was a first – albeit to audiences who had primarily come to see Eric Clapton. Certainly this exposure to a broader audience was bound to create a wider interest in their own timeless music. Sam Gooden, who has sung bass vocal with the Impressions since their formation back in '57 is (along with Fred) a soul survivor. 'We had a big hit with our very first record – 'For Your Precious Love' – and that can be a hard act to follow,' said Sam.

Today Sam (64) and Fred (68) look younger than you might expect, the constant touring in America and their excursions to other countries – they worked ten days in South Africa last year – keeps them both fit. Though thankfully the pace has eased off these days and they can afford to take time out, travel or relax with their families and friends. Of the Clapton concerts, they said, 'We loved the concerts at Albert Hall. But Eric caught a virus and had to cancel one night. He's OK now and we're going to appear with him in Sheffield tomorrow [Monday, 12 February '01] and then to Manchester.'

This collaboration came about when the Impressions were in California to appear at a Memorial Service for Curtis Mayfield, attended by many of his previous associates. One night while they were out having dinner with their manager Marv Heiman, he asked them if they would cut some background vocals with a singer in town, as a favour to him. Before they could phrase the inevitable question, he gestured and said, 'There he is – why don't you come and meet him now,' and they found themselves shaking hands with Eric Clapton. Although both Eric and the Impressions had appeared on the Warner/Mayfield Tribute album in '93, the two parties hadn't actually met before. Eric told them that he wanted to record 'I've Been Trying' and if he could arrange it, were they willing. They were in enthusiastic agreement. 'We went into the studio (Record One I think it was called) and just did the one tune but it went so well that we put down a reggae version too.' As a result of this inspired collaboration, Eric invited them to record on his next album (*Reptile* – Reprise 9 47966-2). 'We began with just a couple of tracks but wound up singing on just about every one,' added Sam (11 out of 14, in fact). In October 1999, shortly after the Impressions picked up a 'Pioneer Award' from the Rhythm & Blues Foundation in New York, they came to London to record a version of the old Prisonaires classic 'Just Walkin' In The Rain' with Eric and they proposed a tour of the States together in June and July 2000.

Before this fortuitous link-up, the Impressions had not been into the recording studio since '93 when they cut that glorious version of Mayfield's 'Fool For You' with Branford Marsalis. In America there was some interest in this collaboration and they performed it together, with a full orchestra, on the 'The Jay Leno Show'. These days the Impressions are a quartet with Vandy 'Smokey' Hampton (54) who left the Chi-Lites 23 years ago to become the Impressions new high tenor lead and has remained there ever since. Ralph Johnson, who also put in a few years with the group, quit in late 2000 and Fred recruited Willie Kitchens Jr (23) in Chattanooga where he runs his own record label and production company. Until this opportunity came his way Willie had worked exclusively in the gospel field, writing and producing for the Inner Ministry's Church. He has also issued solo gospel albums. Smokey is the only Impression who still lives in Chicago and doesn't think he'll ever leave. He too has his own label, Smokestack Records that he runs a small production company through. Smokey and his son Ekima write and produce for artists like Danny Reed and Machine Company Band.

The Impressions were amazed to discover that their illustrious back catalogue has been born again in the UK through Kent Records. 'There's nothing like this available at home – just some hits compilations,' said Fred, '...and I don't believe this "Rarities" album. Does your book cover all these albums?' quizzed Fred.

'Of course,' I said. 'I'll pass on your approval to Trevor Churchill and the team at Kent shall I?'

'Yes, please be sure to do that for us, we really appreciate their efforts on our behalf.'

Both Fred and Sam were most helpful answering all my questions and supplying biographical details and any other minutiae that they could recall. During this enjoyable process. they mentioned a number of events and recollections involving Curtis in the early days. 'He would sleep with that guitar, Curtis was always writing. He would knock on the hotel wall between our rooms and Fred and I would go in and sit on his bed and he would play us a complete song, sometimes more than one, that he'd just written.' They told me that they hadn't seen a great deal of Johnny Pate since they had worked together on the unissued Cotillion album. But they were still in touch though he's now a resident of Palm Springs.

Giants of Soul, a UK series for Radio 2 by Daryl Hall, ran a Curtis Mayfield profile (17 March '00). Hall skipped across the artist's lengthy career playing a predictable selection of Impressions records. From 'For Your Precious Love' to 'People Get Ready' he picked the hits then went fast forward to the formation of Curtom and the hardening of the Mayfield message as he moved to solo success with *CURTIS* and *Superfly*. Daryl was impressed by *Roots* and its impact on the death throws of Vietnam. After 'Future Shock' another quantum leap took us through Disco and Mayfield's accident. Inaccurate research reported Curtis as paralyzed from the waist down and the issue date of his final album *New World Order* a year later than factually accurate. Although this appreciation was only partial and revealed no new information there were some previously unheard quotes from Curtis and the music was as always, great.

The Black Rock Coalition a New York soul/funk/jazz-based quartet played a Curtis Mayfield tribute concert in Joe's Pub, a small venue located in the East Village on Lafayette Street. Joe Papp the Pub's owner founded the Public Theatre, adjacent to the club, which is frequented by an élite crowd of young and mostly black affluent New Yorkers. The Black Rock Coalition had, in the past, featured some great guitarists, among them Lenny Kravitz and more recently Vernon Reid. BRC's Musical Director Gene Williams had been disappointed by the muted response to Mayfield's passing and set about redressing the recognition that he felt Mayfield was due. Faith Aarons was indeed fortunate to be present on the 3 March 2000, the night of the tribute and reported the following. Gene (keyboards) and other band members bassist Ron Monroe, Gary Fitz (percussion) and drummer Lionel Cordew provided a funk solid back up for a rotation of guests who performed Mayfield songs of their choice. The artists on stage included Vernon Reid ('Superfly'), Masa Shimisu ('It's All Right'), Dean Bowman ('People Get Ready'), Nioka Workman ('Keep On Pushing'), Marlene Rice ('Fool For You'), Johnny Kemp ('Here But I'm Gone'), Stephanie McKay ('Hold On/Lets' Do It Again'), Billy Petterson ('If There's A Hell Below') and vocalist GTO who reconstructed 'Pusherman'. Faith reported the audience let BRC know in no uncertain terms, that this concert should become an annual event, like the one that they already perform for Jimi Hendrix.

The UK music business press reported the sale of Castle Music to the Sanctuary Records Group for an estimated £46 million in April '00. That same month Sequel opened the Curtom 2K account with a re-issue of *Curtis Live In Europe* (NEMCD 360) CD, this time with a far more appropriate cover, by Paul Bevoir, whose design for the poster booklet revealed photos taken from the original US issue and not seen in the UK until now. With this album, Sequel had achieved the most complete re-issue of the Curtis Mayfield catalogue ever. They now turned their attentions to Linda Clifford, twinning her first two albums *Linda* and *If My Friends Could See Me Now* (NEMCD 363), three and four *Let Me Be Your Woman/Here's My Love* (NEMCD 364) and five *I'm Yours* with a great compilation *Runaway Love – The singles* (NEMCD 365). Again this marked the most complete issue of Linda's catalogue on CD. Other Sequel releases at this time included *Now* (NEMCD 362) by Ed Townsend (first time on CD) and Rasputin Stash – *The Devil Made Me Do It* (NEMCD 359). Both of these albums had been issued in the UK before on vinyl but research turned up several previously unissued tracks by Stash that along with the two Curtom singles provided nine extra tracks. The *Mystique* album (NEMCD 362) had been more of a rarity in the UK. This time we were fortunate enough to find ten bonus tracks, all which remained of Mystique's recording sessions and these additions effectively made it a double.

The most comprehensive tribute that any UK magazine has paid to

Curtis so far has been by *Record Collector* who contacted me for research and discographical information for a two-part Mayfield tribute that they ran in their March and April (2000) magazines. These excellent features contained many great photos of Curtis and the Impressions, scans of most of his albums, a detailed US & UK discography and articles by Peter Doggett and yours truly. *Record Collector* went a long way towards a contemporary redefinition of the man, his music and influence with these tributes.

A story in *Billboard* (10 June 2000) reported 'Ichiban Headed For The Auction Block', an article by Chris Morris that told of the end of the line for Ichiban Records, whose assets would probably go to auction within the next two or three months. Legal proceedings, said Morris, revealed a claim by Platinum Entertainment Inc (Ichiban's distributors) for $3.2 million in assets and $6.4 million in liabilities. According to this report Ichiban, who had refinanced in March '99 could not convince Platinum that they could repay their debts and that Platinum would be forced to sell the Ichiban masters at auction to recover their money. It was a very sad end to the label that had been suffering a protracted collapse for the past couple of years.

In September the remaining scheduled Sequel/Curtom albums became available on CD in the UK. *Sugar Candy Lady* (NEMCD 361) Billy Butler's only Curtom album had the added bonus of the previously unissued single 'She's Got Me Singing'. 'The Ruby Jones' album also got a new makeover and was now retitled *Stone Junkie* (NEMCD 367) after their best-known UK track. *Jones Girls – The Early Years* (NEMCD 397) was an interesting compilation including Music Merchant and Ember tracks recorded by the talented trio early in their careers. The cuts of most interest, however, are the dozen leased from Curtom, which included not only their rare singles (Curtom and Paramount) but also some great previously unissued tracks that they recorded in Chicago at the Curtom Studios.

The Rhythm & Blues Foundation held their 'Pioneer Awards 2000' ceremony at the Manhattan Centre, New York in early September (it had been 18 months since the previous awards). Chairman of the Board, Jerry Butler opened proceedings by calling for a minute's silence on behalf of missing members Johnnie Taylor, Curtis Mayfield, Doris Kenner (of the Shirelles) and Zeke Carey (of the Flamingos) who had all departed since the last ceremony. Smokey Robinson, who was MC for the event, introduced a number of performers and guests who included Lloyd Price, Chuck Jackson, the Chi-Lites, Sister Sledge, Gerald Levert, Brenda Russell, Betty Wright, Stevie Wonder, Sylvia Robinson, Berry Gordy, Clyde Otis, the Dells, Don Covay, Aretha Franklin, Harvey Fuqua, Berry Gordy, Isaac Hayes, Dionne Warwick, Herbie Hancock, Vanessa Adams and Bonnie Raitt, who also performed with John Sebastian. From what I read about this occasion it was the place to be on that particular evening. My highlight would certainly have been the award to the Impressions, whose earliest line-up (minus Curtis) came together to receive their presentation from Mary Wilson. Jerry Butler, Sam Gooden and Fred Cash seemed to have at last settled some of their differences with Richard and Arthur Brooks as there was no repeat of the clash last time they were honoured by the Rock 'n' Roll Hall of Fame in January '91. This time things were a tad more harmonious as the photograph suggests. (Sam confirmed recently that the photo had been taken at the Brook's Brothers request.) The current Impressions line-up performed 'It's Alright' and 'I'm So Proud' as well as they ever did, their long and continuous career once more on the incline.

Towards the end of 2000 Sequel had by then made most of the Curtom catalogue available in the UK on compact disc. In addition they also released a number of classy collectors 12in edition albums, remastered in 108g heavyweight vinyl. These beautiful reconstructions started with *CURTIS* (NEMLP 965) with original gatefold sleeve and was followed by the two-LP set *CURTIS/LIVE* (NEMLP 400) again with gatefold sleeve, *Roots* (NEMLP 966) had its original US calendar sleeve and *Superfly* (NEMLP 964) had the flap sleeve, left off most early UK LP issues. In addition to these Curtis albums, *The Baby Huey Story* got a new gatefold sleeve and *Hutson* was also faithfully reproduced. The two compilations *Mighty Mighty Soul* (NEMLP 402) and *Funk-Soul Brothers & Sisters* (NEMLP 451) were treated to a vinyl alternative. The UK rights of Sequel/Castle to issue Curtom product had expired by the end of 2000 and the company who had been taken over by

Sanctuary Records Group were undergoing the internal changes that such a takeover imposes.

Due to changes of location and numerous distributors, the Curtom vaults had been falling into some disarray for a number of years. In some cases, during the process of re-issue, difficulties had been encountered in tracking down previously unissued sides and alternative versions. In the mid '90s, an inventory of the entire Curtom product revealed many as yet unreleased recordings by Curtis and a number of other artists that had recorded for the label since '68. Just how much of this product will find future release will depend on a number of factors.

Curtis had registered a number of unreleased songs with BMI but there are over 140 of his tracks identified on master tape in the Curtom vaults. Some of them may be incomplete or at any rate needing some further studio attention but logic dictates that there must be a few more Mayfield recordings awaiting future issue. These include intriguing titles like 'The Great Escape', 'In The News', 'Turn Up The Radio' and 'What's The Situation?' and also listed are tracks recorded as 'Curtis at Montreaux Jazz Festival '87'. Other tracks missing from our collections are the Impressions' 'All Over The World', 'Colours Blow My Mind', 'Double Your Pleasure', 'Exorcist', 'I Get High', 'I Will Overcome', 'Just My Imagination', 'What Happened To A Thing Called Love' and 'Where Is My Love'. Of most personal interest are the live performances from the Impressions, Curtis and Jerry, recorded from their 1982/83 'Silver Anniversary Tour', which (like the other as yet unissued ABC Impressions live at The Club Chicago, recorded in September '66) must see the light of day soon. Ralph Johnson who left the Impressions to form Mystique, then rejoined them around the end of the '80s did try to launch a solo career and recorded an album while still at Curtom and as yet still awaiting digital liberation are 'Take Me Higher', 'Some Things You Gotta Do', 'So In Love', 'Good Guys', 'Back In Love', 'Never Get Over You', 'You're The Music' and 'Good Thing'. Other artists that left tracks behind in the Curtom vaults were Leroy Hutson (19, enough for two albums), Linda Clifford (20, also enough for two albums), Gavin Christopher (ten – an album's worth) and there are still a few tracks outstanding from the Natural Four ('Goodbye', 'Hold On' and 'Searching'), the Jones Girls

('Latin Groove', 'Save The Children', 'So Much Love', 'Too Much Woman' and 'We Got To Live Together') and Major Lance 'Let's Get Together' and yet another version of 'Monkey Time'. There are a number of miscellaneous tapes in the Curtom vault from people like Jermaine Jackson, Joseph 'Lucky' Scott and others that will probably never see the light of day.

A number of Curtom albums originally released on vinyl have not yet found their way on to CD either namely *Love's Happening* (UK *Stay Close To Me*) by the Five Stairsteps, *Patti Miller* by Patti Miller (a rarity that I personally still have been unable to locate) and Bobby Whiteside's *Bittersweet Stories* all of which were originally issued on Curtom/Buddah. Warner distributed Curtom albums *Locked In This Position* by Bunny Sigler & Barbara Mason, and the two Mayfield movie scores *Let's Do It Again* by the Staple Singers and sister Mavis Staples' less successful *A Piece Of The Action* have also not made it to CD. The two albums from the RSO chapter in Curtom's history yet to go digital are *Gavin Christopher* and Ava Cherry's *Ripe* both début solo albums. One previously unissued album from this period that did find a limited UK release on CD was *House Party* on Back To Black/BMG by Fred Wesley.

Although Mayfield's biggest album *Superfly* has been issued and re-issued and *Claudine, Sparkle, Return Of Superfly* and *Short Eyes* have become available on CD, the other three Curtom soundtracks still remain unissued. The rights to these three remaining movies are owned by Warner Brothers (who also own most of Mayfield's songs) and it seems possible at some future date *Let's Do It Again* and *A Piece Of The Action* might be issued as a 2fer and even *Three The Hard Way* might also find a release. Warner could issue all the soundtracks in a series like 'Mayfield at the Movies' or perhaps in a box-set. As the technology of CD and DVD move closer together and as the hardware plays both formats, why not issue the movie and the soundtracks on one disc? This format has all kinds of interesting possibilities for releasing unissued tracks as bonus collectables, the lost *Sparkle* soundtrack for instance.

Jerry Butler's memoirs, *Only The Strong Survive*, was published by Indiana University Press towards the end of 2000. This book, which is yet to be published in the UK, is an absorbing and informative read and well worth acquiring. Some slight differences have occurred in the telling of the Impressions early years together. My interviews with Jerry, Curtis, Sam and Fred revealed certain discrepancies in their various versions of events that occurred in Chicago long ago. Not many of us can accurately recall exactly what we were doing and thinking in 1957. So the precise manner in which they were signed by VJ and the billing of Jerry & the Impressions had some variations in the retelling. Jerry, who bore the brunt of Vee-Jay's decision to call the group 'Jerry Butler and the Impressions' from the outset tells his side of the saga. After all it was this one incident and the reactions it brought from Richard, Arthur, Sam and Curtis, which caused Jerry to leave the group rather sooner than he might have and aggravated a rift between the other members of the group, which still smoulders today. In his book, Jerry relates the mixture of sadness and sweet relief that he experienced after leaving the Impressions. He also tells us about the tours that the quintet made to promote their first hit 'For Your Precious Love' performing on the same bills as Eddie Holland, Lee Andrews and the Hearts, Huey Smith and the Clowns, Robert & Johnny, Ed Townsend, the Coasters and Frankie Lymon, Joe Tex, the Five Keys and Clyde McPhatter etc.

It was just as 'For Your Precious Love' began its rapid climb into Billboard's Hot 100 and the Impressions embarked on their first road tour of America, that an earlier misdemeanor caught up with Eddie Thomas, who had to serve a short jail term just when they needed him the most. It was Irv Nahan who stepped in to act as the group's temporary manager and bridged an important gap until Thomas' return. Whether Eddie could have prevented the manipulation of these five innocents by DJs and promoters along the way is open to speculation but he wasn't there so he didn't. This book contains a discography compiled from two sources: Robert Pruter (*Goldmine*) and David Cole (*In The Basement*). However, there was no sessionography included, which would have revealed much more detail about Jerry's fascinating recording history.

In the late spring of 2001 Bran Van 3000 issued a single on Grand Royal Records (owned by the Beastie Boys and issued by Virgin in the UK) entitled 'Astounded'. Reviewers described the band as a Canadian collective and the music as an alluring groove that ranges from hip hop and soul to '60s west coast psychedelic. Normally this kind of thing is of little interest to me but this time the record's producer James Di Salvio used a previously unissued lead vocal track featuring Curtis Mayfield. Apparently the negotiations to license the track from Curtom were concluded shortly before Curtis' death. A sample from 'Move On Up' was also included in the final mix (or mixes, as two alternatives were issued on the CD single). Some of the mixing on the Mayfield track was done at Olympic Studios in London. The only other name I recognized connected with this project was ex-Cars frontman, Ric Ocasek, who was credited as Co-Producer.

By September, BBC 1 were using a sample from 'Astounded' as the theme music behind trailers for their upcoming annual fundraiser/telethon 'Children In Need 2001'. With so much unused Mayfield master tape available, similar projects to Bran Van 3000's and other future experiments look like they could become a promising reality.

In the summer of 2001 The Isley Brothers issued the exquisite *Eternal* (Dreamworks 450 291-2), their best album for years. In a career spanning 40 years that has grown and evolved, often paralleling Mayfield and the Impressions in many ways, the Isleys have written and recorded some exceptional music. Like Curtis, they pioneered soul music through the many changes of its evolution and still continue to do so today. For the final track on Eternal, Ronald took 'Think' (a Curtis instrumental from the *Superfly* soundtrack) and wrote some lyrics that give the song a whole other dimension. The haunting guitar lines, beautifully recreated by Ernie, weave in and out of the background while Ronald struts his stuff. This inspirational cut was recorded at Westlake Studios, Los Angeles and produced by Jimmy Jam and Terry Lewis and it demonstrates yet another example of Mayfield's enduring influence.

There are a number of Internet sites dedicated to Curtis Mayfield. Some have been around for years, like Johan and Tomas Inkinen's dedicated site www.come.to/curtis.mayfield and others, like darkerthanblue.com are in the process of compiling the most complete Mayfield microsite but also cover a wider spectrum of black music that pays homage to Curtis and other artists with dedicated pages. With so much of his catalogue now available many of the labels like Rhino,

Ace/Kent and Sequel also feature his music and have display pages and interviews online. Compact discs, DVDs, videos and other products can be purchased from Amazon.com, cdnow.com, www.allmusic.com and many others, where fans can browse Mayfield info as they trolley between the virtual isles. Curtis is all over the Internet.

As you cruise around some of these sites you will become aware just how massive the Mayfield influence has been on the hip hop/rap generation. There have been so many versions, part versions, mixes and samples taken from Mayfield's music that it's really hard to keep track of them all. www.galactica.it has listed over two pages of these recordings by artisans like BD Kane, Cookie Crew, Ultramagnetic, Spice1, Camp Lo etc. www.algonet.se also provided a similar service on a table, showing the original Curtis song, the sampling artist and new song (which must be very useful service for any songwriter trying to keep tabs on their royalties). Microsoft Music Central, atlanta.hob.com (Atlanta House of Blues), Goldmine Online and many other sites have also created biographical pages, reviews, interviews, news, gossip and rumour – it varies from site to sight but many of the companies commission well informed writers and have discographies, collaborations, similar artists and other useful research available to view, grab and download.

When reading reviews on the web one often sees references to the political aspects of Mayfield's work. While it is obvious that many of his songs have political implications and some were even used by the civil rights movements and programme/moviemakers as freedom anthems, Curtis always stressed that he was not a political animal and that he would rather leave politics to the elected officials – an opinion that was recently confirmed by two people as close to him as any, Fred Cash and Sam Gooden.

Curtis Mayfield was a free spirit who would not be contained by poverty, racial suppression, or even as in the final decade of his life, almost complete paralysis. Despite a deprived childhood and a sketchy education he taught himself to write, play guitar and to sing. He developed and honed these few precious talents and found a way to deliver them with an honesty and creative style all his own. He was there at the birth of soul when, in his hometown Chicago, he was among those that fashioned the gospel of their childhood into the mainstream of popular American music. He was central in the creation of a unique sound and further developed his own signature that would become indelible in popular music from the early '60s onward.

Mayfield's early work with the Impressions soon brought him widespread attention and clearly indicated long-term possibilities for this bright new talent to evolve. The love songs that he wrote and produced possessed a fresh dimension that set him apart from his contemporaries. Each new record revealed a little more insight into his particular vision and fostered further interest and identification in what he had to say and the style in which he expressed his thoughts and hopes. His poetry encouraged further investigation, a desire to delve deeper into the mysteries of life and love and it is precisely these qualities that give his love songs their timeless but constant fascination.

The evolution of his message songs were a cross fertilization of his early story songs like 'Gypsy Woman', 'At The County Fair' and 'Minstrel & Queen' amongst others, his religious teachings and the development of his own personal moral code. He wanted to say other things in another voice and explore other perspectives. Mayfield often took the role of reporter/observer rather than accuser in his social messages. If criticisms bite, it is because sometimes the truth is tough to face. There was no denying his sincerity as he questioned with the assurance of what he knew to be true. There was no hysteria or phony rhetoric; he concentrated on the realities of life and the effects that they have on people like you and me.

Curtis often issued an uncomfortable invitation to look honestly behind the spin and propaganda of the modern world and to check out what really goes on, both in our personal and public lives. Not only did he suggest that we examine our own personal motivations closely but he encouraged us to confront the suppression of others. To insist on the rights of access to opportunity that should be freely available to all, irrespective of origins or gender and allow true development through education and social progression. A do it yourself utopia, achieved through personal involvement and application.

In America, for those that could see past black, he became a champion for the individual, which didn't make him too popular in some quarters of the biz. Even in the early days he wouldn't sell his songs for $25 to get them recorded, which put him in trouble with the record companies – so he went to the Big Apple to get established and register his own publishing company. Then he could deal on his own terms. Mayfield learned early and often repeated at interviews just how important it was to own as much of yourself as possible, that all too easily you could lose all your creative work, publishing, masters and royalties to sharp businessmen. You had to do it for yourself and that the struggle was continuous. But this kind of personal isolation can have a downside. Curtis was seen by many establishment figures as a renegade ('If There's A Hell Below'), a subversive ('We Got To Have Peace'), a dangerous free-thinking poet ('Choice Of Colors'), the intellectual urban guerrilla ('Mighty Mighty, Spade & Whitey') and worse than that a threat to sponsors ('We're A Winner'). He was not any of these; he was a poet, a troubadour, and a messenger with a question. He wasn't a saint, a superstar or a genius; he was just one of the best singer/songwriter/musicians of all time. The lyrics and music that he left behind will captivate, inspire, inform and entertain for generations to come.

Just move on up
And keep on wishing
Remember your dream
Is your only scheme
So keep on pushing

Take nothing less
But the supreme best
Do not obey
Rumours people say
You can pass the test

Just Move On Up

– 'Move On Up', Curtis Mayfield, 1970

Biographies

I have been writing about Curtis Mayfield and the Impressions for more than 30 years. During that time, I have taken the opportunity to interview many artists who have been associated with him over his lengthy career. When it came time to put these encounters into a book, because Mayfield's influence had been so prolific, I found that it went off in too many directions so in the end I had to cut them from the main text. I had intended to publish much more biographical detail of the artists associated with Curtis, with more discographies, pictures, album sleeves and associated memorabilia but in the end that just wasn't possible. So for those of you out there who like me have a passion for the detail and some might say trivia connected with the Curtis Mayfield story here are some bonus features. Further info not included here can be obtained through SoulMusicHQ.com, which will be launching a website later this year.

ABBEY, JOHN
After establishing his *Blues & Soul* magazine in the late '60s, John Abbey moved into label management. He started Action Records, which were distributed by B&C Records. Both labels were run from offices at 37 Soho Square in London's West End. Action began very well, scoring many hits on the UK soul charts with re-issues from the Mirwood, Duke/Peacock, Swan, Gamble (and other catalogues) but had no crossover success to pop. By early '71, Abbey had launched Mojo, his second label and this time he achieved more consistent chart success. Mojo issued contemporary soul from Glades, DeLite and Atlantic as well as good UK productions featuring Donnie Elbert, The Elephant Band and the Fantastics, as well

as '60s re-issues. He integrated his release programme to coincide with the artists on UK tour, which added to Mojo's success. Singles regularly crossed to the Top 50 but Mojo's biggest UK hits came with Tami Lynn's 'I'm Gonna Run Away From You' (#4 UK pop in May '71), Timmy Thomas' 'Why Can't We Live Together' (#12 UK pop February '73), Joe Simon's 'Step By Step' (#14 UK pop June '73), Formations' 'At The Top Of The Stairs' (#28 UK pop August '71) and the Fascinations' 'Girls Are Out To Get You' (#32 UK pop July '71). Mojo also scored smaller pop hits with James Brown and Millie Jackson. Of course, these records and many other releases sold extremely well in the UK soul/R&B market where the label was seldom out of chart contention.

Contempo, John's third label started trading in early '73 extending further the format that he had created for Mojo to include northern soul. Major Lance and JJ Barnes were among the American singers who recorded here for the label. Unlike Mojo, Contempo had only one notable UK pop hit with Dorothy Moore's 'Misty Blue' (#4 UK pop in June '76) and her UK follow-up 'Funny How Time Slips Away' also managed #38 UK pop (October '76) for them. Their main body of success was again found on the soul chart. Later releases were club/disco orientated but after a proposed link-up with Atlantic fell through, the label folded in early '78. Contempo Raries hit again with a rerun of Tami Lynn's 'I'm Gonna Run Away From You' (#36 UK pop) in May '75.

ABNER JR, EWART

Besides Vivian, Jimmy Bracken and Calvin Carter, the other creative force at Vee-Jay Records was the charismatic Ewart Abner Jr. Ewart had been very helpful to VJ in their early years as they struggled to establish themselves. After four productive years at Chance Records with Art Sheridan, he was invited to join VJ as General Manager. Ewart looked after the marketing and PR for the company and quickly established a reputation as a wheeler dealer with big ideas, energy and vision – and depending who you talked to, a highroller gambling VJ's money away and worse. He also handled the money and by his own admission was a 'bagman' paying off the DJs and greasing the wheels that kept the company turning a healthy profit in a very competitive market.

Abner knew how things really worked and had no illusions about what was necessary to stay out in front. By '61 he had purchased 33 per cent of VJ and had been promoted to company President. Part of his vision for VJ was for it to become a full line company, widening its roster from gospel, the blues and R&B to encompass jazz, rock, pop, C&W and MOR. After a falling out with his other VJ partners in '63, who did not agree with his future plans for the company's expansion, Abner was forced out of VJ. He immediately set up Constellation with 'Bunky' Sheppard and Art Sheridan, taking with him some of VJ's major acts. Despite having all the right ingredients, Constellation scored very few hits and the label was out of business by '66. Meanwhile, Vee-Jay was suffering its own disaster.

This was the lowest point in Abner's career but it proved a temporary setback for this charismatic entrepreneur who by '67 had moved to Detroit and Motown Records as its Vice President. Still moving up he became company President by '73 and he was instrumental in Jerry Butler signing to Motown. Butler, whose work for Motown had not been entirely satisfactory, later followed Abner to Philadelphia International. Abner already occupied the top job at the Gamble/Huff company in '78. He was one of the main characters of the Chicago music scene to which he contributed a great deal; he was one of the handful of men who did what it took to make Chicago soul the highly respected musical genre that it is today. Ewart Abner Jr died in Los Angeles on 27 December '97, aged 74.

ASKEY, GIL

Gil Askey had served a long and fruitful career first as a musician, then developing his skills further into arranging and production. He first played trumpet with Arnett Cobb's Band at the Apollo Theatre in Harlem, when Clyde and the Dominoes performed there in '53. At the Apollo he backed a host of notables like Frankie Lymon and the Teenagers, Chuck Berry and Shirley and Lee, amongst countless others who performed at the theatre over the following five years. This is where he first met Jackie Wilson with whom he later toured America from '58. Askey was on the road with Wilson for years and during this period he also worked with Dizzy Gillespie and Pat Lewis.

After touring with and backing countless outfits for many years, Askey eventually came off the road and settled in Detroit. Gil's earliest success in the Motor City was as a freelance arranger, when in '62 he wrote the charts for 'Baby I Need Your Loving' by the Four Tops. He met James Jameson, Earl Jones and Earl Van Dyke and all four joined the Gordon Staples Symphony Orchestra. This quartet became close friends and stuck together going on to play with Ed Wingate, who led what was to become the Golden World/Ric-Tic house band. This outfit worked with JJ Barnes, Edwin Starr and Barbara Mercer etc and played on the sessions of many other artists who recorded at the Golden World studios. Askey started writing and arranging songs intended for the artists under contract, but the San Remo Strings recorded his earliest songs and had a hit with 'Hungry For Love' (which sold in excess of 700,000 copies). On the strength of this hit, Berry Gordy offered him a job as the Supremes' arranger at Motown in '65. Askey became Diana Ross's right-hand man and remained her personal arranger over the next 20 years, but he also worked closely with Martha Reeves, Billy Eckstine and Kim Weston. It was French composer Michel Legrand who has been previously credited with the music for *Lady Sings The Blues* ('72) and he did write the theme tune but it was, in fact, Askey who wrote the majority of the movie's soundtrack and it was he who was nominated for an Oscar for his work on the movie.

Gil went on to write the soundtrack for *Mahogany* three years later for which he was nominated once again. He also did all the arrangements and much of the musical background work for the *Motown 25th Anniversary TV special*. Askey came to the UK with the Four Tops when they toured in '84. The previous year he had accompanied the Temptations on a similar tour of the USA, with the same band. His family had numerous musical connections including his cousin, the singer Damita Jo and his eldest daughter, Day, who sang with the Brothers Johnson in the mid to late '70s and who was married to Keni Burke.

BURKE, KENI

After leaving the Stairsteps to pursue a solo career, Keni Burke kept his base in New York and recorded his first solo album for Dark Horse *Keni Burke* (DH 3022) in 1977. The album was cut in Los Angeles and mixed in Nashville. Most of the songs included are slow and medium tempo ballads that are easy on the ear and seem natural developments of his songs heard on *2nd Res*. Keni penned all with either writing partners Askey or Vann. 'Day' is a catchy instrumental written for and dedicated to Keni's wife. His deep groove basslines are an integral part of all his records, but feature most on 'Shuffle', which concludes the first side – the strongest side – and 'From Me To You', which is an excellent instrumental alternative to the Stairsteps' version. Produced by Keni, it is a very accomplished collection in most respects, but in total, lacks that little extra something that would include it in the 'great' category. Nevertheless, for a début album, it clearly lays out all of Keni Burke's considerable assets.

It was indeed unfortunate for him, that Harrison's Dark Horse business left little time for public exposure to this album. The distribution deal with Warner was in place but in January '78, George pulled the plug on all Dark Horse product but his own, and Keni's first album disappeared. The two singles 'Shuffle'/'From Me To You' and 'Keep On Singing'/'Day' did little business and Keni temporarily rejoined his brothers in their new group Invisible Man's Band, who had a hit at #9 R&B/45 pop with 'All Night Thing' on Mango (103) in March 1980. Their biggest hit, it was issued in the UK as a 12in on Island but it had already kicked around for months on import.

Later that same year, Keni ran into his old friend Edward 'Chappie' Johnson and together they formed Burjo Productions. He moved his base from New York to Los Angeles and began recording some of the songs that he had written most recently, whilst playing and producing for Bill Withers, Dusty Springfield, Smokey Robinson, Diana Ross, Gladys Knight and Cher amongst others. RCA were impressed when Chappie played them the results of Burjo's first sessions. They signed Keni and Chappie to a deal that initially produced the *You're The Best* album (RCA 4024), recorded in Hollywood and released in mid '81. On this album, which Keni wrote, produced and arranged (with significant contributions from Gil Askey and Wade Marcus), he hit an early creative peak. 'Let Somebody Love You' was chosen as the single but, despite a poor R&B rating, only #66 in May '81, this original song was both written and sung superbly by Keni. Another dancefloor classic, power packed with energy was 'You're The Best', which became an 'all time' club anthem but still did not cross over to greater commercial acceptance. All the tracks on this album, Keni's best to date, benefit from the four-wheel drive of Keni's bass, which is often featured as a lead guitar. It's a great album, but sadly not nearly enough people thought so, otherwise it would have been the monster it deserved to be.

So for the next album, *Changes* (RCA PL 89551), Keni wrote even more uptempo dance tracks in a concerted effort to break into the charts. This time the complete album was recorded in Philadelphia, at Starship One/Sigma by Joe Tarsia. Keni showed plenty of vocal confidence and he compares favourably to his contemporaries of the time, like Al Jarreau and Jeffery Osbourne. 'Risin' To The Top', the album's strongest track was a single that again missed its audience of the time. Who knows why? Burke's bass hooks you straight away – and is rumoured to have been sampled over 50 times by rap and hip hop artists including Mary J Blige. For the CD, RCA (ND 90555) added two tracks taken from the previous and superior *You're The Best* album. Neither of RCA albums sold well enough to chart but did big business on the dancefloor at discos and clubs in America and Europe. Burke managed only two pop hit singles in the UK. The first 'Let Somebody Love You' went to #59 in June '81, remaining on the chart for three weeks and 'Rising To The Top', which only reached a lowly #70 when it was re-issued in April '92.

'The Artist Showcase' (a series of re-issue albums put together by Ralph Tee for the Street Sounds label in '86, a spin off of his magazine) released an album on Keni, which used tracks taken from all three of his solo albums. Keni was elevated to 'Genius' by Tee who, at the time, considered him to be number one in his field. Though he was indeed much respected as a musician/singer/producer, Keni could not maintain a high enough profile to sustain his solo career. He still found plenty of work on other sessions as a studio musician, plus writing and producing in the mid '80s at Philadelphia International. RCA released a second Keni CD in '92 as part of their *Wonderful World of...* (PD 90682) series. This album featured only 15 selected tracks taken from the three albums and contained no unreleased product, but did include an alternative mix of 'Risin' To The Top'. London-based Expansion Records, who Tee became involved with in the late '80s, released one song, 'Friends Or

Lovers', on a CD compilation called *Soul Sauce Volume 1* (CD EXP 1) also in '92. Keni was the youngest of the musically active Burke brothers, until Cubie, the fifth brother and ten years his junior, having finished his full time education also briefly tried his hand as a solo career with 'Down For Double' on Rissa Curissa in '82.

Fifteen years after his last RCA sessions, Keni who had released little as a solo artist tried his luck once again and released a new album *Nothin' But Love* (Expansion XECD 12) in 1998. He breezed through a collection of beautifully self-produced slow to midtempo grooves, starting with 'I Need Your Love' (which includes some vocals by his son Osaze and a rap by Natina), which was issued as a single. Not surprisingly he doesn't have the same compulsion to dance so much these days and has mellowed a little in the intervening years since his RCA recordings. Keni had been content to be working in the studio, playing his bass when required and producing other artists like the Whispers and Keith Sweat during his 16-year layoff as a solo artist. Certainly all the cuts on 'Nothin' But Love' are good to chill to. The cool mood is continuous, with the title track and 'Give Me A Chance' marginally stronger than the others. It's a pity this album didn't receive a little more airtime and a chance to grow but it lacked an instant commercial hook, and was just too cool for the charts anyway. Its release passed most of the media by but Pete Lewis thought it worthy of some attention in *Blues & Soul* with a telephone interview (31 March '98) and column announcing the new album's imminent release.

BUTLER, BILLY

Billy Butler never found the good fortune he deserved to make it as singer, either with one of his groups or as a solo. He got plenty of encouragement from Curtis and brother Jerry but as a performer he never got out from underneath their shadow. He made his initial recordings for OKeh but an early version of 'Gotta Get Away' (which the Impressions cut later) didn't catch on. The insistently uptempo 'Right Track' made #24 R&B in July 1966 after which Billy parted company with OKeh and the Chanters to pursue a solo career with Carl Davis at Brunswick. Incidentally, 'Right Track' was Billy's best-known record in the UK and had some British chart success on Dave Godin's Soul City label later, after being a long-time favourite first with Northern and then the London club scene. Billy's solo efforts made no commercial impact during the next two years but he put out some great records starting with 'Love Grows Bitter' a superb love song written by Jimmy Diggs. Though not quite as prolific as Curtis, his songwriting had regularly supplied other singers with hit records. Gene Chandler recorded 'Bless Our Love', 'A Song Called Soul' and 'No Peace, No Satisfaction'. Lavern Baker, the Artistics and Jackie Wilson also cut his songs. The Opals had 'Does It Matter' and Otis Leavill cut 'Let Her Love Me' and 'To Be Or Not To Be' – the list goes on and on.

BUTLER, JERRY

Jerry Butler had a close association with Curtis from an early age – they grew up together as kids in Chicago and shared a brotherly bond for 50 years. In an interview in '72, Butler said, 'Curtis and I always inspired each other writing and singing. Sometimes we'd fight about this or that, but when it came together it was beautiful.' A testament to this was 'He Will Break Your Heart', which stayed at #1 R&B for seven weeks and was later recorded by many other artists, Ben E King, Freddie Scott and Dawn etc. Jerry Butler became a big star and his success on the R&B and pop charts was awesome. Throughout his long career he hit the R&B chart 58 times and had major pop success too. Some of these hits featured duets, first Betty Everett in '64 with 'Let It Be Me', which actually outsold the Everly Brothers version and charted slightly higher, though both records were million sellers. Betty and Jerry also cut a beautiful interpretation of Charlie Chaplin's 'Smile'. Then later in '71, dueting with Gene Chandler, Butler had 'You Just Can't Win' and 'Ten And Two'.

Between '71 and '73 he had three more hits with Brenda Lee Eager, 'Ain't Understanding Mellow', 'Close To You' and 'Power Of Love'. During the ten-year period that Jerry was associated with VJ they released more than a dozen albums by him as a solo artist. As good and as varied as these albums were, they did not cross over to pop and sold in the main to R&B and soul fans. *Delicious Together* (VJ 1099) was the only exception, charting at #102 in October '64 on Billboard's Top albums chart.

After the VJ collapse in 1966, Jerry moved on to Mercury and a year later 'I Dig You Baby' was a big hit, #8 R&B, just prior to his purple patch with the Kenny Gamble and Leon Huff collaborations 'Never Give You Up', 'Hey Western Union Man', 'Are You Happy', 'Only The Strong Survive', 'Moody Woman' and 'What's The Use Of Breaking Up'. All six hit Top 10 R&B during '68 and '69. When they split in 1970 over royalty disputes, Butler was halfway through his new album *You And Me* (SR 61269). He used Mayfield protégé Donny Hathaway as arranger/producer to finish it off. 'Then it was time to build the Butler Music Workshop,' Jerry later recollected.

The Workshop was an assortment of highly talented songwriters, performers, arrangers and producers based in Chicago. 'If It's Real What I Feel' was an #8 R&B hit written by Charles Jackson for Jerry at the Workshop in '71. 'One Night Affair' went to #6 R&B a year later and was his last top ten hit before Butler left Mercury in '75. During his nine-year period with Mercury, the label released almost 20 albums on Jerry. Eleven made it to album charts including his career best seller *The Iceman Cometh* (SR 61198), which reached #29 in January '69. The follow-up, *Ice On Ice* (SR 61234), also cracked the Top 100 when it reached #41 the following April. Jerry then moved on to Motown for a couple of years, and 'I Wanna Do It To You' hit #7 R&B in February '77.

The material he had to work with there was uneven – the album *Suite For The Single Girl* (M 878) sold reasonably well, but his first duet album with Thelma Houston *Thelma And Jerry* (M 887) went to #53 in June '77. Then in '78, Jerry was reunited with Gamble & Huff and also Ewart Abner, who by then had become President at Philadelphia International Records. 'Cooling Out' hit #14 R&B that year but later releases had disappointing commercial success, the only album to chart being *Nothing Says I Love You Like I Love You* (35510) that went to #160 in January '79. It was time for the Iceman to hang up his pick after a couple of one-shot deals on Fountain (which he re-activated in the mid '80s) and CTI had achieved dwindling success. He quit the music business in the mid '80s and went into local Chicago politics.

Looking back on his success with all those hit records, two of them – 'Only The Strong Survive' and 'Ain't Understanding Mellow' – million sellers, must provide Jerry Butler with a great deal of satisfaction. He wrote some classics too: ('I've Been Loving You Too Long' with Otis

Redding probably being the most famous) plus many more for himself, brother Billy and several others. After coming out of retirement to cut 'Choice Of Colors' for a Mayfield tribute album, Jerry went on to make a fine album for Urgent/Ichiban *Time And Faith* (ICH 1151). Two years later he repackaged his Fountain album *Ice And Hot* and added three new tracks for *Simply Beautiful* on Valley Vue (22006-2) but great as these CDs were, Butler was unable to re-establish his career back to the strong commercial basis that he had enjoyed

CALLIER, TERRY

Over the past couple of years, Callier's music has seen something of a renaissance in the UK, where he has been working recently in response to this latter day interest shown in his music. Terry took a slightly different route to that of his contemporaries – his music is not restricted by the secular boundaries of soul music and its gospel roots but draws from a much wider spectrum that embraces jazz, folk, pop and the blues. Callier's music won't fit easily into the confines of any one category, genre or box – colour him free.

He grew up on the south side of Chicago and went to University of Illinois where he traded his piano for a guitar. Terry had actually begun to write and sing his own songs in the early'60s. He told me in '72 that his earliest inspiration came after he first met Curtis Mayfield. In his early teens, he hung out with childhood friend Larry Wade and the two of them sang their apprenticeship to life within a number of vocal groups from the Cabrini Green area of the city, where they came up alongside Jerry and Billy Butler, Major Lance and Curtis Mayfield. Terry made his first break into recording when he cut a session for Chess Records, from which one single was released. 'Look At Me Now'/'You Gonna Miss Your Candy Man' (originally released by Chess in '62) – though much influenced by the Drifters most commercial Latin period, it missed its audience and quickly slipped into the realms of 'the collectable'.

Two years later Terry got a second chance, this time with the jazz-based Prestige label, for whom producer Sam Charters was in the process of creating a folk music series/outlet. Hence the *New Folk Sound Of Terry Callier* (available on CD in the UK through BGP CDBGPM 101)

was recorded. Although the performance is clearly him, it was not until his first album with Cadet in '71 that Terry really established his unmistakable style within the unique originality of his own superb songs. Shortly before recording *Occasional Rain,* he had joined the Butler Workshop. Through the success that he and Larry were achieving with the great series of songs that they began writing for other artists like the Dells and Jerry Butler, Callier landed a solo deal with Cadet Records.

Terry went to see the John Coltrane Quintet in '64 at Chicago's McKee Disc Jockey lounge. He returned for every performance of their five-night residency. This stunning experience caused the awakening of intensity within Callier that would from that time on give him a unique perspective within his music. With the release of the *Occasional Rain* album and the amazing follow-up *What Colour Is Love* Callier soon earned respect and admiration from his fellow artists and although he commanded a faithful following of fans from his small club and coffee bar appearances, his work did not sell well enough to chart nationally. A third Cadet album *I Just Can't Help Myself* was issued, but this time it was not as well received and it appears that his recorded work could not create quite enough commercial interest. So in '76, he left the Workshop and quit the music business altogether. He went on to take a job with the local council, which enabled him to stabilize his earnings and to provide for his growing family. But he never gave up his music entirely and still continued to write and make the occasional small club appearance.

Terry signed to Elektra in late '77 who got behind the first album *Fire & Ice* and sent Callier on a nationwide tour supporting Gil Scott-Heron. Terry also scored his only R&B singles chart placing with 'Sign Of The Times' that went to #78 in August '79 and this track became the title of his second album for the label.

When his young daughter Sundiata came to live with him in '83, once again Callier's life took another direction and he retrained as a DAT systems analyst in order to put her through high school. This time, Callier's layoff was more permanent but his guitar was never far away. Although he worked his day job at the computer, he would still make 'one off' appearances now and then and managed to cut 'I Don't Want To See Myself' as a single in the mid '80s. It went unnoticed by all but the most faithful followers but a re-issue on UK-based Acid Jazz Records, in August 1990 created some club interest. Intermittent UK gigs followed and Terry began to build a core fanbase. He made several trips to Europe in the early to mid '90s. This process has gradually raised his profile to the present day where he receives quite good airplay (at least on stations like Jazz FM) and has managed a number of TV appearances such as *Later... with Jools Holland* and also played at the Glastonbury Festival '98.

I was fortunate to catch Terry Callier live at the Jazz Café, London on Wednesday 8 November '00 when he appeared as part of Ace Records 25th Anniversary celebrations. Just prior to the concert, I had a chance to talk to Terry and found to my amazement that he was temporarily without a record deal. He introduced me to his band, who later went on to demonstrate just how in tune they are with Callier, his repertoire and audience when they provided an enhanced performance of his songs, both old and new. The café was packed to the max with an enthusiastic crowd who sang, danced and responded with delight to the highly charged atmosphere. Terry began with 'Ordinary Joe', a classic oldie and moved to the newer songs 'Keep Your Heart Right' and 'It's About Time' before returning to his exquisite 'What Colour Is Love' a song of his that has found favour with other artists like Dee Dee Sharp. Callier's spirited versions of 'Holdin' On' and 'Fix The Blame' were very popular with his audience, a large percentage of whom were obvious regulars at his UK gigs. 'C'est La Vie', 'Step Into The Light', 'Lament for AD', 'Four Miles' and 'Sunset Boulevard' were also well received. The band came close to raising the roof with a lengthy rendition of 'Nobody But Yourself' and then they did it all again when they returned for their encore of another early classic 'Dancing Girl'. Such was the clamour that Terry returned one more time to perform a solo of 'Lean On Me', a ballad that has endured and grown over the years. It's easy to see why Callier's gigs are invariably sold out and he fully deserves this level of success and even more. Here's hoping that there are other UK labels like Mr Bongo who will provide enough support for this exceptional artist to flourish and develop.

For those of you who want to recapture these great performances, *Terry Callier – alive* (recorded at the Jazz Café) has been issued on Mr Bongo (MRBCD 19). Since 9/11 'Lament for the late ad' takes on other spooky implications. But this is a great live set where all those present were fused into the special atmosphere of the event. On the cover, a quote from Gil Scott-Heron suggests that everyone should have at least one Terry Callier album. Play this one a few times and soon you will want them all.

In October '01, Mica Paris featured *Occasional Rain* on her Radio 2 programme *Seminal Soul*, which also contained interesting interviews with Terry, his writing partner Larry Wade and the 'Acid Jazzman' Eddie Piller. Great as *Occasional Rain* is, I have always personally preferred the second Cadet album *What Colour Is Love*, which, it transpires, was originally recorded as a double album and no doubt, despite the disappointment of Callier and producer Charles Stepney, was edited by Chess prior to issue. Sadly, it was not this original concept that found its way to us when finally committed to CD by MCA in '98 but perhaps it may find a future release.

Trading on the success of *Timepeace* most of Terry's back catalogue was re-issued on CD in the UK. Charly released *The Best of Terry Callier* back in '92 but in '98 MCA issued *Essential, The Very Best Of...*, the three Cadet albums previously mentioned and Premonition released *First Light*, which featured some unissued tracks. An Elektra 2fer was not forthcoming at that time but they did eventually issue both *Fire & Ice* and *Sign Of The Times* as single CD albums. Talkin' Loud issued their second Terry Callier album *Lifetime* (534 054-2) in the autumnal months of '99. No surprises – he did it again, providing another faultless collection of superb songs that included 'Fix The Blame', 'Holdin' On' and a new version of 'I Don't Want To See Myself', the song responsible for his re-emergence.

CARTER, CALVIN

Calvin Carter is perhaps one of the least celebrated of the great Chicago soul producers. He got into the record business when his sister Vivian and her husband Jimmy Bracken set up Vee-Jay Records in the back of 'Vivian's Record Shop' in Gary, Indiana, circa 1953. As A&R director it was Calvin's job to find new talent and sign them to the label. Once this began to happen, he also took on the role of house producer and began to work with their first signings, The Spaniels and bluesman Jimmy Reed. 'Baby It's You' by the Spaniels was the first song actually recorded, and it was released in Chicago on the Chance label, which, at the time, had a better distribution system than VJ.

Vivian was a protégé of the legendary Al Benson and had become a locally famous radio DJ, and this provided VJ with the opportunity to get their music on the air. By September '53 'Baby It's You' had climbed to #10 on the R&B chart. Their very first recording was a hit. Jimmy Reed's 'High And Lonesome', the first issue at VJ-100, didn't cause much interest. Reed's string of hits began two years later with 'You Don't Have To Go' (#5 R&B, in March '55) but the most popular were 'Ain't That Lovin' You Baby', 'You Got Me Dizzy' and 'Bright Lights, Big City', which all registered at #3 R&B and spanned his eight-year association with VJ.

Once their HQ was located on 47th Street in Chicago, Carter began full steam production and he cut most of the early sessions at Universal Studios. He signed the El Dorados, the 5 Echoes and the mighty Dells who all did good R&B business and began to build VJ's reputation. America began to listen and when 'Goodnight Sweetheart, Goodnight' by the Spaniels hit in May '55 (#5 R&B) it became the first record to cross over to the pop chart for VJ where it reached #24. Carter signed John Lee Hooker in '55.

'Hooker came to us from Detroit and he was one of the most difficult people to record, nobody else could play with him, he was a one man band and I had to get everything in one take. So I put a plywood floor down in the studio to record his footappin' as the drumbeat,' Carter said in '72. Calvin also created the great drum sound on Betty Everett's 'It's In His Kiss' in '64, which was in fact achieved by people stomping on telephone directories.

Three years later they set up their jazz outlet under the control of A&R man Sid McCoy and released memorable early albums from Lee Morgan, Wayne Shorter and Eddie Harris. 'We started Falcon in ... I think '57 because we needed another label, but we changed it after ten records or so, to Abner, to avoid a law suit with a label from the south that already had the name. It wasn't Ewart's label though, as many people assume. We didn't even know about the other Falcon until "For Your Precious Love" went Top 10 in '58.' Within a few short years Vee-Jay grew to be the largest and most successful black-owned record company (prior to Motown) in America. Dee Clark who came to the label as a member of the Kool Gents/Delegates crossed over to the subsidiary Abner in '58 as a solo act and began his hit career with 'Nobody But You', which made both charts in November '58.

Vee-Jay moved into their own building on Michigan Avenue in 1959; Elmore James and Memphis Slim had joined the VJ blues roster and there recorded some of their most famous sides. Their jazz roster also bloomed with the talents of Wynton Kelly and Bill Henderson. Gospel also held its own too, with Swan Silvertones, The Highway QCs (led by Sam Cooke) and the Staple Singers, but by the early '60s, VJ was becoming even more famous for its soul and R&B records. The influential 'Just A Little Bit' by Rosco Gordon made #2 R&B in February 1960 and Gene Chandler's 'Duke Of Earl' was a huge hit when it topped both charts in January '62 and it became the label's first million seller. Gene had joined VJ in '61 as part of the Dukays with his producer William 'Bunky' Sheppard (and the Sheppards) as part of the package. He went solo with a name change and his first record went gold.

Carter had the closest working relationship and the most consistent sales with Jerry Butler though. In addition to the homegrown songs of Mayfield, Butler and brother Billy, he often shopped at the Brill Building and in New York for the right songs. 'That's how I found "Moon River", "Make It Easy On Yourself" and "Giving Up On Love" for Jerry. Later it worked again for Betty Everett when I got "Shoop, Shoop", "I Can't Hear You No More", "Getting Mighty Crowded" and "You're No Good" although Betty didn't do the original on that one. But we had the first hit with the song.' (Dee Dee Warwick cut the original record that also became a #1 for Linda Ronstadt in '75).

Early in '62 Vee-Jay signed the Four Seasons. Their first record 'Sherry' went to #1 on both charts and the follow-up 'Big Girls Don't Cry' followed suit. They also got the Beatles in a deal with Frank Ifield. In '72 Carter said, 'We got stung on the Four Seasons deal, the more records they sold the less money VJ got. We got behind with their royalties and that caused an internal shake up. You see, Ewart was still running that side of the label, like a store...we needed a better business approach. He had to go.' Whilst they were in the middle of their management shuffle and Randy

Wood, who headed their LA office, was appointed as the new President, the label began to shatter before their eyes. Abner and Sheppard left to set up their own new label Constellation taking Chandler, Dee Clark and the Sheppards with them.

It will not have passed unnoticed that the Beatles took the American charts by storm at the beginning of 1964, just prior to their incredibly successful US tour that began that February. It seemed at first that Capitol had exclusive rights to release Beatles records but in fact a five-year deal had previously been struck between EMI and Vee-Jay. Calvin had this to say on the subject, 'We had some deals with England, and we got the Beatles as a throw in with Frank Ifield! They said "We got a group here, will you take it?" So we took the Beatles, put out a record "Please Please Me" – nothing. We put out another record "From Me to You" – nothing. Then Beatlemania hit and zap, everything happened. That was the cause of our demise. We had a five-year contract with the Beatles but EMI had bought Capitol and so litigation started. Hey! We would have won but we were like up to here in taxes. And we grossed twenty million the year we went out of business!!'

During that period of litigation, VJ held on to two Beatles hits, 'Please Please Me' (#3 pop) and 'Thank You Girl' (#35 pop) but the others went to Capitol, Swan, MGM and Atco. Vee-Jay was squeezed out by the majors and never really recovered. Capitol exclusively released and distributed Beatles records in America from August 1964 onwards.

Meanwhile, the Four Seasons sued their producer Bob Crewe, who had them under contract and in turn he sued Vee-Jay Records and they left for Phillips. EMI pulled out of the Ifield and Beatles deal and all of a sudden it was raining lawsuits. 'We had more than 50 lawsuits against VJ in something like a two-year period, and at the time we were selling more records than we ever had. We had gold records on six of our artists and several big R&B hits as well.' Carter kept on doing what he was best at in the studio with Jerry, Betty and many others.

Meanwhile, VJ split in two and was managed from the west coast. 'As fast as we were making money in Chicago, they were blowing it in LA. In May '65 Vivian and Jimmy had had enough and they bought out the west coast management.' The Brackens rehired Abner and set up once more in Chicago, but Vee-Jay was too badly damaged and never regained its momentum. A year later it was all over and they filed for bankruptcy. Jerry Butler was the last artist to leave, his contract expiring at the end of May, and he signed with Mercury. 'VJ could have been as big as Motown, if the suits had taken care of business like the artists did,' Carter said as a postnote in '72. Calvin Carter carried on producing as an independent and cut two hit singles with the Players, 'He'll Be Back' and 'I'm Glad I Waited' and followed through with an album that featured excellent Riley Hampton arrangements on a mixture of original songs and standards.

He recorded Steeler on Date in '69, Betty Everett on Fantasy in '70 and Bobby Rush on Galaxy in '71. He was one of the co-founders of the Butler Workshop and Fountain Productions with Jerry Butler in '69 and he started his own label 'On Top' in '71. Sadly, it lasted no longer than a year, gaining only local interest for the Bobby Rush and Shades of Brown product. He produced for Jerry Butler, again in '73, this time for the Mercury album *Sweet Sixteen* (which was a celebration of Butler's first 16 years in the music business). Calvin moved to California in '75 but couldn't make much headway out there either and he retired to Indiana where he died in obscurity in July 1986. Jerry Butler was the only celebrity to attend the funeral.

During his most creative period at VJ Records and just after, Calvin Carter produced some of the best R&B records of all time, but it seems in recent years he has become a forgotten man, and little recognition has been given to this great artist. Sadly the only album Vee-Jay issued under his name was *Twist Along With Cal Carter* (VJ 1041) a rather uninspiring collection of instrumentals issued in '61.

Jerry Butler who perhaps knew him best, described him thus – 'Calvin was a strange mixture of talents – he was a politician, an actor – he was the non musicians musician, he couldn't play anything but he could hear everything, we all called him "The Ear" because of his reputation in Chicago for hearing a hit before anyone else. Cal was the creative force at Vee-Jay Records, produced hits on everyone there in the field of blues, gospel, soul – there is no end to his achievements. He was responsible for bringing me into the business as a solo act – we cut a few records together. You won't see his like again.'

CHURCHILL, TREVOR

Trevor landed his first job in music as Label Manager for EMI between '65 and '69. He then moved over to Bell Records as International Manager between '69 and '70 – his successes at Bell were 'Cry Like A Baby' (by the Box Tops), 'Keep On' (Bruce Channel), 'Captain Of Your Ship' (Reparata & the Delrons), 'A Way Of Life' (Family Dogg) and 'Love Grows' (Edison Lighthouse). He considers his biggest failure was not breaking the Delfonics, which didn't happen until after he left.

For the next three years, he worked as European Manager for the Rolling Stones label in the London office. He considers that his biggest contribution to the Stones was researching their tape vaults and coming up with enough material to make *Exile On Main Street*, a double album, for which they got half as much again in advances. He also gave Allen Klein 'Metamorphosis'. Getting the opportunity to work with Marshall Chess there, was in his own words 'a great privilege'. Churchill has few regrets about the past but one was not having established their label with other artists.

Next move was to Motown UK as A&R manager between '73 and '75. The only big success Trevor had at Motown was 'Dan The Banjo Man', which was a number one smash hit in Germany on Rare Earth, but they couldn't break it anywhere else. Trevor brought Peter Anders and Kenny Laguna over from the States (as ALI Productions) to produce at Motown UK and they placed two songs in the David Essex film *That'll Be The Day* but never had a hit with them, though they came close with 'Dirty Work' by the Flirtations (Polydor '74). Trevor then moved to Hamburg where he lived and worked for 18 months as product manager for Polydor International. 'My biggest contribution at Polydor was recommending the signing of Jean Michel Jarre, who went on to have giant success with them. We also purchased Capricorn and I remember a crazed evening of celebration spent with Phil Walden and Frank Fenter down by the harbour.'

He was tempted back to the UK by an offer to join forces with Ted Carroll and Roger Armstrong at Chiswick Records in '77. Together they set up Ace Records, which has since grown into the most respected UK independent label. Today, 25 years since its launch, Ace encompasses almost 20 labels including Kent, Blue Horizon, Fantasy, Prestige, Stax and Vanguard, and their musical sphere embraces all vital areas of the contemporary and archive music genres. So far Trevor had been responsible for the UK issue of seven Impressions CDs, which contain all the records that Curtis and the group cut during their seven-year period with ABC.

DAVIS, CARL

When Davis left the USAF in the mid '50s, he spent a few rootless years drifting from job to job. Once he had found his niche, Davis worked through a number of jobs in music promotion, sales and distribution. Within five years he was Regional Promotion Manager with Columbia Records.

Carl set about creating a roster of talent for Columbia, which included Walter Jackson, who he had discovered singing in Detroit, the Duotones, Otis Clay, Joyce Davis and Gerald Sims. Carl produced three singles on Walter, with the first 'I Don't Want To Suffer', creating mostly local interest. His most successful Columbia release came with 'The Bird' a dance-orientated piece by the Duotones. Soon after joining the company Davis met and became great friends with Bill 'Bunky' Sheppard who was trying to get a break on some groups he was promoting. Carl and Bill teamed up and created their own production company PAM (named after Davis's daughter) in early '61. They founded three independent labels of their own: Nat, Wes (William E Sheppard) and Pam, and began looking for upcoming attractions.

The first acts they found were the Starlets, the Dukays and the Sheppards who Bunky put together from two earlier groups that he had managed, the Ballads and the Bel-Aires. In '61 their earliest productions began to make an impact. 'Better Tell Him No' by the Starlets (Pam 1003) climbed to #24 on the R&B chart (#38 pop) by June, though their follow-up 'My Last Cry' didn't register. The Dukays' first record on Nat, 'The Girl Is A Devil', created a ripple of interest when it entered the low end of the Hot 100. Davis and Sheppard were short of money and had to borrow to fund their upcoming session at which was scheduled 'Nite Owl' and 'Duke of Earl' and featured Eugene Dixon as lead on both tracks. Contractual obligations to their New York distributor meant that The Dukays could choose their next A-side. They chose 'Nite Owl' as the follow-up.

Meanwhile, Calvin Carter had heard 'Duke Of Earl' and his radar told him it was a big hit, so naturally he wanted it for VJ. 'Carl explained to me that Dixon was tied to the Dukays under contract,' Cal said in '72, 'so I said that I only wanted the song and Gene as a solo, so why couldn't we find a new lead singer and take him out of the group. Carl wasn't completely happy at first, so we thought about it for a while and after some discussions with Vivian and Jimmy I offered to take the whole company into VJ and also offered them an in-house production deal.' The Nat label released 'Duke of Earl' by the Dukays just before this all came about, but Dixon promptly changed his name to Chandler (Jeff Chandler was his favourite movie star at the time) and went solo with 'Duke Of Earl', this time on VJ, who then took the Dukays with their new lead Charles Davis plus the Sheppards as part of the deal. 'Duke of Earl' by Gene Chandler became the label's biggest hit when it topped both charts in January '62.

The credits on Chandler's future VJ sides read 'A Bunky Sheppard Production' but it soon became common knowledge around town that it was Carl Davis who was responsible for the records. Sensibly, Dave Kapralik of Columbia moved Carl into their A&R department with considerable personal flexibility to operate his freelance activities and this soon led to Davis's rejuvenation of OKeh that began in 1962.

OKeh was Columbia's independently distributed R&B subsidiary, which had languished virtually unused for several years and badly needed a new direction. OKeh had released many great records in the jazz, blues, country, R&B and soul fields since its inception in 1918. Curtis joined Davis in late '62 as associate producer at OKeh and began working with Carl. Freelance arrangers Johnny Pate, Riley Hampton and Sonny Sanders were recruited and a super session group was formed around the nucleus of Mayfield, Phil Upchurch, Gerald Sims, Billy Butler and Kermit Chandler on guitars, Bernard Reed and Louis Sattersfield on bass and Maurice White (later to head up Earth Wind & Fire) and Al Duncan on drums to lay down the music for a talented group of vocalists under contract to OKeh. These were the guys who created and delivered the Chicago sound from OKeh with 'Monkey Time', 'It's All Right', 'Um, Um, Um, Um, Um, Um' and many others.

As Mayfield and Pate began to concentrate more on their ABC

commitments and OKeh's success began to diminish, Davis brought in Billy Butler, whose guitar style was closest to Curtis, and began to use Riley Hampton for arrangements, more in an effort to maintain the Chicago soul sound that he had been producing since 'Monkey Time' in '63. The results came amazingly close, but were not as commercially successful. Davis began to rely more on the writing and production services of Gerald Sims who also recorded at OKeh as a solo artist. A boardroom shuffle at Columbia left Davis reporting to Len Levy, who didn't share Kapralik's flexible attitude to Carl's freelance activities, the upshot of which was that Davis quit under a cloud in late '65.

OKeh spluttered on for another five years and did well with some of Davis' back catalogue. Ted Cooper produced some excellent sides with Walter Jackson including 'My Ship Is Coming In' and a superb remake of Clyde McPhatter's hit 'Deep In The Heart Of Harlem'. The label also had hits from Larry Williams and Johnny 'Guitar' Watson, Ray Thompson and the Vibrations in the late '60s, but Richard Parker's talents could not halt its demise. During his tenure Parker headed A&R for less than a year and the label closed in 1970. Some of Columbia's board members just had not grasped the fact that Carl Davis and the talent he had assembled were OKeh Records from '62 onwards, but that's the music business.

Davis carried on producing as a freelance through Jalynne Publishing, which he co-owned with Irv Nahan. He provided hits for Mary Wells and created 'Whispers' with Barbara Acklin and Gerald Sims. This record relaunched Jackie Wilson's career in October '66 when it became a US #5 R&B/11 pop hit. It occurred to Nat Tarnopol who ran Brunswick at the time, that Carl could do his magic once again for them and rejuvenate the label's flagging fortunes at the same time. Davis was hired as A&R Director and a flood of Chicago talent began once more to beat a path to his door. OKeh soon felt the chill of desertion as artists and musicians moved over to Brunswick drawn by the magnet of Carl's reputation. In addition to the hits he created for Wilson, he also continued to chart with the Young-Holt Trio, Artistics, Gene Chandler and Barbara Acklin.

He decided that he wanted to start another label of his own in '67 and he founded Dakar Records with Otis Leavill as his Vice-President. Davis took the name Dakar from the infamous town that is the capital of Senegal and was at one time, the centre for the embarkation of slaves. Carl enlisted the talents of Willie Henderson, Leo Graham, Otis Leavill and Richard Parker and soon reaped big rewards when 'Can I Change My Mind' by Tyrone Davis went to #1 R&B/5 pop in December '68 and launched both the label and artist on a very successful run that lasted eight years. After this hit, Carl decided to distribute Dakar through Atlantic and Tyrone's next single became the biggest success of his career 'Turn Back the Hands Of Time' (#1 R&B/3 pop).

Carl Davis' final label venture Chi-Sound and its demise, were a sad epitaph to all those great Chicago soul labels big and small like VJ, Constellation, Chance, Chess and all the others that had illuminated addresses on Record Row. An epitaph also to those Carl was directly responsible for – OKeh, Nat, Brunswick and Dakar that had gone before. It marked the end of an era when Chicago could no longer lay claim to the accolade of the 'World's Leading City Of soul/R&B'. Carl Davis was the man who kept Chicago's reputation so high for so long. He was also one of the original founders of what became known as the 'Chicago sound' along with Mayfield, Butler, Carter, Pate, Hampton and a few others.

FISHER, BOB

Bob's first job in the music business came in late '75 when he moved from Leicester to London to take a job as Press Officer for the Motown label. He had been a fan of all kinds of music since his mid teens, collecting records and specialist magazines like *Shout, Blues & Soul* and *SMG*, while in the evenings he frequented local clubs like Burlesque and the Night Owl. He began assisting John Stretton at the Blues Society and was inspired when he read a Charlie Gillett piece that stated, 'anyone who really likes black music should try to write about it.' Fisher began by reviewing new releases for *Cream*, and then moved on to *Let It Rock* and the *NME*. He interviewed notable US artists who appeared on tour in Leicester and other northern venues and was soon supplying articles to a number of magazines. He travelled down to London at request of EMI's Keith Peacock to do an interview with BT Express, which never happened but the journey wasn't wasted because Peacock informed him about the vacant post of Motown's UK Press Officer, which he applied for and got. Bob set about the enviable task of promoting many of the Motown stars when they visited the UK. But it was not long before he moved over to label management for Fantasy and EMI International, where he worked with Harvey Fuqua and had big success with Sylvester and 'You Make Me Feel Mighty Real' (#8 UK pop, August '78). He also had steady success with the Salsoul label and 'I Got My Mind Made Up' by Instant Funk and 'And The Beat Goes On' by Ripple, amongst others. Fisher left EMI in '80, to work on the respected Orbis 'History Of Rock' part work magazine series and compilation CDs. He extended his activities to freelance compilations of blues and soul CDs for a number of companies including Ace, Charly and EMI. Charly offered Bob a permanent consultancy and during his tenure there, he worked his way up to Deputy Managing Director. By late '89 he realized a long-held aspiration when, through Castle, he launched his very own label Sequel in '89. Within a short time, Sequel had established itself in the re-issue market and rightly gained a reputation for good value and high quality product and their catalogue was bristling with a wide variety of great music of all kinds. Fisher directed operations from his compact West Hampstead office, producing accessible design and informed sleevenotes. He was responsible for the UK Curtom renaissance through Sequel, which he began in the in the '90s. Bob Fisher has always had a great appetite for the music and an innovative approach that comes through in any project he's involved with.

FOUNTAIN PRODUCTIONS

Jerry Butler and Calvin Carter set up Fountain Productions in 1969. Billy had formed Infinity with ex-Chanter Erroll Banks, Phyllis Knotts and Larry Wade. When the their first record 'Get On The Case' took off, it raced to #41 R&B within a few days of release. This caught Stax (Fountain's distributor) on the hop as they were struggling to get out of a deal with Gulf Western and couldn't supply enough records to meet public demand. Billy said later, 'We had plenty of airplay but the records were not in the shops. In a panic we took Fountain to Mercury with a new deal but it was all too late for 'Get On The Case''.

Infinity put this disappointment behind them and stayed with Mercury for their next two singles. 'That Ain't Water It's Pollution', Butler's ode to ecological demise and 'Winter Of The Loving Heart' both went AWOL and Mercury's distribution did no better for Fountain, which gradually evolved into the Butler Workshop. Undaunted, the Brothers Butler set up their next venture, Memphis Records in 1970 whose roster included the Unifics, James Spencer, the Girls, Ollie & The Nightingales and, of course, Infinity. 'I Don't Want To Lose You'/'Free Yourself', the label's third release, rose and faded. Jerry Butler had this to say in '72: 'Billy's probably been one of the unluckiest guys around with records – good records. He had some stuff with OKeh that was fixin' to happen and they faded out the label. "Right Track" was fixin' to be bigger than bubble gum when Columbia just said, "We're getting out of the black record market. Close everything up in Chicago." Billy's record had already sold 100,000 in Chicago and LA but Columbia had said they weren't gonna deal with Carl Davis, and bing, Billy's record went down. Then he had "Get On The Case" with Infinity on the Fountain label and we got caught up in the Stax thing. They were playing games too, and the record was very strong, especially in Chicago. We switched distribution from Stax to Mercury and they were goin' crazy. There was a whole power struggle and Mercury didn't have their stuff together at all. Irv Green was leaving the company and everybody was hustling to see who'd be next president. There wasn't nobody taking care of business. Then came "I Don't Want To Lose You" which we put out on Memphis, and we did 53,000 copies in this city and there was no place else in the country where we could get airplay. We just didn't have the wherewithal by ourselves to do all the necessary things so we lost three potentially big records. I doubt if I'll start any more labels. I have a bad taste for it now.' Jerry in fact temporarily reactivated Fountain Records ten years later.

Another single that almost slipped by unnoticed was their only outing on Uni, in '72, 'In The Darkness'/'Do Your Thing Like Jesus'. However the Infinity single on Memphis wasn't to go completely to waste for in '72 they put it on their only album *Hung Up On You* (Pride 0018). In an interview later that year Billy said 'MGM (Pride's parent company) is basically pop oriented, they've never really been selling to the black market and they are trying hard to break in – black airplay, etc. I have great hopes that if we provide the material the company will get it to the people.' It was not to be and of the three Pride singles released only 'Hung Up On You' crept into the R&B chart in April '73 at #48. On the album of the same name issued on Pride (0018) were ten songs of their best work, produced by Billy, James Blumenberg and Gerald Sims. It was to be Infinity's epitaph and the group splintered shortly afterwards.

Billy and Larry immersed themselves in the Butler Workshop and had much success writing and producing for the likes of Terry Callier, the Dells, the Independents and brother Jerry. Of Infinity, Larry Wade later said, 'It was a very creative time, despite all the business hang ups, we had fun and I believed in the material, maybe it was ahead of its time – who knows?' Billy (and Jerry) wrote and produced many more great songs at the Workshop like 'What Do You Do?', 'How Did We Lose It?' and 'Special Memory'. At Curtom he linked up with Curtis once again of whom he had to say, 'I think Curtis Mayfield is such a great writer. You know the images he projects – he never fails to amaze me. The way he can manoeuvre into different images and situations. His conviction keeps you totally involved. He says things in a hip way but always with the truth, like it is. To me Curtis has always been one of the great poets, because he cares little about grammar, he's not restricted by it, he just writes naturally and sometimes the words may sound wrong but when he sings them they're so right.'

GILLETT, CHARLIE

Charlie Gillett gained international respect as a music historian and writer with a string of books starting with his masterwork *Sound Of the City* ('70), which was adopted as essential reading by many US college media courses. *Making Tracks* (the story of Atlantic Records) followed in '75 and Charlie edited a jackdaw of musical items *Rock Files* ('72), and other volumes followed in '74 etc. I discovered him through the pages of *Soul Music* magazine who he began writing for in early '68 while teaching social studies at Kingsway College in London. Then Charlie began to contribute to the best pop music weekly of its time *Record Mirror* ('68–'72). He went on to be associated with a number of UK music publications such as *Cream, Let It Rock* and *NME*.

I first met Charlie at a Drifters Press Reception at Polydor Records in September '71, when he invited me to appear in a BBC TV documentary on the Drifters called *Sounding Out*, which he was directing for producer Tony Cash. Gillett was also a working DJ at a number of clubs in the early days but by '72 he was presenting his own radio programme *Honky Tonk* for BBC Radio London. The following year he was co-editor of BBC Radio 1's *Story Of Pop* series. Charlie with partner Gordon Nelki has run Oval Records since '72 where they have had hits with Ian Dury, Lene Lovich (on Stiff) and Paul Hardcastle. As a music consultant, he has had success in advertising (Levi's Campaign) and selecting music for movie soundtracks like *My Son The Fanatic* ('98) amongst others.

Gillett soon developed his much wider musical interests with the pioneering *World Music* programmes for Capital Radio from '80. He was awarded the Sony Gold Award for 'Broadcaster Of The Year' in '91 and since May '95 he has produced and presented *Saturday Night* for BBC GLR relaunched as 'London Live' in April 2000 and the popular 'Radio Ping Pong' with celebs (between 8 and 10pm). Charlie also researched and presented a series of *Soul Pioneers* for Radio 2 '98–'00, which included his Curtis Mayfield tribute. I supplied some research and appeared on his programme, which is one of the best UK radio tributes so far produced.

HATHAWAY, DONNY

Had 'I Thank You' achieved the success it deserved to at Curtom, Donny Hathaway's vocal career would have blossomed sooner. As it was, he set his sights on New York and created a series of great arrangements for another Howard University classmate, Roberta Flack and thereby contributed much to her early Atlantic success. Roberta and Donny dueted on a number of occasions, gaining their biggest hit at #1 on R&B and #5 pop with 'Where Is The Love?' in June '72.

When Curtis launched Mayfield (his second independent record label) in '66, he began to work with Guy Draper, a young talent trying to get started. Draper also had Howard connections, where by now Hutson and Hathaway were both finishing their sophomore year of study. They cut their earliest tracks as part of the Mayfield Singers, on which Donny also played piano. 'I've Been Trying' was a distinctive single and, though it did no chart business, it was a great start and later the source of intense collectable interest. Draper linked up with the Unifics and became their manager. He used Hathaway's writing and arranging talents on the Unifics early sessions. The group's superb début 'Court Of Love', written by Guy and arranged by Donny, was a huge hit for the team (#3 R&B/25 pop in September '68). In a telephone interview in late '72 Hathaway stated, 'The Unifics gave me my first big hit and after that, I began to gain a belief that I could really begin to communicate with others through my music. I suddenly had the confidence to spread my ideas around and after that, I found it easier to see the direction in which I wanted to go. It was like I was in the clear and all sorts of opportunities came my way.'

Donny formed a production company Don-Ric Enterprises Inc and a publishing house Don-Pow Music with Rick Powell and began to freelance. He joined Curtom in Chicago where he began to write and arrange for the Impressions (he also toured as their MD for a period) and other acts on the roster. At the same time, he recorded new acts for many other Chicago labels. Hathaway was drafted in to complete Jerry Butler's *You And Me* album when Gamble & Huff quit after a royalty dispute with Mercury in 1970. Donny co-produced the album with Jerry and arranged seven of the ten tracks, most of which were written by members of the Butler Workshop. Whilst *You And Me* and the follow-up ... *Assorted Sounds*, which Hathaway was also involved in, did not hit the commercial highs of Butler's two previous albums (*The Iceman Cometh* and *Ice On Ice*) they have since been raised to the status of classic by collectors and journalists alike.

Curtis Mayfield introduced Donny to King Curtis who took him to the Atco label in late '69. 'The Ghetto' Donny's first solo single was an R&B smash, going to #23 on the R&B chart but only went to #87 on the Hot 100 in the first month of 1970. The first album *Everything Is Everything* (Atco 332) was cut in Chicago all with Hathaway arrangements. Good as this album is, it is a little uneven and when it was released it stiffed. It was not until after the success of the second album *Donny Hathaway* (360), this time produced by Atlantic wizards Arif Mardin and Jerry Wexler that *Everything...* went to #73 on the album chart in May '71. But if the public didn't catch on right away, the artists did and Hathaway was soon in great demand for his writing, arranging and production skills on many other people's records. He cut sessions with Carla Thomas and the Staple Singers at Stax, Garland

Green at Cotillion and others. He went back to Chicago in '71 to contribute to Jerry Butler's 'Special Memory' hit single and his *The Sagittarius Movement* album on which he was very much involved. This album was to become Butler's biggest since *Ice On Ice* two years earlier and put his career back in the ascendance. Atlantic recorded some of the best moments from Hathaway's '71 tour appearances in venues like the Troubadour and the Bitter End and issued a *Live* (386) set in March '72, which went as high as #18 on the album chart.

While Donny was collaborating with Roberta on her next album, it was Jerry Wexler who had the bright idea of putting the two of them together on record as a duet. The resulting *Roberta Flack & Donny Hathaway* (Atlantic 7216) album became his career peak when it went to #3 in May '72 and stayed on the album chart for 39 weeks. 'You've Got A Friend' the Carole King classic was chosen as their first single and it went to #8 R&B/29 pop giving both Donny & Roberta their first hit single and winning a Grammy for the duo. 'Where Is The Love' went to the top of the R&B singles charts in June '72 and also crossed over to #5 on the pop charts. At this point, Curtom were sharp enough to re-issue 'I Thank You (Baby)' the Hathaway/Conquest duet and this time it went to #41 R&B/94 pop. Curtom switched flipsides from the original issue of 'I Thank You' and this time they released a great version of 'Just Another Reason', previously cut as an A-side by the Fascinations. It is one of Donny's least known but most excellent records. Atlantic got behind the album with a Roberta & Donny nationwide tour, which was a big success and pushed their records even harder.

Hathaway wrote the score for the movie soundtrack for Mark Warren's *Come Back Charleston Blue* ('72) a violent sequel to another Chester Himes story 'Cotton Comes To Harlem' both of which starred Godfrey Cambridge and Raymond St Jacques. He teamed up with Atlantic stablemate Margie Joseph to cut the vocal tracks. This was Donny's most successful period. Previously his solo Atco singles had done good R&B business but hadn't crossed over to pop as well as hoped for. His final album *Extension Of A Man* (7029) could not match the sales of Donny's duet album with Roberta and this was a bitter pill for Hathaway to swallow. Perhaps he feared being stuck behind an ampersand for evermore.

'Magdalena' a great track that not often gets much recognition, was originally written and recorded by Danny O'Keefe in '73 for his exquisite *Breezy Stories* (Atlantic 7264) album. Donny was present on those O'Keefe/New York sessions that provided the outstanding vehicle for Danny's dark and emotionally tortured poetry. Hathaway played keyboards on seven of the 11 tracks and his electric piano contributed significantly to the atmosphere of the whole album. His work is particularly good on 'Angel Spread Your Wings', 'She Said "Drive On Driver"' and 'Mad Ruth/The Babe'.

During this period, Donny was also involved in the sessions that became Aretha Franklin's *Let Me In Your Life* album for which he wrote arrangements and on which he played, and which went to #14 on the album chart. He had worked with Aretha earlier on the *Young Gifted And Black* (which was a #11 album) sessions and had supplied the spirited keyboards for her version of 'Spanish Harlem' (#1 R&B/2 pop).

Inner turmoil, self doubt, over sensitivity and nervous breakdowns are all things that we think that we know something about. Some of us may know how it is to plumb the depths of clinical depression but none of us can really feel another's pain, no matter how much we sympathize. It is clear, from written reports, that Donny had some kind of breakdown and was unable to maintain a consistent level of work. He dropped out of the public view for a few years and any music projects that he was involved with stayed low profile.

Donny briefly re-emerged from the wasteland in '78; he managed to put his demons behind him and began to work again. He made some contributions to Joe Cocker's comeback album, which gave him sufficient confidence to make a redux of his own. Donny re-signed with Atco and began work on a second album of duets with Roberta and they were immediately rewarded with a huge hit 'The Closer I Get To You', which topped both US charts in February '78 and earned the duo their second gold record. Inspired by this success, Donny began to cut more solo sides and 'You Were Meant For Me' went to #15 R&B but went nowhere on the pop chart. Again, it was well received by black music fans but he could not recapture any interest from the larger white market.

On 13 January 1979 the devastating news broke that Donny

Hathaway had fallen to his death from a 15th floor suite in New York's 'Essex House Hotel'. Suicide was suspected but many of Hathaway's closest friends and associates found this hard to believe. He was just 33 years old. There have been few celebrations of his excellent work written since that time, possibly because it is scattered across a wide variety of different artists recordings and record labels. Donny was not generally a lyricist but a musician/arranger/singer and sometimes it is difficult to establish exactly just what he did or did not write but whatever his involvement with a project, his positive contributions seem to shine through and recordings were always enriched by his involvement.

In the UK, Donny's solo success had been consistent on the soul charts but his duets with Roberta had broken through to pop. 'Where Is The Love' and 'The Closer I Get To You' had been Top 40 records but their biggest hit came after his death, when 'Back Together Again' went to #3 pop in May '80 and earned another gold record, selling better here than in the States where it had managed a respectable #18 R&B but couldn't make it into the Top 40.

After Hathaway's tragic demise there were not enough tracks to complete and issue a whole album but Roberta's *Featuring Donny Hathaway* did include the two duet tracks, 'Back Together Again' and their other hit single, the Stevie Wonder song 'You Are My Heaven' (#8 R&B/47 pop). Events on that fateful January night in '79 closed the last chapter in Donny's short and generally unappreciated but intensely brilliant career. In the years since then, his music has slowly gained a more flattering and wider perspective of appreciation and as his legacy gradually becomes more accessible, his reputation will continue to grow.

INVISIBLE MAN'S BAND

The Invisible Man's Band consisted of former Stairsteps members, the Burke Brothers Clarence, Dennis, James, and Keni (temporarily), plus Alex Masucci, Dean Gant, Greg Fowler and guest musicians who included Steve Ferrone (of the Average White Band) and Lee Jaffe (of Earth Wind and Fire) plus a host of background singers. The *All Night Thing* album (Mango 9537) was recorded in New York City's Soundmixers studios and featured six extended tracks, which were produced by Clarence

Burke and manager Alex Masucci, with Island supremo Chris Blackwell giving his executive support. It begins with 'Full Moon', a cacophony of sounds and voices that are woven together in a complex pattern of intriguing and refreshing audio design. 'All Night Thing' is driven by Keni's bass and is an EW&F inspired dance groove aimed at the charts, where it scored high placings. 'X Country' has a spoof country start, which gives way as the bass breaks it down to funk in this overlong piece, which is written and performed by the extended group.

On '9 x's Out Of 10', another highlight, Clarence leads a midtempo ballad on which he leaves himself no choice but to gamble against the odds. Keni takes the lead on his song 'Rent Strike', which is a critique of landlords and proffers recommendations for action to redress the situation. The payback will be 'nothin' for nothin''. 'Love Can't Come'/'Love Has Come' the album highlight, uses shared vocals with most going to Clarence – the track is crammed with individual signatures, immersed in a multi-level arrangement with layers rising and falling in tempo. *All Night Thing* was entirely written and performed by the brothers Burke (and the extended group) as only they can. Though this was a different persona to that of the Stairsteps, it is inevitable that comparisons were made and of course there are some similarities. There seems little doubt, however, that they were trying to get away from their previous identity.

The cover has an excellent photograph of model Maggie Hann (by Mark Ledzian) and is similar in design to those of the early Roxy Music sleeves. Whilst they have made obvious concessions to the commercial marketplace of the time, nevertheless (in places) this album shows another step forward in the brothers' constructive development as they continued the evolution of their completely unique style of vocal harmony. The progressive arrangements were by Chris White and Clarence Burke. Three months later Island issued the excellent 'Love Can't Come'/'Love Has Come' as a 12in in the UK but despite the borrowed commercial edge of Earth Wind and Fire, they still could not chart here. Despite positive reviews, follow-ups failed to break through to pop in the US or the UK. The album was also liked by reviewers and charted at #90 on Billboard's US album chart in May 1980 but made little impact at all in the UK, despite many positive recommendations.

In an interview in '83 Keni Burke had this to say, 'After the Buddah deal finished we all went back home to find ourselves once more. Some of us wanted to devote time to catching up on education. During the lay-off we tried to become better writers and musicians. We all knew we'd make a comeback – but not until the time was right. Then when Billy Preston offered us Dark Horse, we just knew that was it. You know we were the very first family of soul, and on the scene long before the Jacksons. I guess we were a gimmick act but that wasn't our intention – it just happened that way. We made some records that we are all proud of though, and now we have separate careers, but naturally we're all still a very close family and actively involved in and about each other's successes and achievements.' Keni's wife Day Askey-Burke who had joined the Bros Johnson in '76 was also planning a solo album, which Keni was set to write and produce for her, but unfortunately it did not materialize.

The Invisible Man's Band signed to Boardwalk Records at about the same time as Curtis (in '81). *Really Wanna See You* (33238) became their only album for Boardwalk and it was produced by Burke Jr and Masucci for Sensation Productions. Whilst one would expect that the line up of IMB might be slightly mysterious, it is evident that James and others of the Burke dynasty were still involved. The album reveals Clarence, Alex & Co still trying to develop their own strain of post-disco dance music. Whilst they do show some other funk/groove influences, IMB manage to retain enough of their own individuality on the six tracks that go to make up this album. Despite a distinctive sleeve, the album passed almost unnoticed and was not even issued in the UK. After Boardwalk folded, IMB went to Move 'n' Groove and their 'Sunday Afternoon' single managed #77 on the R&B singles chart, and sometime during the next couple of years the group was rumoured to have cut another album. As most of their records catered to the club audiences of the time, they went unheard by the larger public they needed to reach to survive. It seems inconceivable that individuals with this much creative ability will not resurface at some time in the future and take their rightful place as leading exponents of their musical culture.

JACKSON (CHARLES) AND YANCY (MARVIN)

Charles Jackson and Marvin Yancy Jr first came together as a songwriting team in '71 when Jackson, newly hired by the Butler Workshop, was scouting for a writer/partner and spotted Yancy playing keyboards with Albertina Walker, at brother Jesse Jackson's Black Expo. Chuck had already written 'If It's Real What I Feel' (#8 R&B/69 pop March '71) by then for Jerry Butler. The duo cut a demo of their first collaboration 'Just As Long As You Need Me' and acting on the advice of Eddie Thomas, they quickly created a group that were dubbed the Independents and recut the record for Scepter. It had gone to #8 R&B/84 pop by April '72 and the Independents went on to create seven more hit singles, including their biggest 'Leaving Me' that went gold and scored #1 R&B/21 pop in March '73. Scepter also released two albums on the Independents; *First Time We Met* that sold well and *Chuck, Helen, Eric, Maurice* (Christian names of the group) that flopped. Jackson and Yancy had written and produced all the Independents' hits and when the group broke up in late '74, they began to work their magic for others.

They set up their own production/publishing company and went right through the roof with their first project that became *Inseparable*, Natalie Cole's first gold album for Capitol in '75, which was cut at Curtom Studios. Whilst at Curtom the duo wrote and produced for the Notations, the Impressions and the Natural Four, between '75 and '76. They also created the first hit in three years for Ronnie Dyson, with 'The More You Do It' and went on to create and produce his album, also at Curtom. Their second album with Cole simply entitled *Natalie* was considered by many to be their best work with her and also went gold. In addition to the albums, Marvin and Charles provided Natalie with a dozen hit singles including five R&B number ones and two gold records on 'I've Got Love On My Mind' and 'Our Love' both in '77.

Marvin and Natalie married in '77 and the writing team took this opportunity to move operations to Los Angeles where Mr and Mrs Yancy set up home, whilst all three of them concentrated on her career. *Unpredictable* ('77) and *Thankful* (also '77) went platinum but Natalie filed for separation in '79 and divorced Marvin the following year. These events ended the trio's partnership but their last album collaboration *I*

Love You So rode high on the album charts and they struck gold once more in 1979.

Charles Jackson decided to stay put and mounted a career at Capitol in '78. His first album *Passionate Breezes*, produced by Yancy and Gene Barge was critically well received but commercially it did poorly: he had better success with a version of the title song later with the Dells. Meanwhile, Charles wrote songs and produced sessions for Aretha Franklin, Michael Henderson and Phyllis Hyman. A second solo album did no better than the first and Jackson returned to Chicago. Tragically, Marvin Yancy Jr died of a heart attack in '85; at the time he had a successful gospel album on the R&B chart entitled *Heavy Load*. During their seven-year partnership Charles Jackson and Marvin Yancy burned the brightest in their contemporary creative circle. Most of the music they produced could be described as gospel-based soul, which got as close to the supper club pop and the disco as it had to, in order to break Natalie Cole on the pop charts.

JACKSON, WALTER

Walter Jackson's career was a brief but magical one. He contracted polio at an early age and despite the hardship and problems this disability created during the 23 years of his career, he produced maximum vocal magic. He made many great records: 'Uphill Climb To The Bottom', 'Corner In The Sun', 'Speak Her Name', 'No Butterflies' and many more. The majority of his work is to be found on the ten albums he made for various labels both during and after his departure from OKeh. His voice and vocal delivery were unique, he had the ability to make any song his own and delivered in a particularly soulful way. After Walter's death from a brain haemorrhage in June 1983, Carl Davis who had produced most of his records said, 'I feel privileged that I knew Walter Jackson for more than 20 years. I knew him foremost as a fan, and as a fan I was privileged to be his producer. Walter has left a rich legacy and this his last album is testimony to that legacy.' (This quote comes from the sleeve of *Bluebird LPBR 1001*.)

KILLBOURN, BOB

Bob Killbourn who took over from John Abbey as Editor of *Blues & Soul* had previously worked at EMI where he managed a number of labels for them. He was born and grew up in the area of South London (pronounced 'Sarf' if you come from thereabouts) known as Peckham. Bob's first job was in advertising where he worked alongside Charlie Watts. They became good buddies travelling to Paris to check out the local jazz clubs and the like. Charlie joined an insignificant R&B band as their drummer and Bob went to EMI Records in '61 to design record sleeves. He soon became more interested in the music and increasingly involved in licensed American repertoire. In due course, he began to manage UK labels including Stax, ABC, Impulse, Bluesway, Musicor and Paramount. He was responsible for releasing 'Hot Buttered Soul' by Ike Hayes and 'Private Number' by William Bell and Judy Clay as well as 'Wandering Star' by Lee Marvin!! So everything wasn't entirely soulful. Killbourn was in at the formation of Stateside Records and responsible for much of their early success. At that time, EMI had numerous records being submitted by small US independents and the thinking was that it would be sensible to have a corporate label releasing everything they secured and elected to release through indies.

Around '68 Bob received an offer from John Abbey to join him at the launch of his Mojo label and he started writing for *B&S* within a year. After Abbey's move to America, the new owners of *B&S* appointed Killbourn as Editor in August '79 – a position he has held ever since. But Bob says that he still harbours a few dreams of playing for Spurs and Kent – someday. Highlights of the Editorship have been many and numerous: discussions with Stevie and Marvin being amongst the most cherished alongside a meeting with Muhammad Ali when he visited the UK to launch his movie *The Greatest* ('77). Bob feels honoured to have occupied such a privileged position within the world of black music and long may he continue to do so. Other great soul magazines have come and gone but today *Blues & Soul* maintains a healthy survival despite all the changes of style and impingement's on the soul music field over the years. It has changed with the times and today its range has expanded to a wider coverage of contemporary black music like rap, hip hop, nu soul, etc but it still keeps its finger on the pulse of the '60s/northern soul and the club scene that had inspired its original creation. Over the years. many of the writers like Sharon Davis, Richard Searling, Tony Monson,

Lewis Dene, Tony Rounce, Ralph Tee, and many others too numerous to mention have been published in *B&S* and remained associated with the magazine. Bob supplied me with the first Impressions' ABC discography in '68, which inspired my series of articles entitled the 'Curtis Mayfield Story' that *Blues& Soul* went on to publish. Their photographic library is second to none and is in constant demand by the UK record companies, music journalists and other magazines.

LANCE, MAJOR

Major Lance and Mayfield's paths criss-crossed during their teenage years. He was a fellow student at high school, ambitious and energetic in his quest for fame. Major's closest school friend was Otis (Cobb) Leavill who even became his sparring partner, when he took up amateur boxing for a while. Lance was a hustler and there were many stories of his exploits and the stunts that he pulled on his quest to 'make it' as a boxer, a dancer and finally a singer. He persuaded Curtis to write him songs, badgered Carl Davis until he gave him some studio and eventually became the most prominent of the singers associated with Chicago soul (other than Mayfield himself).

Major Lance invented great dance routines, which he would perform on stage – one of the most memorable was the 'Matador', which he co-wrote with Davis and Billy Butler and which gave him another Top 20 US hit. After 'Monkey Time' reactivated OKeh he went on to have a dozen more R&B/pop hits with the label. In total, Major Lance achieved 16 hits on the R&B chart, only five of which were not from the pen of Curtis Mayfield. His biggest album was *The Best Of Major Lance* (OKeh 12106), which only reached #100 on the US album charts in mid '64. His albums were not initially released in the UK but it was his dance-orientated singles that put Lance at the very forefront of what was later to become known as northern soul. He signed to Volt but had no hits there, though he did quite good UK soul chart business.

Things seemed to be going better for him in England, so he moved his family here. His popularity was solid in the UK but despite constant live appearances, especially on the northern circuit, his records on Contempo and Warner Bros did not sell well enough and within two years he had returned to Atlanta. In October '74 Lance turned up again with a second stab at 'UM 6' on Playboy and went through a spate of re-runs with his old hits like 'Sweeter'. His last hit was 'You're Everything I Need' that came out on his own Osiris label and crept in at #50 R&B in July '75. After that, things went from bad to worse and the records that he cut for Columbia went nowhere. Eventually Otis Leavill came to his rescue and gave him some behind the scenes work at ChiSound Records. Together they relaunched Major's recording career with an album *Now Arriving* (S7-751R1), which they co-produced on Soul for Motown, but recorded in Chicago. Good as this comeback material was, it could not get his career back on track. He tried to keep going and toured extensively through the States and Europe but his performing career hit bottom in 1979 when he served a three-year prison term for selling cocaine.

After his release Lance came out to nothing, no family and no career. He would have to start all over again and went back to a spot on the bill in many '60s revival shows. Soul music had something of an American revival in the early '80s with 'Beach' music and a few of his OKeh sides were re-issued, which led to some renewal of interest from record companies. In 1983 he recorded an album for Kat Family Records *The Major's Back* (FZ 38898), which found no chart success and contained re-runs of his past hits including 'Monkey Time' and 'Gypsy Woman'. He toured the UK again in '84 and recorded his last *Live* album here but still could not muster the kind of interest he had received at his peak. Despite suffering an acute case of glaucoma, Lance headlined the Chicago Blues Festival in July '94 with Gene Chandler and Barbara Acklin, and according to reviews, transported a young and enthusiastic audience back 30 years with excellent renditions of his hits, whilst still managing to maintain his reputation as a truly great performer. At that time no one was aware that this would be the Major's final public appearance, for he was to die from a heart attack just a few weeks later on 3 September '94 in Decatur, Georgia.

Ace (UK) released a 22-track CD *Soul Soldiers* in '88, which featured the Volt recordings of Darrell Banks, Jimmy Hughes, JJ Barnes and Major Lance. A year after his death, Legacy released a two-CD set *Best* album containing 40 of Major's OKeh sides, which includes all his greatest hits plus a few rarities and excellent sleevenotes from Bill Dahl.

MARLEY, BOB AND JAMAICA

'I Gotta Keep On Movin' ' was one of the many Impressions records that had great impact in Jamaica, even allegedly influencing Bob Marley to write 'I Shot The Sheriff'. The Wailers recorded their own version of the song and in '89 yet another version, this time by UB40, was used on the soundtrack of *The Mighty Quinn* (an average actioner set in Jamaica and starring Denzel Washington). Bunny, the only remaining Wailer recorded a solo version in '93 for the Shanachie *Tribute* album. Curtis and the Impressions had been revered by the Wailers and many other Jamaican groups, who copied their vocal style and writing techniques in the mid '60s. The Wailers had been heavily influenced and inspired by early '60s soul music and their earliest work recorded between 1963 and 66 at Studio One, Kingston's answer to the Motown studios, clearly shows the influences of the Drifters, Chuck Jackson and the Impressions amongst others. Their producer and the studio owner Clement Seymour Dodd (aka Coxsone Dodd) had encouraged them to study the soul music of the period in addition to the gospel work of the Pilgrim Travelers, the Highway QCs and the Soul Stirrers.

The Wailers were originally a quintet, who in addition to the big three (Bob Marley, Peter Tosh and Bunny [Neville Livingston] Wailer) featured Junior Braithwaite and Beverly Kelso. All five took their turn singing lead but the majority went to Marley, whose tenor better reflected Ben E King, the Drifters and Sam Cooke. It was Tosh whose baritone echoed Jerry Butler and Chuck Jackson, and Bunny whose high tenor traced those of Curtis Mayfield, Ronald Isley and Smokey Robinson. The Wailers were very taken not only with the sound, but the look of the Impressions. Their first album *The Wailing Wailers* (S-100) has the group working through their influences and Mayfield's mark comes through indelibly. Heartbeat Records put together two CDs of these early Wailers' recordings in '94 (40 tracks, some of them demos), which illustrate through audio collages a rich mixture of influences in which they borrowed riffs, lines and verses from the songs that they had studied. The cover uses early photographs of the trio paying homage to the pictures that they had seen on the Impressions' early ABC albums. They regularly restyled songs for their own use and wrote new lyrics, music and arrangements for the bits that they wanted changed and this is the way that they cut their own versions of 'Talking About My Baby', 'Amen', 'I'm Still Waiting' and 'I Gotta Keep On Movin'' etc.

'People Get Ready' has also been reconstructed a number of times by the Wailers on 'One Love', Marley on 'People Get Ready' and Burning Spear on 'Get Ready'. The Wailers style and approach quickly evolved as the three personalities began to emerge in their own right. 'Simmer Down' was a big Jamaican hit, but outside Kingston it was not seen as radically different to those reggae, ska and bluebeat records that had been making waves in the European danceclubs and discothèques for the past couple of years. At home in Trenchtown, both this song and 'One Love' became anthems. Immediately the Wailers were elevated to the status of cult poets in the tradition of Woody Guthrie.

Marley, Tosh and Wailer, however, had drawn their early inspiration in the main from Dylan, Cooke and Mayfield and therefore as early as '64 they were regarded by many as 'militant'. Marley and the Wailers of course grew into icons by articulating the concerns of their generation but in addition to the Mayfield sound, it was the lyrics from the songs of social injustice that Curtis had written for the Impressions that were to provide some of Marley's earliest inspiration. When interviewed in '92, Peter Tosh admitted, 'We used to practice off Curtis Mayfield and the Impressions, even tried to look like 'em – Yeah, the Impressions was bad.' Marley's later political songs of revolution grew from the influence of songs like 'People Get Ready', 'Keep On Pushing' and 'We're A Winner'.

Mayfield's popularity in Jamaica was not confined to the Wailers – his songs have been recorded by many artists there. 'Minstrel and Queen' seems to have caused the most interest, the song has a royal twist in Jamaica, and many versions have been cut under the title of 'Queen Majesty' by the likes of Dennis Alcapone, the Techniques, Bunny Brown, the Chosen Few and U Roy. It seems that the Jamaican focus was on the songs that were recorded by the Impressions for ABC between 'Gypsy Woman' and 'You Must Believe Me' with a couple of exceptions like 'Choice Of Colors' and 'This Is My Country', which were later cut for Curtom. Michael Turner, in his tribute to Curtis Mayfield, 'Keep On Moving', that appeared in *The Beat* (May '96) discusses many of these records in some detail, as he looks closely at the legacy created by their influence. In *Reggae – The Rough Guide* (by Steve Barrow and Peter Dalton), Mayfield is affirmed as the 'godfather of reggae' on a dedicated page that goes some way in an appreciation of his influence on Jamaican music. It concludes with the observation that Mayfield's songs were recorded in great numbers in the mid to late '60s, reworked and updated in the '70s, went through the dancehall revival in the '80s, and in the digital '90s were once more getting new treatments bringing Mayfield's influence into ragga.

MAXWELL, HOLLY

Curtom issued just one single on Holly Maxwell who had begun singing as a schoolgirl in female vocal groups. She had a classical music background and her family wanted more for her than soul music success, an ambition that slowed her down at first. Bill 'Bunky' Sheppard discovered Holly in '64 and recorded and produced her on Constellation where he released her singles 'One Thin Dime' and 'Only When You're Lonely'. In '66 she moved to Star Records where she worked with Monk Higgins who produced 'Philly Barracuda' a novelty dance item that had Holly performing on table tops. She also cut a version of 'Blueberry Hill' and Higgins took her to Chess in '67 where she cut 'Heartbeat'/'It Was A Very Good Year' on Checker, but like all her other great records she couldn't get a hit with it. In the early '70s Holly moved out to the west coast and ran a night-club in California. She spent three years singing jazz with organist Jimmy Smith's Band and then two years singing lead and touring extensively with the Ike Turner Review after Tina left.

PRIDE, LOU

Lou Pride's career had started back in the late '70s when he began recording for a small label/studio out of El Paso called Sue Mie Records. Pride grew up in North Chicago, where as a child he began singing at the First Baptist Church. When he returned from Germany after serving out his military service in the early '60s he began performing as one part of duo JC & Lou (in the Sam & Dave mode) but soon went solo. He was based in Texas and New Mexico for the best part of 20 years and it was here that he got his first break recording. 'I'm Comin' Home In The Mornin'' was a very accomplished début, which had Lou promising his imminent return. This cult classic really moves along but finishes in a discordant, abstract jazz deconstruction that's not to everyone's taste. After his brief spell with Curtom, Lou went on touring and recording for many other labels but his popularity was strictly within the blues and R&B field.

REED, JOHN

John Reed took a sabbatical year as Editor of the Student Union newspaper when he was studying at Brunel University, Uxbridge. He had studied Material Science there from '84 but also found lots of time to DJ at club nights and gigs at the campus venue. Music was always a major passion with John who soon found ways to combine a wish to learn journalistic talents with his musical interests. He worked at *Record Collector* magazine for nine years but during that period also freelanced for many magazines including *Uncut* and *Mojo* and wrote sleevenotes for a number of record labels. John wrote a biography of Paul Weller entitled *My Ever Changing Mood* (published by Omnibus '96), which sold upwards of 35,000 copies. To his new post as a record label manager when he joined Sequel in '98, he brought enthusiasm, energy, fresh ideas and a good understanding of the collector's market. John and I worked together in a combined effort to issue (in the UK) as much of the Curtom label's output on CD, until their deal came to an end in 2000.

SIMON, LOWRELL

Simon created a body of great work in songwriting and record production, which puts him among the Chicago élite of Butler, Mayfield, Davis, Carter, Jackson, Yancy, Hutson etc. As legend has it, by '79 he had published over 2000 songs, some of which he had written for Jackie Wilson, the Natural Four, the Chi-Lites, Johnny Mathis, the O'Jays and Barry White amongst many others. Lowrell was destined to become another of the great but generally unsung Chicago singer/songwriter/producers.

Lowrell fronted the LaVondells who soon cut to the Vondells and had a sizeable local hit with 'Lenore' on Marvelow in '64. When Simon formed Lost Generation in '68, the group crackled with creativity. Soon they had developed as exciting performers and had written a bagful of songs. Carl

Davis snapped them up for Brunswick in 1970 and Eugene Record produced the first two hits 'Sly Slick And Wicked' (which went to #14 R&B/ 30 pop in May '70) and 'Wait A Minute' (which scored a #25 R&B in November) but pop sales dropped out. The following year, Lost Generation hit middling twice more on the R&B chart but still could not interest the pop fans. Lowrell's creative influence was evident in all their work, his reworkings of other people's songs like 'Didn't I Blow Your Mind This Time' and 'Thin Line Between Love And Hate' cut for the two albums they made for Brunswick showed an interesting and individual approach. But none of their other singles took and in '74, the Lost Generation moved over to Innovation, another Carl Davis label, to record their last chart record 'Your Mission (If You Decide To Accept It) Pt 1', which peaked at #65 R&B in September '74. A short time later, the group broke up with Lowrell and Larry pursuing studio and songwriting opportunities.

Lowrell found work at Curtom where he began an association with Richard Tufo and started to write and produce for the Impressions. Tufo and Simon teamed to create and produce the Impressions' *Three The Hard Way* soundtrack in '74, Richard and Lowrell also combined in a similar way for the Natural Four. When brother Fred and Larry joined Ralph Johnson in Mystique, Lowrell also made more Curtom contributions. He made a solo album for AVI Records in '78 called *Lowrell* and recorded three R&B chart singles the highest 'Mellow, Mellow Right On', registering at #32 in October '79. The singles were dance/disco items but reviewers (with little imagination) compared his vocal style to Marvin Gaye. He recorded for the Zoo York label in '74 and had a lowish #58 hit with 'Love Massage', which needs no further description here.

ST PIERRE, ROGER
Now working as Editor of *Holiday & Leisure World* magazine and three publications for American Express, Roger St Pierre is the author of more than 50 books published on a wide variety of subjects ranging from cycling (he helped edit the official Tour de France guide for a number of years) through the movies to travel (including the best-selling *AA guide to Orlando*) but he is perhaps best known to the readers of this book for his prolific work as a music journalist and author. He began writing for

fanzines in the mid '60s and soon had columns in *Music Now, Musical Express* and *Record Mirror*. He also made regular contributions to *Melody Maker, Sounds* and *Blues & Soul* amongst many others and his work could be found in *Music Week, Financial Weekly, Smash Hits*, and *Sky TV News*. St Pierre became a stringer for the *Daily Mirror, London Evening News* and *Evening Standard*. He also edited *Record Buyer Magazine*. Roger was co-author of *The Rock Handbook* (total sales to date 3.7 million) and has written books on celebrities such as Tom Jones, Marilyn Monroe, James Dean, Tina Turner, Jimi Hendrix, Bon Jovi and Ah-Ha. He's even written the official history of McDonald's!

Down the years St Pierre has worked successfully as publicist on UK and European tours for the Jackson Five, Jerry Lee Lewis, Diana Ross, James Brown, BB King, the Drifters, KC & The Sunshine Band, George McCrae and many other major artists and has promoted their records too (scoring six #1 hits). He owned and ran both Now! and Energy Records, he also launched Beacon (with whom he got #3 UK hit in March '68 via the Showstoppers' 'Ain't Nothing But A House Party'). Roger promoted the UNICEF Peace For Christmas concert in '69, which headlined John & Yoko, George Harrison and featured Delaney & Bonnie, Billy Preston, Young Rascals, Jimmy Cliff and others. As a broadcaster Roger has DJ'd his own shows for BBC Radio Medway and Skyline Radio and hosted a 20-minute 'Sound Advice' slot on the much-missed GLR. These days he can be found on a UK satellite channel near you called Solar Radio where he has his own weekly two hour R&B Revival Show, sponsored by *Blues & Soul* (Wednesday 8–10pm on Sky Digital 944 or at www.solarradio.com).

THE STAIRSTEPS

When Curtis wound up his first two labels, Windy C and Mayfield, there was still almost a year to go before his Curtom Records was to be launched. While waiting for the new label set up to happen, the Five Stairsteps recorded temporarily for Buddah where they put down some excellent sides at the RCA studios in Chicago. The first of these was 'Something's Missing' and it hit #17 R&B in December '67. The precocious Clarence Burke Jr took over production of the sessions for Kama Sutra. 'A Million To One' featured Kenneth, who sang lead on few Stairsteps records but was destined to become a solo artist later as Keni Burke. These singles were included in their new album, which came in a gatefold sleeve entitled *Our Family Portrait* (BDS 5008) and featured all the family in turn. At that time the group was billed as 5 Stairsteps & Cubie (who was the youngest member of the family at 2+ years). Cubie was featured on 'New Dance Craze', Alohe on the Bacharach/ David standard 'The Look Of Love', Papa and Mama dueted on 'I Remember You' and 'Windows Of The World'. James got the excellent 'You Make Me So Mad' and Dennis had 'Find Me'. The album had great highs but some low lows, Clarence Jr sang on just four tracks. The third Buddah single 'Shadow Of Your Love' was not included and when it didn't chart, was destined for collectable status. The record to make most impact on the UK soul club scene was 'Under The Spell Of Your Love' where it was periodically flavour of the month.

After a spell at Curtom, the Stairsteps returned to Buddah where they were teamed with Stan Vincent who produced most of their records over the next three years. Their biggest hit was 'Ooh Child', which was a million seller and hit #8 on the Hot 100 but only made #14 on R&B, selling less than 'Baby Make Me Feel So Good' and 'World Of Fantasy', but it broke the band internationally and the song became a pop classic. Consequently the first Buddah album *Stairsteps* (BDS 5061) sold very well. The album showcased a wide variety of songs including two from Lennon/McCartney, 'Getting Better' and 'Dear Prudence', and also contained the excellent 'Because I Love You' that was written by and features Clarence Burke Jr at his finest.

However, the Stairsteps, as they became, could not sustain this kind of success and, though their next album *Step By Step* (BDS 5068) also sold well (especially as it was a mixture of old Windy C and Curtom tracks – plus the hit), the final Buddah album – also called *Stairsteps* (BDS 5079) – flopped. Two singles, 'Didn't It Look So Easy' scored #32 R&B and 'I Love You – Stop' #40 R&B, were taken from it and became the only other two Buddah singles to chart. A short while later, the Stairsteps retired to pursue other things. Clarence Jr and Kenneth remained active in music. Keni Burke, as he became, worked on many sessions, playing, writing and producing. He was much sought after and later recorded with Bill Withers, the O'Jays, the Jones Girls and Billy Preston on numerous studio projects.

As a result of their meeting and extensively working together whilst Keni was a member of Billy's road band, Preston rediscovered the Stairsteps and took them to George Harrison's Dark Horse label in late '75 where the quartet recorded the *2nd Resurrection* (SP22004) album. Keni had been on the point of joining the Brothers Johnson at that time, with George Johnson who had also been a long-time member of Preston's entourage. Fortunately the Dark Horse deal came up instead. Preston produced and together they created their biggest R&B hit 'From Us To You', which reached #10 R&B in January '76. This album is not so much conceptual as a thematic resurrection by the Stairsteps, who had no records released since they had left Buddah in '72. Since then the brothers' skills and attitudes developed and had been refined immeasurably. They all made valuable contributions with both lyrics and outstandingly dexterous individual musicianship. 'From Us To You' acts as a perfect intro and was their first choice as a single. The excellent 'Pasado' features Clarence's superb vocal treatment of his lyrics set to brother James' music. Like most of this album, after a few plays, this song begins to haunt the listener, soon appearing in the subconscious, often unannounced. James Burke also wrote and played guitar on the first of the instrumental tracks, 'Theme Of Angels'.

'Lifting 2nd Resurrection' is a song written by Dennis and Clarence, with Dennis taking lead vocal. Later the vocal lead switches around between all the brothers. 'All Praise To You' is just one reference that suggests that there are some Islamic influences at work here. On 'Time' (as in the dimension of time), Clarence adds his thoughts to the long ongoing philosophical debate in passing. 'Throwing Stones Atcha' is an amazing vocal performance by them all, to a fast but shifting tempo – again great individual performances and close collective understanding is what makes this kind of vocalizing possible. 'Far East' the second instrumental, shows clear west-east influences in the memorable melody. Possibly the last track to be appreciated is 'In The Beginning', which is a plea that gets so intense in places that it at first evokes unwelcome memories, but is so well handled and performed that it also soon becomes a favourite. 'Tell Me Why', like the opening track, is Keni Burke singing lead on his own song and signals his first solo album, which was to appear a year later.

The Stairsteps made their exit with the beautiful 'Salaam', which features all the brothers jamming with Billy Preston, who contributed great production and keyboard work on these sessions. It showcases the fantastically fluid lead guitar of Dennis, as it glides through borrowed eastern origins and this just shades being the best of the three instrumentals contained here. With no criticism implied, it is hard to see '60s soul music fans going for this album en masse, though it did reach the Top 30 on R&B/soul albums shortly after its release in March '76, both here and in the US. The reviewers of the time were very divided in their opinions also, which isn't the least bit surprising given the variety and creative scope of the work. Dave Godin, the man credited for coining the terms 'northern soul' and 'deep soul' was enamoured with the album and between '75 and '77 wrote glowingly in premier UK music journal *Blues & Soul* about the Stairsteps.

John Abbey, the Editor of *Blues & Soul* at the time, reviewed the *2nd Resurrection* album in March '76 with a degree of enthusiasm, but compared the music to that of Stevie Wonder and ended up saying 'Personally speaking, this isn't really my type of soul, I must admit.' So opinions varied, even at *B&S*. But sales and chart statistics reveal that Abbey's remarks were a barometer of the public's taste in this particular case, as they often were.

So, perhaps predictably, the *2nd Resurrection* didn't take and brothers Dennis, Clarence and James went back to New Jersey to reform under another identity, the Invisible Man's Band.

THOMAS RECORDS

Eddie Thomas set up the Thomas label in 1965 and it was originally a subsidiary of Satellite Records, using the distribution services of the St Lawrence Corp. Thomas was later distributed by a number of different outfits including Chess, ChiSound, Atlantic (300 series) and Buddah (800 series). Monk Higgins was one of the principal early producers for the label. The most celebrated of the early Thomas releases was Jamo Thomas's re-run of Luther Ingram's 'I Spy For The FBI', which was not a hit in America but scaled the soul singles chart a couple of times in the UK. The Amazers' 'It's You For Me'/'Without A Warning' also caused northern soul interest in the UK. After Richard and Arthur Brooks had flopped as their version of the Impressions on Swirl, Eddie gave the brothers another break four years later. He recorded them under their own name on the Thomas label, where they cut 'You Got Something Baby'/'Come See'. It made no commercial impact and even more obscure was 'Looking For A Woman', one of the sides, which they put down for Tay Records a short time later.

Eddie relaunched his Thomas label in '69 with 'Bring It On Down To Me (pt 1)' by Bobby Franklin's Insanity. The side had been recorded and produced by Curtis for issue on Curtom but Thomas wanted it for his new deal with Buddah. Though none of the ten new issues charted anywhere, they were to become some of the most sought after by collectors in later years. Donny Hathaway and Mayfield produced Nolan Chance (pka ex-Dukays lead singer Charles Davis) on 'I'll Never Forget You'. Hathaway also arranged two great Jesse Anderson singles for the label: 'I Got A Problem'/'Mighty Mighty' and 'Let Me Back In'/'Readings in Astrology'. Other notables include releases by Donald Jenkins, the Triplett Twins and Dewi Cheetum and Howe. By the end of 1970, sadly, the Thomas label ceased production.

PATE, JOHNNY

Johnny worked at ABC with other acts on the roster, as well as freelancing for Curtom. He was sacked, then reinstated after management changes at ABC brought in a new breed. He moved operations to New York in '72 and began to get commissions from the movies, so he moved again, this time to LA, and composed the scores for *Shaft In Africa* ('73), *Bucktown* ('75) and *Dr Black And Mr Hyde* ('76). Cotillion, who had the Impressions under contract, hired Johnny to cut an album (SD 5303) for them in the summer of '77 in New York, but sadly this record was not issued, so he returned to the west coast, where he made successful records with Peabo Bryson on Capitol, but soon returned to jazz, his first love, and cut an album with Jimmy Smith on Milestones Records in '88 called *Some Serious Blues*. Johnny and his wife, Carolyn decided that they did not want to bring their son up in LA, and the Pates retired to Las Vegas, where they still live today. Rumour has it that he is an underground cult in Europe. He cut several albums under his own name, of which *Set The Pattern* (ABC) and *Outrageous* (MGM) are the best known. To the rest of the world, he will always be remembered for his great arrangements and co-productions with Curtis for the Impressions' greatest hits.

Appendix 1: the Impressions
General Sessionography And Discography

GENERAL SESSIONOGRAPHY 1

Compiled by Peter Burns for Echo Archive. Acknowledgements: Trevor Churchill, Rob Hughes. Calvin Carter, Jerry Butler, Bernie Harville Jr, Sam Gooden

CHICAGO 1957-58	Demos recorded on OR tape in CMs basement and kitchen **The Impressions:** Jerry Butler (lead), Curtis Mayfield (± lead), Sam Gooden, Arthur Brooks, Richard Brooks
	'Pretty Betty' (B Harville) – Design LP 201, Wynoote LP W9100, LP 1018, (E) JSP 4501
	'Sweet Was The Wine' (Jerry Butler)
	'My Baby Loves Me' (JB) – Design LP 201
	'I've Got A Girl' ± (Curtis Mayfield)
	'Sweet Was The Wine' / 'Take 2' (JB)
	'You Are The Only One' ± (CM)
	'Your Precious Love' (R Brooks / A Brooks / J Butler)

UNIVERSAL STUDIOS, CHICAGO	
25 June '58	**The Impressions:** Jerry Butler (lead), Curtis Mayfield (± lead), Sam Gooden, Arthur Brooks, Richard Brooks. Produced Calvin Carter. Arranged Riley Hampton. Musicians: Johnny Pate (double bass), Gene Chandler (handclaps)
58.890	'Sweet Was The Wine' (JB) – Vee-Jay 280, Falcon 1013/Abner 1013, VJ 396, VJLP 1029, 1075, Upfront LP 102, Lost Nite 266 (E), London HL 8697, Oldies 20, DJM 26086, Charly 2023, *VJCD NVD2 719, Collectables 7239, (E) Charly CD 1105, CDRB 30, CD 54, Black Tulip 725, Neon NE 34537,*
58.891	'For Your Precious Love' (R Brooks/A Brooks/J Butler) – Falcon 1013/Abner

1013, VJ 280, 396, VJLP 1027, 1048, 1075, 1021, Upfront LP 102, Abner LP 2001, Exodus 309, Sire LP 3717/2, OLD 8005, Lost Nite 266, (E) Joy LP104, TL 5246, London HL 8697, Oldies 20, DJM 26086, Charly 2023, Buddah 4001, *R2 71463, VJCD NVD2 719, Collectables 7238, 7239, (E) Charly CD 1105, CDRB 30, CD 54, EAB CD 050, CPCD 8254/2, Black Tulip 725, Neon NE 34537*

('FYPL' appeared on many collection albums and bootlegs not listed here)

58.892   'Lovers Lane' (± CM) – VJLP 1075, Custom 1031 (E) Joy LP 104, DJM 26086, Charly 2023, *VJCD NVD2 719, Collectables 7238, (E) Charly CD 1105, Black Tulip 725, Neon NE 34537*

58.893   'Don't Drive Me Away' (R Staples) – VJLP 1075, Upfront 102, Robin Hood 140, (E) Joy 104, DJM 26086, Charly 2023, *VJCD NVD2 719, Collectables 7238, (E) Charly CD 1105, Black Tulip 725, Neon NE 34537*

UNIVERSAL STUDIOS, CHICAGO
21 July '58   **The Impressions:** same. Produced Calvin Carter. Arranged Riley Hampton.

58.956   'The Gift Of Love' (JB/CM/RB) – Abner 1023, VJ 574, Oldies 77 VJLP 1029, 1048, 1075, SUS 5216, Exodus 309, (E)Joy 104, DJM 26086, Charly 2023, Buddah 4001, *VJCD NVD2 719, Collectables 7238, 7239, (E) Charly CD 1105, Black Tulip 725, Neon NE 34537*

58.957   'At The County Fair' (± CM) – Abner 1023, VJ 574, Oldies 77, VJLP 1075, 1029, Upfront 102, Custom 1031, OLD 8005, (E) Joy 104, DJM 26086, Charly 2023, *VJ CD NVD2 719, Collectables 7238, (E) Charly CD 1105, CPCD 8254/2, Black Tulip 725,*

58.958   'Come Back My Love' (R Hamilton/C Otis) – Abner 1017, VJLP 1027, 1034, 1048, Abner 2001, Exodus 309, (E)Joy 104, DJM 26086, Buddah 4001, Charly2023, (E) TL 5246, *VJCD NVD2 719, Collectables 7239, (E) Charly CD 1105, EAB CD 050, CPCD 8254/2, CDRB 30, Black Tulip 725, Neon NE 34537*

58.959   'Love Me' (A Brooks) – Abner 1017, VJLP 1027, 1034, 1038, Abner 2001, Upfront 102, (E) Joy 104, DJM 26086, Charly 2023, *VJCD NVD2 719, (E) Charly CD 1105, Black Tulip 725, Neon NE 34537*

CHICAGO
11 Nov '58   **The Impressions:** Curtis Mayfield (lead), Sam Gooden (>lead) Fred Cash, Arthur Brooks, Richard Brooks. Produced Calvin Carter. Arranged Riley Hampton.

58.1034   'Young Lover' (CM) – VJLP 1075, Upfront 102, Robin Hood 140, (E) Joy 104, DJM 26086, Charly 2023, *VJCD NVD2 719, Collectables 7238, (E) Charly CD 1105, CPCD 8254/2, Black Tulip 725, Neon NE 34537*

58.1035   'Lovely One' (>RB) – Abner 1025, (E) DJM 26086, Charly 2023, *VJCD NVD2 719, Charly CD 1105, Black Tulip 725, Neon NE 345377*

58.1035/2   'Lovely One' > / 'Take 2' (RB) – *VJCD NVD2 719, Black Tulip 725*

58.1036   'A Long Time Ago' (CM) – VJLP 1075, 1051, Upfront 102, (E) Joy 104, DJM 26086, Charly 2023, Robin Hood 139, *VJCD NVD2 719, Collectables 7238 (E) Charly CD 1105, Black Tulip 725, Neon NE 34537*

58.1037   'Senorita I Love You' (CM) – Abner 1025, VJ 424, 621, VJLP 1075, Upfront 102, Custom 1031, (E) Joy 104, DJM 26086, Charly 2023, *VJCD NVD2 719, Collectables 7238, (E) Charly CD 11051, Black Tulip 725, Neon NE 34537*

HALL RECORDING STUDIOS, CHICAGO
27 April '59   **The Impressions:** Sam Gooden (lead), Curtis Mayfield (± lead), Fred Cash, Arthur Brooks, Richard Brooks. Produced Vi Muszynski. Arranged Riley Hampton

Ba 4546   'Listen' (J Butler) – Bandera 2504, Port 70031, Design LP 201, Wynoote LP W 9100, (E) JSP 4501, *Westside WESM 525*

Ba 4547   'Shorty's Got To Go' (± C Mayfield) – Bandera 2504, Port 70031, Design LP 201, (E) JSP 4501

          'Shorty's Got To Go' ± BA 45472/ 'Take 2'

CHICAGO
9 Dec '59   **The Impressions:** Curtis Mayfield (lead), Sam Gooden / Jerry Butler (* lead) Fred Cash, Arthur Brooks, Richard Brooks (< lead). Produced Calvin Carter. Arranged Riley Hampton.

59.1324   'Give Me Your Love' (* RB) – VJLP 567, 1029, (E) SS 252, *VJCD NVD2 719, Collectables 7239, Black Tulip 725, Neon NE 34537*

59.1325   'That You Love Me' (CM) – Abner 1034, VJ 424, VJLP 1075, Upfront 102, Custom 1031, (E) Joy 104, DJM 26086, Charly 2023, *VJCD NVD2 719, Collectables 7238, (E) Charly CD 1105, Black Tulip 725, Neon NE 34537*

59.1326   'A New Love' (CM) – Abner 1034, VJLP 1075, (E) Joy 104, DJM 26086, Charly 2023, *VJCD NVD2 719, Charly CD 1105, Black Tulip 725, Neon NE 34537*

59.1327   'Believe In Me' (< RB) – VJLP 1075, Upfront 102, Robin Hood 139, (E) Joy 104, DJM 26086, Charly 2023, *VJCD NVD2 719, Collectables 7238 (E) Charly CD 1105, Black Tulip 725, Neon NE 34537*

59.1328   'Let Me Know' (CM) – VJLP 1075, (E) Joy 104, DJM 26086, Charly 2023, *VJCD NVD2 719, Collectables 7238 Charly CD 1105, Black Tulip 725, Neon NE 34537*

GENERAL SESSIONOGRAPHY 2

Compiled by Peter Burns. Acknowledgements: Trevor Churchill, Bob Killbourn, Rob Hughes.

NEW YORK
13 July '61   **The Impressions:** Curtis Mayfield (lead), Sam Gooden, Fred Cash, Arthur Brooks, Richard Brooks. Session 626. Produced Curtis Mayfield / Mal Williams. Arranged Roy Glover

10441   'Gypsy Woman' (CM) – ABC 10241, (E) HMV POP 961, ABCLP 450, 515, 727, ABCX 780/2, Sire 17/372, ABCL 5104, ABC 1232, (E) Charly CRB 1063, HMV CLP 1935, GTSP 201, Kent 005, ABSD 303, *MCAD 31338, Kent CDKEND 923, HMNCD 005, MCAD2 10664, Pickwick PWKS 4206,   Remember RMB 75051, Kent CDKEND 126, R2 72583, MCAD 11837, MCAD 22175*

10442   'As Long As You Love Me' (CM) – ABC 10241, (E) HMV POP 691, ABC LP 450, (E) Kent 005, *Kent CDKEND 126*

NEW YORK
22 Nov '61   **The Impressions:** same. Session 679 A Mal-Max Production. Arranged Roy Glover.

10602   'Can't You See' (CM/J Butler) – ABC10289, *(E)CDKEND 170*

10603   'Grow Closer Together' (CM) – ABC 10289, ABCLP 450, 515, 727, ABCX 780/2, (E) CLP 1935, ABCL 5104, CSD 1642, GTSP 201, Kent 005, ABSD 303, *Kent CDKEND 923, MCAD2 10664, Kent CDKEND 126*

NEW YORK
21 March '62   **The Impressions:** Curtis Mayfield (lead), Sam Gooden (> lead), Fred Cash, Arthur Brooks, Richard Brooks. Session 738. A Mal-Max Production. Arranged Roy Glover

10834   'Minstrel & Queen' (CM) – ABC 10357, ABCLP 450, 515, (E) CLP 1935, ABCL 5104, Kent 005, ABSD 303, *Kent CDKEND 923, MCAD2 10664, Kent CDKEND 126, HMNCD 005*

10835   'I Need Your Love' (> R Brooks) – ABC 10386, (E) POP 1129, ABCLP 450, Pickwick SPC 3502, (E) Kent 005, ABSD 303, *AVID AVC 516, Kent CDKEND 126*

10836   'Little Young Lover' (CM) – ABC 10328, ABCLP 450, SPC 3502, (E) Kent 005, ABSD 303, *Kent CDKEND 923, MCAD2 10664, Kent CDKEND 126, HMNCD 005*

10837   'I'm The One Who Loves You' (CM) – ABC 10386, (E) POP 1129, ABCLP

450, 515, 727, ABCX 780/2, (E) CLP 1935, ABCL 5104, Kent 005, ABSD 303, GTSP 201, *Kent CDKEND 923, MCAD2 10664, Kent CDKEND 126, HMNCD 005*

10838   'Never Let Me Go' (J Scott) – ABC 10328, ABCLP 450, 515, 727, ABC 1225, ABCX 780/2, PWKS 4206, (E) CLP 1935, ABCL 5104, CRB 1063, Kent 005, GTSP 201, *MCAD2 10664, Kent CDKEND 126*

NEW YORK
22 March '62   **The Impressions:** Curtis Mayfield (lead), Sam Gooden, Fred Cash, Arthur Brooks (* lead), Richard Brooks. Session 741. Produced Curtis Mayfield/Mal Williams. Arranged Maxwell Davis.

10846   'Love Is A Mystery' (* CM) – ABCLP 504, Spartan 504, *(E) CDKEND 170*. (Applause was added later for inclusion on the album *Shindig*.)

10847   'You've Come Home' (CM) – ABC10357, ABCLP 450, (E) CRB 1063, Kent 005, *Kent CDKEND 126*

10848 / 1   'Emotions (Won't You Let Me Cry)' (CM) – *(E) CDKEND 170*

10848 / 2   Emotions (Won't You Let Me Cry)

10848 / 3   'Emotions (Won't You Let Me Cry)' (CM) – (E) Charly CRB 1063

10849   'Can't Work No Longer' (CM) – ABCLP 505, ABCX 780 / 2, LP 90097, (E) CLP 3548 (aka 'Work Song'), CRB 1063, Kent 012, GTSP 201, *CDKEND 130, HIPD 40002*

NEW YORK
1962   **The Impressions:** Richard Brooks (lead), Arthur Brooks, plus others.

ZTSP 81246   'Don't Leave Me' (R Brooks) – Swirl 107, Gramercy

ZTSP 81247   'I Need Your Love' (R Brooks) – Swirl 107, Gramercy

UNIVERSAL STUDIOS, CHICAGO
24 Jan '63   **The Impressions:** Curtis Mayfield (lead), Sam Gooden, Fred Cash. Session 836. Produced Curtis Mayfield. Arranged Johnny Pate.

11314   'Sad, Sad Girl And Boy' (CM) – ABC 10431, ABCLP 450, 515, 727, ABCX 780 / 2, (E) CLP 1935, ABCL 5104, Kent 005, ABSD 303, Kent 923, MCAD2 10664, GTSP 201, *Kent CDKEND 126*

11315   'I Thank Heaven' (CM) – ABCLP 493, (E) ABCL 5104, Stateside SSL 10279, Kent 009, *Kent CDKEND130*

11316   'Twist And Limbo' (CM) – ABC 10413, ABCLP 450, (E) Kent 005, *Kent CDKEND 126*

UNIVERSAL STUDIOS, CHICAGO
21 Aug '63   **The Impressions:** same. Session 907. Produced Curtis Mayfield. Arranged Johnny Pate (Johnny Pate.co-produced Chicago Sessions).

11680	'It's All Right' (CM) – ABC 10487, (E) POP 1226, ABCLP 450, 515, 727, ABCX 780 / 2, Sire 3717 / 2, ABC 1232, (E) ABCL 5104, Kent 005, ABSD 303, CRB 1063, GTSP 201, *MCAD 31338, Kent CDKEND 923, MCAD2 10664, RMB 75051, PWKS 4206, Kent CDKEND 126, R2 72583, MCAD 11837 MCAD 22175, HMNCD 005*
11681	'You'll Want Me Back' (CM) – ABC 10487, (E) POP1226, (E) Stateside SSL 10279, *CDKEND 170*
11682	'Sister Love' (CM) – ABCLP 468, (E) CLP 1743, Kent 008, *Kent CDKEND 126*
11683	'That's What Love Will Do' (CM) – ABCLP 468, (E) CLP 1743, Kent 008, *Kent CDKEND 126, HMNCD 005*

UNIVERSAL STUDIOS, CHICAGO
1 Nov '63   **The Impressions:** same. Produced CM. Arranged Johnny Pate. Session 934.

11807	'Girl You Don't Know Me' (CM) – ABC 10537, ABCLP 468, (E) CLP 1743, Kent 008, ABSD 303, *Kent CDKEND 923, HIPD 40002, Kent CDKEND 126, HMNCD 005*
11808	'Talking About My Baby' (CM) – ABC 10511, (E) POP 1262, ABCLP 493, 515, 727, ABCX 780 / 2, Sire 3717 / 2 (E) CLP 1935, 7EG 8896, ABCL 5104, CRB 1063, Kent 009, ABSD 303, GTSP 201*MCAD 31338, Kent CDKEND 923, 130, MCAD2 10664, PWKS 4206, R2 72583, MCAD 11837 MCAD 22175, HMNCD 005*
11809	'A Woman Who Loves Me' (CM) – ABC 10537, ABCLP 468, (E) CLP 1743, Kent 008, *Kent CDKEND 126, MCAD 22175*
11810	'Never Too Much Love' (CM) – ABC 10511, (E) POP 1262, (E) SSL 10279, *CDKEND 170*

UNIVERSAL STUDIOS, CHICAGO
26 Dec '63   **The Impressions:** same. Session 952. Produced CM. Arranged Johnny Pate.

11881	'Little Boy Blue' (CM) – ABCLP 468, (E) CLP 1743, Kent 008, *Kent CDKEND 126*
11882	'I Gotta Keep On Movin'' (CM) – ABCLP 468, (E) CLP 1743, Kent 008, *Kent CDKEND126*
11883	'Satin Doll' (D Ellington / J Mercer / B Srayhorn) – ABCLP 468, (E) CLP 1743, Kent 008, *Kent CDKEND 126*
11884	'Lemon Tree' (J Holt) – ABCLP 468, (E) CLP 1743, Kent 008, *Kent CDKEND 126*
11885	'You Always Hurt The One You Love' (Roberts / Fisher) – ABCLP 468, (E) CLP 1743, Kent 008, *Kent CDKEND 126*

11886   'September Song' (K Weill / Anderson) – ABCLP 468, (E) CLP 1743, Kent
         008, *Kent CDKEND 126*

11887   'Ten To One' (CM) – ABCLP 468, (E) CLP 1743, Kent 008, *Kent
         CDKEND 126*

11888   'I'm So Proud' (CM) – ABC 10544, (E) POP 1295, ABCLP 468, 515, 727,
         ABCX 780 / 2, Sire 3717 / 2, (E) CLP 1743, Kent 009, ABCL 5104, GTSP
         201, *MCAD 31338, Kent CDKEND 923, MCAD2 10664, RMB 75051,
         PWKS 4206, Kent CDKEND 126, MCAD 11837, HMNCD 005, CPCD
         8254 / 2*

CHICAGO, UNIVERSAL STUDIOS
10 March '64   **The Impressions:** same. Session 984. Produced CM. Arranged Johnny Pate.

11984   'I Made A Mistake' (CM) – ABC 10544, (E) POP 1295, ABCLP 493, (E)
         Kent 009, *Kent CDKEND 923, 130, HIPD 40002*

11985   'We're In Love' (CM) – ABCLP 504, LP 90097, (E) CLP 3548, Kent 012,
         Kent CDKEND 130, HMNCD 005, HIPD 40002

11986   'Keep On Pushing' (CM) – ABC 10554, (E) POP 1317, ABCLP 493, 515,
         727, ABCX 780 / 2, Sire 3717 / 2, (E) CLP 1935, ABCL 5104, Kent 009,
         GTSP 201, *MCAD 31338, MCAD 22175, Kent CDKEND 935, 130,
         MCAD2 10664, RMB 75051, PWKS 4206, R2 72583, MCAD 11837,
         7243 8358 1825*

11987   'I Love You (Yeah)' (CM) – ABC 10554, (E) POP 1317, ABCLP 493, (E)
         Kent 009, *CDKEND 130, MCAD 22175*

CHICAGO, UNIVERSAL STUDIOS
10 June '64   **The Impressions:** same. Session 1024. Produced CM. Arranged Johnny
               Pate. Musicians: Freddy Robinson (g).

12148   'I've Been Trying' (CM) – ABC 10622, (E) POP 1408, ABCLP 493, 654,
         ST 91540, (E) SSL 10279, Kent 009, CRB 1063, *MCAD2 10664, HMNCD
         005, Kent CDKEND 923, 130, PWKS 4206*

12149   'Long, Long Winter (CM) – ABC 10602, (E) POP 1492, ABCLP 493, (E)
         Kent 009, *Kent CDKEND 130, HMNCD 005*

12150   'You Must Believe Me (CM) – ABC 10581, (E) POP 1343, ABCLP 505,
         515, 727, ABCX 780 / 2, Sire 3717 / 2, (E) CLP 1935, 7EG 8896, ABCL
         5104, CRB 1063, Kent 009, GTSP 201, *MCAD 31338, Kent CDKEND
         923, 130, MCAD2 10664, RMB 75051, PWKS 4206, R2 72583, MCAD
         11837, HMNCD 005*

12151   'I Ain't Supposed To' (CM / J Butler) – ABCLP 493, (E) Kent 009, *Kent
         CDKEND 130*

UNIVERSAL STUDIOS, CHICAGO
20 June '64   **The Impressions:** same. Session 1027 Produced CM. Arranged Johnny Pate.

12160   'Amen' (CM / J Pate) – ABC 10602, (E) POP 1492, ABCLP 493, 515, J Hairston (originally) 654, 727, ABCX 780 / 2, ST 91540, ABC 1234, Sire 3717 / 2, (E) CLP 1935, ABCL 5104, Kent 009, GTSP 201, *MCAD 31338, Kent CDKEND 923, 130, MCAD2 10664, RMB 7502. PWKS 4206, R2 72583, MCAD 11837, MCAD 22175, HMNCD 005*

12161   'See The Real Me' (CM) – ABC 10581, LP 90097, (E) POP 1343, ABCLP 505, (E) Kent 012, *MCAD2 10664, Kent CDKEND 130, MCAD 22175*

12162   'Don't Let It Hide' (CM) – ABCLP 493, (E) Kent 009, *Kent CDKEND 130*

12163   'Dedicate My Song To You' (CM / A Beard) – ABCLP 493, Kent 009, *Kent CDKEND 130*

12164   'Somebody Help Me' (CM) – ABCLP 493, Kent 009, *Kent CDKEND 130*

UNIVERSAL STUDIOS, CHICAGO
26 Oct '64   **The Impressions:** same. Session 1070. Produced CM. Arranged Johnny Pate.

12349   'Woman's Got Soul' (CM) – ABC 10647, (E) POP 1429, ABCLP 506, 727, ABCX 780 / 2, Sire 3717 / 2, LP 90097, (E) CLP 1935, 7EG 8954, ABCL 5104, Kent 012, GTSP 201, *MCAD 31338, Kent CDKEND 923, 130, MCAD2 10664, PWKS 4206, R2 72583, MCAD 11837, MCAD 22175, HMNCD 005*

12350   'Emotions' (CM) – ABCLP 505, ABCX 780 / 2, LP 90097, (E) CLP 3548, Kent 012, GTSP 201, *Kent CDKEND 130*

12351   'Sometimes I Wonder' (CM) – ABC 11135, ABCLP 505, ABCX 780 / 2, LP 90097, (E) CLP 3548, Kent 012, GTSP 201, *Kent CDKEND 130*

12352   'Just Another Dance' (CM) – ABCLP 505, LP 90097, (E) Kent 012, *Kent CDKEND 130, HIPD 40002*

Session 1071
12353   'People Get Ready' (CM) – ABC 10622, (E) POP 1408, ABCLP 505, 654, 727, ABCX 780 / 2, ST 91540, Sire 3717 / 2, (E) CLP 1935, Probe 584, 7EG 8954, ABCL 5104, Kent 012, ABDS 303, CRB 1063, GTSP 201, *MCAD 31338, Kent CDKEND 923, 130, MCAD2 10664, RMB 75051, PWKS 4206, R2 72583, MCAD 11837, HMNCD 005*

12354   'I've Found Out That I've Lost' (CM) – ABC 10670, (E) POP 1446, ABCLP 505, LP 90097, (E) SSL 10279, Kent 012, *Kent CDKEND 130, HIPD 40002*

12355   'Hard To Believe' (CM) – ABC 10932, ABCLP 505, LP 90097, (E) SL 10239, 10279, Kent 012, *MCAD2 10664, Kent CDKEND130*

| 12356 | 'Get Up And Move' (CM) – ABC 10647, (E) POP 1429, ABCLP 505, LP 90097, ABCX 780 / 2, (E) Kent 012, GTSP 201, *Kent CDKEND 130, HIPD 40002* |

UNIVERSAL STUDIOS, CHICAGO
5 Jan '65   **The Impressions:** same. Session 1105. Produced CM. Arranged Johnny Pate.

| 12430 | 'Never Could You Be' (CM) – ABC 10710, (E) POP 1472, ABCLP 545, (E) ABDS 303, *CDKEND 170, HIPD 40002* |

| 12431 | 'I Need You' (CM) – ABC 10710, (E) POP 1472, ABCLP 545, SPC 3502, *Kent CDKEND 923, 152, MCAD2 10664, MCAD 11837, HMNCD 005* |

| 12432 | 'Too Slow' (CM) – ABC 10789, (E) POP 1526, ABCLP 545, 654, ST 91540, SPC 3502, (E) CLP 3548, *Kent CDKEND 152, HIPD 40002* |

| 12451A | 'Man Oh Man (I Want To Go Back)' (CM / B Krass) – ABC 10750, (E) SL 10239, *MCAD2 10664, 7243 8358 1825, CDKEND 170* |

UNIVERSAL STUDIOS, CHICAGO
14 April '65   **The Impressions:** same. Session 1157. Produced CM. Arranged Johnny Pate

| 12600 | 'Meeting Over Yonder' (CM) – ABC 10670, (E) POP 1446, SPC 3502, Sire 3717 / 2, (E) CLP 1935, 7EG 8954, ABCL 5104, (E) *MCAD 31338, Kent CDKEND 923, MCAD2 10664, MCAD 11837, HMNCD 005* |

| 12601 | 'Ridin' High' (CM) – ABCLP 545, 727, ABCX 780 / 2, (E) CLP 3548, CRB 1063, GTSP 201, *Jap CD MVCM 22034, Kent CDKEND 152* |

| 12602 | 'No One Else' (CM) – ABC 10789, (E) POP 1526, ABCLP 545, (E) CLP 3548, *MVCM 22034, Kent CDKEND 152* |

| 12603 | 'Right On Time' (CM) – ABCLP 545, (E) CLP 3548, CRB 1063, *PWKS 4206, MVCM 22034, Kent CDKEND 152* |

| | Session 1158 |
| 12604 | 'Mona Lisa' (J Livingstone / R Evans) – ABCLP 523, Sparton 523 (E), *Kent CDKEND 152* |

| 12605 | 'Twilight Time' (M Nevins / B Ram / A Nevins / A Dunn) – ABC 10725, ABCLP 523, Sparton 523 (E), *Kent CDKEND 152* |

| 12606 | 'Nature Boy' (E Ahbez) – ABCLP 523, Sparton 523 (E), *Kent CDKEND 152* |

| 12607 | 'Answer Me' (C Sigman / G Winkler / F Rauch) – ABCLP 523, Sparton 523 (E), *Kent CDKEND 152* |

UNIVERSAL STUDIOS, CHICAGO
9 June '65   **The Impressions:** Curtis Mayfield (lead), Sam Gooden (lead), Fred Cash (* lead). Session 1172. Produced CM. Arranged Johnny Pate.

12662   'My Prayer' (J Kennedy / G Boulanger) – ABCLP 523, Sparton 523 (E), *Kent CDKEND 152*

12663   'I Wanna Be Around (S Vimmerstedt / J Mercer) – ABCLP 523, Sparton 523 (E), *Kent CDKEND 152*

12664   'Without A Song' (B Rose / E Eliscu / V Youmans) – ABCLP 523, Sparton 523 (E), *Kent CDKEND 152*

12665   'I Want To Be With You' (C Strouse / L Adams) – ABCLP 523, Sparton 523 (E), *Kent CDKEND 152*

UNIVERSAL STUDIOS, CHICAGO
11 June '65   **The Impressions:** same. Session 1173. Produced CM. Arranged Johnny Pate.

12666   'Just One Kiss From You' (CM) – ABC 10725, (E) POP 1498, ABCLP 523, Sparton 523, SPC 3502, (E) SSL 10279, ABDS 303, *Kent CDKEND 923, 152, HIPD 40002*

12667   'Lonely Man' (CM) – ABCLP 523, Sparton 523, (E) SSL 10279, *Kent CDKEND 152*

12668   'Falling In Love With You' (CM) – ABC 10761, (E) POP 1516, ABCLP 523, Sparton 523, (E) SSL 10279, *Kent CDKEND 152*

12669   'It's Not Unusual' (L Reed / G Mills) – ABCLP 523, Sparton 523, (E) CLP 3548, *Kent CDKEND 152*

UNIVERSAL STUDIOS, CHICAGO
1 Oct'65   **The Impressions:** same. Session 1229. Produced CM. Arranged Johnny Pate.

12914   'This Must End' (CM) – ABC 10831, (E) POP 1545, ABCLP 654, ST 91540, (E) SSL 10279, *CDKEND 170*

12915   'I Need A Love (I'd Need Her Love)' (CM) – (E) SSL 10279, *CDKEND 170*

12916   'Since I Lost The One I Love' (CM) – ABC 10761, (E) POP 1516, SPC 3502, (E) SSL 10279, ABDS 303, *Kent CDKEND 923, HIPD 40002*

UNIVERSAL STUDIOS, CHICAGO
4 Oct '65   **The Impressions:** same. Session 1231. Produced CM. Arranged Johnny Pate.

12921   'You've Been Cheatin'' (CM) – ABC 10750, (E) POP 1498, ST 91540, SPC 3502, Sire 3717 / 2, (E) SSL 10279, ABDS 303, 7EG 8954, *MCAD 31338, Kent CDKEND 923, MCAD2 10664, PWKS 4206, MCAD 11837, HMN CD 005*

12922   'Man's Temptation' (CM) – ABCLP 545, (E) CLP 3548, CRB 1063, *MVCM 22034, Kent CDKEND 152*

12923 'You Ought To Be In Heaven' (CM) – ABC 10964, ABCLP 606, (E) CLP
    3631, *Kent CDKEND 155*

UNIVERSAL STUDIOS, CHICAGO
20 Oct '65 **The Impressions:** same. Session 1240. Produced CM. Arranged Johnny Pate.

12954 'Gotta Get Away' (CM) – ABCLP 545, (E) CLP 3548, *MVCM 22034, Kent*
    CDKEND 152

12955 'I'm A Telling You' (CM) – ABCLP 545, (E) CLP 3548, *MVCM 22034,*
    Kent CDKEND 152

12956 'That's What Mama Say' (CM) – ABCLP 545, (E) CLP 3548, *MVCM*
    22034, Kent CDKEND 152

12957 'I Need To Belong To Someone' (CM) – ABCLP 545, (E) CLP 3548, *MVCM*
    22034, Kent CDKEND 152

12958 'Let It Be Me' (M Curtis / G Becaud / P Delance) – ABCLP 545, *MVCM*
    22034, (E) CLP 3548, SSL 10239, *CDKEND 152*

UNIVERSAL STUDIOS, CHICAGO
7 Feb '66 **The Impressions:** Curtis Mayfield (lead), Sam Gooden (> lead), Fred Cash.
    Session 1278. Produced CM. Arranged Johnny Pate.

13081 'Little Girl' > (CM) – ABC 10900, ABCLP 606, (E) POP 1581, (E) CLP
    3631, *Kent CDKEND 155*

13082 'Rainbow' (CM) – Unissued

13083 'What Now' (CM) – Unissued

13084 'It's All Over' (CM) – ABC 11022, ABCLP 606, (E) CLP 3631, CRB 1063,
    Kent CDKEND 155

UNIVERSAL STUDIOS, CHICAGO
21 June 1966 **The Impressions:** Curtis Mayfield (lead), Sam Gooden (> lead), Fred Cash.
    Session 1356 Produced CM. Arranged Johnny Pate.

13411 'Love's A Comin'' > (CM) – ABC 10869, ABCLP 606, (E) CLP 3631, *Kent*
    CDKEND 155

13412 'Can't Satisfy' (CM) – ABC 10831, (E) POP 1545, ABCLP 654, SPC 3502,
    Kent CDKEND 923, MCAD 11837

RECORDED LIVE AT THE CLUB, CHICAGO
2 Sept '66 **The Impressions:** Curtis Mayfield (lead), Sam Gooden (> lead), Fred Cash.
    Session 1399. Produced CM.

13558 'It's Alright' – Unissued

13559	'See The Real Me' – Unissued
13560	'Amen' – Unissued

Session 1400
13561	'You've Been Cheatin'' – Unissued
13562	'Woman's Got Soul' – Unissued
13563	'I've Found Out That I've Lost' – Unissued
13564	'Wade In The Water' (R Lewis) – ABC 10869

Session 1401
13565	'Can't Satisfy' – Unissued
13566	'Medley Gypsy Woman' – Unissued
	'I'm So Proud' – Unissued
	'You Must Believe Me' – Unissued
	'Somebody Help Me' – Unissued
	'People Get Ready' – Unissued
	'Keep On Pushing' – Unissued
	'I've Been Trying' – Unissued

UNIVERSAL STUDIOS, CHICAGO
19 Jan '67 **The Impressions:** same. Session 1476. Produced CM. Arranged Johnny Pate.

13823	'You Always Hurt Me' (CM) – ABC 10900, (E) POP 1581, ABCLP 606, (E) CLP 3631, ABDS 303, *Kent CDKEND 923, 155, MCAD 22175, HIPD 40002*
13824	'You've Got Me Runnin'' (CM) – ABC 10932, (E) Stateside SS 2083, (E) SSL 10239, *CDKEND 170, HIPD 40002*

UNIVERSAL STUDIOS, NASHVILLE
5 April '67 **The Impressions:** Curtis Mayfield (lead), Sam Gooden (> lead), Fred Cash. Session 1525. Produced CM and Johnny Pate. Arranged Johnny Pate.

13945	'Isle Of Sirens' (CM) – ABCLP 606, (E) CLP 3631, *Kent CDKEND 155*
13946	'Aware Of Love' > (CM) – ABCLP 606, (E) CLP 3631, *Kent CDKEND 155*
13947	'I Can't Stay Away From You' (CM) – ABC 10964, ABCLP 606, (E) CLP 3631, SPC 3502, *Kent CDKEND 155, HIPD 40002*

Session 1526
13948	'She Don't Love Me' (CM) – ABCLP 606, 654, (E) CLP 3631, *Kent CDKEND 155*
13949	'I'm Still Waiting' (CM) – ABCLP 606, (E) CLP 3631, *Kent CDKEND 155*
13950	'100lbs Of Clay' (B Elgin / E Dixon / K Rogers) – ABCLP 606, (E) CLP 3631, *Kent CDKEND 155*

UNIVERSAL STUDIOS, CHICAGO
15 Nov '67   **The Impressions:** same. Session 1668. Produced CM and Johnny Pate. Arranged Johnny Pate.

14403   'We're A Winner' (CM) – ABC 11022, (E) SS 2083, ABCLP 635, 654, 727, ABCX 780 / 2, ST 91540, Sire 3717 / 2, (E) SSL 10239, ABDS 303, GTSP 201, *MCAD 31338, Kent 923, 155, MCAD2 10664, PWKS 4206, RMB 75051, R2 72583, MCAD 11837, HMNCD 005*

14404   'I Loved And I Lost' (CM) – ABC 11103, ABCLP 635, 654, ST 91540, (E) SSL 10239, ABDS 303, *MCAD2 10664, Kent 923, 155, MCAD 11837*

14405   'Little Brown Boy' (CM) – ABCLP 635, (E) SSL 10239, *Kent CDKEND 155*

UNIVERSAL STUDIOS, CHICAGO
22 Nov '67   **The Impressions:** Curtis Mayfield (lead), Sam Gooden, Fred Cash (* lead). Session 1671. Produced CM. Arranged Johnny Pate.

14475   'Up, Up And Away' (J Webb) – ABC 11103, ABCLP 635, (E) SSL 10239, *Kent CDKEND 155*

14476   'Let Me Tell The World' * (CM) – ABCLP 635, (E) SSL 10239, *Kent CDKEND 155*

14477   'Romancing To A Folk Song' (CM) – ABCLP 635, (E) SSL 10239, *Kent CDKEND 155*

14478   'Moonlight Shadows' (CM) – ABCLP 635, (E) SSI 10239, *Kent CDKEND 155*

            Session 1672
14516   'I'm Gettin' Ready' (CM / P Upchurch) – ABCLP 635, (E) SSL 10239, *Kent CDKEND 155*

14517   'No One To Love' (CM) – ABCLP 635, (E) SSL 10239, *Kent CDKEND 155*

14518   'Nothing Can Stop Me' (CM) – ABCLP 635, (E) SSL 10239, *Kent CDKEND 155*, CRB 1063

UNIVERSAL STUDIOS, CHICAGO
15 March '68   **The Impressions:** same. Session 1748. Produced CM. Arranged Johnny Pate.

14867   'We're Rolling On' Pt 1 (CM) – ABC 11071, ABCLP 654, 727, ST 91540, ABCX 780 / 2, (E) SSL 10279, Probe 584, ABDS 303, GTSP 201, *MCAD2 10664, Kent CD KEND923, 170, MCAD 11837, (E) CDKEND 170, HMNCD 005*

14868   'We're Rolling On' Pt 2 (CM) – ABC 11071, ABCLP 654, (E) SSL 10279, *CDKEND 170*

14869   'Don't Cry My Love' (CM / O Brown Jr) – ABC 11135, ABCLP 668, SPC 3554, (E) SSL 10279, ABDS 303, CRB 1063, *CDKEND 170*

UNIVERSAL STUDIOS, CHICAGO
10 April '68   **The Impressions:** same. Session 1773. Produced CM. Arranged Johnny Pate.

14945   'Just Before Sunrise' (M David) – ABC 11188, *(E) CDKEND 170*

14946   'East Of Java' (M David) – Unissued.

14947   'East Of Java 2' (M David) – ABC 11188, ABCLP 668, SPC 3554, *(E) CDKEND 170*

UNIVERSAL STUDIOS, CHICAGO
4 June '68   **The Impressions:** Curtis Mayfield (lead), Sam Gooden, Fred Cash. Produced CM. Arranged Johnny Pate.

15162   'Yesterday' (J Lennon / P McCartney) – ABCLP 668, SPC 3554, *(E) CDKEND 170*

15163   'All Of My Trials' (CM / Trad) – *(E) CDKEND 170*

15164   'The Look Of Love' (B Bacharach / H David) – ABCLP 668, SPC 3554, *(E) CDKEND 170*

15165   'Thanks To You' (J Butler / CM) – *(E) CDKEND 170*

15166   'Sermonette' (J Adderley / J Hendricks) – ABCLP 668, SPC 3554, *(E) CDKEND 170*

15167   'Once In A Lifetime' (A Newley / L Bricusse) – ABCLP 668, SPC 3554, *(E) CDKEND 170*

15168   'Puppy Love' (CM) – *(E) CDKEND 170*

15169   '(Bring A Little Water) Sylvie' (CM / trad) – *(E) CDKEND 170*

15170   'Oo You're A Livin' Doll' (J Pate) – ABCLP 668, SPC 3554, *(E) CDKEND 170*

15171   'Fool On A Hill' (J Lennon / P McCartney) – ABCLP 668, SPC 3554, *(E) CDKEND 170*

15172   'Devil In Your Soul' (CM / J Butler / E Thomas) – *(E) CDKEND 170*

15173   'This Is The Life (L Adams / C Strouse) – ABCLP 668, SPC 3554, *(E) CDKEND 170*

GENERAL DISCOGRAPHY

Compiled by Peter Burns for Echo Archive.

US SINGLES		UK SINGLES
VEE-JAY		
2806 / 58	'For Your Precious Love' / 'Sweet Was The Wine'	
FALCON		
1013 7/58	'For Your Precious Love' / 'Sweet Was The Wine'	
ABNER		**LONDON HL**
1013 8/58	'For Your Precious Love' / 'Sweet Was The Wine'	8697
1017 10/58	'Come Back My Love' / 'Love Me'	
1023 11/58	'The Gift Of Love' / 'At The County Fair'	
1025 2/59	'Senorita I Love You' / 'Lovely One'	
1034 4/60	'A New Love' / 'That You Love Me'	
BANDERA		
2504 5/59	'Listen' / 'Shorty's Got To Go'	
PORT		
70031 '62	'Listen' / 'Shorty's Got To Go'	
VEE-JAY		
3969 '61	'For Your Precious Love' / 'Sweet Was The Wine' (JB)	
4246 '62	'Senorita I Love You' / 'That You Love Me'	
5742 '64	'At The County Fair' / 'The Gift Of Love'	
621 10/64	'Senorita I Love You / That You Love Me'	
SWIRL		
107 '62	'Don't Leave Me' / 'I Need Your Love'	
GRAMERCY		
	'Don't Leave Me' / 'I Need Your Love'	
ABC		**HMV (POP)**
10241 9/61	'Gypsy Woman' / 'As Long As You Love Me'	961
10289	'Can't You See' / 'Grow Closer Together'	
10328	'Little Young Lover' / 'Never Let Me Go'	
10357	'Minstrel & Queen' / 'You've Come Home'	
10386	'I'm The One Who Loves You' / 'I Need Your Love'	1129
10431	'Sad, Sad Boy And Girl' / 'Twist And Limbo'	
10487 9/63	'It's All Right' / 'You'll Want Me Back'	1226
10511	'Talkin' 'Bout My Baby' / 'Never Too Much Love'	1262
10544	'I'm So Proud' / 'I Made A Mistake'	1295
10554	'Keep On Pushing' / 'I Love You (Yeah)'	1317
10581	'You Must Believe Me' / 'See The Real Me'	1343
10602	'Amen' / 'Long Long Winter'	1492
10622	'People Get Ready' / 'I've Been Trying'	1408

10647	'Woman's Got Soul' / 'Get Up And Move'	1429
10670	'Meeting Over Yonder' / 'I Found Out That I've Lost'	1446
10710	'I Need You' / 'Never Could You Be'	1472
10725	'Just One Kiss From You' / 'Twilight Time'	
10750	'You've Been Cheatin'' / 'Man Oh Man'	
	'You've Been Cheatin'' / 'Just One Kiss From You'	1498
10761	'Since I Lost The One I Love' / 'Falling In Love With You'	1516
10789	'Too Slow' / 'No One Else'	1526
10831	'Can't Satisfy' / 'This Must End'	1545
10869	'Love's A Comin'' / 'Wade In The Water'	
10900	'You Always Hurt Me' / 'Little Girl'	1581
10932	'You've Got Me Runnin'' / 'It's Hard To Believe'	
10964	'I Can't Stay Away From You' / 'Man's Temptation'	
11022	'We're A Winner' / 'It's All Over'	Stateside SS
	We're A Winner' / 'You Got Me Runnin''	2082
11071	'We're Rolling On' Part 1 / 'We're Rolling On' Part 2	
11103 7/68	'I Loved And I Lost' / 'Up, Up And Away'	
11135	'Don't Cry My Love' / 'Sometimes I Wonder'	
11188	'Just Before Sunrise' / 'East Of Java'	
	Can't Satisfy / You've Been Cheatin'	2139
	'People Get Ready' / 'We're Rolling On'	Probe 584 4 / 73
		JSP
	'Shorty's Got To Go' / 'Pretty Betty / Listen'	4501

VINYL ALBUMS (tracks)

VJ 1075	*For Your Precious Love* (12). UK issues (16).	JOY 104 (Aug '68), DJM26086 (Nov '76)
	The Impressions With JB (12)	CRM 2023 (Dec '81)
Custom 1031	*Betty Everett And The Impressions* (4)	
Design 201	*Impressions With JB And BE* (4)	
Upfront 102	*Winners* (10)	
Pickwick 3502	*Impressions Chartbusters* (9)	
ABC 450	*Impressions (It's All Right)* (12)	Kent 005
ABC 468	*Never Ending Impressions* (12)	HMV CLP 1743 (July'64), Kent 008
ABC 493	*Keep On Pushing* (12)	Kent 009
ABC 504	*Shindig* (1)	Spartan 504
ABC 505	*People Get Ready* (12)	Kent 012
ABC 515	*Greatest Hits* (12)	
	Impressions Big 16	HMV CLP 1935, CSD 1642 (Dec '65), ABCL 5104 (Feb '75)
ABC 523	*One By One* (12)	
ABC 545	*Riding High* (11) / (14)	HMV CLP 3548 (July '66)
ABC 606	*Fabulous Impressions* (11)	HMV CLP 3631 (Sept '67)
ABC 635	*We're A Winner* (10) / UK (14)	Stateside SS10239 (July '68)

ABC 654	Best Of The Impressions (11)	
	The Impressions' Big 16 Volume 2	Stateside 10279
ABC 668	Versatile Impressions (10) / (9)	Pickwick 355
ABC 727	16 Greatest Hits	
ABC 780 / X2	Curtis Mayfield And The Impressions (20)	
Sire 3717 / X2	The Vintage Years JB / CM And The Impressions (28)	
	Impressions Originals (28)	ABC 303 / X2
	Right On Time (16)	Charly CRB 1063

EPs

| | It's All Right (4) | HMV 7EG 8896 (June '65) |
| | Soulfully (4) | HMV 7EG8954 (Sept '66) |

US	**CDs**	**UK**
	For Your Precious Love (16)	Charly CDCD 1105 / 93
VJ NVD2-719	Complete Vee-Jay Recordings (18)	Black Tulip 725
MCAD 31338	Greatest Hits (12)	
	Definitive Impressions (28)	Kent CDKEND 923 / 89
	This Old Heart... (8)	December RMB 75051 / 92
MCAD2 10664	Anthology / CM And The Impressions (30)	
	All The Best Impressions, Featuring CM (15)	Pickwick 4206 / 94
MCAD 22175	It's All Right (10)	
	People Get Ready / Best (23)	Half Moon 005 / 97
	Changing Impressions (2-CD box) (39)	Charly CPCD 8254 / 2 / 96
Hippo 40002	Further Impressions (14)	
MCAD 11837	The Greatest Hits (16)	
Rhino R2 72583	Very Best Of The Impressions (16)	
Rhino R2 72262	People Get Ready Box (3-CD) (12)	
	For Your Precious Love (15)	Neon NE 34537 / 2K

COLLECTABLES

7238	For Your Precious Love / Folk Songs (23)	
	Doctor Good Soul (1)	Westside WESM 525 / 98
	Impressions / Never Ending... (24)	Kent CDKEND 126 / 95
	Keep On Pushing / People Get Ready (24)	Kent CDKEND 130 / 96
	One By One / Ridin' High (23)	Kent CDKEND 152 / 98
	Fabulous Impressions / We're A Winner (21)	Kent CDKEND 155 / 98
	Impressions / ABC Rarities (26)	Kent CDKEND 170 / 99

JAPANESE CDs

	Impressions (It's All Right) (12)	Jap MVCM 22031
	People Get Ready (12)	Jap MVCM 22033
	Ridin' High (11)	Jap MVCM 22034
	We're A Winner (11)	Jap MVCM 22035

See 'Curtom Discography' for further releases by The Impressions

Appendix 2: The Impressions Curtom Sessionography And Discography

CURTOM SESSIONOGRAPHY

Compiled by Peter Burns for Echo Archive. Acknowledgements: Trevor Churchill, Sam Gooden.

RCA STUDIOS, CHICAGO
1968   **The Impressions:** Curtis Mayfield (lead), Sam Gooden, Fred Cash. Produced Curtis Mayfield. Arranged Johnny Pate / Donny Hathaway. Musicians: Donny Hathaway (kbds).

'**This Is My Country**' – Curtom CRS 8001, (E) Buddah 203 012, Get Back GET 8001, *NEM CD 782, CDGR 108*

'Fool For You' (CM) – Curtom 1932, 8004, (E) 2011.021, Active Gold 22, *MCAD2 10664, CPCD 8254 / 2, MCCD 360, R2 72583, CD LAB 107, NEECD 322, NEECD 321*

'They Don't Know' (CM)

'Gone Away' (CM / D Hathaway) CRS 8004, Active Gold 28, *CPCD 8254 / 2, MCCD 360, NEECD 321*

'So Unusual' (CM)

'I'm Lovin' Nothing' (CM) – CR 1932, (E) 2011.021, Active Gold 22, *NEECD 321*

'Love's Happening' (CM)

'You Want Somebody Else' (CM / DH) – CR 1937, *NEECD 321*

'Stay Close To Me' (CM)

'Merry X-mas Happy New Year / SP3

RCA STUDIOS, CHICAGO
10 Oct '68   **The Impressions:** same. Produced CM. Arranged Donny Hathaway / Johnny Pate.

'This Is My Country' (CM) – CR 1934, CRS 8004, SPC 3325, RAG 23, *MCAD2 10664, CPCD 8254 / 2, R2 72583, MCCD 360, CD LAB 107, NEECD 322, NEECD 321,*

'My Woman's Love' (CM) – CR 1934, RAG 23

RCA STUDIOS, CHICAGO
1968   **The Impressions:** same. Produced CM. Arranged Donny Hathaway / Johnny Pate.

'Young Mods Forgotten Story' – Curtom CRS 8003, (E) 2359.003, *Curtom CD 2013, NEM CD 782, CDGR 108*

'Young Mod's Forgotten Story' (CM) – *NEMCD 402, NEECD 321*

'Choice Of Colors' (CM) – CR 1943, (E) 2011.062, CRS 8004, RAG 25, *MCAD2 10664, NEECD 321, EAB CD 050, CPCD 8254 / 2, MCCD 360, R2 72583, NEECD 322, (J) TECW 20096*

'The Girl I Find' (CM) – CR 1940, RAG 24.

'Wherever You Leadeth Me' (CM) – CR 1948, CRS 8004, RAG 27, *CPCD 8254 / 2, MCCD 360*

'My Deceiving Heart' (CM) – CR 1937, RAG 30, *NEECD 322, NEECD 321*

'Seven Years' (CM) – CR 1940, RAG 24, *CPCD 8254 / 2, CD LAB 107, NEECD 322, NEECD 321*

'Love's Miracle' (CM)

'Jealous Man' (CM)

'Soulful Love' (CM) – CR 1954, (E) 2011.045, *NEECD 321*

'Mighty Mighty (Spade And Whitey) (CM) – CR 1943, (E) 2011.062, CRS 8004, RAG 25, *CPCD 8254 / 2, MCCD 360, NEECD 321*

RCA STUDIOS, CHICAGO
1969   **The Impressions:** same. Produced CM. Arranged Johnny Pate / Donny Hathaway. Musicians: Robert Lewis (tpt, fl hrn), Clifford Davis (ten), Leonard Druss (sax, fl), Phil Upchurch (gtr), Henry Gibson (perc), Sol Bobrov (vln), John Howell, Harold Lepp, Loren Binford, Patrick Ferreri, Richard Single, Rudolf Stauber, Donald Simmons, Harold Dessent, Ronald Kolber, Harold Klatz, John Ross, Sam Heiman, Elliot Golub, Robert Sims, Gary Slabo.

'Best Impressions' – Curtom CRS 8004, (E) 'Amen' 2359.009, Amen '70 (CM / J Pate)   CR 1948, RAG 27, (E) 2011.099, *CPCD 8254 / 2, NEECD 321*

'Keep On Pushing' (CM) – RAG 28, (E) 2011.099, *EAB CD 050, CPCD 8254 / 2, NEECD 321*

'Gypsy Woman' (CM), – RAG 29, *EAB CD 050, CPCD 8254 / 2, NEECD 321*

'I'm So Proud' (CM) – CR 1957, RAG 30, (E) 2011.068, *CPCD 8254 / 2, NEECD 321*

'I've Been Trying' (CM) – RAG 29, *EAB CD 050, CPCD 8254 / 2, NEECD 321*

'Say You Love Me (CM) – CR1946, RAG 26, (E) Windmill WMD 114, *NEECD 322, NEECD 321.* (Remaining tracks previously credited.)

RCA STUDIOS, CHICAGO
July/Aug '70   **The Impressions:** same. Produced CM. Arranged Riley Hampton / Gary Slabo.

'**Check Out Your Mind**' – Curtom CRS 8006, (E) Buddah 2318.017, *NEM CD 843*

'Check Out Your Mind' (CM) – CR 1951, (E) 2011.030, RAG 98, *MCAD2 10664, EAB CD 050, CPCD 8254 / 2, MCCD 360, R2 72583, CD LAB 107, NEECD 322, NEECD 321*

'Baby Turn On To Me' (CM) – CR 1954, (E) 2011.045, *EAB CD 050, CPCD 8254 / 2, CD LAB 107, NEECD 322, NEMCD 451, NEECD 321*

'You'll Always Be Mine' (CM) – CR 1946, RAG 26,

'Madam Mary (CM) – *NEECD 321*

'We Must Be In Love' (CM) – CR 1964, *CPCD 8254 / 2, MCCD 360,*

'Can't You See' (CM / J Butler) – CR 1951, (E) 2011.030, *NEECD321*

'You're Really Something, Sadie' (CM) – *NEECD 321*

'Only You' (CM)

'Do You Want To Win' (CM) – CR 1959, 2011.087

'Ain't Got Time' (CM) – CR 1957, (E) 2011.068, *EAB CD 050, CPCD 8254 / 2, MCCD 360, CD LAB 107, NEECD 322.* (RH arrangement available on single only.)

RCA STUDIOS, CHICAGO, 1971
NEW YORK BELL SOUND STUDIOS, NY, 1972
'71 / '72   **The Impressions:** Leroy Hutson (lead), Sam Gooden (> lead), Fred Cash (* lead). Produced CM. Arranged Riley Hampton / Leroy Hutson / CM.

'Times Have Changed' – Curtom CRS 8012, (E) 2318.059, *NEM CD 843*

'Stop The War'* (CM)

'Potent Love' (CM) – *CPCD 8254 / 2*

'Times Have Changed' (CM) – CR1970, 1977, 1982, 1994, *CPCD8254 / 2, NEECD 321*

'Inner-City Blues' (M Gaye / J Nyx Jr) – CR 1964, RAG 98, (E) 2011.099, *EAB CD 050, CPCD 8254 / 2, CD NEW 110, NEMCD 451*

'This Love's For Real' (L Hutson / M Hawkins) – CR1970, (E) 2011.124, *NEECD 321,*

'I Need To Belong To Someone' > (CM) – CR 1973

'Our Love Goes On And On' (CM) – (E) 2011.124, *NEECD 321*

'Love Me' (CM) – CR 1959, 1973, (E) 2011.087, *NEECD 322*

'Love Me 2' (CM) (single version, previously unissued) – *NEECD 321*

CURTOM STUDIOS, CHICAGO
1972   **The Impressions:** Fred Cash (lead), Sam Gooden (> lead), Reggie Torian (tenor). Produced and arranged Rich Tufo. Master: Henry Gibson (perc).

'Preacher Man' (RT) – CRS 8016, *NEM CD 866*

'What It Is' (RT) (instrumental featuring Henry Gibson)

'Preacher Man' (RT) – CR 1982, *EAB CD 050, CPCD 8254 / 2, MCCD 360, CD LAB 107, NEECD 321,*

'Simple Message' (E Story)

'Find The Way' (RT)

'Thin Line' (RT) – CR 1985, (E) 2011.167, *EAB CD 050, CPCD 8254 / 2, MCCD 360, NEECD 321*

'(I'm Lost) Color Us All Grey' (J Thompson / E Dixon) – *NEECD 321,*

'I'm Loving You' (RT) – CR 1985, (E) 2011.167

CHICAGO
1973   **Curtis Mayfield And Friends** with Gerry Butler, Brenda Lee Eager, Mattie Butler, Diedra Teig, live at WTTW-TV Studios, Chicago. Engineer Roger Anfinsen. Produced CM / Richard Tufo. Musicians: Carolyn Johnson (fem vcl), Philip Upchurch (g).

'Curtis In Chicago' – Curtom CRS 8018, (E) 2318.091, BDLH 5009, K 56250, *(E) CPCD 8046, JICK89418, NEMCD 400*

'Superfly' (CM) – Curtis Mayfield – *(J) TECW 20095*

'For Your Precious Love' (J Butler / A&R Brooks) – The Impressions: JB, CM, SG, FC

'I'm So Proud' (CM) – The Impressions CM, SG, FC – *(E) CPCD 8065*

'For Once In My Life' (Miller / Murden) – The Impressions: RT, SG, FC – *EDM CD 009*

'Preacher Man' (R Tufo) The Impressions: FC, SG, RT

'If I Were Only A Child Again' (CM) – Curtis Mayfield – CR 1991,

'Duke Of Earl' (Edwards / B Williams / E Dixon) – Gene Chandler – *EDM CD 009*

'Love Oh Love (L Hutson / L Hawkins / J Hutson) – Leroy Hutson

'Amen' (CM / J Pate) – complete cast – *(J) TECW 20096*

CURTOM STUDIOS, CHICAGO
1973   **The Impressions:** Ralph Johnson (lead), Reggie Torian, Sam Gooden, Fred Cash. Produced Rich Tufo / Lowrell Simon. Arranged David van de Pettite.

'Finally Got Myself Together' – CRS 8019, (E) BDLP 4003, *NEM CD 866*

'If It's In You To Do Wrong' (AJ Tribble / G Davis) – CR 1994, *CPCD 8254 / 2, NEECD 321*

'We Go Back A Ways' (L Simon / AJ Tribble / S Davis) – *MCCD 360*

CURTOM STUDIOS, CHICAGO
1973   **The Impressions:** same. Produced Rich Tufo / Lowrell Simon. Arranged RT.

'I'll Always Be Here' (L Simon / L Brownlee / G Davis) – CR 1997, (E) BDS 403, *EAB CD 050, CPCD 8254 / 2, NEMCD 402*

PRODUCED RICH TUFO / LOWRELL SIMON, ARRANGED RENE HALL
'Don't Forget What I Told You' (L Simon / AJ Tribble)

'Guess What I've Got' (E Townsend)

'Try Me' (ET)

PRODUCED ED TOWNSEND, ARRANGED RENE HALL
'Miracle Woman' (ET) – CMS 0103, (E) Curtom K 165635, SS 13

'Finally Got Myself Together' (ET) – CR 1997, (E) BDS 403, A8R 8012, *EAB CD 050, NEECD 321, CPCD 8254 / 2, MCCD 360, R2 72583, NEECD 322*

CURTOM STUDIOS, CHICAGO
1974   **The Impressions:** Ralph Johnson (^ lead), Reggie Torian (lead), Sam Gooden, Fred Cash. Produced Rich Tufo / Lowrell Simon. Arranged Rich Tufo. Musicians: Phil Upchurch (gtr), Quinton Joseph.

'Three The Hard Way' – CRS 8602 (movie score)

'Make A Resolution' (RT / LS) – *CPCD 8254 / 2, NEECD 321*

'Wendy' ^ (RT / LS)

'That's What Love Will Do' (RT / LS)

'Something Is Mighty, Mighty Wrong' (RT / LS / T Green) – CR 2003, *EAB CD 050, CPCD 8254 / 2, NEECD 321*

'Mister Keyes' (RT / LS)

'Having A Ball' (RT / LS / P Upchurch)

'On The Move' (RT / LS)

'Three The Hard Way' (chase and theme) (RT / LS) – CR 2003

CURTOM STUDIOS, CHICAGO
1975   **The Impressions:** Ralph Johnson (lead), Reggie Torian (^ lead), Sam Gooden, Fred Cash (lead). Produced Ed Townsend. Produced Rich Tufo / Joseph Scott. Arranged Rich Tufo / Rene Hall

'**First Impressions**' – Curtom CU 5003, (E) K 56143, RSO RSS 9, *NEM CD 867*

'Sooner Or Later' (ET) – CMS 0103, (E) K 16565, SS13, *CUR 2006, CPCD 8254 / 2, R2 72583, CD LAB 107, CD NEW 115, NEECD 322, NEECD 321*

'Same Thing It Took' (ET / C Jackson / M Yancy) – CMS 0106, *CUR 2006, NEECD 322   CPCD 8254 / 2, R2 72583, NEECD 321*

'Old Before My Time' * (ET) – (E) K 16638, *CUR 2006*

'First Impressions' (ET) – CMS 0110, (E) K 16638, *CUR 2006, PWKS 4206, EAB CD 050, CPCD 8254 / 2, MCCD 360, NEECD 322, NEECD 321*

'Groove' (ET) – *NEECD 321*

'I'm So Glad' (V McCoy) – CMS 0106, K 16736

'How High Is High' (ET) – *CD NEW135*

'Why Must A Love Song Be A Sad Song' ^ (ET)

CURTOM STUDIOS, CHICAGO
Aug '75   **The Impressions:** Ralph Johnson (lead), Reggie Torian, Sam Gooden (>lead), Fred Cash. Produced Chuck Jackson and Marvin Yancy, Rich Tufo, CJ, MY and ET. Executive Ed Townsend. Arranged Rich Tufo, R Evans, Rene Hall.

'**Loving Power**' – Curtom CU 5009, (E) K56211, RSO RSS 10, *NEM CD 867*

'Loving Power' (CJ / MY) – CMS 0110, *CUR 2006, EAB CD 050, NEECD 321, CPCD 8254 / 2, MCCD 360, NEECD 322*

'Sunshine' (B Sigler / P Hurtt) – CMS 0116, *CUR 2006, CPCD 8254 / 2, NEECD 321*

'I Can't Wait To See You' (CJ / MY) – *CUR 2006*

If You Have To Ask' (ET) – *CUR 2006, NEECD 321*

'You Can't Be Wrong' (ET)

'I Wish I'd Stayed In Bed' (ET) – CMS 0116, (E) K 16736, *NEECD 321*

'Keep On Trying' > (ET) – *NEECD 321*

UNRELEASED CURTOM MASTERS
'All Over The World' – Unissued
'Colors Blow My Mind' – Unissued
'I Get High' – Unissued
'Whatever Happened To A Thing Called Love' – Unissued
'Where Is My Love' – Unissued
'Double Your Pleasure' – Unissued
'I Will Overcome' – Unissued
'Just My Imagination' – Unissued
'Exorcist' – Unissued

CHICAGO
1976   **The Impressions:** Nate Evans(lead), Reggie Torian (lead), Sam Gooden, Fred Cash.

32806   'I Saw Mommy Kissing Santa Claus' (T Connors) – Cotillion 44211

32807   'Silent Night' (trad) (edited from 32681 and 32680) – Cotillion 44211

Note: Master numbers erroneously shown as 32807 and 32808 on Cot 44211.

BARNUM STUDIOS, CALIFORNIA
1976   **The Impressions:** Nate Evans (lead), Reggie Torian (lead), Sam Gooden, Fred Cash. Produced McKinley Jackson. Arranged HB Barnum. All Rhythm arrangements McKinley Jackson. Musicians: John Barnes, Sylvester Rivers, Ronald Coleman, Mervin Seals, McKinley Jackson (kbds), Ray Parker Jr, Lee Ritenour, Ben Benay (gtr), James Jamerson, Scott Edwards (bs), Jack Ashford, Eddie (Bongo) Brown, Gary Coleman (perc), James Gadson, Ed Greene, Ollie Brown (ds).

'It's About Time' – Cotillion SD 9912

32810   'Same Old Heartaches' (Marvin Steals / Melvin Steals)

32811   'I Need You' (MS / MS)

ABC STUDIOS, LOS ANGELES
1976   **The Impressions:** same. Production and arranged by McKinley Jackson.

32809   'You'll Never Find' / 2 (MS / MS)

PARAGON STUDIOS, CHICAGO
1976   **The Impressions:** same. Production McKinley Jackson. Arranged Gil Askey

32808   'In The Palm Of My Hands' (MS / MS)

32814   'I'm A Fool For Love' (P Richmond / D Ellis) – 44210

WALLY HIEDER STUDIOS, HOLLYWOOD, CALIFORNIA
1976   **The Impressions:** the same. Produced McKinley Jackson. Arranged Gene
              Page.

32815   'What Might Have Been' (MS / MS)

32812   'This Time' (McJ / S Jones) – Cotillion 44210

32813   'Stardust' (MS / MS) – Cotillion 44214

NEW YORK, JANUARY1977 (edited from 32809)
33108   'You'll Never Find' (3.40) (MS / MS) – Cotillion 44214

33109   'You'll Never Find (6.05) (MS / MS) – DSKO 85 (12")

KENDUN RECORDERS, BURBANK, CALIFORNIA
1977   **The Impressions:** same.

33650   'Bicentennial Christmas' – Unissued

33651   'Passin' On' – Unissued

ATLANTIC STUDIOS, NEW YORK CITY
2 Sept '77   **The Impressions:** same. Produced and arranged: Johnny Pate. Executive
              producers: Bill Traut and The Impressions. Unissued album (SD 5203).

34215   'Dance' (P Richmond / R Torian) (6.19) – Disco DSKO 103 (12")
34216   'You're So Right For Me' – (Totillion) 44222
34217   'Take My Time' – Unissued
34218   'Illusions' – Unissued
34219   'Pressure' – Unissued
34220   'Inside Out' – Unissued
34221   'Let's Talk It Over' – Unissued
34222   'Who You Been Loving' – Unissued
34223   'Can't Get Along' – Cotillion 44222

UNIVERSAL STUDIOS, CHICAGO
1979   **The Impressions:** Reggie Torian (lead), Nate Evans (tenor), Sam Gooden, Fred Cash. Produced Carl Davis. Arranged Sonny Sanders.

'**Come To My Party**' – Chi-Sound T596, *CDGR 126, Westside WESM 582*

'Come To My Party' (E Record / T Washington) – *MCCD 360*

'All I Want To Do Is Make Love To You' (ER) – *CPCD 8254 / 2*

'This Can't Be Real' (G Davis / L Simon / F Cash / S Sanders)

'Sorry' (J Scott / F Cash) – Chi-Sound 2418

UNIVERSAL STUDIOS, CHICAGO
1979   **The Impressions:** the same. Produced Carl Davis. Arranged James Mack.

'Whole Lot Of Good Lovin'' (E Record)

'I Could Never Make You Stay' (J Thompson / E Dixon) – *MCCD 360*

'Maybe I'm Mistaken' (J Thompson / EDixon) – Chi-Sound 2438, *MCCD 360*

UNIVERSAL STUDIOS, CHICAGO
1981   **The Impressions:** Nate Evans (lead), Reggie Torian (lead), Sam Gooden (> lead), Fred Cash (* lead). Produced Carl Davis, Eugene Record. Arranged Tom Tom 84.

'**Fan The Fire**' – Chi-Sound T624, (E) 20th Century T 624, *CDGR 126, Westside WESM 582*

'Fan The Fire' (E Record / P Henderson) – Chi- Sound 2491, (E) 20 Century TC 2500, *EAB CD 050, CPCD 8254 / 2*

'You're Mine' * (F Cash / J Scott)

'I Don't Mind' (E Record / P Henderson)

'For Your Precious Love' (J Butler / A Brooks / R Brooks) – Chi-Sound 2491, (E) 20 C TC2500, *CPCD 8254 / 2, MCCD 360*

CHICAGO, UNIVERSAL STUDIOS
1981   **The Impressions:** same. Produced CD / ER. Arranged Sonny Sanders.

'I Don't Wanna Lose Your Love' (P Richmond) – *CPCD 8254 / 2, Westside WESM 582*

'**Love Love Love**' (E Record)

'I Surrender' (PR)

'Take Everything' (ER)

VARIOUS US CITIES – LIVE, SILVER ANNIVERSARY TOUR, '82-'83

Late '82 / '83   **The Impressions:** Nate Evans (lead), Vandy 'Smokey' Hampton (lead / ten), Fred Cash, Sam Gooden. Also featuring Curtis Mayfield and Jerry Butler with backgrounds by Debra Henry and Mattie Butler. Arranged and produced by Curtis Mayfield. Musicians: 12-piece orchestra under the direction of Lawrence Hanks, including Henry Gibson (perc), Gary Thompson (gtr), Tracey Mayfield (bass), Eric Hackett (keyboards) and Ira Gates (drums).

'For Your Precious Love' (Unissued) / 'Gypsy Woman' / 'It's Alright' / 'Amen' / 'People Get Ready' / 'Keep On Pushing' / 'We're A Winner' / 'Fool For You' / 'Choice Of Colors' / 'Finally Got Myself Together' (plus others)

CURTIS MAYFIELD

'If There's A Hell Below' / 'Freddie's Dead' / 'Superfly' (plus others)

JERRY BUTLER

'He Will Break Your Heart' / Only The Strong Survive' (plus others)

50 MUSIC GRAND STUDIO, CHICAGO

'86 / '87   The Impressions: Vandy 'Smokey' Hampton (lead / ten), Sam Gooden, Fred Cash.

'Can't Wait Until Tomorrow' – MCA 52995

JERRY MICHAEL STUDIOS, NASHVILLE

1989   **The Impressions:** Ralph Johnson (lead 1), Vandy 'Smokey' Hampton (lead 2), Fred Cash (tenor / lead 3), Sam Gooden (bass / lead 3). Arranged and produced by Jerry Michael for Michael Productions. Executive producers Don Grierson, John Lappen. Jerry Michael (synths)

'Draw The Line' – (RJ) – Unissued
'In The Middle' – (RJ) – Unissued
'I Found You' – (RJ) – Unissued
'Tired Of Being Alone' – (A Green / RJ) – Unissued
'What A Feeling' – (RJ) – Unissued
'Winning Combination' – (RJ) – Unissued
'Sad, Sad Boy And Girl And Boy' (CM) – SH – *(E) PIE SD 265*
'Choice Of Colors' (CM) – SH – *(E) PIE SD 265*
'Say You Love Me' (CM) – *(E) PIE SD 265*
'Check Out Your Mind' (CM) – SH – *(E) PIE SD 265*
'I Loved And I Lost' (CM) – SH – *(E) PIE SD 265*
'For Your Precious Love' (JB / RB / AB) – SG – *(E) PIE SD 265*
'Grow Closer Together' (CM) – SH – *(E) PIE SD 265*
'I'm So Proud' (CM) – SH – *(E) PIE SD 265*
'Find Yourself Another Girl' (CM / JB) – SG – *(E) PIE SD 265*

JERRY MICHAEL STUDIOS, NASHVILLE

1989   **The Impressions:** Ralph Johnson (lead 1), Vandy 'Smokey' Hampton (lead 2), Fred Cash (tenor / lead 3), Sam Gooden (bass / lead 4). Arranged and produced by Jerry Michael for Michael Productions. Executive producers Don Grierson, John Lappen. Jerry Michael (synths).

'Keep On Pushing' (CM) – SH – *Edel ED 12392, (E) PIE SD 265*
'It's Alright' (CM) – SH – *Edel ED 12392, (E) PIE SD 265*
'Talkin' 'Bout My Baby' (CM) – SH / SG – *Edel ED 12392, (E) PIE SD 265*
'People Get Ready' (CM) – SH / SG – *Edel ED 12392, (E) PIE SD 265*
'You Must Believe Me' (CM) – SH – *Edel ED 12392, (E) PIE SD 265*
'Woman Got Soul' (CM) – SH / SG – *Edel ED 12392, (E) PIE SD 265*
'You've Been Cheatin'' (CM) – SH / – *Edel ED 12392, (E) PIE SD 265*
'I'm The One Who Loves You' (CM) – SH – *Edel ED 12392, (E) PIE SD 265*
'Amen' (CM / JP) – SH / group – *Edel ED 12392, (E) PIE SD 265*
'I've Been Trying' (CM) – SH / SG / FC – *Edel ED 12392, (E) PIE SD 265*
'Gypsy Woman' (CM) – SH – *Edel ED 12392, (E) PIE SD 265*
'Somethin' Said Love' (Jerry Michael / Wood Newton) – FC / RJ – *Edel ED 12392*

'Whatever It Is' (J Michael / M Gray / E Setser) RJ – *Edel ED 12392*
'I Can Make It Go Away' (V Hampton / H Hicks) – RJ – *Edel ED 12392*
'Never Too Much Love' (CM) – RJ – (missing from CDs)

SIGMA STUDIOS, WEST HOLLYWOOD, LOS ANGELES

1993   **The Impressions:** Vandy 'Smokey' Hampton (lead), Ralph Johnson (ten), Fred Cash (tenor), Sam Gooden (bass). Arranged Branford Marsalis. Produced Branford Marsalis for Two Coon Productions. Musicians: Branford Marsalis (ten, sop sax), Kenny Kirkland (pno), Tony Maiden (gtr), Matt Finders (tromb), Sal Marquez (tpt)

'Fool For You' (CM) – Warner Bros 9362 45500 2

2000   'Reptile': Eric Clapton with the Impressions on backing vocals.

CURTOM DISCOGRAPHY

Compiled by Peter Burns for Echo Archive.

SINGLES

UK Curtom CR		UK Buddah
SP 3, Dec '68	'Merry Xmas Happy New Year'	
1932, Aug '68	'Fool For You' / 'I'm Loving Nothing'	2011.021
1934	'This Is My Country' / 'My Woman's Love'	2011.032

1937	'My Deceiving Heart' / 'You Want Somebody Else'	
1940	'Seven Years' / 'The Girl I Find'	
1943	'Choice Of Colors' / 'Mighty Mighty Spade And Whitey'	2011.062
1946	'Say You Love Me' / 'You'll Always Be Mine'	
1948	'Amen 1970' / 'Wherever She Leadeth Me'	
1951	'Check Out Your Mind' / 'Can't You See'	2011.030
1954	'Baby Turn On To Me' / 'Soulful Love'	2011.045
1957	'Ain't Got Time' / 'I'm So Proud'	2011.068
1959	'Love Me' / 'Do You Want To Win'	2011.087
1964	'Inner-City Blues' / 'We Must Be In Love'	
	'Inner City Blues' / 'Amen' / 'Keep On Pushing'	2011.099
1970	'This Love's For Real' / 'Times Have Changed'	
	'On And On' / 'This Love's For Real'	2011.124
1973	'Love Me' / 'I Need To Belong To Someone'	
1982	'Preacher Man' / 'Times Have Changed'	
1985	'Thin Line' / 'I'm Loving You'	2011.167
1994	'If It's In You To Do Wrong' / 'Times Have Changed'	
1997	'Finally Got Myself Together' / 'I'll Always Be Here'	BUD403
2003	'Something's Mighty, Mighty Wrong' / '3 The Hard Way'	

CMS

0103, Mar '75	'Sooner Or Later' / 'Miracle Woman'	K16565
0106	'Same Thing It Took' / 'I'm So Glad'	
0110	'Loving Power' / 'First Impressions'	
	'First Impressions' / 'Before My Time'	K16638
0116	'Sunshine' / 'I Wish I'd Stayed In Bed'	
	'I Wish I'd Stayed In Bed' / 'I'm So Glad'	K16736

COTILLION, 1976

44210, Oct	'This Time' / 'I'm A Fool For Love'	
44211, Nov	'I Saw Mommy Kissing Santa Claus' / 'Silent Night'	
44214	'You'll Never Find' / 'Stardust'	
44222, 8/77	'Can't Get Along' / 'You're So Right For Me'	
DSKO 85	'You'll Never Find' / 'You'll Never Find' (12")	
DSKO 103	'Dance' / 'Dance' (12")	

CHI SOUND, 1979

2418	'Sorry' / 'All I Want To Do Is Make Love To You'	
2435	'Maybe I'm Mistaken' / 'All I Want To Do Is Make Love To You'	
2438	'Maybe I'm Mistaken'	
2491	'For Your Precious Love' / 'You're Mine'	
2499	'Fan The Fire' / 'Love, Love, Love'	
	'Fan The Fire' / 'For Your Precious Love' (12")	20C TCD 2500 (Aug '81)

MCA, 1987
52995   'Can't Wait Until Tomorrow'

RIPETE, 1989
R45 3001   'Something Said Love' / 'Whatever It Is'

CURTOM ALBUMS (tracks)
CRS
8001	*This Is My Country* (10)	Buddah 203.012
8003	*Young Mod's Forgotten Story* (10)	Buddah CD 2013
8004	*Best Impressions* (12)	UK Amen 2359.009
8006	*Check Out Your Mind* (10)	Buddah 2318.017
8012	*Times Have Changed* (8)	Buddah 2318.059
8016	*Preacher Man* (7)	
8018	*Curtis In Chicago* (5)	Buddah 2318.091
8019	*Finally Got Myself Together* (8)	BDLP 4003
8602 3	Three *The Hard Way* (8)	

CU
5003	*First Impressions* (8)	K56143
5009	*Loving Power* (7)	K56211
	This Is My Country	Get Back GET 8001

ADAM VIII LTD
A8R 8012   *Soul Train* (1)

COTILLION
SD 9912   *It's About Time* (8)

CHI-SOUND
T596   *Come To My Party* (7)
T624   *Fan The Fire* (8)

CURTOM CDs
CUR 2006   *Lasting Impressions* (8)
CUR 2013   *Young Mods' Forgotten Story* (10)

RHINO
R2 72583   *The Very Best Of The Impressions* (16)
R2 72262   *People Get Ready* (3-CD box) (12)
R2 75568   *Gospel / Curtis Mayfield And The Impressions* (13)

MCA
D2 10664	*Anthology / Curtis Mayfield And The Impressions* (30)	
	Changing Impressions (2-CD box) (39)	Charly CPCD 8254, Feb '96
	The Masters (19)	Eagle EAB CD 050, '97

Check Out (19)	Music Club MCCD 360, '98
Indelible Impressions (2-CD set) (45)	Sequel NEECD 321, '99
The Curtom Story (2-CD set) (7)	Charly CDLAB 107, '99
Curtis In Chicago (5)	Charly CDCD 8046
Curtis Live / Curtis In Chicago (5)	Sequel NEMCD 400, '99
Curtom Superpeople (1)	Charly CDNEW 110, '97
Curtom Superpeople 2 (1)	Charly CDNEW 125, '97
Curtom Soul Trippin' (1)	Charly CDNEW 115, '98
Curtom Soul Trippin' 2 (1)	Charly CDNEW 135, '98
Curtom Chartbusters (2-CD set) (14)	Sequel NEECD 322, '99
Mighty Mighty Soul (2)	Sequel NEMCD 402, '99
Funk-Soul Brothers And Sisters (2)	Sequel NEMCD 451, '99
This Is My Country / Young Mod's... (20)	Charly CDGR 108, '96
This Is My Country / Young Mod's... (20)	Sequel NEM CD 782, '96
Check Out Your Mind / Times Have Changed (18)	Sequel NEM CD 843, '96
Preacher Man / Finally Got Myself Together (15)	Sequel NEM CD 866, '97
First Impressions / Loving Power (15)	Sequel NEM CD 867, '97
Come To My Party / Fan The Fire (15)	Charly CDGR 126, '97
Come To My Party / Fan The Fire (15)	Westside WESM 582, '99

D/C © PWB 5/68, 0203

EDEL
ED112392   *The Impressions: A Tribute To The Memory of Curtis Mayfield* (14)
Curtis Mayfield, Jerry Butler And The Impressions   Raven RVCD 125 / 01
(2-CD set)

Remembering Curtis (20)   Pie PIESD 265 / 01

Appendix 3: Curtis Mayfield Sessionography And Discography

CDs

Compiled by Peter Burns for Echo Archive

CURTIS
RCA STUDIOS, CHICAGO

July / Aug
'70

Curtis Mayfield. Vocal background The Impressions. Produced CM. Arranged Riley Hampton and Gary Slabo. Engineer Roger Anfinsen. Vocal overdubbing: Record Plant, New York. Musicians: Leonard Druss (fl / alt sax), John Howell (tpt), Harold Lepp, Loren Binford (tbone), Patrick Ferreri (gtr), Richard Single, Rudolph Stauber (horns), Donald Simmons, (perc / dms), Robert Lewis (tbone / fl horn), Harold Dessent, Ronald Kolber, Harold Klatz (v / viola), John Ross, (kbds), Sol Bobrob, Ronald Kolber (b sx), Sam Heiman, Elliot Golub (strings), Clifford Davis (saxes), Henry Gibson (perc), Robert Sims (dms), Gary Slab, Philip Upchurch (gtrs / bs).

Distributed by Buddah Records) – Curtom CRS 8005, *CUR CD 2012*, (E) 2318.015, (E) BDLP 5005, K56252, NEMLP 965, *Charly (E) CPCD 8036*, *Charly CPCD 8189 / 2*, 74026, *Jimco JICK 89413*, 8122-79932-2, *Sequel SSC 998*, *NEM CD 965*

'If There's A Hell Below' (CM) – CR 1955, (E) Buddah 2011.055 (single edit), 8122-79932-2,*CUR2 2902 / CD*, MCAD2 10664, CCS CD 806, MUSCD 007, LL 12364, (E) CPCD 8034, *102.802*, *Eagle EDM CD 054*, NTMCD 538, R2 72584, *Summit SUMCD 4119*, *Recall SM CD 105*, *Beechwood CURTIS CD1*, *(J) TECW-20171*, 20096, *Rhino R2 72262*, *(E) Sequel NXT CD 286*, NEECD 320, *SELCD 568*, 7243 8324 3822, DC 3027

'If There's A Hell Below' (demo) – 8122-79932-2

'The Other Side Of Town' (CM) – CR 1987, (E) 2011.187, *EDM CD 009*

'The Makings Of You' (CM) – CR 1955, (E) 2011.055, MCAD2 10664, *(E) CDCD 1211*, *(J) TECW 20096*, R2 72584, *306532*, *Music Club MCCD 314*, *CUR 9502*, VICP60429, JICK89411

'We People Who Are Darker Than Blue' (CM) – CUR2 2902 / CD, MCCD 314, SM CD 105, R2 72262, NXT CD 286, SELCD 568, Victor VICP 60292, 7243 8358 1825

'Move On Up' (CM) – CR 1974, (E) 2011.080,12, BDS 410, 7CUR101, FBS 23, (single edits) BDLP 4015, MCAD2 10664, MUSCD 007, TL 1333, LL 12364, CUR2 2902 / CD, CD LAB 107, (E) CPCD 8034, 8065,1211, 8189 / 2, SSC CD 998, (J)TECW 20095, 20171, 20096, VICP60429, NTMCD 538 Audiophile 102.802, CCS CD 806, R2 72584, EDM CD 054, Hallmark 306532, SM CD 105, Pickwick PWKS 4206, ESL / Gold 30359 00112, MCCD 314, SUMCD 4119, CURTIS CD1, R2 72262, NXT CD 286, Delta 47 022, NEECD 320, SELCD 568, JICK89411, DC 3027

'Miss Black America' (CM) – (E) BDLP 4015, (E) CDCD 1211, 306532, Delta 47 022

'Wild And Free' (CM) – (E) BDLP 4015, (E) CPCD 8034 , EDM CD 009, NTMCD 538, MCCD 314, Delta 47 022

'Give It Up' (CM) – CR 1960, (E) 2011.080, BDS 410, EDM CD 009, MCCD 314, CURTIS CD1, CPCD 8189 / 2, Delta 47 022

'Check Out Your Mind' (instrumental, not used on Curtis) – R2 72836, CD NEW 125,

'70 / '96   'We People Who Are Darker Than Blue' (CM) – Warner 946348.2

LOVE PEACE UNDERSTANDING
RCA STUDIOS, CHICAGO
1970   **Curtis Mayfield.** Produced and arranged by CM. Musicians include Curtis Mayfield (vcl / gtr), Craig McMullen (gtr), Henry Gibson (perc), Joseph 'Lucky' Scott (bs), Tyrone McCullen (dms).

UK only – (E) Sequel NXT CD 286, Sequel 'Love' NEM CD 967

'Power To The People' (CM) – 8122-79932-2
'Underground' (CM) (demo) – R2 72836, 8122-79932-2
'Ghetto Child' (CM) – R2 72836, 8122-79932-2
'Readings In Astrology' (CM) – 8122-79932-2
'Suffer' (CM / D Hathaway) – 8122-79932-2
'Miss Black America' (CM) – 8122-79932-2
'Woman's Got Soul' (CM)
'I Loved And I Lost' (CM)
'Talkin' 'Bout My Baby' (CM)
'You Must Believe Me' (CM)
'Minstrel And Queen' (CM)
'Romancing To A Folk Song' (CM)
'Little Brown Boy' (CM)
'I Thank Heaven' (CM)

'Man's Temptation' (CM)
'Little Boy Blue' (CM)
'Love's Miracle' (CM)

CURTIS/LIVE
THE BITTER END, NEW YORK CITY
1970   **Curtis Mayfield.** Produced and arranged by CM. Musicians: CM (vcl / gtr), Henry Gibson (perc), Craig McMullen (gtr), Joseph Scott (bs), Tyrone McCullen (drs)

Curtom CRS 8008, (E) 2659.004, K56252, BDLP 2001, K 66047, *Movie Play Gold CD 74176, (E) CPCD 8038, JICK89414, NEMCD 400*

'Mighty, Mighty Spade And Whitey' (CM) – CR 1963, (E) BDLP 4015, *EDM CD 054, CUR 9502, (J)TECW 20095, MCCD 314, R2 72262,VICP60429, JICK89411, NEECD 320*

'I Plan To Stay A Believer' (CM) – *NXT CD 286*

'We're A Winner' (CM) – CR 1966,1968, *(E) CPCD 8043, EDM CD 009 (J)TECW 20096*

'We've Only Just Begun' (P Williams / R Nichols) – *(E) Sequel NXT CD 286, (J) TECW-20171, (J) TECW-20093, VICP60429, JICK89411*

'People Get Ready' (CM) – (E) 2011.101, BDLP 4015, *(E) CPCD 8043, EDM CD 054, EDM CD 009, MCCD 314, (J) TECW-20171, 20096, NTMCD 538, CURTIS CD1, Metro CD008*

'Stare And Stare' (CM) – *(E) Sequel NXT CD 286,*

'Check Out Your Mind' (CM) – *R2 72262*

'Gypsy Woman' (CM) – *EDM CD 009,(J)TECW 20096*

'The Makings Of You' (CM) – *VICP 60292*

'We People Who Are Darker Than Blue' (CM)

'If There's A Hell Below' (CM) – *CUR 9502*

'Stone Junkie' (CM) – (E) 2011.119, *(J) TECW 20095, CUR 9502. R2 72262, NXT CD 286, VICP60429, JICK89411*

ROOTS
RCA STUDIOS, CHICAGO
1971   **Curtis Mayfield.** Background vocals: Mr and Mrs L Hutson, Mr and Mrs M Hawkins. Produced CM. Arranged Riley Hampton / Johnny Pate (John Pate Jr copyist). Master Engineer Roger Anfinsen. Musicians: Curtis Mayfield (vcl / gtr), Craig McMullen (gtr), Henry Gibson (perc), Joseph 'Lucky' Scott (bs), Tyrone McCullen (dms).

Curtom CRS 8009, (E) 2318.045, BDLH 5006, K 56249, NELP 966, *MPG 74027, (E) CPCD 8037, JICK89415, Sequel NEM CD 966, Rhino R2 78569*

'Get Down' (CM) – CR 1966, *(E) CPCD 8034, EDM CD 054,102.802,* NTMCD 538, CURTIS CD1, CPCD 8189 / 2, R2 72262, NXT CD 286, *Delta 47 022, NEECD 320, SELCD 568, DC 3027*

'Keep On Keeping On' (CM) – (E) 2011.119, BDLP 4015, *(E) CPCD 8043,* NXT CD 286, NTMCD 538, MCCD 314, SM CD 105, *Delta 47 022, SELCD 568, NEECD 320*

'Underground' (CM) – CR 1974,1975,1978, (E) 2011.141,*MCCD 314, CD NEW 110,*

'We Got To Have Peace' (CM) – CR 1968, (E) 2011.101, BDLP 4015, *102.802,* CCS CD 806, CPCD 8189 / 2, NTMCD 538, *R2 72584,* MCCD *314,* SM CD 105, *R2 75568, R2 72262,* NXT CD 286, *Delta 47 022, NEMCD 402, SELCD 568, NEECD 320, DC 3027*

'Beautiful Brother Of Mine' (CM) – CR 1960 1972, (E) 2011.080, *MCAD2 10664, (E) CPCD 8034, CPCD 8189 / 2,102.802, R2 72262, SELCD 568, VICP 60292, NEECD 320, DC 3027*

'Now You're Gone' (CM / J Scott) – *(E) CPCD 8034*

'Love To Keep You In My Mind' (CM) – CR 1972, *(E) CDCD 1211, 306532,*

SUPERFLY
RCA STUDIOS, CHICAGO / BELL STUDIOS, NEW YORK
1972   **Curtis Mayfield.** Produced CM. Arranged CM / Johnny Pate.

Curtom CRS 8014, CD CUR 2002, (E) 2318.065, BDLP 4015, 4018, RSO RSS5, NEMLP 964, *MPG 74028, (E) CPCD 8039, JICK89416, Rhino R2 72836, Sequel NEM CD 964, Charly NEW CD 130-2*

'Little Child Runnin' Wild' (CM) – (E) 12,7CUR 101, *(E) CPCD 8034,* CURTIS CD1, Metro CD008

'Pusherman' (CM) – MCAD2 10664, MUSCD 007, TL 1333, CRS 8014 EP, LL12364, *(E) CPCD 8034, EDM CD 009 102.802,* CCS CD 806, CUR 9502, NTMCD 538, R2 72584, CURTIS CD1, Metro CD008, R2 72262, NXT CD 286, Delta 47 022, SELCD 568

'Freddie's Dead' (CM) – CR 1975, (E) 2011.141, MCAD2 10664, *PWKS 4206,* MUSCD 007, TL 1333, LL 12364, CPCD 8034, EDM CD 054, CPCD 8189 / 2, (J) TECW-20171, 20096, CCS CD 806, 102.802, NTMCD 538, R2 72584, SUMCD 4119, 30359 00112, SM CD 105, CURTIS CD1, DC 3027, R2 72262, NXT CD 286, *Delta 47 022,NEECD 320, SELCD 568,VICP 60292 (single), Metro CD008*

'Junkie Chase' (CM) (instrumental) – CRS 8014 EP

'Give Me Your Love' (CM) – (E) 2011.156, BDLP 4015, CRS 8014 EP, *MUSCD 007, LL 12364,(E) CPCD 8043, EDM CD 054, (J)TECW 20095, 20096, CCS CD 806, NTMCD 538, SUMCD 4119, SM CD 105, CUR 9502, CURTIS CD1, R2 72262, NEMCD 451, VICP 60292, Metro CD008, Planet PML 1065*

'Eddie You Should Know Better' (CM) – CRS 8014 EP,*(E) CDCD 1211, 306532, CURTIS CD1*

'No Thing To Me' (CM) – *(J) TECW 20095, CURTIS CD1, CD NEW 125, VICP60429, JICK89411, Metro CD008*

'Think' (CM) (instrumental) – CR 1991,CRS 8014 EP *CUR 9502*

'Superfly' (CM) – CR 1978, (E) 2011.156 (single edit), BDLP 4015, RSO 68, 12 CUR 108 MCAD2 10664, TL 1333, LL 12364, CCS CD 806, *(E) CPCD 8034,1211, 8189 / 2, CD LAB 107, (J) TECW-20171, 20096, SM CD 105, 102.802, NTMCD 538, R2 72584, 306532, MCCD 314, CURTIS CD1, R2 72262, NXT CD 286, Delta 47 022, NEECD 320 SELCD 568, Metro CD008, DC 3027*

'Pusherman' (take) – *Rhino R2 72836, Charly CD 130-2*

'Freddie's Dead' (take) – *CD NEW 125*

'Junkie Chase' (take)

'No Thing On Me' (take)

'Militant March' (CM)

'Eddie You Should Know Better' (take)

'Radio Spot#1'

'Radio Spot #2'

NEWPORT IN NEW YORK
RADIO CITY MUSIC HALL, NEW YORK
6 July '72   **Curtis Mayfield Live.** Produced Don Schlitten.

Atlantic 40439 (E) NEMCO 634

'Stone Junkie' (CM)
'Pusherman' (CM)

RAPPING
CURTOM STUDIOS, CHICAGO
1972   **Curtis Mayfield.** Produced CM. Arranged Rich Tufo

Curtom CRS / SP, *NEMCD 448*

Interview with Mayfield made for promotional reasons. Not originally issued as an album but containing six previously recorded tracks.

BACK TO THE WORLD
CURTOM STUDIOS, CHICAGO
1973   **Curtis Mayfield.** Produced CM. Arranged Rich Tufo.

Curtom CRS 8015, (E) 2318.085, BDLH 5008, K 56251, *MPG 74026, (E) CPCD 8040, JICK89417, Sequel NEM CD 967*

'Back To The World (CM) – (E) 2011.187, BDLP 4015 (single edit), *NXT CD 286, EDM CD 009, MCCD 314, CD NEW 135, CUR 9502, NEECD 320*

'Future Shock' (CM) – CR 1987, A8R 8012, *EDM CD 054, CPCD 8189 / 2, 102.802, SUMCD 4119, SM CD 105, R2 72262, NXT CD 286, NEECD 320, SELCD 568, DC 3027*

'Right On For Darkness' (CM) – CR 1999, (E) BDS 402, *(E) CPCD 8034, EDM CD 009, NTMCD 538, SM CD 105, CURTIS CD1, NEMCD 451, VICP 60292, 7243 8358 1825*

'Future Song' (CM) – CR 1993

'If I Were Only A Child Again' (CM) – CR 1991, (E) BDLP 4015, *(E) CPCD 8034 EDM CD 054, (J) TECW-20171, 102.802, CPCD 8189 / 2, MCCD 314, R2 72262, NEECD 320, SELCD 568, DC 3027*

'Can't Say Nothin'' (CM) – CR 1993, *102.802, R2 72584, R2 72262, NEECD 322, SELCD 568*

'Keep On Trippin'' (CM) – *(E) CPCD 8034, VICP60429, JICK89411*

CURTIS IN CHICAGO
LIVE AT WTTW-TV STUDIOS, CHICAGO
1973   **Curtis Mayfield And Friends,** with Gerry Butler, Brenda Lee Eager, Mattie Butler, Diedra Teig. Produced CM / Richard Tufo. Musicians: Carolyn Johnson (fem vcl), Philip Upchurch (g), Curtom Rhythm Section.

Curtom CRS 8018, (E) 2318.091, BDLH 5009, K 56250, *(E) CPCD 8046, JICK89418, NEMCD 400*

'Superfly' (CM) – Curtis Mayfield – *(J) TECW 20095,*

'For Your Precious Love' – (J Butler / A&R Brooks) – The Impressions: JB, CM, SG, FC

'I'm So Proud' (CM) – The Impressions: CM,SG,FC, – *(E) CPCD 8065*

'For Once In My Life' (Miller / Murden) – The Impressions: RT, SG, FC – *(E) EDM CD 009*

'Preacher Man' (R Tufo) – The Impressions: FC, SG, RT

'If I Were Only A Child Again' (CM) – Curtis Mayfield – CR 1991,

'Duke Of Earl' (Edwards / B Williams / E Dixon) – Gene Chandler – *(E) EDM CD 009*

'Love Oh Love (L Hutson / L Hawkins / J Hutson) – Leroy Hutson

'Amen (CM / J Pate) – complete cast – *(J) TECW 20096*

SWEET EXORCIST
CURTOM STUDIOS, CHICAGO
1974   **Curtis Mayfield.** Produced CM. Arranged Rich Tufo, Gil Askey.

Curtom CRS 8601, (E) 2318.099, BDLH 5001, K 56284, *(E) CPCD 8047, JICK89419, Sequel NEM CD 966*

'Ain't Got Time' (CM)

'Sweet Exorcist' (CM) – CR 2005, *(E)CPCD 8043, (J) TECW-20171, CPCD 8189 / 2, CUR 9502, R2 72262, SELCD 568, NEECD 320, DC 3027*

'To Be Invisible' (CM) – *CPCD 8189 / 2, R2 72262, NXT CD 286, VICP 60292, DC 3027*

'Power To The People' (CM) – *(E) CDCD 1211, 306532,*

'Kung Fu' (CM) – CR 1999, (E) BDS 402,*CPCD 8043, EDM CD 054, 102.802, R2 72584, SM CD 105, CPCD 8189 / 2, CUR 9502, R2 72262, NEECD 320, SELCD 568, DC 3027*

'Suffer' (CM / D Hathaway) – CR 2005, *(E) CPCD 8065, SM CD 105*

'Make Me Believe In You' (CM) – *NEMCD 451, SELCD 568*

THE BITTER END YEARS
BITTER END, GREENWICH VILLAGE, NEW YOROK
1974   **Curtis Mayfield Live.** Musicians: Curtis Mayfield (vcl / gtr), Craig McMullen (gtr), Henry Gibson (perc), Joseph 'Lucky' Scott (bs), Tyrone McCullen (dms).

Chelsea (E) 2336108

'Gypsy Woman' (CM)

GOT TO FIND A WAY
CURTOM STUDIOS, CHICAGO
1974   **Curtis Mayfield.** Produced CM. Arranged Rich Tufo.

Curtom CRS 8604, (E) BDLP 4029, *(E) CPCD 8048, JICK89420, Sequel NEM CD 965*

'Love Me' / 'Right In The Pocket' (CM) – CR 2006, (E) BDS 426, *VICP 60292*

'So You Don't Love Me' (CM)

'A Prayer' (CM) – *R2 75568, CUR 9502*

'Mother's Son' (CM) – CR 2006, (E) BDS 426, *(E) CPCD 8043, DC 3027, CPCD 8189/2, (J) TECW 20095, CD NEW 110, CUR 9502, R2 72262, NEECD 320 SELCD 568,*

'Cannot Find A Way' (CM) – *SM CD 105,*

'Ain't No Love Lost (CM) – *MUSCD 007, TL 1333, LL 12364, (E)CPCD 8043, CD 1211, (J) TECW-20171, 306532, VICP 60292, JICK89411, Metro CD008*'

BLACK CAUCUS CONCERT (LIVE)
CAPITOL CENTER, MARYLAND
25 Sep '74   Curtis Mayfield with War, Kool And The Gang, Gladys Knight And The Pips, Jimmy Witherspoon. Produced Jerry Goldstein, Lonnie Jordan, Howard Scott. Engineer Andrew Berliner. Remix Ed Barton

Chess GCH 8033, (E) Greenline GCH 8033 CD

'Give Me Your Love' (CM)

'On And On' (CM) – with Gladys Knight And The Pips

THERE'S NO PLACE LIKE AMERICA TODAY
CURTOM STUDIOS, CHICAGO
1975   **Curtis Mayfield**. Produced CM. Arranged Rich Tufo. Distributed by Warner Bros Records.

Curtom CU 5001, (E) BDLP 4033, CD CUR 2003, *(E) CPCD 8069, JICK89434, Sequel NEM CD 401*

'Billy Jack' (CM) – *(J) TECW 20096, MCCD 314, CPCD 8189 / 2, R2 72262, NXT CD 286, VICP 60292, DC 3027, Planet PML 1065*

'When Seasons Change' (CM)

'So In Love' (CM) – CMS 0105, MCAD2 10664, CUR2 2902 / CD, *MUSCD 007, TL 1333, LL 12364, SM CD 105, (E) CPCD 8043, EDM CD 054, (J) TECW-20171, 102.802, CCS CD 806, NTMCD 538, R2 72584, SUMCD 4119, CPCD 8189 / 2, R2 72262, DC 3027 NXT CD 286, Delta 47 022, NEECD 320*

'Jesus' (CM) – *R2 75568, VICP 60292*

'Blue Monday People' (CM) – *EDM CD 009*

'Hard Times' (CM) – CMS 0105, *CUR2 2902 / CD, MUSCD 007, TL 1333, LL 12364, (E) CDCD 1211, SM CD 105, (J) TECW-20171, 306532, SUMCD 4119, Delta 47 022, VICP60429, JICK89411, Planet PML 1065*

'Love To The People' (CM) – CMS 0118, *(E) CPCD 8043, R2 75568*

GIVE, GET, TAKE AND HAVE
CURTOM STUDIOS, CHICAGO
1976   **Curtis Mayfield**. Produced CM. Arranged Rich Tufo.

Curtom CU 5007, CD 2011(E) BDLP 4042, *Century CD (J) CECC 00349, (E) CPCD 8070, JICK 89435, Sequel NEM CD 401*

'In Your Arms Again (Shake It)' (CM) – MUSCD 007, *LL 12364, (E) CDCD 1211, EDM CD 009, (J) TECW-20171, (J) TECW 20095, 306532*

'This Love Is Sweet' (CM) – *(J) TECW-20093, VICP60429, JICK89411*

'PS I Love You' (CM) – CMS 0122

'Party Night' (CM) – CMS 0122, *EDM CD 054, CPCD 8189 / 2, R2 72262, NEECD 320*

'Get A Little Bit' (Give, Get, Take And Have) (CM) – CMS 0135, *(E) CPCD 8065, VICP 60292*

'Soul Music' (CM) – *MUSCD 007, LL 12364,(E) CPCD 8065, (E) CDCD 1211, NXT CD 286, JICK89411, EDM CD 054, (J) TECW-20093, 306532, SUMCD 4119, CPCD 8189 / 2, VICP60429, JICK89411, Metro CD008, DC 3027, Planet PML 1065*

'Only You Babe' (CM) – CMS 0118, *MCAD2 10664, CUR2 2902 / CD, TL 1333, (E) CPCD 8043, EDM CD 009, R2 72584, SM CD 105, CPCD 8189 / 2, R2 72262, NEECD 320, DC 3027,*

'Mr Welfare Man' (CM) – *R2 72262, NXT CD 286, Metro CD008*

NEVER SAY YOU CAN'T SURVIVE
CURTOM STUDIOS, CHICAGO
1977   **Curtis Mayfield**. Produced CM. Arranged Rich Tufo, James Mack.

Curtom CU 5013, CD 2010, K56352, *Century CD (J) CECC 00356, (E) CPCD8049, JICK89436, NEMCD 440*

'Show Me Love' (CM) – CMS 0125, *CPCD 8043, EDM CD 054, CPCD 8189 / 2, R2 72262, NEECD 320, DC 3027*

'Just Want To Be With You' (CM) – CMS 0125, *CPCD 8065, (J) TECW-20093, VICP60429, JICK89411*

'When We're Alone' (CM) – *R2 75568, VICP60429*

'Never Say You Can't Survive' (CM) – *NXT CD 286, MCCD 314, VICP 60292*

'I'm Gonna Win Your Love' (CM) – *CPCD 8065, CPCD 8189 / 2, DC 3027*

'All Night Long' (CM) – *CPCD 8065, EDM CD 009*

'When You Used To Be Mine' (CM)

'Sparkle' (CM) – *EDM CD 009, 20096*

SHORT EYES (MOVIE SOUNDTRACK)
CURTOM STUDIOS, CHICAGO
1977   **Curtis Mayfield.** Backing: Mystique. Produced CM. Arranged Rich Tufo. Musicians: Curtis Mayfield (vcls / gtr), Richard Tufo and Floyd Morris (kbds), Gary Thompson (r / gtr), Joseph Scott (b), Henry Gibson (perc), Don Hagen (ds).

Curtom CU 5017, (E) K56430, *JICK89437, CPCD 8183, Sequel NEM CD 964*

'Do Do Wap Is Strong In Here' (CM) – CMS 0131, *MCAD2 10664* (single edit), *CUR2 2902 / CR, MUSCD 007, TL 1333, (J) TECW-20171, LL 12364, CPCD 8043 NTMCD 538, R2 72584, R2 72584, CPCD 8189 / 2, R2 72262, NXT CD 286, Delta 47 022, SELCD 568, VICP 60292 (single), NEECD 320, Metro CD008, DC 3027*

'Back Against The Wall' (CM) – *Metro CD008, Planet PML 1065*

'Need Someone To Love' (CM) – CMS 0131, *EDM CD 009, CPCD 8189 / 2, DC 3027*

'A Heavy Dude' (CM) – *Metro CD008*

'Short Eyes' (CM) – *CPCD 8189 / 2, DC 3027*

'Freak, Freak, Free, Free, Free' (instrumental) (CM) – *CPCD 8189 / 2, DC 3027*

'Break It Down' (CM)

'Another Fool In Love' (CM) – *EDM CD 009*

'Father Confessor' (instrumental) (CM)

DO IT ALL NIGHT
WALLY HEIDER RECORDING, LOS ANGELES / LAS VEGAS RECORDING CENTRE/ CURTOM STUDIOS, CHICAGO
1978   **Curtis Mayfield.** Produced CM. Arranged Gil Askey.

Curtom CUK 5022, *(E) Charly CPCD 8050, JICK89438, NEMCD 440,*

'Do It All Night' (C Mayfield / G Askey) – CMS 0141, *CPCD 8043, EDM CD 009, EDM CD 054, CPCD 8189 / 2, R2 72262, NEECD 320, DC 3027 Planet PML 1065*

'No Goodbyes' (CM / GA) – CMS 12 0049, (E) LV1, *(J) TECW 20095, NEECD 320*

'Party, Party' (CM / GA) – CMS 0141, CMS 12 0049, (E) LV1

'Keeps Me Loving You' (CM) – CMS 0142, *CDCD 1211, (J) TECW-20093, 306532,*

'In Love, In Love, In Love' (CM) – CMS 0142, *VICP60429, JICK89411, NEECD 320*

'You Are, You Are' (CM) – CMS 0135, *CUR2 2902 / CD, MUSCD 007, TL 1333, LL 12364, (J) TECW-20171, 20093, CPCD 8043, SM CD 105, R2 72262, NEMCD 448, NEECD 320*

HEARTBEAT
SIGMA SOUND STUDIOS, PHILADELPHIA
1979   **Curtis Mayfield.** Executive Production CM. Produced Norman Harris and Ronald Tyson. Arranged NH. Engineer Joe Tarsa.

Curtom / RSO RS 1 3053, (E) RSS 4, *Century (J) CD CECC 00351, (E) CPCD 8071, JICK89431, NEMCD 446,*

'Tell Me, Tell Me (How Ya Like To Be Loved)' (N Harris / R Tyson) – *EDM CD 009*

'Victory' (NH / RT) – *(J) TECW-20093*

BLANK TAPES INC, NEW YORK
KENDUN RECORDERS, BURBANK, CALIFORNIA
1979   **Curtis Mayfield.** Produced Bundino Siggalucci (Bunny Sigler). Arranged Fred Wesley.

'What Is My Woman For?' (B Sigler / D Robinson) – *EDM CD 009, Planet PML 1065*

'You Better Stop' (J Sigler)

'Over The Hump' (J Sigler)

CURTOM STUDIOS, CHICAGO
1979   **Curtis Mayfield.** (Duet: CM and Linda Clifford.) Produced CM. Arranged Gil Askey.

'Heartbeat' (CM / GA) – *EDM CD 009, (J) TECW-20093, CUR 9502, Planet PML 1065*

'You're So Good To Me' (CM / GA) – RSO 941, (E) RSO 43, *CPCD 8065, CURTIS CD1, (J) TECW-20171, 20095,20096, CCS CD 806, CUR 9502, CPCD 8189 / 2, R2 72262, DC 3027*
'Between You Baby And Me' (CM) – RSO 941, (E) RSO 43,*CUR2 2902, TL 1333, CPCD 8065, (J) TECW-20093, R2 72584, CPCD 8189 / 2, R2 72262, NEECD 320, DC 3027*

'This Year, This Year' (CM) – RSO 919,(E) RSO 28, *CUR2 2902 / CD MUSCD 007, TL 1333, LL 12364, DC 3027, CPCD 8065, (J)TECW-20093, SM CD 105, CPCD 8189 / 2, NEMCD 448, NEECD 320*

'79 / '96   'It Was Love That We Needed' (CM) (not issued on *Heartbeat*) – Warner 946348.2

SOMETHING TO BELIEVE IN
CURTOM STUDIOS, CHICAGO
1980   **Curtis Mayfield.** Produced Gil Askey, Curtis Mayfield. Arranged GA. Produced CM, Keni Burke.

Curtom / RSO 3077, CD 2005, (E) 2394 271, CPCD 8073, JICK 89532, NEMCD 446

'Love Me, Love Me Now' (CM) – RSO 1036, CPCD 8065, R2 72262, NXT CD 286, NEECD 320

'Never Let Me Go' (J Scott) – MUSCD 007, (J) TECW-20093, CUR 9502, Planet PML 1065

'Tripping Out' (B Sigler) – RSO 1046, CUR2 2902 / CD, TL 1333, LL12364, CPCD 8065, EDM CD 009, CCS CD 806, DC 3027, (J) TECW-20171, 20093, 20095, NTMCD 538, SUMCD 4119, CPCD 8189 / 2, R2 72262, Delta 47 022, NEECD 320, Metro CD008

'People Never Give Up' (CM) – 12,7CUR 106, NXT CD 286, Metro CD008

'It's Alright' (CM) – (E) RSO 43, (E) RSO 68, (J) TECW-20093, NEECD 320

'Something To Believe In' – (CM) RSO 403, CPCD 8065, CPCD 8189 / 2, CUR 9502, R2 75568, NXT CD 286, DC 3027

'Never Stop Loving Me' (K Burke / D Burke / CM) – MUSCD 007, LL 12364, EDM CD 009, SM CD 105, (J)TECW-20093, 20095, CUR 9502, VICP 60292, Planet PML 1065

THE RIGHT COMBINATION
SIGMA SOUND STUDIOS, PHILADELPHIA
1980   **Curtis Mayfield.** Produced Norman Harris, Bruce Gray, Curtis Mayfield. Arranged NH.

Curtom / RSO 3084, (E) 2394 269, CPCD 8072, JICK89535, NEMCD 448

'It's Lovin' Time (Your Baby's Home)' (B Gray)

'Body Guard' (NH / RT) – CRC 2001, JICK89536, NEMCD 447

CURTOM STUDIOS, CHICAGO
1980   **Curtis Mayfield And Linda Clifford.** Produced Gil Askey and CM. Arranged GA

'Rock You To Your Socks' (Carbobe / Lambert)

'The Right Combination' (K Echols / Sanderson / Miller) – CPCD 8065, SUMCD 4119, CUR 9502, Delta 47 022

'I'm So Proud' (CM) – *(J) TECW-20093*

'Love's Sweet Sensation' (Bleu) – RSO 1029, *CPCD 8065 , EDM CD 009, CPCD 8189 / 2, R2 72262, Delta 47 022, NEECD 320, DC 3027*

CURTOM STUDIOS, CHICAGO
1980   **Curtis Mayfield And Linda Clifford.** Produced CM. Arranged Gil Askey

'Ain't No Love Lost' (CM) – *CUR2 2902 / CD, CPCD 8065, EDM CD 009, (J)TECW 20095,*

LOVE IS THE PLACE
QUANTUM STUDIOS, TORRANCE, CALIFORNIA
WALLY HEIDER STUDIOS, HOLLYWOOD, CALIFORNIA (STRINGS ONLY)
1981   **Curtis Mayfield.** Produced Dino Fekaris and CM. Arranged Gene Page.

Boardwalk / Curtom 33239, *JICK89534, NEMCD 783*

'She Don't Let Nobody But Me' (D Fekaris / CM) – Boardwalk 122, *CUR2 2902 / CD, TL 1333, (J) TECW-20171, 20093, 20096, CCS CD 806, R2 72262, NXT CD 286, NEECD 320*

'Toot An' Toot An' Toot' (CM) – Boardwalk 132, *NEECD 320*

'Babydoll' (D Fekaris)

'Love Is The Place' (D Fekaris) – *NXT CD 286*

'Just Ease My Mind' (CM)

'You Mean Everything To Me' (CM)

'You Get All My Love' (D Fekaris) – Boardwalk 122

'Come Free Your People' (CM) – Boardwalk 132, *NXT CD 286*

HONESTY
WEB IV RECORDING STUDIOS / AXIS SOUND STUDIOS, ATLANTA
1982   **Curtis Mayfield.** Produced CM. Arranged Richard Tufo, CM.

Boardwalk / Curtom 33256 (E) Epic 25317 *Century (J) CECC 00352, JICK89535 NEMCD 783*

'Hey Baby (Give It All To Me)' (CM) – Boardwalk 155, *CCS CD 806, NEECD 320*

'Still Within Your Heart' (CM) – *SM CD 105,*

'Dirty Laundry' (CM) – 12 CUR 108, *CUR2 2902 / CD, TL 1333, NXT CD 286, (J) TECW-20093, SM CD 105, NEECD 320*

'Nobody But You' (CM)

'If You Need Me' (CM)

'What You Gawn Do?' (CM) – *CUR 9502*

'Summer Hot' (CM) – Boardwalk 155

WE COME IN PEACE WITH A MESSAGE OF LOVE
CURTOM RECORDING STUDIO, ATLANTA
1985   **Curtis Mayfield**. Produced and arranged CM. Distributed Jewel-Paula-Ronn Records

CRC 2001, *JICK89536, NEMCD 447*

'We Come In Peace' (CM)

'Baby It's You' (CM) – CRC 001, (E) 12 / 98.6 Curt 1T, 98.6 Curt 1, *EDM CD 054, CCS CD 806, CPCD 8189 / 2, DC 3027, CUR 9502, R2 72262, NXT CD 286, NEECD 320, Planet PML 1065*

'Breakin' In The Streets' (CM / J Scott / B Scott) – CRC 001, 12 / 98.6 Curt 1T, 98.6 Curt 1

'Everybody Needs A Friend (CM) – *SM CD 105, Planet PML 1065*

'We Gotta Have Peace' (CM)

CURTOM RECORDING STUDIO, ATLANTA
1985   **Curtis Mayfield**. Produced CM. Arranged Rich Tufo, CM.

'This Love Is True' (CM) – CRC 2001, *JICK89536*
'Tomorrow Night For Sure' (CM) – *NEMCD 448 , CUR2 2902*

LONDON
May '87   **Curtis Mayfield And The Blow Monkeys** (collaboration). Produced Dr Robert. (Engineered by Andy Mason).

'Celebrate (The Day After You)' (Dr Robert) – RCA Monk 6, *RCA PD 74191* / 'It's Not Unusual' (live) (10", withdrawn)
/ 'Beautiful Child'
/ 'Smile On Her Face (Sweet Murder)'

LIVE IN EUROPE
July '87   **Curtis Mayfield**. Produced CM. Musicians: Curtis Mayfield (vcl / gtr), Henry Gibson (perc), Buzz Amato (kbds) Lebron Scott (bs), Lee Goodness (drs).

Curtom CUR 2 2901,*CD 2901, JICK89537*. Distributed Ichiban Records – *Sequel NEMCD 360*

'Intro – Ice 9' (B Amato) (featuring Henry Gibson)
'Back To The World' (CM)
'It's Alright' (CM) / 'Amen' (CM / J Pate) – *R2 75568*
'Gypsy Woman (CM)
'Freddie's Dead' (CM)
'Pusherman' (CM)
'We've Gotta Have Peace' (CM) – 12 CUR 108
'We've Only Just Begun (P Williams / R Nichols)
'People Get Ready' (CM)
'Move On Up' (CM) – 12CUR 101
'If There's A Hell Below' (CM)
'When Seasons Change' (CM)

PEOPLE GET READY – LIVE AT RONNIE SCOTT'S
LONDON
31 July'88   **Curtis Mayfield.** Produced Stephen Cleary, Robert Lemkin. Instruments: CM (vcl / gtr), Buzz Amato (kbds), Benny Scott (bs), Lee Goodness (drs), Luis Stefanell (perc).

(E) Castle / Essential *ESMCD 003, Spectrum 551258-2, CMRCD 078*

'Little Child Running Wild' (CM)
'It's All Right' (CM)
'People Get Ready' (CM)
'Freddie's Dead' (CM)
'Pusherman' (CM)
'I'm So Proud' (CM)
'We've Gotta Have Peace' (CM)
'Billy Jack' (CM)
'Move On Up' (CM)
'To Be Invisible' (CM)

TAKE IT TO THE STREETS
CRS STUDIO, ATLANTA
1990   **Curtis Mayfield.** Produced, arranged and orchestrated CM.

Curtom CUR 2008 – CD / tape / vinyl (Euro numbers same as US), *JICK89538, NEMCD 447*

'Homeless' (CM) – 12,7CUR 106, *CPCD 8189 / 2, R2 72262, NXT CD 286, NEECD 320, Planet PML 1065*

'Got To Be Real' (T Brown / M Brown) – 7CUR 107, 12CUR 107, *EDM CD 009,VICP 60292*

'Do Be Down' (CM) – 12CUR 107,7CUR 107 (single edit), CUR2 2902 / *CD TL 1333, (J) TECW-20093, R2 72584, CPCD 8189 / 2, NEECD 320, R2 72262, NXT CD 286, DC 3027*

'Who Was That Lady' (CM) – 12CUR 108, *Planet PML1065*

'On And On' (CM) – *SM CD 105,*

'He's A Fly Guy' (CM) – 12,7CUR 102, *EDM CD 009*

'Don't Push' (TB / MB)
'I Mo Git U Sucka' (CM) – 12,7CUR 102, *NEECD 320*

'Tomorrow Night For Sure' (CM) – CUR2 2902 / CD, *TL 1333*

All Ichiban / Curtom, available in 12", 7" vinyl LP, CD and CDS and on tape

RETURN OF SUPERFLY (MOVIE SOUNDTRACK)
CURTOM / CRS STUDIO, ATLANTA
1990   **Curtis Mayfield.** Produced CM / Lenny Kravitz.

Capitol *CDP 79 4244 2*

'Superfly 1990' (CM) – with Ice T *CDCL 586*
'Superfly 1990 – Mantronix Remix' – 12CL 586 / CD
'Superfly 1990 – Fly Mix' – 12CL 586 / CD
'Superfly 1990 – New Jack Swing Mix' – 12CL 586
'Superfly 1990 – Bonus Mix' – *CDCL 586*
'Showdown' (CM)
'Forbidden' (CM)
'Superfly 1990 – Hip-Hop Instrumental'
'For The Love Of You' (CM)

CURTIS MAYFIELD LIVE IN CONCERT
LONDON TOWN AND COUNTRY CLUB, KENTISH TOWN,
BBC RADIO 1 LIVE IN CONCERT
Spring '90   **Curtis Mayfield.** Produced Pete Dauncey. Musicians: Curtis Mayfield
(vcl / gtr), Frank 'Buzz' Amato (kbds), Randy Brown (bs) Luis Stefanell
(perc), Lee Goodness (ds)

(E) *Windsong CD052*

'Superfly' (CM)
'It's Alright' (CM) / 'Amen' (CM / JP) – medley
'I'm So Proud' (CM)
'Billy Jack' (CM)
'Freddie's Dead' (CM)
'People Get Ready' (CM) – *(J) TECW-20093*
'We've Gotta Have Peace' (CM) – *(J) TECW-20093*
'Homeless' (CM)
'Move On Up' (CM)
'Invisible' (CM)
'Don't Worry...' (CM)

A TRIBUTE TO CURTIS MAYFIELD
ATLANTA CRS STUDIOS, RIVER SOUND NYC
'94   **The Repercussions And Curtis Mayfield**. Nicole 'Bubba Diva' Willis (lead vcl), Genji Siraisi, Daniel Wyatt and The Repercussions. Produced Gary Katz

Warner Bros.9362 45500 2

'Let's Do It Again' (CM) (contains a sample from a Staple Singers original)

ATLANTA
1995   **Curtis Mayfield**. Interview about the *Superfly* movie and songwriting, taped by David Dorn – R2 72836

NEW WORLD ORDER
CURTOM STUDIOS, ATLANTA
late '95   **Curtis Mayfield**. Executive producer Curtis Mayfield. Produced Curtis Mayfield, Bryan Fleming, Carlos Glover and Rosmary Woods. Backgrounds Rosmary Woods, Brian Fleming, Raimundo Thomas. (Duet with Sandra St Victor – Backgrounds: Diamond.)

Warner Bros 9 46348.2

late '95   New World Order (CM / B Fleming / R Thomas) – CD 9175682

'I Believe In You (CM / R Woods) – remixed at Purple Dragon Studios in Atlanta by Mike Peterson and Tim Harrigan

last in '95   'Let's Not Forget' (CM / A Hemmings)

PURPLE DRAGON STUDIOS, ATLANTA
early '96   **Curtis Mayfield**. Produced Curtis Mayfield. Drum sequencing and mixing Carlos Glover. Backgrounds Rosmary Woods, Raimundo Thomas, Robert Scott Jr. Rappers Blaise Mayfield and Lisa Coates.

'Just A Little Bit Of Love' (CM / C Glover / R Thomas) – CD W0403CD Curtis Mayfield in duet with Mavis Staples and Organized Noize. Produced Organized Noize

'Ms Martha' (CM / Organized Noize)

'Here But I'm Gone (CM / Organized Noize / M Etheridge / A Martin / M Matias)

CURTOM STUDIOS, ATLANTA
'96   **Curtis Mayfield**. Produced Naranda Michael Walden. Backgrounds Aretha Franklin (added later).

'Back To Living Again' – (CM / R Woods)

'The Got Dang Song' (CM / NM Walden / R Woods)

'Oh So Beautiful' – (CM / NM Walden / E Hicks)
Produced Curtis Mayfield, Daryl Simmons. (Daryl Simmons kbds / progamming.)

'No One Knows About A Good Thing (CM / D Simmons) – CD 974062. Producer Roger Troutman. (Roger Troutman kbds / programming / remixing. Duet vocal Shirley Murdock.)

'70 / '96   'We People Who Are Darker Than Blue' (CM)

'79 / '96   'It Was Love That We Needed' (CM)

DOPPLER STUDIOS, ATLANTA

'96 ('87)   **Curtis Mayfield**. Produced Curtis Mayfield, Carlos Glover. Remixed by Curtis Mayfield and Carlos Glover. Original track: Buzz Amato (kbds), Lebron Scott (bs), Curtis Mayfield (all other instruments).

'The Girl I Find Stays On My Mind' (CM)

EVE'S BAYOU: THE COLLECTION
DOPPLER STUDIOS, ATLANTA

1996   **Erykah Badu** with Terence Blanchard. Producer Curtis Mayfield. Arranged Terence Blanchard. Remixed by Madukwa Chinwa. Recorded by Carlos Glover and Terence Blanchard.

MCA MCACD 11670

'A Child With The Blues / 1' (CM)
'A Child With The Blues / 2' (CM)

THE MOD SQUAD (SOUNDTRACK)
KENDAL STUDIOS, ATLANTA

1998   **Lauryn Hill** and **Curtis Mayfield** (duet). Produced CM, Organized Noize. Added production Lauryn Hill.

Elektra 62364-2

'Here But I'm Gone Pt 2' (CM)

CURTOM STUDIOS, CHICAGO
OLYMPIC STUDIO, LONDON

2001   Original Mayfield tracks. Engineers: Rod Shearer, Martin Rouillard and The Brothers Grand. Mixed by Mark 'Spike' Stent. **Bran Van 3000** featuring Curtis Mayfield (lead vocal samples). Produced James Di Salvo. Co-produced by Rik Ocasek and The Brothers Grand.

'Astounded' (J Di Salvo / C Mayfield / G McKenzie) – Grand Royal Records

Long Radio Edit – *(E) Virgin 7243 897538 20 VUSCD 194*
Album Version
MJ Cole Master Mix

CURTIS MAYFIELD DISCOGRAPHY

Compiled by Peter Burns for Echo Archive

US	SINGLES	UK
CURTOM		BUDDAH
1955 / '70	'If There's A Hell Below' / 'The Making's Of You'	2011.055
1960	'Beautiful Brother Of Mine' / 'Give It Up'	
	'Move On Up' / 'Beautiful Brother Of Mine' / 'Give It Up'	2011.080
1963	'Mighty Mighty Spade And Whitey (Live)' / Pt 2	
1966	'Get Down' / 'We're A Winner'	
1968	'We Got To Have Peace' / 'We're A Winner'	
	'We Got To Have Peace' / 'People Get Ready'	2011.101
1972	'Beautiful Brother Of Mine' / 'Love To Keep You In My Mind'	
	'Keep On Keeping On' / 'Stone Junkie	2011.119
1974	'Move On Up' / 'Underground'	
1975	'Freddie's Dead' / 'Underground'	2011.141
1978	'Superfly' / 'Underground'	
	'Superfly' / 'Give Me Your Love'	2011.156
1987	'Future Shock' / 'The Other Side Of Town'	
	'Back To The World' / 'The Other Side Of Town'	2011.187
1991	'If I Were Only A Child Again' / 'Think'	
1993	'Can't Say Nothin'' / 'Future Song'	
1999	'Kung Fu' / 'Right On For Darkness'	BDS402
	'Move On Up' / 'Give It Up'	BDS410
2005	'Sweet Exorcist' / 'Suffer'	
2006	'Mother's Son' / 'Love Me (Right In The Pocket)'	BDS426
CMS		CURTOM
0105	'So In Love' / 'Hard Times'	
0118	'Only You Babe' / 'Love To The People'	
0122	'Party Night' / 'PS I Love You'	
0125	'Show Me Love' / 'Just Want To Be With You'	
0131	'Do Do Wap Is Strong In Here' / 'Need Someone To Love'	
0135	'You Are, You Are' / 'Get A Little Bit'	
0141	'Do It All Night' / 'Party Party'	
	'No Goodbyes' / 'Party Party' (12")	Curtom LV1
0142	'In Love, In Love, In Love' / 'Keep Me Lovin' You'	

RSO   RSO
919   This Year, This Year / This Year (instrumental)   28
941   Between You Baby And Me / You're So Good To Me   43
            (w / Linda Clifford)

1029   'Love's Sweet Sensation' / 'Love's Sweet Sensation' (instrumental)
1036   'Love Me, Love Me Now' / 'It's Alright'
1046   'Tripping Out' / 'Never Stop Loving Me'
            'It's All Right' / 'Superfly'   68

BOARDWALK
122   'She Don't Let Nobody But Me' / 'You Get All My Love'
132   'Toot An' Toot An' Toot' / 'Come Free Your People'
155   'Hey Baby' / 'Summer Hot'

CRC
001   'Baby It's You' / 'Breakin' In The Streets' – 7 / 12 98.6 Curt1 / (1T)
            Celebrate (The Day After You) / It's Not Unusual (live)
            RCA Monk 6 (with The Blow Monkeys)
            'Beautiful Child' / 'Smile On Her Face (Sweet Murder)' – 10" withdrawn

CURTOM   CURTOM
101   'Move On Up' / 'Little Child Runnin' Wild' /   7 / 12 CUR101
            'Move On Up (Live)'

102   'I Mo Git U Sucker' / 'He's A Fly Guy'   7 / 12 CD CUR102
106   'Homeless' / 'People Never Give Up'   7 / 12 CUR106
107   'Do Be Down' (LV) / 'Do Be Down' / 'Got To Be Real'   7 / 12 CUR107
108   'Dirty Laundry' / 'We Gotta Have Peace' / 'Superfly' /   7 / 12 CUR108
            Who Was That Lady?

CAPITOL
CDCL 586   'Superfly '90' / 'Superfly Mantronix Remix' / 'Superfly Fly Mix' / 'Superfly
            Bonus Mix (with Ice T)
CL 586   'Superfly '90 / 'Superfly Fly Mix Edit'

WARNER BROS
1996   'New World Order' – CD 9175682
1996   'No One Knows A Good Thing (Radio Edit)' / 'We People Who Are Darker
            Than Blue' – CD 2-17406
July 1997   'Back To Living Again' (NMW Remix)' CD
August 97   'Just A Little Bit Of Love' – CD W0403CD

GRAND ROYAL RECORDS
            Bran Van 3000: 'Astounded' (various mixes). Performed by CM. *Virgin
            VUSCD 194 ('01)*

US	EPS	UK
8014 EP	'Pusherman' / 'Think' / 'Give Me Your Love' / 'Eddie You Should Know Better' / 'Junkie Chase' (with Superfly cover)	

US ALBUMS (tracks)		UK
CURTOM CRS		BUDDAH
8005	Curtis (8)	2318.015, BDLH 5005, K56252, CLP 8036, NEMLP 965
8008	Curtis/Live (16)	2659.004, BDLP 2001, K566047, NEMLP 400
8009	Roots (7)	2318.045, BDLH 5006 K56249, NEMLP 966
8014	Superfly (soundtrack) (9)	318.065, BDLP4018, RSS5, NEMLP 964,
8015	Back To The World (7)	2318.085, BDLH 5008, K56251,
8018	Curtis In Chicago (4)	2318.091, BDLH 5009, K56250,
8601	Sweet Exorcist (7)	2318.099, BDLH 5001, K56284,
8604	Got To Find A Way (6)	BDLP 4029,
	Move On Up (11)	BDLP 4015

ATLANTIC		
Atl 40439	Newport In New York '72 (live) (2)	Sequel
CRS / SP	Rapping (rare interview, pressed for US radio play only)	
Chelsea	The Bitter End Years 1974 (1)	Chelsea 2336 108
Chess GCH 8033	Black Caucus 1974 (2)	Greenline GCH 8033

CURTOM		CURTOM
5001	There's No Place Like America Today (7)	BDLP 4033, CUR 2003
5007	Give, Get, Take And Have (8)	BDLP 4042,
5013	Never Say You Can't Survive (8)	K56352,
5017	Short Eyes (soundtrack) (9)	K56430,
5022	Do It All Night (6)	

RSO CUR		
3053	Heartbeat (8)	RSO RSS4,
3077	Something To Believe In (7)	2394.271, RS 13077,
3084	Right Combination (7) (with Linda Clifford)	2394.269,

BOARDWALK		
33239	Love Is The Place (8)	
33256	Honesty (7)	Epic 25317,

CRC		
2001	We Come In Peace, With A Message Of Love (7)	

ARISTA
AL 8574   *I'm Gonna Git You Sucka* (soundtrack) (1)

CURTOM
22901   *Live In Europe* (14) (double)   CUR 2901,

2008   *Take It To The Streets* (8)   2008

Capitol CDP
79 42442   *Return Of Superfly* (soundtrack) (5)

US	CDs	UK
CURTOM		
2012	*Curtis* (8)	CUR 2012, CPCD 8036, (J) JICK 89413, 74026, NEM CD 965
	Curtis/Live (16)	CDMPG 74176, (J) JICK 89414 CPCD 8038, NEM CD 400
	Roots (7)	CDMPG 74027, (J) JICK 89415 CPCD 8037, NEM CD 966
2002	*Superfly* (soundtrack) (9)	CDMPG 74028, (J) JICK89416, CPCD 8039, NEM CD 964
	Back To The World (7)	CDMPG 74029, (J) JICK89417, CPCD 8040, NEM CD 967
	Curtis In Chicago (4)	(J) JICK89418, CPCD 8046, NEM CD 400
	Sweet Exorcist (7)	(J) JICK89419, CPCD 8047, NEM CD 966
	Got To Find A Way (6)	(J) JICK89420, CPCD 8048, NEM CD 965

CHESS
GCH 8033   *Black Caucus* (2)
         Love (17)   NEM CD 967

CURTOM
2003   *There's No Place Like America Today* (7) CUR CD2003, (J) JICK89434, CPCD 8069, NEM CD 401

2011   *Give, Get, Take And Have* (8)   CURCD 2011, (J) CECC00349 (J) JICK89435, CPCD 8070, NEM CD 401

2010   *Never Say You Can't Survive* (8)   CURCD 2010, (J) CECC00350, (J) JICK89436, CPCD 8049, NEM CD 440

         Short Eyes (soundtrack) (9) (J) JICK89437, CPCD 8183, NEM CD 964
         Do It All Night (6) (J) JICK89438, CPCD 8050, NEM CD 440
         Heartbeat (8) (J) CECC00351, (J) JICK89531, CPCD 8071, NEMCD 446

         Something To Believe In (7) CURCD 2005,(J) JICK89532, CPCD 8073, NEMCD 446

         Right Combination (7) (with Linda Clifford) (J)JICK89533, CPCD 8072 NEMCD 448

         Love Is The Place (8) (J) JICK89534, NEMCD 783

Honesty (7)	(J) CECC00352,(J) JICK89535, NEMCD 783	
We Come In Peace, With A Message Of Love (7)	(J) JICK89536, NEMCD 447	
Choices (Blow Monkeys) (CM) (1)	RCA PD 74191 CD / 89	

CURTOM   CURTOM

22901   *Live In Europe* (14) (double)   CUR 2901 CD, CPCD 8178 (J) JICK89537

             People Get Ready – Live (10)   Essential ESMCD 003 / 90

             aka *Curtis Mayfield Live At Ronnie Scott's* (11)   Spectrum 551258-2

                                                                     CMRCD 078

2008   *Take It To The Streets* (8)   CUR 2008 CD, (J) JICK89538,

                                                          CPCD 8179, NEMCD 447

CAPITOL CDP

79 42442   *Return Of Superfly* (soundtrack) (5)   Capitol 79 42442 / 90

             BBC Radio 1 Live In Concert (11)   Windsong WINCD 052 / 93

WARNER BROS

946348.2   *New World Order* (13)   Warner Bros 946348.2 / 97

MCA

MCAD 11670 *Eve's Bayou* (soundtrack) (2)

US	CD COMPILATIONS	UK
CURTOM		
2902	*All-Time Classic Collection* (16)	CUR 22902 / 90, (J) CECC 00255
CUR 9501	*Curtis Mayfield*	
CUR 9502	*Living Legend* (20) (2-CD set)	

MCAD2

10664   *Anthology 1961–77* (10)

             A Man Like Curtis (16)   Music Club MUSCD007 / 92

             Hard Times (16)   Traditional Lines 1333 / 93

Warner Bros

9362 455002 *Tribute To Curtis Mayfield* (CM And The Percussions) (1)

	Curtis Mayfield (16)	LaserLight 12364 / 94
	Get Down To The Funky Groove (13)	Charly CPCD 8034 / 94
	Groove On Up (15)	Charly CPCD 8043 / 94
	Tripping Out (17)	Charly CPCD 8065 / 94
	Power For The People (12)	Charly CDCD 1211 / 94
	Very Best Of Curtis Mayfield (16)	Castle CCS CD 806 / 96
	Curtis Mayfield Definitive Collection (34) (2-CD set)	Charly CPCD 8189 / 2 / 96
	The Curtom Story (2) (2-CD set)	Charly CDLAB 107 / 99
	Curtom Superpeople (2)	Charly CDNEW 110 / 97

Curtom Superpeople 2 (4)	Charly CDNEW 125 / 97
Curtom Soul Trippin' (1)	Charly CDNEW 115 / 98
Curtom Soul Trippin' 2 (1)	Charly CDNEW 135 / 98
The Impressions Featuring Curtis Mayfield (2)	Pickwick PWKS 4206 / 94
The Impressions Featuring Curtis Mayfield (2)	Essential 3035900112 / 96
Move On Up (13)	Audiophile 102.802 / 95
The Best Of Curtis Mayfield (15)	Nectar NTMCB 538 / 97
Move On Up (12)	Hallmark 306532 / 97
Give It Up (14)	Music Club MCCD 314 / 97
The Best Of Curtis Mayfield (29) (2-CD set)	VAL 108-2
The Best Of Curtis Mayfield (11)	Summit SUMCD 419 / 97
The Ultimate Curtis Mayfield (29) (2-CD set)	Recall SMD CD 105 / 97
Curtis Mayfield – The Masters (33) (2-CD set)	Eagle EDM CD 009 / 97
The Masters (17)	Eagle EDM CD 054 / 97
Love's Sweet Sensation (16)	Delta 47 022 / 99
Move On Up (18)	Select SELCD 568 / 99
Curtis – The Very Best (14)	Beechwood Curtis CD1 / 98
Sequel Soul Cellar (1)	SSC CD998 / 96
Beautiful Brother / The Essential (15)	Metro CD008 / 2K
Greatest Hits (32) (2-CD set)	Double Classic DC 3027 / 99
Love Peace Understanding (3-CD box) (49)	Sequel NXT CD 286
Love Is The Place / Honesty (15)	Sequel NEMCD 783 / 96
Curtom Chartbusters (10) (2-CD set)	Sequel NEECD 322
Mighty Mighty Soul (1)	Sequel NEMCD 402
Funk / Soul Brothers And Sisters (3)	Sequel NEMCD 451
Superfly / Short Eyes (soundtracks) (17)	Sequel NEMCD 964 / 98
Curtis / Got To Find A Way (14)	Sequel NEMCD 965
Roots / Sweet Exorcist (14)	Sequel NEMCD 966
Back To The World / Love (24)	Sequel NEMCD 967
Curtis Live / Curtis In Chicago (22)	Sequel NEMCD 400 / 99
...America Today / Give, Get, Take And Have (15)	Sequel NEMCD 401
Never Say You Can't Survive / Do It All Night (14)	Sequel NEMCD 440
Heartbeat / Something To Believe In (15)	Sequel NEMCD 446
We Come In Peace... / Take It To The Streets (15)	Sequel NEMCD 447
Move On Up – The Singles (39)	Sequel NEECD 320 / 99
Curtis And Linda (rapping interview) (20)	Sequel NEMCD 448
Curtis Mayfield Live In Europe (13)	Sequel NEMCD 360 / 2K
Soul Music (14)	Planet PML 1065 / 01
Curtis Mayfield, Jerry Butler And The Impressions (2-CD set)	Raven RVCD 125 / 01

RHINO

R2 72262	*People Get Ready* (51) (3-CD box)	
R2 72584	*Very Best Of Curtis* (18)	
R2 72836	*Superfly* (23) (2-CD set, 25th anniversary edition)	Charly NEW CD 130-2
	Superfly (2-CD set, 25th anniversary edition) CSAND 507CD	Eagle

R2 75568	*Gospel* (13)
R2 78569	*Roots* (11)
R2	*Superfly*
R2 79972	*Love Songs* (16)
R2 79932-2	*Curtis* (17)
R2	*Curtis Live*

Chicken Soup For The Soul (1)
Pop Culture Box
Soul Train 1972
Soul Train 1973
Millennium Funk Party
Rhino Instant Party – Whole Lotta Soul
(Other Rhino issues also.)

MCAD
116700   Eve's Bayou (2)

ELEKTRA
62364-2   *The Mod Squad* (soundtrack) (1)

JAPANESE CDs	**JAPAN**
Groovy Curtis (14)	Victor VICP60429 / 98
Groovy Curtis (14)	Jimco JICK89411
Mellow Curtis	Jimco JICK89412
The Best Of Curtis Mayfield	Jimco JICK89484-5
New Soul Rebels '68 / '75	Teichiku TECW 20092
Dancing Away (20)	Teichiku TECW 20093
Folksy Curtis	Teichiku TECW 20094
Club Curtis (13)	Teichiku TECW 20095
Choice Of Covers (17)	Teichiku TECW 20096
The Very Best (17)	Teichiku TECW 20171
The Ultimate / The Curtom Years / Curtom 30th Anniversary (16)	
	Victor VICP 60292 / 98

DC © PWB 5/68, 02/03